About the Author

Robert Sardello, Ph.D. is co-founder with Cheryl Sanders-Sardello, Ph,D. of the School of Integral Spiritual Psychology, which began in 1992. Robert Sardello began the work of this form of spiritual psychology in 1980, which was prepared for with his work in phenomenological psychology which began in 1970.

He taught at the Duquesne University, the University of Dallas (where he established a Ph.D. program in phenomenological psychology) and at the Dallas Institute of Humanities and Culture (of which he is one of the founders), and at the Chalice of Repose Project.

He is the author of eight books and six monographs.

The School of Integral Spiritual Psychology held courses in practically ever state in America as well as in Canada, the United Kingdom, the Czech Republic, the Philippines, Ireland, and Australia

The Collected Notes of Integral Spiritual Psychology

Foundations for a Spirituality of the Future

by

Robert Sardello

VOLUME I - FOUNDATIONS

Goldenstone Press
Granbury, Texas

Published by Goldenstone Press.
417 W. Doyle
Granbury, Texas 76048

Library of Congress Cataloging-in-Publication Data
Sardello, Robert J., 1942 -

Collected Notes in Integral Spiritual Psychology: Foundations of a Spiritual Psychology of the Future

Volume I / Robert Sardello.

ISBN 9798685654618

1. Spiritual Life 2. Integral Psychology.

GOLDENSTONE PRESS seeks to make original spiritual thought available as a force of individual, cultural, and world revitalization. The press is an integral dimension of the work of the School of Spiritual Psychology. The mission of the School includes restoration of the book as a way of inner transformation and awakening to spirit. We recognize that secondary thought and the reduction of books to sources of information and entertainment as the dominant meaning of reading places in jeopardy the unique character of writing as a vessel of the human spirit. We feel that the continuing emphasis of such a narrowing of what books are intend to be needs to be balanced by writing, editing, and publishing that emphasizes the act of reading as entering into a magical, even miraculous spiritual realm that stimulates the imagination and makes possible discerning reality from illusion in the world.

CONTENTS

Acknowledgements

Mary Jane Taylor drew rendered in color the image that graces the cover of this book. There could be no better way of entering the writing than to contemplate this image for a while each time you start to read a section, for an inner alignment will occurs when the image is held in a moment of inner silence.

Mary Jane has engaged with the work of the School of Integral Spiritual Psychology since 1992. It is as if the book cover holds the soul of the whole of the work.

Trudie A. Thibodeaux took on the work, the artistic work, of the design of the cover, and has done so in such a way that the contemplative image is held in exquisite beauty. Trudie also did the work of formatting this unusual book, a book with the flaws deliberately retained, when, I am sure she had to hold back from making corrections. Thank you, Trudie, for holding back.

The Nature of these Notes

These writings are either written papers from the years of work of the School of Integral Spiritual Psychology or are notes for classes or talks. In the past, the collections of such writings would have been printed in their original handwritten form. It is now almost impossible to print handwritten material, so there was no alternative to transcribing notes into printed text.

Almost no editing was done as the aim is to have a record of the 45 years of work, research documents rather than completed texts, although many of the papers are quite complete.

The papers and the themes are not arranged in some logical order nor chronological order; these notes are not historical because the soul does not date itself in terms of a calendar.

If read receptively, contemplatively, the way the material is intended to be read, a transformation from mentalness into soul-consciousness will occur — not if sampled, but if there is a dedicated attempt to enter into the work. That is the purpose of this collection and the additional volumes

Important

These writings are notes from courses, publications, distance and internet courses, as well as ongoing research. All have been left essentially as they were when created. This volume and further volumes are not books in the usual sense of a book.

In earlier times, documents comprising the mark of a life of research would be donated to a library somewhere. In this age it becomes possible to make such a work available to everyone interested rather than having to search out where such documents of an individual are held and go to that institution to find and work with the documents.

These documents have not been edited. The errors are part of what constitutes a work in process and provide the opportunity to observe the arising and working through of ideas unencumbered by the demands of publication.

These writings are also not arranged in a historical timeline. Most of the time, I did not even include a date in what I was researching and writing. That proves to be a wonderful way of retaining the wholeness of a life work rather than placing a historical overlay onto it.

Introduction

Integral Spiritual Psychology has a long history, and has had quite a few names, so a short review of how it has unfolded might be helpful.

I received a Ph.D in psychology from St. Louis University in 1969 after going through four years of hell there. I had expected psychology to be the study of the psyche, the soul, or at the very least be concerned with understanding the nature of human experience. Instead, psychology was presented as a "would be if it could be" natural science like chemistry, biology, or physics. It was laughable, and extremely dull. I was also shocked to find that I was the only graduate student to feel any passion in relation to this field, or held any concerns and questions concerning the nature of psychology as a field of study as well as a practical endeavor. Everyone was solely interested in getting the degree in order to get a good job. In many ways, they were all more talented than I was as I was unable to hold back trying to enter into deep questions with the professors, and argued with them all the time in classes. I was nearly thrown out of the program at least five different times. I could not get any of the professors interested in the question of human experience. That also meant that dissertations had to be some sort of an empirical study. I choose to do my dissertation in the field of verbal learning and was sponsored by the head of the department as that was his field. For my 'empirical/experimental' study I devised an experiment to prove that human beings can think, for people saying they could, is not "scientific." In experimental psychology, the primary theory of thinking was that it was an automatic associative process and did not involve any creative activity. It is strange to try and prove something that everyone already knows. William James accused psychology of this sort of triviality many, many years earlier.

After graduate school, my first teaching position was at Duquesne University in Pittsburg. I choose to teach there rather than a position I was offered at Georgetown University because Duquesne had a very unique graduate program in existential-phenomenological psychology. It was a wonderful program involving working with great texts in phenomenology like those of Edumund Husserl, the founder of phenomenology, as well as Maurice Merleau-Ponty, who wrote on the fully human meaning of behavior, and the classic book titled "The Phenomenology of Perception".

And, we - each of the professors, would sit in on each others classes — out of interest and the deepening of the community.

Phenomenology is the philosophy/study of experience. The program at Duquesne was unique, even in that area of study because the department was founded by a group of people from Holland who, with Adrian Van Kaam, began what was called existential-phenomenological psychology. This important development expanded phenomenology to include not only consciousness but world-consciousness with concerns like the "lived body", the "life-word", and the experience of time. The program not only involved working with lively texts, but also taught the 'doing' — that is, how to carefully track and express human experience.

I became uneasy at Duquesne, though, when I became interested in the phenomenon of imagination. For unknown reasons for which I could never determine the cause or history, this dimension of experience was not only excluded, it was looked down upon as somehow illegitimate. My conjecture is that the hope there at Duquesne was to establish psychology as a "Human Science", and there was fear that imagination would not remain only a necessary theme of experience to study, but that it would infect this aim to start a new form of science. That is, the work itself might become imaginal, that is, a form of soul-work, rather than scientific and literal.

I was at Duquesne for several years, and was then invited to begin a psychology program at the University of Dallas—- all the way from undergraduate school through the Ph.D. The University absolutely did not want a program in behavioral or cognitive or so-called 'scientific' psychology. It was an amazing experience to develop the program there. The undergraduate program worked with classic texts in psychology — such as William James, C. G. Jung, Freud, and many others. The aim was to get away from 'text books' and enter into the imagination of the great psychologists. The graduate program was in phenomenological psychology. All the graduate students in psychology were also required to take a minor in Literature alongside their courses in phenomenological psychology — a way of promoting the development of true imagination,

The University of Dallas was a prominent, small, liberal arts college with a truly gifted president, Dr. Donald Cowan, and the director of the Literature program and the graduate dean, Dr. Louise Cowan.

The graduate program in phenomenological psychology yearly attracted as many applications as all the rest of the graduate programs combined.

Universities, though are filled with teachers who hate their disciplines and become identified with working on power in various committees and sub-committees and sub-sub committees. The popularity of psychology became a point of contention with people who ran the graduate council, for example. The politics of the school, after ten years, became unbearable and a group of us — not only from psychology, but from other disciplines revolted for other reasons and left to begin the Dallas Institute of Humanities and Culture — in downtown Dallas.

Several years prior to this founding in 1980, James Hillman, an extremely significant thinker at the C.G. Jung Institute in Zurich, who developed a particular approach to the psychology of C. G. Jung that was named Archetypal Psychology came to the University of Dallas to be a guest teacher at the invitation of the psychology department — and subsequently moved to Dallas and also taught at the university. He too left and was one of the founders of the Dallas Institute. Dr. Gail Thomas who was director of a Master's degree program in The Center for the City at the University of Dallas and who had received the doctorate there in psychology also left and became director of the Dallas Institute. Dr. Joanne Stroud, who received a dual graduate degree in Literature and psychology left too, and became director of Publications.

While spiritual psychology developed well at the Institute, it was also always in the background and much of my time was engaged being Director of Studies, and I could feel that spiritual psychology would develop awfully slowly. So, the next move was to Great Barrington, Ma., where the School of Spiritual Psychology was started by Dr. Cheryl Sanders-Sardello and myself in 1992. Here, another dimension of spiritual psychology also developed — a relation to the work of Spiritual Science, Anthroposophy, which was started by the extraordinary thinker, and spiritual seer, Rudolf Steiner, who died in 1925. He did not develop a psychology, but did develop many cultural endeavors, including Waldorf Education, Biodynamic Farming, Anthroposophical Medicine, Eurythmy, a form of movement, and many other cultural endeavors. He was prolific as a thinker, a lecturer of some 6000 presentations, and deeply engaged in practical activities. He said this concerning psychology:

Psychology must be founded anew out of the consciousness soul: this psychology is not to be a theory but rather a spiritual activity. The purpose

of this psychology is to work agains the decline of the psychic in the world.
that is its anthroposophical task.

This description matched, almost precisely, the aspirations and
endeavors of the School of Spiritual Psychology. Except we were not
attached to the rather rigid way that Anthroposophy had developed. And,
we were shocked to find that anthroposophists were quite antagonistic to
psychology, except for a few, including Christopher Bamford, who was the
head of the Anthroposophic Press, which headquartered in Great
Barrington. He was the reason we went there, and have remained close
friends since.

For something like ten years, we traveled from the home base of Great
Barrington, offering courses in spiritual psychology in nearly every state in
the US, as well as in Canada, Ireland, Australia, Italy, the Philippines,
England, and other countries. After harpist and singer Therese Schroeder-
Sheker participated in a conference on angels at the Dallas Institute of
Humanities and Culture, I taught for a decade at the Chalice of Repose
Project, the music-thanatology organization which she founded.

Then, in 2002, we moved the School of Spiritual Psychology to
Greensboro, North Carolina at the invitation of a group of students there
who we had worked with for several years. About 7 years later, we moved the
School to Benson, North Carolina, near Raleigh, as we found a very large
9000 sq. ft. residence there that made possible having a center where
students could come and study. And, they did come.

Cheryl died tragically in 2015. She was integral to the School. She
co-taught every course with me and was executive director of the School. I
devised the courses, wrote notes and longer papers as well as eight books.
Cheryl would read the course notes before the classes and present parts of
each course. Almost no courses were repeated, and those that were did not
remain the same. Many students took the "same" course more than once.
We also established a yearly Sophia Conference that went on for seven
years. We traveled some, but the main work was with the students who came
from everywhere in the U.S. and many other countries. It was here that
Spiritual Psychology matured. Here is the way it was described in an
introductory booklet:

The School of Spiritual Psychology provides a foundation for meeting change, turmoil, and instability. This dynamic moment is an opportunity for the beginning of a new spiritual culture that escapes imprisonment in a materialistic outlook, but does not abandon the beauty of the world. Spiritual Psychology unites the highest (spirit) with the deepest (soul) and views the individual as the chalice of this union. This endeavor might aptly be called a "Grail Psychology". It coordinates a disciplined approach to the inner life with soul and spirit qualities of the outer world and recognizes that individual development is not for one's sake alone, but for the Earth, the World, and the Community, orienting the individual toward conscious work in relation with the spiritual worlds. The aim is to stir the depths of soul, develop the capacity of imagination, awaken an individual sense of spirit, and bring practical forces of renewal to the world.

The work of the School, while it was always phenomenological, that is, descriptive rather than theoretical, also involved developing inner practices in order to bring about transformations of consciousness — a deepening as well as an elevating, **always with an interest in the evolution of consciousness in the world much more than for personal fulfillment, though that always happened also.** But, it was never a direct intention, for that would only serve to increase self-wisdom, disconnected from world transformation.

Along with the development of the phenomenology of many aspects of soul and spirit life, further developments of the work of spiritual psychology occurred. First, the foundations of this psychology were developed. Then, a series of classes developed particular areas of endeavor, which will become clear in this collection of writings — they are fairly standard as psychological topics - emotions, relationships, those sorts of interest, again, though, developed far differently than other modes of psychology. Then, there was a series of very different themes — for example a two-year course called "Sacred Service", and another two-year course called "Caritas: Caring for Those who have Died", and another two-year course named "Spirit Healing." We also developed a two-year training program in Spiritual Direction.

Staying always within developing the capacities to notice and track experiences, and, most importantly recognize the significance of body-awareness with every phenomenon studied led directly to a concern with the heart, working to develop practices of heart-awareness as a way of being present with all the phenomena and areas of interest mentioned and more to come.

The previously mentioned course work resulted in significant transformations of the people who did this work — it was not merely cognitive study. We could see the development of a heart-intelligence occurring, and that led to a direct concern with heart-consciousness, both as a method and as a transformative way of being. Thus, a two year course called "Heart-Initiation" was inaugurated.

Another area of spiritual psychology began to emerge — a concern with the Soul of the World, addressed through a series of courses on Sophia and other significant Sophianic spiritual figures such as Mary Madeleine, Mary, the Black Madonna — all in relation to developing sensibility to the imaginal presence of these figures here and now. That is, we did not slide either into quasi-religion nor the now fashionable work of calling these figures "archetypes." This work led to another focus — that of the Spiritual-Earth, which, for a while was called "Earthosophy." Then, finally, still in keeping with the courses on the spiritual-earth, a series of courses on the particular nature of the land of America unfolded along with developing the capacities of earth-consciousness — not consciousness-of-earth, as for example is done in certain approaches in ecology and as well, interests in the "Sacred Earth", which simply assumed Earth-as-Sacred, and then often developed rituals in relation to Earth. We recognized that the human body is of the same substance as Earth, and awakening to Earth-Consciousness correlated with awakening to body-consciousness (again, different than consciousness of the body).

The most recent development of spiritual psychology, a concern with the integral character of this work also names this series of volumes of notes — **Notes in Integral Spiritual Psychology**. This psychology alway works with the unified Wholeness of body, soul, spirit, earth, the Divine. The integral way of the work of the School now, though, became informed by the astounding work of Sri Aurobindo and his partner, Maria Alfassa, who was known as The Mother, the work of "Integral Yoga". There were no courses that were directly concerned with what they did, but rather a complete re-orienting of the whole work of the School that recognized explicitly what was previously more or less simplicity — that spirit/soul transformation could not be world-transformation unless occurring integrally.

Soul Writing

We listen with our eyes when we read. When we write, we speak with our hands. That makes all writing sign language, a gesture of the body. Typewriting puts a motor to our gestures, and the computer typewriter electrifies them, making us forgetful of the body of writing. Let's try to remember.

The great mystery of writing is how the soul can find its way through the mechanics of writing to rise from the page to speak that which no single word alone can, what the series, taken as a series, does not say. How does the commonality of terms continually say uncommon things?

Where do our words come from? Even though we have learned them, where do those we employ at a given moment come from? We do not store them in our brains as in a file cabinet; the speed of a computer cannot match the manner with which words arrive one after another, all together. Words are with us everywhere, available for speaking sentiments, speeches, gossip, news – and occasionally, beauty. A writer somehow plays upon the happy accident of the arrival of beauty, making it into a skill. The "accident" may be no more than a cover for our ignorance, glossing over a highly mysterious process. The way into the happy accident may remain forever a mystery – but learning to follow it – that is a matter of education.

Whoever can follow falling into beauty begins the search for those rare sentences which outlast all utility, leap across time, outlast fashion and fad to make something permanent.

A deep desire exists to steward such sentences into the world, sentences which outlive the maker and awaken the soul of the reader, leaving behind the hand that made them, the mouth that spoke what the fingers form and electricity dulls. Such sentences become genuine charms, magical marks that ward off insecurity; they let us know that speech does last longer than granite. Anyone attempting to write writes from this desire to make something that escapes becoming a hostage of the author.

To relegate writing to desire is just the beginning of the task. It is too easy to slip into platitudes about genius, talent, inspiration, or the muses. One would not speak so lightly about physics or mathematics. True writing is rare, like a bolt of lightning in the blue sky or snow in the Sahara. It is a kind of oddity, and for that reason, of great psychological interest. It may be a psychological anomaly — we all have a bit of it somewhere within us, though few are those who act out. Like psychological oddballs, we are a bit afraid to look very closely at the soul of writing, for fear that we might become even more infected. We would rather hear the marvelous stories of perverted geniuses, tormented by day, writing, drinking late into the night, taunted by characters of imagination who keep them to the pen and the bottle. Yes, we would like to know about them, but not to imitate them.

Who wants to enter the torment of writing? Or writing as torment? It is as tightly held a secret as the tortures of love. Not a love manual can is available that tells it like it is – that love is supposed to be torturous, and no less so are the torments of writing. Desire never sheds the garments of pain; ecstasy is the shallow side of the story. So, to begin with, I suspect that one has to be a kind of pervert to want to write. One has to be able to enjoy suffering. What redeems the work from pure perversion is some knowledge of the inner life of such torture, and where and how it can go wrong, and recognize the mysteriousness of it going right.

When I look at what the great psychologists say concerning writing and speech, Freud rather than Jung is more interesting. It is not surprising to find that Freud was more the writer, a kind of master of the detective story; Jung, more the prophetic, wise old mystic that makes us want to be visionaries rather than writers, seers rather than makers.

The underlying metaphor of all of Freud's work is libido – a wonderful word, untranslatable either as desire or sex. It connects with the word 'lips' which places one in the locality of both speech and receptive sexual organs at the same time. Very early on, Jung substitutes the word 'psychic energy' for libido, and this seems to me to be an abstraction, one that perhaps covers more ground, but at the expense of the body of desire, the incarnation of imagination in gesture and speech.

At the same time, Freud has an extraordinary proclivity for rationalistic explanations. Jung is more the phenomenologist, able to stay with exactly what appears. Thus, in this exploration of writing, we shall have to try to be as bodily as Freud, as imagistic as Jung.

Words ooze out of us like pee or excrement. Or, should I say sounds, for words are something else. A writer is a craftsman of sound, staying close to the poop and the pee, feeling an urgent demand to fashion what comes out into art. The connection between sound and excretion makes for good bodily fantasy. We emerge from the womb peeing, shitting, cooing, and babbling. The possibility of speech presents itself from the beginning; the creative writer can stay close to those beginnings. That is to say, writing emanates from the bowels, the depths, not from the head, and much of writing must concern re-establishing the connection to the purity of bodily will.

It is the physicality of language that we are after. Babbling may be its purest expression. It shows itself in writing as rhythm and pace, intonation, and overtone – all that communicates ahead of any understanding.

Writing involves the art of clearly communicating that which cannot be understood, which nevertheless acts as if it can, and therefore is. The successful fiction of any writing, including so-called "non-fiction," which is itself a fiction, involves the communication of gesture as if it could be understood, conveying all of our sacred bodily grunts under the guise of understanding. Language without physicality has no soul. However conceptually well-connected, pure knowledge remains lifeless.

The most primary dimension of the body of writing is not what is said, but the way one says it. It is a matter of tact, of being tactual and tactile in acceptable ways, and therefore saying the unacceptable. The depth of desire is always publicly unacceptable. Freud noted that it was tactless for the child to say that he wanted sexual pleasure from mom, but it has the right touch to say that one wants to be like dad when one grows up. The unfriendly editors accompany us in all writing. We are required to write and rewrite until the guardians are satisfied, and we do not lose our satisfaction in the process.

With writing, style comes first, and without thinking, and as the civilizing of desire, ecstasy composing itself. The ambition is never wrong, but the formulation may be off base by being too base. The inner editors do not wish to shut the door on desire, merely to help us learn the art of acceptable disguise. A good deal of effort must go into learning to distinguish the difference between denying desire and denying specific formulations of desire. That involves getting to know the inner editors who are never against desire and merely try to tell us to say it another way.

Freud acquaints us with our editors. Mommy does not let the child play with its stools, but finger-paints are perfectly alright, and so are rolls of clay and lumps of wet sand. It's a matter of getting the message across without its most profound meaning too quickly revealed, and doing this in the most transparent way possible. If the meaning is too clear, losing the body, it will be sent back for a rewrite. A lessor editor will send it back if the formulation is unclear.

The problem of writing is how to be soul-aware and social at the same time. It's a matter of noticing the bureaucrats of the mind, of which there are many. We must remember, they are not there to stop the desire, but its formulation must satisfy them all. There is the moral editor, the family editor, the society editor, the public-relations editor. How to get through all of these?

First, becoming a writer requires that one be an avid reader, and the avid reader reads moving one's lips, one who reads with juicy libido. Such "libidoship" provides a large stock of formulations on which to draw. If there are no formulations, no signs to draw up, the desire will bump around in the dark without any formula with which it might try to be satisfied.

The first formulation is likely to be refused – and now comes the pain. Pure desire does not get through, and what was supposed to be pleasure turns into torment. Many inner editors exist, but each of them is also sly, devious, inconsistent, divided, throwing writing into total confusion, while thee editors sit back and laugh.

The struggle serves but one purpose – to sharpen the pen into the sword, which can finally make a mark, which is not a final victory. To come upon an acceptable sentence is, in one way, to be sentenced — imprisoned in the notion that because the revision worked this time, similar sorts of changes will work from now on. That is, our success proves to be our failure – there is no final victory. Anxiety increases — can it be done again and with consistency? Repeating while remaining originating indicates the mark of the writer as distinguished from the dabbler. Being repetitive in an original way takes up residence within anxiety, coupled with calm.

One who writes consistently makes some alteration in the difficulties thus far presented. And the joy of writing comes from beginning to sense these alterations. The internal editorial staff gives way to a wide though discriminating sense of taste; the writer detects the value of writing by tasting it. The guardians also open the gate when the script is no longer for the world but the word-as-world. Writing is not to tell the world something, but rather offering, just by the speaking, repair. The destructive urges within desire constitute the basis for creative activities, but the calls to engage with love form that same basis.

Urges for destructiveness do not differ much from the urges for love – when our demons flee, so do the angels. It is only when the two feel extraordinarily similar that we give up the fantasy that dark impulses may be satanic. Relinquishing such an illusion cannot happen without repeatedly practicing putting the gesture of words into writing, not as an attempt to freeze the darkness, but to allow its equality with the light.

One who writes starts becoming a writer when an inchoate desire to become the word begins to arise. This moment promises an end to the crazed dynamic of the love triangle of writer, word, and world. Finding the word finds the world. The point of writing, of its struggles, pains, hurts, is to lose ourselves as word, to wholly give our breath to the sentence so that it might have soul; that it might be a freed sentence, not a prison-sentence by acting as if it belonged to someone. Such is the wish expressed by those who say, "I want to become a writer." It is a kind of death wish, sufficiently disguised so as not to betray its meaning. The sentence says "I want to become a writer," not "I want to be one who writes." It does not even say "I want to become one who uses words." The secret desire of the writer is to become the word. The gesture rather than the completion keeps one writing.

Soul Reading

There are several traditions of soul-reading. Soul-reading aims to move away from reading only for information and concepts and letting the words become living speaking that impress into the life of the soul.

There is the monastic tradition of Lexio Divina. While this form of reading centers on sacred texts in the monastic tradition, we can learn much from it. In this tradition, reading constitutes a supreme act of listening. The words of a book cannot be glossed over, read for informational content only. Language consists of two simultaneous forms happening at the same time. La Lingua, and La Parole, is the way the French linguists speak of these two forms. La Lingua concerns the grammatical structure of the language and its content. La Parole involves the living word. In the tradition of Lexio Divina, the attempt in reading is to hear the living word, as if someone were speaking, and, in fact, someone does speak through the writing ….. the author, the tradition, maybe even the spiritual beings of the word.

This level of reading comes alive when reading aloud. Feel the texture, the qualities of the words. Slow down reading. The soul moves slowly; it loves to linger, making images of what the words are saying. When you read, try to be in the imagination of being read-to.

Remember what it was like to hear stories when you were a child. Approach any writing as if it were a story. Become interested in the words… not just listening through the words into the concepts. Read with your whole body, not only with your eyes.

There is the other great tradition of reading that comes from the medieval world, also centered in the spiritual tradition, the reading of Sacred Texts. However, Dante extended this tradition into all writing and reading. Every text can be simultaneously read at four levels: the literal level, the moral level, the allegorical level and the anagogical level.

Without going into these levels in detail, notice that the first level is the literal level. This is the words as they present themselves. You have to start at this level. You have to get what is said. Thus, always read a text through for an initial understanding – but while doing so, other levels are simultaneously speaking.

Example of the four levels:

If a biblical text says: "Israel went out of Egypt"

The literal level — the Jewish people left Egypt

The moral level — This phrase refers to the conversion of a soul from a sinful life.

The allegorical level — The text is an allegory speaking of redemption through Christian conversion.

The anagogical level — Anagogical means "mystical". The text at this level speaks of the movement of life from temporal to eternal states of being.

It is not necessary to 'analyze' the levels of a text. It is essential to try to hear the polyphony of language, to hear many things being said in a text, and try to take them all in, though all are not taken in through the literal reading going on. Soul and spirit participate and are the real guides of what literally speaks. The literal level is thus important, but most people get completely stuck, caught at the literal level.

Soul Reading is a particular kind of reading in which, through the literal level one tries to hear, or to live in the question: What is being said to the soul and by the soul in this speaking – and, what and how does the soul hear? Unanswerable questions but living experiences easily felt happening.

In order to read in this way, it is necessary to pause a lot in your reading. In the pauses, let what you just read sink from the region of the head into the region of the heart. Then, listen within and try to be aware of the response you hear from within the region of the heart; the answer will not be content but heart-feeling. Try, though, to hear, in an inner way, the soul repeating imaginally what was read and understood mentally when you read the text.

The soul does not speak English – or any other language, so the "hears" images, hears imaginally. If alert, you may re-hear, not in words, but in the many images that come pouring in – probably too fast to get hold of, or too distracting to keeping concentration on the reading. It is unnecessary to hold such images, though some might hold you, and how that happens has importance, for such images will stay and work with and on you. It is only necessary, though, to read with image-awareness as you simultaneously 'believe' you understand what is being said. It is more you are being-understood —- presences "stand under," "stand in and for" your reading. Sometimes they are listening – and when they do, we find ourselves deeply moved, changed. After reading, ask yourself – What stays with you now of what you read? Not necessarily an intellectual content... rather, how are you moved, and if you are not, then either the writing was not originating and creating, but was secondary, or, you read with the intellect alone.

The third imagination of soul reading comes from the practice of hermeneutics. Hermeneutics is the philosophy ...and the art of interpretation. Interpretation here, however, does not mean saying what you think something means. The word "hermeneutics" concerns the art of living at the boundaries of soul, Hermes' gift. He is also the god of communing, of healing, and many other qualities, such as 'telling' you where you are – the 'herm', a standing stone in the middle of nowhere when one is traveling, marking the crossroads where you are and where you are going... herme..neutics. The word means "carrying across."

Hermes is the messenger, moving between the gods and the mortals and the underworld and the mortals. Soul reading moves into the between, feeling the many regions in the text occupied by the souls –of the past and the dead, and the regions occupied by the spirits, and the regions occupied by the humans. Hear a text in this way, as a kind of message from the spirit/soul worlds, clothed in the language of the human world.

The main work of soul reading is to refrain from restricting our reading and the discussion of our reading to: a) "This is what I got out of the reading."
b) "This is what the author means." c) "Let's discuss the reading together." d) "I agree or disagree." Refrain from asking questions as questions move the reading to confinement with the intellect only. Reading listens.

Try instead to re-say what the reading says, speaking now from the viewpoint of the soul. If, for example, a text says: "The soul resonates" — what does the soul hear in these words? How can you say what you hear the soul saying in these words? Take a text as a mystery — as something to enter into more and more deeply, not as something to master and take the living blood out of so you can take the informational knowledge and pack it away

Foundations for a Spirituality of the Future

somewhere. At the same time, respect, respect, respect the literal level of any text. If you do not "get" the literal level, the soul/spirit levels of will always, always, always be wrong, off, artistically bad.

Imagine a text as someone, a soul being, or a spirit, speaking to you.

We cannot live into writing all writing in these ways. Secondary writing – writing that consists of putting together thoughts that have already been thought – "thoughting" rather than creating-thinking – thinking happening as if for the first time — cannot be heard as soul/spirit speaking. Most writing these days consists of a "talking about" rather than "the within emerging" and taking the reader to where it emerges from – that is, the bulk of what passes as writing seldom opens to the soul/spirit dimensions because these dimensions are not present.

Since most writing is not soul/spirit presence, readers have become used to reading with non-presence, and indeed, are educated to read in this manner. Thus, when writing of some depth and awakening is encountered, it will be read as 'non-presence,' for we are used to reading in this manner. Such non-presence exemplifies what now comes over digital devices, so here, special caution, special awareness, must be present, for here, quick reading is the norm. Skimming over the top of soul/spirit writing harms not only the reader, the writing also suffers, for soul and spirit intent has been curtailed.

Foundations of Spiritual Psychology I
A Short Course

I. Introduction
A. Description of the School of Spiritual Psychology

- purpose of the School
The School of Spiritual Psychology has its aim to help people develop embodied conscious soul life that is open and receptive to the spiritual worlds. The work is of individual importance, but the individual in this work is never separated from the earth, culture, and the wider world. The purpose of the work of spiritual psychology is to bring soul life to bear on the challenges and opportunities in the world and to help capacities of spiritual perception and knowledge.

- when we began
The School of Spiritual Psychology began in 1992.

- what we do
The School offers seminars throughout the country, soul retreats, a correspondence course series, individual consultation in Spiritual Therapeutics, a yearly conference, a website, and a blog.

- how the school functions
The programs of the School of Spiritual Psychology are practically oriented. It is not a School per se that we offer, but a Schooling – various practices to help develop embodied, conscious soul life that is open and receptive to the spiritual worlds. The School is not academic in nature, though the work is thoughtful and requires the development of inner discipline, reading, and study.

B. Texts for this course:
Love and the World, by Robert Sardello. Lindisfarne Press, 2001.

Parzival by Wolfram von Eschenbach. Penguin books. Helen Mustard, translator.

C. Instructions for this Correspondence Seminar

Begin by reading through this booklet. First, simply read through the whole booklet. Do not try to understand everything you read. Just read through it, take it in as a whole. This step is important because spiritual psychology always works as a whole. So, you want to begin by taking in the whole of what is presented. It will then begin to work on your soul. The booklet looks small, but it is packed.

Then, a couple of days after you have simply sat down and read the whole document, begin to read now for deeper understanding. Proceed at a pace that is comfortable for you. When you come to something that is puzzling or seems to be difficult, stop. Try to think of an experience that seems to relate to what the text presents. When you feel you have an inner image of what is being talked about, proceed. If you have lingering questions, write them down.

There are four assignments in this seminar. Send in two assignments a time. Do not do the next two assignments until you hear back from the School with a response to your first two assignments. When you do hear back, then go over the comments made to your work. Then, go back and read the whole of this booklet over again. Then, when you are ready, complete the second two assignments and send them to the School. You will receive comments back. When you receive the second set of comments, this will complete this seminar. Send all assignments to:

Robert Sardello

> You must enclose a stamped, self-addressed
> envelope with your assignments if you wish to
> receive comments on your work.

Expect that it will take a week for your assignment to reach the School from the time of mailing. The School will take about two weeks to work with your assignment, putting it in line with other assignments that come it. Then, expect another week for the comments to be returned to you.

II. On the Discipline of Spiritual Psychology
A. The word - "Psychology"

Psychology, "psyche-logos". This word means, "the speech of the soul." Rather than the study of the soul, psychology as an inner discipline asks, in the word itself, for us to learn to listen to soul. Psychology is very different than other disciplines because the only way of knowing the life of the soul is through engagement. You have to "step" into the soul realm to know soul. Soul is known through soul. What today passes as psychology in the world is not typically about the soul but attempts to be a science of human behavior. This kind of psychology recognizes only what is observable and measurable. Or psychology is seen to be a particular way of being of help to others.

Only the tradition of depth psychology holds that all psychology begins with self-knowledge and never leaves that starting point behind. Spiritual psychology draws on Jung's psychology and the Archetypal psychology of James Hillman because of the emphasis on the soul's inner life. Spiritual Psychology also draws on phenomenology because the aim of spiritual psychology, like phenomenology, is not to construct a theory of the soul, but rather to develop the capacities needed to be consciously present in soul and describe soul from within. Spiritual psychology also draws on the Spiritual Science of Rudolf Steiner, Anthroposophy, because Anthroposophy has developed a disciplined approach to spiritual life, and also because the work of Anthroposophy is capable of engaging the world in practical ways – through education, Medicine, architecture, painting, drama, movement, agriculture, etc. Thus, there is much to learn from Anthroposophy concerning the practical dimensions of soul life oriented to spiritual awakening.

Spiritual Psychology is a way of knowing the world as well as oneself. It is not primarily content to be learned as information. No discipline is founded on information alone. For example, if someone wants to become a medical doctor, the studies required consist of learning information, but also of learning to see the human body differently than seen in ordinary life. If someone wants to be a physicist, training in perception is involved that enables the physicist to see what others cannot. Any discipline is a mode, a way of knowing, as well as content. However, only psychology demands that we are aware of the method of knowing as well as the content of knowledge because, in psychology, the mode of knowing is the same as the content known. In this respect, psychology is entirely unlike other disciplines. You can know the soul only as deeply as you have gone into your soul, to paraphrase Jung. Spiritual psychology requires the development of inner capacities, so that spirit/ soul life becomes conscious, and, in a certain sense, even visible, though not visible through the usual senses.

B. Why there are so many different approaches to psychology
- the necessity for continually re-founding the discipline
There are so many different psychologies in the world because the soul is continually changing. Soul is not like a 'thing', not even an invisible 'thing'. Soul evolves, is highly complex, and exists as an activity, an action, not a static thing. Soul is process, the internal process of constantly imagining, not the inner mental presentation of images already made. Also, in the West, we have a pretty poor sense of the complexity of soul life. There are many levels of soul. Spiritual traditions in the East recognize the soul's complexity. Spiritual psychology is concerned with the spirit-soul, which can be provisionally imagined as the border between soul life and spiritual life. At the moment, it is not necessary to try to define either soul or spirit. Each word is a symbol that carries worlds of meaning. If a definition is attempted, there is a narrowing of complex experience to rational and abstract knowledge. Think of soul as the innerness of all things, and spirit as the creating activity of the innerness of all things. Thus, we do not limit soul to the individual. Everything has soul.

C. The Three Founding Streams of Spiritual Psychology
1. Existential Phenomenology
Phenomenology is concerned with being present to what is present. The word itself means "the speech, the logos, of phenomena." Phenomenology intends to allow phenomena of every sort to reveal themselves rather than imposing theories to explain phenomena. As a component of spiritual psychology, phenomenology lets inner experience show its form, character, and content.

There are several approaches to phenomenology, the discipline founded by Edmund Husserl in the last century. He recognized that human beings were rapidly losing the capacity to be present to the world's immediacy and others. Theories are replacing this immediacy. We forget the theories and take the forgotten theories to be reality. For example, consider the human body. The lived body is not the same as the body of anatomy, physiology, and Medicine. Nonetheless, we now live the scientific/medical conception of the body. We have lost connection to the living body as conscious experience, which is quite different from body sensations or feeling. We rely on pre-conceptual experience of the body to get along in the world, but we have lost the logos of the body. We think, for example, that the heart is a pump, not recognizing that this is but one theory of the heart. But people and indeed a whole culture has become enamored, we could say, enchanted, with this theory and have a deep emotional attachment to it. Try to suggest to someone that the heart is not a pump, and you will immediately see that this theory is taken as fact. Once a belief like 'the heart is a pump' is established, then indeed the viewing and understanding of the phenomenon narrows to that belief and 'facts' support that belief. (On the way belief works, see the amazing work of Phineas Quimby, the founder of the "New Thought" movement).

The particular approach to phenomenology, which is the discipline of returning to the immediacy of experience and developing the capacity to describe what we experience, is existential phenomenology. This approach to phenomenology began in the Netherlands and was brought to this country primarily by Adrian Van Kaam to Duquesne University.

Some Texts:

William Luijpen, Existential Phenomenology

Stephen Strasser Phenomenology and the Human Sciences

Erwin Straus, Phenomenological Psychology

Medard Boss, Existential Foundations of Psychology and Medicine

Adrian Van Kaam, Existential Foundations of Psychology

Maurice Merleau-Ponty, Phenomenology of Perception

J. H. Van den Berg, A Different Existence

2. Some of the founding principles of Phenomenological Psychology
On the nature of consciousness as intentional

Phenomenology begins with the sense of the inherent intentionality of consciousness – consciousness is always consciousness-of-something. Consciousness always has an object, and the object of consciousness cannot be separated from consciousness itself. This founding principle, based on observation, has the implication that we must always look to particular instances in order to understand the operations of consciousness. If we just speak of 'consciousness' we are speaking an abstraction. For example, emotional consciousness is the bodily and psychic act of holding something in affective regard. We need a sense of what an emotion concerns – what is its world? its time? its space?

Being-in-the-World

Existential phenomenology understands the human being as ex-isting, that is, as standing out in the world. We belong to the world. Human beings are not in the world the way in which apples are in a box. The world is not just a container. We co-exist with the world. We do not create our reality, but are together with the world and together, exist in our fundamental being as creating beings, the mode of perception needed to perceive our living presence in the world. That is, to perceive the operation of soul within and within the world, a creative act of perception is needed. This creative act of perception has to be prepared for. We have to develop the capacity to perceive through soul as in our ordinary consciousness this capacity is asleep.

Being-in-Time

Human beings are time beings. We do not just exist in a neutral world with time as an independent factor that is now measured by the clock. Lived-time is very different than clock time. There is work-time, leisure-time, love-time, depression-time, and many, many other kinds of time. Soul-time never heard of the clock.

Being embodied

To be human is to be embodied, but the living body is not the same as the body known by science, biology, biochemistry, and Medicine. The living body is the place from which the whole of the world opens for us. The living body is the power to move around in the world. The phenomenologist Maurice Merleau-Ponty describes the living body as the "I am able." The living body is inherently expressive.

The phenomenological method

Phenomenology is not a theory but a method. We now have to undergo a discipline to be able to be present to the immediacy of experience. This discipline begins with the conscious work of placing what we already 'know' into brackets, that is consciously attempting to put aside for a while what we know and attempt to be present to the immediacy of experience. This immediacy does not mean going to the level of feelings or of sensations, because these too are now covered over by conceptual constructions. For an excellent example of the practice of phenomenological description in psychology, see the writings of J.H. Van den Berg. The work is to simply be present to a phenomenon without imposing what we think about it, and let the phenomena itself shape the way we speak it. This method is central to the work of Spiritual Psychology.

Here is an example of a description of an experience. The event was a phone call from a friend in difficulty. After receiving the call, this description was written with the purpose of serving as an example of what a description of immediate experience is like:

> *T. calls me in a panic. The panic is palpable; it comes through the phone and is as if it leaks out the receiver into my ear and through my body, like liquid ice. He speaks of feeling completely betrayed by four people he has worked with for twelve years as their supervisor, their director. The experience of the call, the initial moment —it is as if a voice comes to me out of the depths of the darkness. This quality of darkness announces itself, as if saying this is not an ordinary call. The darkness is not blackness in spite of the bleakness of the voice. The person calling is located somewhere in that darkness; in fact, all that is left of him is a voice, as if supported by the darkness. His voice pushes out of the darkness and gradually becomes more forceful while filled with pleading. I have to work to be able to listen in a way that allows him to speak, not so much to me, as into a different kind of field. I do not feel I am perceived by this person as an individual right now. It is more like a voice in the darkness is searching for some familiarity. My listening is called upon to let the voice from the darkness move out instead of round and round in circles. He needs someone to hear his plight, as if hearing it will turn on a light. He has tangled with these feelings of betrayal alone, as if only inside his head. I feel that I am being dumped on and also that I am going to be*

asked to do something, and that the call is somewhat manipulative. I work
to back away from these feelings and to re-open and remain with the sense
of the field that has the qualities of depth. My effort is in that direction. To
let the panicked voice find a resting place.

I find it enormously difficult to hold to this deep and open field and he is so
caught in the emotion of what has happened to him that it is most difficult
to just be in silence together even for a moment. As a way of trying to
keep the field open, I, without thinking about it, try to focus on the details
of what happened, to hear the story. I find myself doing this because the
emotion expressed is so overwhelming that I can feel it crushing the open
and dark space of the field. He is full of emotional judgments concerning
those four people. How terrible they are. What they have done to him
after all that he has done for them. My focus does not get out of the
emotion but gives the emotion something to stick to so that it does not float
around in a circular way and go right back into him. But, in the process it
feels as if a film of goo oozes onto me and breathing becomes an effort.
I begin to feel his anxiety. The anger is laced with anxiety and they attack.
I work to breathe in what is being said into the heart and breath out
through the solar plexus. I do this because I feel the anxiety in the solar
plexus, and I am trying to get free enough of the anxiety of this person that
I can just listen. There are only fragmentary moments that I can just
listen. I either want to console or to offer advice about what to do, or offer
to do something. It is as if I have to keep fighting off the anger and the
anxiety, which come at me as if there were autonomous beings. It is like
suddenly being in a swirl; it feels like walking unawares into a hornet's
nest. There are too many negative things coming at me. I can't find the
space of listening.

I have a moment of feeling that the fears this person is feeling and
emotions this person is feeling do not only have to do with what has
happened to him. The call is not so much about the betrayal. It is that the
betrayal took the ground from beneath my friend and he does not know
where he is or what is coming next. The betrayal severed the support of
the past, the support my friend has relied on. This is a huge transitional
time for this person, a liminal time, a threshold. His time with these people
is at an end and he is thrown into not knowing where he is or who he is. I

*have only a slight and momentary sense of this threshold and that sense
helps give a contour to the initial experience of a voice coming toward me
out of the depths of darkness. In this place, the past is gone and there is no
sense of the future. That is what comes to this person. That is the
darkness. But I now feel the darkness differently. As the angel of
darkness. What comes to my friend is the protection of a mantle of
darkness. He cannot sense this, though. And I cannot say this without
objectifying it. I rest, though, in the darkness surrounding his voice now.*

Assignment #1

A. Write an experiential description of an inanimate object, such as a
pencil or a cup, something quite simple. However, you must put aside what
you know and simply perceive what is in front of you and describe the
immediate experience of the way the object presents itself. This description
is to be no longer than a single, double-spaced, typed page.

B. Write an experiential description of something in the natural world. For
example, write a description of your immediate sensation (sensation, not
perception – perception is filled with our concepts, for example our concepts
of what a tree looks like, neglecting the other senses) of a tree, or of a plant,
or of a sunset, or clouds. Again, put aside what you know and simply
perceive what is in front of you and describe the immediate experience. This
description is to be no longer than a single, double-spaced, typed page. Be
sure to describe the object of your experience, not just your experience of
the object. That is, phenomenological description is non-dualist. Experience
is not subjective! Experience is not just your reaction to something!
Experience is not private. It includes both your presence and the object you
are present with –both at once.

C. Write an experiential description of an experience of fear that you have
felt. This description takes us further into the soul realm. To write this
description, it is necessary to describe the circumstances of the experience,
the fear process itself, how fear came into you, what it was like, what

happened to it, and how you were after the fear. This description is to be no longer than a single, double-spaced, typed page.

1. The Stream of Jung and Archetypal Psychology
Jung's depth psychology and its extension into Archetypal Psychology is important to the foundations of Spiritual Psychology.

Jung was, in part, a phenomenologist of soul life. There is also a great deal of theory in Jung, so it is necessary to tease out the phenomenology of the soul in his works. James Hillman's extension of Jung into Archetypal Psychology is highly important because of its emphasis on soul-as-image. Further, Hillman's work develops a language of the phenomenology of soul life and provides a significant bridge to being present to soul life not only within the individual but also within the world.
Some texts:

C. G. Jung	Collected Works
James Hillman	Re-Visioning Psychology
James Hillman	The Myth of Analysis
James Hillman	The Thought of the Heart and the Soul of the World
James Hillman	The Soul's Code
Gerhard Wehr	Jung and Steiner: The Birth of a New Psychology (Introduction by Robert Sardello)

2. The Stream of the Spiritual Science of Rudolf Steiner
The Spiritual Science of Rudolf Steiner is important to the development of spiritual psychology because spirit is central to Steiner's work. Anthroposophy, a term which means "the wisdom of the human being" looks upon the human being archetypally. This differs from depth psychology where archetypal imagination is confined to the psyche of the human being. Spiritual Psychology differs from depth and Archetypal psychology because it is concerned with the spirit- soul, but the spirit-soul as lived and expressed in our humanness. In Jung, soul and spirit are more or less haphazardly mixed. Jung is concerned at times with spirit archetypes, but that interest is solely a soul interest. In other places what is soul and what is spirit in Jung is mixed up. The spirit/soul is not a separate soul, but can be

best imagined as the level of soul that is open and receptive to the beings of the spiritual worlds.

Some anthoposophical texts relevant to psychology:

Rudolf Steiner   A Psychology of Body, Soul, and Spirit
(Introduction by Robert Sardello)

Rudolf Steiner   Psychoanalysis and Spiritual Psychology
(Introduction by Robert Sardello)

III. Psychology and the Consciousness Soul

A. Guiding thought of the whole course

"Psychology must be founded anew out of the consciousness soul. This psychology is not to be a theory, but rather a spiritual activity. The function of this psychology is to work against the decline of the psychical in the world; that is its anthroposophic purpose." - Rudolf Steiner

(Note: Steiner sometimes uses the term 'consciousness soul', which means the same as the spirit-soul.)

B. Working with this statement

- characterizing the consciousness soul

The consciousness soul, on the one hand, characterizes our ordinary consciousness. In ordinary consciousness there is a split between inner consciousness and its objects and consciousness of the outer world and its objects. We do not experience belonging to that which we perceive in the world. The inner life is either neglected or it is focused on obsessively and egotistically. When we begin to work with this typical consciousness, however, we find that it is the same as the spiritual soul. By 'working' with it, I mean, engaging in certain exercises, such as the phenomenological descriptions you are writing, that begin to help us be aware of the union between the inner life and the outer world. Not identity, but union. When we delve further into the characteristics of this union, we begin to have intimations that our consciousness is not completely ours but that what we call consciousness is the working of spiritual beings through us. This recognition begins to sound like archetypal and depth psychology, except the beings are here imagined as real beings, independent and autonomous. Not psychic beings, and even more than archetypal beings. More because the spiritual beings that work through us have more to do with the future, with possibility, with what we can become as human beings than, as with depth and archetypal psychologies, beings of the deep past.

- difference between working out of a theory and engaging in spiritual activity
Jung and even Archetypal psychology are theory bound. The only way the depths of the spiritual soul can be known is through engagement. We have to find the ways, the methods, to come into direct experience of the depth of the spirit-soul, and then be able to describe such experiences. And, since the innerness of the world coheres with the spirit- soul, the kinds of experiences described will always have a world component. That is, spiritual psychology is inherently a world soul psychology and a cultural psychology.

- on the decline of the psychical in the world; the effects of this decline
Steiner, in around 1910, already recognized that soul was being lost in the world. This endangerment of the life of the soul has only increased since that time. It has come to the point that very few people understand what is meant by the term soul. It has become a specialized term, in spite of the fact that soul is as or more important to being human than having a heart, that is, a physical heart, for the imaginal heart intimately functions with and even as soul.

IV. The Myths Backing different kinds of Depth Psychology

One of the valuable contributions of Archetypal Psychology is its insistence on 'seeing through' what we usually take as content. This 'seeing through' extends to the discipline of depth psychology itself. When there is a psychological act of "seeing through" experience deeply, we come to some mythic form, some myth that is backing the psychology. For Psychoanalysis, the founding myth is the Oedipus Myth. Thus, when Psychoanalysis is "seen through" we see this myth as founding the discipline. For Jung's psychology and Archetypal psychology, the founding myth is the Eros and Psyche story. And for Spiritual psychology, one of the essential founding myths is the Grail Myth.

A. Psychoanalysis and the Oedipus Myth

- there is much more to the story of Oedipus than the desire of the boy child to kill his father and marry his mother; this is a degraded understanding of what Freud was about. While there is something to this level, at the most, it is a reflection of deeper matters, matters of which Freud had significant intuitions:

- the Oedipus myth is a myth of the beginning of ego-consciousness and of the ending of ancient forms of clairvoyance.

- the story: story of Laius, king of Thebes, and his wife, Queen Jocasta. They had no offspring; Laius inquired of the Oracle at Delphi whether he might not have a son. The Oracle said: "If you want to have a son, then it will be such a one that he will kill you."

- A son was born; Laius became afraid the prophecy would be fulfilled; he took the boy, pierced his feet (Oedipus means "pierced feet) and abandoned him. A shepherd found Oedipus in Corinth. When he grew up, he searched for his parents; along the way, he came across an individual, got into a fight, and killed him; he did not know it was his father. He went on to Thebes, which was under the siege of a monster. The monster was killing everyone and said that the city would be spared only if someone could answer the riddle of the Sphinx: "What walks on four legs in the morning, two at midday, and three in the evening?" Oedipus answered the riddle – it is Man

- and he saved Thebes. He received the hand of the Queen, Jocasta. Oedipus did not know this was his mother; ruin came to the city; Oedipus finds out what he had done and blinds himself.

B. What the Myth Concerns

Oedipus is removed from the past, from memory, from the memory residing in the blood, which is a source of natural clairvoyance. In times when blood memory was strong, so also was clairvoyance. Even today, people who are spontaneously clairvoyant inherit this capacity, which is in their bloodline. Oedipus is one of the first individuals to establish an independent sense of the "I", of ego-consciousness. In this independence, though, he does not realize what has been lost; this memory capacity of the blood; consequently, he does not recognize his parents, when, if blood memory was awake, he would have felt a connection. The Oedipus myth functions as a myth of the ego, the story of the founding of ego-consciousness.

(A "definition" of myth: Myth is something that never happened but is always happening.)

C. Why Psychoanalysis places this Myth at the Center of its psychology

- there is a level of the soul where this myth does reflect a soul reality; we imagine ourselves to be independent of our family, of the past; this forgetting brings untold difficulties; so, for Freud, anamnesis, un-forgetting, is essential to the health of the soul. In addition, of far greater importance, is Freud's method through which memories are brought forth; the method of association, and the method of the talking cure, of which the phenomenon of transference is central. Transference is a psychological term that actually is an imagination of a new kind of love, the love of the soul.

What is most important, though, is that the enterprise of psychoanalysis involves the act of remembering; the active work of re-membering the past; which is also a training of imagination, for memory is never literal, never just factual. What was previously given, in earlier times, as a natural capacity

- to be in connection with the deep past through the blood, now has to be a conscious task.

D. Jung and the Eros-Psyche Myth

A myth also backs the depth psychology of Jung - the Eros and Psyche Myth. James Hillman worked with this myth as central to Jung's psychology in <u>The Myth of Analysis</u>. The story is from a longer tale, <u>The Golden Ass,</u> written in about the 4th century A.D. The story concerns Lucius, who is turned into an ass by a witch, and of the adventures of Lucius to find redemption from his fate. He goes through many trials and many adventures. Embedded within the tale there is this most beautiful story of Eros and Psyche.

- a telling of the story
Some essential elements of the story. Psyche is the most beautiful of all mortals. She is honored by all. Venus is enraged because the honor due her is being given instead to Psyche. But, no one will marry Psyche. Psyche's father goes to the Oracle and asks what to do to get Psyche married. The Oracle says to take Psyche to a high mountain and leave her and someone will come to her. In the meantime, Venus, in her rage, sends her son, Eros, to infect Psyche with love. Psyche is thus stricken by Eros and taken from the mountain top to his abode. She lives in the beautiful palace, but she never

sees her husband, Eros. He only comes in the dark of night to visit her. Psyche's sisters are envious, and they instill doubt in Psyche about the identity of her husband. They say, 'how to do you who you have married, what kind of person he is. He could be a monster." So, one night, when Eros comes, Psyche had made a plan to see him. She had hidden a lit candle, and when he comes to her, she turns the light on him. The moment she sees him, he flees. Psyche then has to go in search of Eros. She goes through a series of significant trials. She has to separate a large pile of different kinds of seeds. She succeeds through the help of ants. She has to retrieve the golden fleece. She also has to retrieve a vial from the deep. In the meantime, Eros works out a deal with Hermes that allows him to return to Psyche and Venus to be placated. Psyche and Eros are re-united and have an offspring, Joy.

E. The significance of this myth

- like the Oedipus myth, this story also begins with the visit by a father to the Oracle; and the Oracle actually announces that a new form of love would come and be united with Psyche. When Eros is present, then Psyche lives in fantasy, in images. Psyche's sisters, who might be called Envy and Jealousy, come along and question the imagination that she is living; they actually, in a certain sense, are of great service to her, because her imagination is undifferentiated. When Psyche finally sees Eros, he flees. She must go in search of him and go through the series of trials. The first trial is a picture of the work we must go through to differentiate our emotions, a work of separating; the second trial pictures how passion cannot be dealt with directly, head on, and the need for the right rhythms; the third trial pictures the need to die to our fantasies of love and realize that love comes as a gift of the gods.

- This story, too, speaks of a level of the soul, what Rudolf Steiner speaks of as the intellectual soul; the intellectual soul does not mean abstract thought; it also refers to the capacities for distinguishing one thing from another, not just the intellectual capacity to do so, but also the emotional and instinctual, and most importantly, the psychic capacity to do so.

- This story also shows that our fantasies, our imaginations have an archetypal character to them. When we fall in love, for example, there is an awakening of fantasy; these imaginations have very little to do with the actual person but are the medium through which we connect soul to soul. Image is the medium and content of soul.

- this story also shows that psychic reality becomes conscious only when there is Eros. That is, love is necessary and intrinsic to soul experience. We cannot be in connection with soul life unless we feel the inner sense of love of the soul. This is a most important point.

F. The Grail Story as the Myth backing Spiritual Psychology
(for elaboration, read *Parzival* by Wolfram von Eschenbach)

A. *The Imagination of the Grail*

- The Grail is imaged as a vessel; a vessel has the quality of receiving and the quality of giving forth what one needs
- ancient mysteries of the concave object have to do with the relationship between the Earthly and the Divine – the earthly as the receiving vessel of the fluid, spiritual worlds.
- e.g. Earth-mound cave at New Grange in Ireland; over 6000 years old At this site, at a particular time of the year, a priestess would go deep inside the earth-mound. At one place there would be an opening in the mound that would allow the light of a particular star to shine in at a particular moment of the year. When this happened, the light would shine in on a concave object of crystal. The priestess at that moment would go into a vision in which she saw the whole mystery of creation happening. The priestess would then share this vision with the community. This event is perhaps one of the earliest versions of the Grail – the coming together of the divine and the earthly in such a way that all of creation is given to us through community.

B. *On Sacred Vessels of Plenty – there are versions of the Grail Object in every spiritual tradition:*

Buddhist - focuses on the rice bowl as a sacred object of meditation
Taoist - focuses on the three-legged cauldron of Bronze - the I-Ching
Jew- passes the Seder cup, which contained knowledge of the Cabala, the sacred word of the Divine
Christian - takes communion from the Chalice
- Other sacred Vessels:
Irish - Dagda's Cauldron; could feed an entire army without becoming empty
Nordic - Vessel of Sinnreger; contains wisdom and inspiration

Welch - Basket of Gwyddno Gahanhir; place food for one person in the basket; sustenance for a hundred.

-The Chalice of the Last Supper - Joseph of Arimathea is imprisoned in a tower for many years, and yet needs no food or water. He receives everything he needs from the Chalice.

C. *Wolfram Von Eschenbach's* <u>Parzival</u>

(Read <u>Parzival</u> by Wolfram von Eschenbach in conjunction with this section)

Read this translation, available on Amazon Books:

Here is a website that summarizes Parzival:

<u>https://www.mcgoodwin.net/pages/otherbooks/we_parzival.html</u>

- written down in the 12th century A.D. a story, an initiation document for the time of the consciousness soul

- a new understanding of the Grail; no longer an outer object that mediates between the human and the divine

- The Grail is now each and every individual, who is called to go through the process of inner development to form themselves into a vessel - of receiving and giving creative love

- <u>Parzival</u> is not a work of literature; an initiation document; instructions on this process, written in the form of a veiled story; the source of the story – the stars. In the book we are told that the story came from a reader-of-the-stars. This does not mean astrology. It refers to someone who had the capacity to see the movement of the stars and feel within this story unfolding in the movement of the stars.

- How we will approach this story:

we will not explicate the whole of the story;

- it is a text to be lived with for a very long time; Note; Freud does not explicate the Oedipus Myth; Jung does not explicate the Eros/Psyche myth; we are not engaged in mythical analysis or literary criticism; let the whole imagination of the story live within.

V. Spiritual Psychology and Our Relation to Our Past

A. Beginning of the Story

- Gamuret, the father of Parzival

- his father dies; inheritance left to his brother; his brother generously offers to share his inheritance

- Gamuret declines accepting anything; he speaks of a yearning in the region of the heart, a passionate yearning

- Gamuret does not know what the yearning is about; he thinks it is a yearning for adventure; he changes the emblem on his coat of arms - from a panther to an anchor; he goes East, joins the army of the Baruch of Baghdad

- comes to the castle of Petalamunt - it is under siege, 16 gates; half under a Moorish army; half by a white army; esoteric significance – this has to do with the 'throat chakra'; the throat chakra has 16 petals. Eight of these petals were opened for humanity in the past. The work of the consciousness soul is to open the other 8 petals. Then, there is the soul-creating of the word. Spiritual psychology is a work to come to the soul-creating of the word.

- Queen Balakane – this name means "Pelican"; Gamuret marries her; does not stay with her; she has a son, Fierefis.

- Gamuret continues following Lady Adventure; comes to another castle; Herzeloide – this name means "Heart's Sorrow"; Gamuret falls in love with her; marries her; a son from this union, Parzival – This name means "Pierce through the Middle"

- Gamuret leaves after a while; engages in more battles; his death, due to sorcery; an alchemical preparation of the blood of a goat; hot, poured on the diamond of Gamuret's helmet; melts the diamond, Gamuret loses his strength

B. Psychological Reflection

- the putting aside of what Gamuret was given; an intimation of what is necessary to enter into spirit-soul; don't live by what you have been given; all this must be made conscious and seen through; esoterically, in the past, spiritual connection was given through the past in the old ways of the soul; but this is the new way. We have to put aside the past, know it thoroughly, and know how it affects us, but be able to put it aside

- what we have learn to put aside (this does not mean forget it, it will come back, but in a new way, when the capacities of the spiritual soul are developed)

- what we have been given by family, education, church, society, others; this will all come back, given in a new way.

- the change of the coat of arms; what Gamuret lives - the heat of the panther; what he needs; anchoring in the watery element of soul

- Gamuret's error; he confuses his passion with his spiritual yearning; cannot tell one from the other. They are still mixed in him. Often, our passion is really spiritual yearning, but we think it is a passion for someone. Then when we get what we want, we find the passion, the deep sense of longing is still present. Gamuret is like this. He keeps moving from one passion to the next and cannot see that his passion is actually spiritual longing.

-Gamuret changes the coat of arms of the anchor back to the panther; his passion is his downfall, the place where he is subject to attack, his confusion;

- an important note; do not take the figures of this story as having to do with men and women; nor with the masculine and the feminine; reflect on the qualities to come to what the images speak of the spirit-soul.
Gamuret's passion - his relation to Belakane- soul abandonment
Gamuret's passion - his relation to Herzeloide - heart sorrow

VI. Parzival's Birth and Upbringing
A. Herzeloide
- takes Parzival into the woods of Soltaine, away from culture, education, religion, civilization; he is not even told his name. She did not want him to know anything about knights because she knew he would want to be a knight. She feared that he would be killed as her husband was killed.
B. Parzival
- the incident of shooting birds with bow and arrow. One day, young Parzival was in the woods, shooting birds with his bow and arrow. He hits a bird and it falls to the ground, dead. Parzival spontaneously begins crying. He does not know about death but feels something deeply.

- meeting with King Arthur's knights in the woods. One day Parzival is walking through the woods when all of a sudden, an immense, bright light flashes, like fire from the sky. Parzival drops to his knees and says that God is present. The light is caused by the sun gleaming off the suits of armor of a group of King Arthur's knights. They laugh at naïve Parzival. When he finds out who they are, he knows that he must become a knight.

- leaves his mother; she dies, he does not know this.
- his encounter with Jeschute. On his journey, Parzival comes to a tent. He goes in and sees a beautiful woman, asleep. He sits down, eats her food, and takes her brooch and leaves. When Jeschute's husband comes home he thinks that she has been unfaithful to him and punishes her by making her ride, clothed in rags, on a nag, behind him for years. Parzival's mother had told him a story involving a ring and brooch. It was a story that was a way of telling Parzival about taking favors from women, a kind of instruction in proper ways of treating women. Parzival, at this stage is a complete literalist, and takes the story literally.
- his encounter with Sigune. Later in the story, Parzival comes to a clearing in the woods. A woman sits in the center of the clearing, holding her dead fiancé. Parzival is interested in what he sees because he has never seen a dead knight. But he has no capacity of compassion for Sigune.
- His encounter with Cunneware
- marriage to Condwiramurs - "bringer of love"

His encounter with Kundry. Just at the point where Parzival is about to become an Arhurian knight, a strange being rides into camp. She is quite ugly. She shouts at Parzival, telling him that he is not worthy to be an Arthurian knight. He then goes wandering, lost for a long time, until he can come to his own destiny.

C. Psychological Reflection

- Again, the theme of leaving everything that one has been given behind. We saw this theme with Parzival's father, Gamuret. Here it is again. Herzeloide leaves everything behind to take Parzival into the unknown. In order to enter into the spirit-soul, it is necessary to leave the past, that is, not be governed by the past, but to find the way to the heart, and from within the heart, be awake to incoming destiny and develop the capacity to create the images to carry out the sense of destiny calling from the future. We are, in spiritual psychology, called to what we can be, more so than derive our identity from what pushes us from the past. While other psychologies emphasize the importance of the past, and thus, of fate, spiritual psychology emphasizes the future, possibility, the not-yet --- our destiny.

- Parzival; initially an image of the idealism of spirit without soul. We see that spirit without soul is completely literalistic; it takes everything literally, and in doing so brings great harm to others, but this harm is not seen. After Kundry confronts Parzival, he has to go on a journey in which he becomes aware of all the harm his naïve and literalistic idealism has caused others.

-his relation to Jeschute like our first connection with the soul level. He approaches Jeschute the way we approach our dreams. We want to take what is bright and shiny from our dreams and do not recognize that we are supposed to give over our ego and enter into the imaginal process of the dream.

-his relation to Sigune - no capacity of compassion at first. He has no soul connection to Sigune, nor to suffering.

- note; the story is not about the spirit and about the soul; it is about the process of becoming conscious in soul and spirit

- note; the importance of the encounter with Kundry; she is his angel, the one who knows and guides his destiny; he is not destined to be an Arthurian knight but a Grail knight; note, how the worst things that happen to us may well be the work of our angel protecting our life destiny

-what happens to Parzival after he leaves King Arthur's camp - he wanders, essentially alone, for five years, finally giving up, giving the reins over and letting his horse find the way; an image of relinquishing the egotism of our idealism; this does not lead to intertia, giving up, but to giving over

VII. Yearning and Sorrow

A. How to put aside the past, beliefs, assumptions, etc. This is the first and a most central aspect of Spiritual Psychology. We must be aware and in good connection with our past, but have to quite consciously put it aside, put it on the shelf for a while, so that we can be open to destiny experience that is coming from the future. That is, we want to work to become aware of what we can become. As long as we are occupied, usually unknowingly, by the past, we cannot live our destiny, but are caught in our fate. Here are some ways to work at become aware of and putting the past into brackets for a while:

Assignment #2

1. Backward review of the day. Each day, before going to sleep, review each event of the day in backward order. (Note: this exercise is different that an exercise recommended by Rudolf Steiner, which is to review the events of the day in backward order and also to imagine the events themselves as moving backward). You begin with the event that occurred closest to the end of the day, review it as it happened. Feel remorse for hurts caused and opportunities missed, and gratitude for help given and received. This requires, of course, objective observation and intelligent judgment and evaluation of these events. This exercise should not become a cause for brooding or depression or guild feelings. The events reviewed must be put out of mind after the review is completed

This exercise offers several important benefits. (1) It trains us to be observant; (2) It empties the 'subconscious mind", freeing us from the inner psychological festering of unresolved events; (3) It develops the most important capacity of the *witness* – the capacity of our individual spirit to observe the events we are living while being fully engaged with them.

When you have done this exercise for one full month, then write a description of your experience of this exercise. What was it like doing the exercise? What happened? What seems to be the result of doing this exercise?

2. Recall of the events of your life, one by one, starting from the present and working backward; that is, take several weeks and review your life, starting with the most recent events of note and working backwards. It is an excellent way to put the past on the shelf. Many spiritual traditions advise doing this kind of retrospective look. It is important to be impartial and objective, as if you were looking at someone else. Write out this backward life review and then, in a separate section, describe the effects on you of doing this exercise as you see them showing up in daily life

B. The Qualities that Remain as we become aware of our Lived Assumptions

- a quality of <u>yearning</u>; note: this quality characterizes Gamuret and Parzival

- a quality of <u>sorrow</u>; note: this quality characterizes Belakane, Jeschute and Sigune

- we tend to literalize the quality of yearning, imagine that there is something in the world that will satisfy this yearning - things, power, position, love, religion; and then we try to get this thing; never learn to work with yearning in a healthy way.

- there is an object to our yearning, but it is ineffable; need to be aware that the yearning we feel is also a yearning for us; that is, the object of yearning is yearning, and not something that will satisfy it; need to be aware of the object of yearning; the work is to be present to the yearning without needing to satisfy it; an elemental spiritual quality; a way of characterizing the experience of spirit; develop the capacity to follow the yearning without expecting its completion

- note how yearning moves outward - tends to get way ahead of itself; wants the completion rather than the process

- note how every yearning, when literalized, increases the inner quality of sorrow; this can also happen with our spiritual yearnings

- working with our sorrow is somewhat different; note how sorrow moves inward rather than outward; a quality of depth

- a strong tendency to want to get rid of our sorrow; attribute as a cause of our sorrow something that happened to us in the past; feel that if we could know what this cause is, we could rid ourselves of the sorrow;

- need to work at being true to our sorrow; what we think caused our sorrow is not the cause but a gateway to sorrow that has been opened;

-be present to the sorrow without trying to get rid of it; it is necessary to work on becoming aware of the doorways in order to work with sorrow in a healthy way; need to develop the capacity of stillness

VIII. Spiritual Psychology as an Intelligence of the Heart
A. Holding yearning and sorrow together

- tendency is very strong for these two qualities to separate; and the separation then becomes institutionalized, or even legitimized as:

-the masculine and the feminine
these qualities do not just float around; they become our institutional/
cultural structures and bias; and then, we try to solve the split in ways that it
can never be solved.

- an image of the holding together of yearning and sorrow: Parzival's first
visit to the Grail castle; the Grail castle is the place of imagination; it is
something very real, but not literal; Parzival enters imagination, but he is
not aware of doing so; for him, it is more like entering a trance state.

- note: Parzival does not ask any questions; his mother told him not to,
and his first teacher told him to only ask the right questions; an image of not
being fully alert, fully conscious; a kind of sleepy consciousness

- Note; Spiritual Psychology requires the awakening of imagination;
imagination while fully awake; different than imagination in Freud and Jung;
this is not an altered state; not a shamanic state; not a trance state; it is a
more comprehensive consciousness of the type we experience in ordinary
waking life, but much more intensified in the direction of the subtle and the
invisible.

- an image of the intention of the Grail castle as the place of
imagination: The Grail procession

- an individual enters the room holding a sword - the capacity of
differentiation

-a second individual enters the room carrying a bleeding lance; an image
of the fallenness of desire

- the Grail procession led by Repanse de Shoy - the imagination of the
creating beings and activities of the cosmos

-Amfortas - the imagination of love, but an old kind love, no longer what is
needed – Amfortas was the guardian of the Grail, and was the one who was
supposed to bring a new form of love, creative love, into the world. He fell
back into romantic love.

- What begins to occur as we learn to hold together yearning and sorrow:

      Yearning develops into the conscious capacity to love
      Sorrow develops into the conscious capacity of compassion

Assignment #3

Remember an inner block that seemed to be a hindrance in your life. Where in your past did this hindrance seem to originate? Now take the same inner block and describe how this block in fact is a shaping force that does not come from the past, but is rather a signaling of your movement, first, into a time of unknowing and confusion, which then opens to your discovering new capacities and a creative way into the future. Describe the experience of entering into unknowing and confusion – what happened, what was it like. Then describe how your life shifted and you moved into something quite new and unexpected. Note. This kind of life-movement is something very different than the clique that we learn from our difficulties, that we can, in certain circumstances overcome our difficulties. We are looking here for an instance in which the spirit-soul comes into momentary consciousness, a moment in which we suddenly see that we are not governed by the past but are open in freedom to what comes to us from the unknown future. This is a Grail experience.

IX. Spiritual Psychology as Radical Receptivity
A. Grieving as a turn-around of soul life
a) The women of the Grail; these women figures are all imaginations of aspects of soul.

B. Radical Receptivity and Developing Stillness
1. The Grail stories of Sigune and Cunneware
a. Cunneware and the waiting for the one most deserving of the highest praise.

Recognition indicated by laughter (recognition of Parzifal, not at him, but because of his entering the hall. Parzifal carries the possibility for, and is currently, the one most deserving of the highest praise). The act of re-cognition is perception of the future coming into the present, not obscured by the past.
b. Sigune is a figure engaged in the activity of receiving the innerness world through the holding of Schionatulander throughout the events of the story. Her dead fiancé is the figure of the things, the inner contents of

the world in their utter physical qualities, and their symbolic and spiritual aspects. Sigune holds the evidence of the world in its injury and sacrifice. The activity of holding invites the soul of the world through the individual discipline of acceptance without judgment and expectation. When, for example, we enter into grieving, holding suffering without expectation, we notice that the world begins to be more vivid. We have to be, in a way, empty in soul in order to become available for the time current of the future to enter into soul life and to begin to have a sense of living our destiny rather than our fate. It is thus necessary to understand something of the nature of time and the soul.

C. Time and the Soul

This section on Time and the Soul is a contribution by Cheryl Sanders-Sardello

1. The element of perception of destiny in the activity of Radical Receptivity

The nature of Time:

2. The Time of Life - duration - time as a river, a flow. the time of harvest, sleep, play, work, love, birth, death. weaving experience into context; perception into relationship and interrelationship; knowledge into wisdom. Introduction of the calendar begins to dull this sense of time as duration.

3. The Time of the Clock - rhythm - the measure of time through seconds and minutes and hours. One can count seconds because they are not time but space. We begin to attempt to measure and count time since we cannot hold it still. We delineate the passage by counting off the singular demise of each passing moment.

4. The Time of the Schedule - pace - a sacrifice of the present to the past to be in control of the future. That is, with the schedule we are always thinking of the future, but this is not the future that is known through creative love. It is the unknown future that we are trying to control by scheduling it. We begin to sacrifice what is now for the illusion of making now be like what was, for the sake of prescribing what will be. (Onset of addictive thinking)

a. addictive thinking: almost every thought we have is given to us, not just in its content, but also in the form of the thoughts. How to think becomes directed and defined by what to think and the very capacity to think at all.

b. thought forms become repetitions of what has come before, and when we cannot break out of the given form, we are addicted. Addicted thinking is the part that is most dead in our lives.

5. the past - which becomes our most reassuring reality, because we think it can be known. The forms of addicted thinking are the calendar, the clock, the schedule and the program.

6. creating an historic future. An 'historic future' takes what it wants from the past to construct a theory of the future; an abstraction, usually created by fear. The historic future cuts off the possibility to engage in the act of receptivity - it does not allow for living into the future as an unknown. In the historic future we cannot participate in lived time, thus we are no longer aware of having, or living a destiny. With no destiny we lose purpose, and hope.

7. The Time of the Program - computer time - the loss of time altogether as a personal experience. The advent of having "no time" to accomplish the activities proscribed by life, much less any sense of personal time, for an inner life. Program time loses all purpose or sense of destiny because the model for time itself is based on the instantaneousness of the computer and the seemingly endless capacity of the computer to call up (re-call) or combine bits of information instantly. The sense that this is a capacity rather than a tool confuses our imagination of what intelligence is.

From this point we have gone two ways. One is the courageous individual who embarks on "new beginnings," a heart activity in the world. Courage as the activity of the heart.

The other route, usually valued as the more rational, is to take up the time of the Program - the collapse of time, the beginning of "No Time" - the sacrifice of time and space to the image of the achievement of goals defining the qualities of life, directed and formed through the nature of the computer program. The seemingly instantaneousness of the computer becoming the model for the activity of the individual. When our movement is modeled on the computer speed for retrieving and processing information, we lose the connection we have to a sense of destiny and purpose. With no purpose, we have no relationship to the time from the future, we are only about the past, thus are inwardly "dead". We are no longer Time, for we have NO time.

D. Living Into Time

1. Living into time is like a musical chord. All the tones blend to make a new sound, but individual tones are still distinct. Unlike colors, which, to stay separate without blending they have to stay next to each other in space - they cannot occupy the same space. But notes can occupy the same space and remain separate. This is Time.

2. Developing inner strength and capacities to distinguish the individuality within the chords of our relationships is developing Radical Receptivity.

a. First we must learn to Hold Still (whatever Still is? or, whoever Still is.)

b. Stillness in our time is scorned, reviled, even feared. Still threatens, - it looms - it is feared for its potential unknown, next moment, over which one may have no control.

c. Stillness is where we are taught the sacredness of the act of radical receptivity.

3. Radical Receptivity points to the moment in which we may meet Time as its equal, not it's lackey.

a. A moment in which we could be thrown into radical receptivity is one which we hold a loved one who has died in our arms one last time. Time opens into stillness. The phenomenon of Still-ness does not exist in our Time.

b. Holding Still - or the attempt to do so, is a practice in radical receptivity - "radical" because it is not commonly deemed acceptable, but also because it is extreme, revolutionary, original. Receptive - as the act of receiving is opening, becoming vulnerable, losing the walls of the ego to expose the immensity of the soul.

X. Spiritual Psychology as an Activity of Love; What Amfortas Needed to Know

A. The Purpose of Love in the World

- love as nourishment for the gods - the nectar and ambrosia of the gods; love must circulate; necessity for the future of the Earth; difficulties with love stem from the blockage of the circulation - we wish to keep it for ourselves. Love nourishes the gods, the spirits, the angels, the dead. Earth as the planet of love; we are responsible for developing this force. The various modes of love with which we are familiar are preparations for developing the capacity to create love in the world. It is necessary to be able to experience all the modes of love in some degree in order to be able to come to the capacity of creative love. In depth psychology, as we saw above, there is a fundamental connection between psyche and eros. Love is necessary to soul. In spiritual psychology there is also a necessary connection between love and soul. To be able to be conscious in the spirit-soul, however, the kind of love needed is creative love. When we develop the capacity to create love where there does not seem to be any, then the spiritual dimension of the soul awakens. This is the aim of spiritual psychology.

The Modes of Love:

A. *Sexual Love*

The attraction of sex - an instinct, unlike other instincts at the human level; a commingling of wisdom and love; instinct - belongs to the realm of wisdom; the love of the body for the body; a strong impersonal component; helpful to be in touch with this dimension; Wisdom sees to it that love is introduced into the human realm in a way that that body will not be abandoned; note: in relation to spiritual disciplines that turn away from the body, there is an abandoning of the body, which typically returns in pathological forms.

Sex - not an instrument for something else - eg. Procreation; it has its own significance; see Vladimir Soloviev - The Meaning of Love. It is the force of love working through the body. Shows that love flows through the body, and our work is to make ourselves proper instruments through which love can work. Love works through us, right into the body, through the body into the world, where it re-shapes, creates things anew.

B. *Love as a Force in the Blood*

Up until a few hundred years ago, love between individuals was a matter of blood relationships; one did not meet and fall in love with a stranger; marriage occurred within blood lines; memory and the blood; a form of natural clairvoyance (see the section on Oedipus above.)

This form of love - as connection of the blood - is still very strong; e.g. easier to love one's own child; adopted children who locate their blood parents have an immediate and extremely strong feeling of relationship with them; but this form of love also becoming more destructive; eg. Nationalisms are, or can become a form of 'blood-lust' – that is why nationalistic wars are so difficult to bring to an end; in our time, connections of blood are often related to various forms of abuse; " my child as my possession"; a change occurring - relationships in time to relationships in space. When love lives in the blood, our love relationships have to do with time and memory. As we become free of the blood, love concerns our relationship in freedom to the person who stands next to us in space. As love evolves in the world it will become more and more necessary to re-imagine the family. The present imagination of family comes from Roman times and is based on the blood.

C. *Emotional Love*

Love between individuals mediated by images, fantasies; Love is never just you and me - it's you and me and a fantasy; Images keep changing. Need to work to be aware of what fantasy we are engaged in together. Emotional love as karmic – it has to do with work that needs to be done between two people; love as a debt to be paid; we usually do not recognize this debt at the outset; when the karmic work sets in, often individuals separate; what to do when the karmic work is done - no longer feeling between the individuals; how to recognize when habit has taken over; this form of love may last a short while, or for a lifetime. Most psychologies of relationship are based on this form of love, that is, emotional love. Psychology has not yet learned how creative love is involved in relationship and must come into play when emotional love come to a stopping place or else the relationship either moves into living in habit or the relationship simply ends.

D. *Self-Love*

Much misunderstanding these days surrounds this form of love; inherent with individuality of consciousness; to the extent that I have some sense of myself as an individual ---"I am an I" – there is self-love. Self-love cannot be supplied from the outside; the difficulty with building self-esteem; self-affirmations; self-esteem education. When there is a sense of individuality, there is self-love. Work is to provide the freedom that makes development of individuality possible; note -- individuality is not individualism. A most confusing form of love; when we say we love another, this usually means - "I love the me in you." Self-love directed outward is an error. Individual consciousness as self-love, the way we come to self-knowledge; we do not know ourselves as we know objects in the world. Through self-love we discover ourselves as creating beings who create through love.

E. What is Discovered through the Golden Threads of the Gifts of Love

Love permeates every aspect of our being - the body, blood, emotions, self; human beings are beings of love. Love in its various form has been but a preparation; now we are called upon to develop the next form of love - to become creators of love; not for our own sake, but for the sake of the world. **For psyche to become conscious, love, in all its forms, is a necessity.** Creative love does not simply evolve from the other forms of love. There is a kind of natural development of love, up to and including self-love. Creative love does not evolve naturally. Rather, there is a kind of breakdown that happens. A time in life when love as a gift seems to be gone. This void, this time of emptiness and loneliness is an important transition as it is a time of developing a radical receptivity of soul, necessary in the development of the capacity of creative love. The development of radical receptivity is revealed in the images of the Grail story of Parzival in the stories of the women figures.

Assignment #4

Remember a time in your life when there seemed to be an inner emptiness, a real soul-loneliness. Not a time of depression or feeling sorry for yourself for feeling so alone. Just a time in which there was an inner emptiness, even if everything in your outer life seemed to be going well. Describe the circumstances of this experience, and describe your inner experience of this emptiness. What then happened? What came that changed this inner state? Carefully describe exactly what happened, the inner sense of what happened. Describe how what happened to change the inner sense of emptiness was related to receptivity of soul. Describe the inner experience of coming out of the emptiness, the inner quality of what came. Even if an outer event or person seemed to instigate a turn-around for you, describe the inner experience of this turn-around and the relation of this turn-around to love. Then describe what happened after the turn-around. How was your outlook in life different? What new or different capacities did you experience?

Foundations of Spiritual Psychology II

I. Spiritual Psychology as the development of the capacities of the Heart

A. The Grail Story of Gawain

- the Grail Castle and the Castle of Wonders

The Castle of Wonders is an inversion of the Grail Castle. You can't find the way into the Grail Castle, but you can't find your way out of the Castle of Wonders. Four hundred women are trapped in the castle, including Arthur's mother. Also, the men and the women are separated in this castle. When Parzival first approaches the Grail Castle, he sees a man on a boat in the center of a lake wearing a heat with the feather of a peacock. The peacock color is a sign of having achieved a certain level of initiation – the level of imagination. The man in the boat is the wounded Grail King. When Gawain comes to the Castle of Wonders, the interior entrance to the castle is painted in peacock colors. This indicates that for Klingsor, the king of the Castle of Wonders, imagination is selfishly turned inward for his own use. Another interesting characteristic of the Castle of Wonders is the crystal pole at the top of the castle. This is a device that allows anyone who looks into it to see what is going on in a radius of six miles. It is a kind of technological wonder and shows us something about the way in which technology is a double of spiritual capacities. For example, through inner development it is possible to be in instantaneous spiritual connection with others. Technology makes us forget we have such capacities and substitutes a kind of double of them. For example, we can be in almost instantaneous touch with others through cell phones. Being in spiritual connection is certainly not the same thing but having these technical devices can lead to a forgetfulness of our spiritual gifts. We also have the hint of how to begin thinking about the spiritual psychology of technology with the picture of this castle. For example, the confinement of the 400 women. This picture, read imaginally, indicates that technology concerns keeping the feminine soul trapped and confined. Electronic technology is a kind of 'all spirit' invention. It is all out there, no interior; and as such, it tends to be manic as spirit without soul always is.

- Klingsor; the room with the wonder-bed

Klingsor is a magician of dark magic. He, like the Grail king, was wounded
with a wound that would not heal. He was caught in bed with the wife of a
king and was castrated. In his bitterness and anger, Klingsor went off to
Sicily and learned black magic, which he now uses against the forces of
good. In the Castle of Wonders there is a magic bedroom. Gawain, as he is
trying to free the women from the castle, come to this bedroom. The floor of
the room is polished so slick that it is not possible to walk on it without
falling, so Gawain jumps from the door to the bed. Then, there is a moment
of silence. A volley of arrows comes flying through the air, and Gawain
catches them with his shield, an asbestos shield. Then, there is a moment of
silence and a strange man dressed in fish scales and holding a club comes in
and says there is more to come. A lion jumps on the bed. The bed has ruby
rollers and begins to spin faster and faster as Gawain fights the lion. He cuts
off the paw of the lion and is almost defeated by the lion. He kills the lion
and then seems to expire. One of the women comes to him and holds a
feather to his nose and determines he is still breathing. The women nurse
him back to health.

This whole scene pictures the inner work of entering into the interior of
the heart. When we first do this we are confronted with the uncontrollable
force of passion. Gawain barely gets through this, and he does so wrongly.
The lion is an alchemical image. In alchemy there is a famous engraving of
cutting off the paws of the lion. This image indicates that in order to
progress spiritually it is necessary to stop desire from reaching out to the
world for whatever it wants, but rather to learn to experience desire without
needing to satisfy desire. Gawain is supposed to ride the lion, not kill it.
Riding the lion is an alchemical image that says when confronted with the
full force of the desire of the heart the only thing one can do is ride it out,
give oneself over completely to the spiritual worlds. This does not mean
seeking to satisfy the desire, but rather to experience the full force of desire
without seeking to bring it to completion.

With this section of *Parzival* , we are brought into the mysteries of the
heart, which are central to the practice of spiritual psychology. We thus need
to enter into a consideration of the heart, followed by a series of heart
meditations that are at the center of spiritual psychology and other
meditative practices that are oriented toward coming to be able to be
present to the life of the soul in full consciousness. Remember, spiritual

psychology is an incarnational psychology. One of the things incarnational means is that it is embodied psychology. Thus, when we speak of the heart, we simultaneously mean the actual organ of the heart as well as the spiritual/ soul qualities of the heart. When we speak of heart, we do not primarily mean the heart chakra, though it is certainly involved. But, the meditations on the heart have to do with the physical heart which is also a spirit/soul organ. It takes a good deal of inner work to rid ourselves of the medical notion of the heart, that the heart is just a pump that shoves blood around in the body. This view of the heart is a theory, one that has had application to be sure, but the heart is not really a pump. Let us go into the understanding of the heart as given in anthroposophy and then take this view of the heart and work with it in terms of spiritual psychology.

II. The Spiritual Psychology of the Heart
A. Heart as the Organ of the Middle

One of the primary accesses to an imagination of the organs is to begin always by paying attention to the location of the organ within the body. The heart is located between the head and the organs of the abdomen. This location is important. We would be decidedly different beings if our heart was located, say in the left leg.

Alchemy spoke of the body as consisting of three primary activities - note, we say activities, for it is important to begin to be able to imagine the organs as the locus of relationships rather than as entities. The three primary bodily activities are the Salt processes, the Mercury processes, and the Sulfur processes.

Salt refers to the activities of the body concerned with solidifying, bringing to form, hardness. The nerve-sense processes of the body are Salt; they are centered primarily in the head region of the body, but also are to be found in each and every organ of the body. These processes have to do with the hardening element, with sclerosis, with head and brain and nerves, with what is cold rather than warm.

The Sulfur processes of the body have to do with the life processes of the body - with warmth, heat, body-forming processes, growth, reproduction, digestion, the transformation of a thought into movement, the metabolism. These processes are centered primarily in the lower part of the body, the abdomen and genital regions, but they too are to be found occurring in every organ of the body.

The Mercury processes have to do with balance, with rhythm, with the middle region of the body, with heart, breathing, and the circulation of the blood. The heart is the primary organ of this middle region and its processes having to do with balance.

B. The Heart as Mercury

Within this picture of the Salt, Mercury, and Sulfur processes of the body, the heart is the primary Mercury process. Thus, the location of the heart in the middle region indicates that the work of this center is to bring balance to the hardening forces of Salt and the dissolving forces of Sulfur. Any heart difficulties, except perhaps certain congenital heart difficulties, concern what happens when there is lack of balance between Salt and Sulfur processes. For example, when brain-nerve processes are two strong, then these forces move too strongly into the region of the heart, and the result is angina or sclerosis. When the Sulfur or metabolic processes are too strong, as for example, when through alcoholism the liver processes become out of balance, then the metabolic or Sulfur processes works too strongly into the middle region, and the result is an enlarged heart, or congestive heart disease.

Note, the heart, in itself, would not become diseased. Heart disease is a result of imbalance of the other two polarities. This leads us to a second image, also related to Salt, Sulfur, and Mercury. These processes also, at the same time, describe soul and spirit processes. Salt has to do with thinking; Sulfur with willing; and Mercury with feeling. As we proceed, the importance of this imagination will become apparent.

C. The Salt, Sulfur, and Mercury Processes of the Heart

In the alchemical way of imagining the body, every organ of the body is the whole body; the part is also the whole. Thus, it is possible to speak of the Salt, Sulfur, and Mercury processes of the heart in its activity. It is thus possible to consider, on the one hand, the nerve-sense processes of the heart, which also have to do with the way in which the heart is a certain kind of thinking. Within the heart, the Salt processes relate to the small bundle of nerves at the opening of the right chamber of the heart - known as the sino-atrial node (and, as well, the bundle of nerves known as the auricular-ventricular node of the heart). This bundle of nerves, like all nerves - indicate that the heart has a capacity to sense. What happens is something like this: When blood enters the right chamber of the heart, the valve closes, and for a brief moment, the blood is stopped in the heart chamber. In this brief moment, the nerve bundles senses the qualities of the blood - all kinds of qualities, such as chemical composition, but most importantly, what is sensed is the warmth of the blood. The blood is different temperatures at different places in the body - for, example, the blood is warmest at the place of the liver; it is coldest in the lungs because here there is direct connection with the outer world; and the blood in the brain is colder than that in the abdominal region. If the qualities of the blood are such that the whole of the body is not in balance, then the heart starts beating either faster or slower - an attempt to restore balance. This is really a kind of thinking located within the heart.

Then, Sulfur processes also occur in the heart. Sulfur has to do with the soul activity of willing, and with the metabolic activity of the muscles. The heart is also a muscle, and thus we can speak of the will of the heart. There are some extraordinary things about this muscle. First, it is one of two hollow muscles of the body, and only women have them both, for the other hollow muscle is the womb. Thus, there is an intimacy between the heart and the womb, and this intimacy has to do with creating. Women have, I would say, a much more intimate connection to the heart than men and know in a bodily way that the heart has to do with creation of life in the world as the womb has to do with the creation of life within. Another most important feature of the heart as a muscle is that this muscle is between what are known as smooth muscles and muscles that are striated. Smooth muscles, for example, like those lining the wall of the stomach, are characterized as being involuntary. Striated muscles, such as those of the arms and legs, are characterized as being voluntary. The muscles of the wall of the heart are between smooth and striated, tending toward striated. This indicates the most amazing fact that the heart is gradually evolving toward becoming a conscious organ, able to be worked with voluntarily. When, for example, we say of someone that their heart is open or their heart is closed, this has in fact a physical dimension to it. Another most important aspect of the wall of the heart is that it consists of seven layers of muscles; and at each layer, these muscles are seen to move in a different direction - if one could put all seven layers into a single image, what would be seen is the form of a spiral. This spiral form indicates that the heart is always, always in connection with the spiritual worlds.

Finally, the heart is primarily concerned with the Mercury processes of balance, as already pointed out. Mercury, though, has to do with the soul process of feeling. It does not have to do with emotion - but with feeling. From the other heart processes, it is possible to say that the two ground - feelings of the heart - that from which all of feeling life originates, is the feeling of devotion and the feeling of courage. Devotion - related to the intimate, unending engagement of the heart in its observation of the qualities of the blood; not detached observation, but fully involved, and never resting - this is devotion. Courage has to do with the unending enthusiasm with which the heart is always at work balancing Salt and Sulfur. Since this act of courage is always present, it is difficult to experience; it is experienced only at times when it stops - for example in an attack of angina. At such a time a person feels terrible fear, a fear that cannot be taken away - for example, by trying to calm the person down.

III. The Heart is Not a Pump; The Heart as the Organ of Spiritual/ soul Imagination

A. The prevalent medical conception of the heart is that it serves to pump the blood through the body, keeping the blood circulating. The researches of anthroposophical medicine, and particularly those of Rudolf Steiner, indicate that the heart is in fact not primarily a pump. First, it is to be noted that this can be verified through our own experience of the heart. When, for example, we feel a moment of joy, the heart leaps in the chest - and this is more than a metaphor. And when we feel anguish, the heart sinks. A mechanical pump simple does not do this; it just sits there and mechanically beats. Further, when the heart beats, it moves within the body with a torque. A mechanical pump does not move at all. The torque movement of the heart is related to the seven-layered spiraling muscles of the wall of the heart.

Now, in a certain way, the heart does function like a pump, but more like the kind of pump known as the "battering ram" than a pump with cylinders, etc. The pumping action of the heart, however, is not what is responsible for the circulation of the blood in the body. The pump-like action of the heart increases the pressure so that the blood can get from head to toe - it increases pressure but is not primarily responsible for circulation. The interesting question then arises - where does the circulation of the blood come from. Here, we have to look more closely at the capillaries. The capillaries are where blood becomes so fine that it lines up one cell next to another - like in the extremities near the skin. When the blood cells are lined up like this, a surface area is formed, and this surface area - is in close connection with the outer world - these capillaries come very close to the skin. In this close connection with the outer world, it is the circulation of the sun that is responsible for the circulation of the blood in the body - though the circulation of the blood occurs in a different periodicity than the circulation of the sun.

IV. Developing Soul Consciousness of the Heart

The approach taken here to developing consciousness of the heart is incarnational. We mean by 'incarnational' that we are working with the actual organ of the heart, which is at the same time, the spiritual, and soul center of our being. We are not working in a direct way with the heart chakra. The particular gift that Spiritual Psychology offers to the world is instruction in developing the capacity to work from the center outward and doing so in such a manner that the sacramental nature of the human body is always reverentially respected.

The sequence of heart meditations that follow gradually develop the capacity to center our consciousness in the interior of the heart. For a long time, this heart-centering occurs only periodically, when we are actively doing the meditations. In time it becomes possible to live consistently within this new form of consciousness. You will find this transformation happens something like the learning of a new language happens. With consistent practice we awaken one day to find ourselves speaking differently.

These meditations have different sources, primarily from alchemical works and from meditations from anthroposophy suggested by Rudolf Steiner and others. However, each meditation has been adapted to the work of spiritual psychology and of Sacred Service, so if you find a meditation you recognize, do not be alarmed in seeing that it does not precisely follow the way it was first presented. In any case, as with all meditation, these meditations are to be the source of individual research. They are not to be done thoughtlessly or automatically. It is very important to observe what happens as you do the meditations and keep ongoing journal notes of your experiences, precisely described. You may almost certainly find that further adaptations will be necessary for you. Central to this research is to make these modifications without changing the intent of the meditations.

The meditations are to be done in the sequence listed below. It is suggested that you do one meditation a day, though that meditation can be done twice a day. The next day you move to the next meditation, and so on. At the end of the sequence, take two days of not meditating, and then begin again.

(1) Heart Alignment Exercise
Always begin any of the heart meditations with this heart-alignment exercise:

Focus your consciousness at the center of your forehead, near the bridge of the nose, at the interior there. As your consciousness is focused there, say, in an interior way, "I am."

Move your consciousness, now centered at the center of your forehead and dwelling in the experience of the words "I am", move your consciousness down to the center of the throat area, again at the interior there. As your consciousness is focused there, san, in an interior way, "It thinks."

Move your consciousness back to the center of your forehead and focus there. Then move your consciousness down through the throat region to the region of your heart. As your consciousness is focused there, say, in an interior way, "She feels."

Move your consciousness back to the center of your forehead and focus there. Then move your consciousness down through the throat region and through the region of the heart to the region of your solar plexus. As your consciousness if focused there, say, in an interior way, "He wills."

Let your consciousness be within these four areas for a few minutes. Then open your eyes.
The whole exercise does not take any longer than about seven minutes.

(2) Entering the Heart and Emptying
Think of a difficulty or a worry you are currently experiencing in your life. Make this difficulty into an inner mental image. Then shift this image from the region of the head into the center of the heart. It disappears there as a

worry or concern, and this is a simple method for shifting into heart consciousness in a way that you can feel the difference between head consciousness and heart consciousness.

Then, stay in the heart—keep your consciousness centered in the deep interior of your heart. Then, with an act of will, empty your heart-consciousness of any content and apply just enough will-force to keep it empty. Try to feel the currents that are active in the interior of your heart. Do this exercise for no more than five minutes.

(3) Cardiodiagnosis and Strengthening

Take a fairly good-sized stone, but one that is not particularly beautiful or outstanding in any way--- and ordinary stone--- and carefully observe it. Hold it in your hand and look at it carefully, turning it over, seeing it from all sides. After doing this observation for a few minutes, make an inner image of this rock. At first it is likely that this will be a mental image of the rock. You can tell if it is a mental image if you "see" the rock with your interior eye as if you are looking at the rock; that is, you mentally see only one side of the rock. Move the image down into the interior of your heart; that is, now "see" the rock with the heart's eye. You will have the feeling of seeing all sides of the rock at once, something like a hologram. Simply hold the rock there, in the interior consciousness of the heart, for a few minutes...two or three minutes. Then, consciously erase the image of the rock and remain in the empty void as long as you can. Then open your eyes.

This meditation strengthens the capacity to stay in heart-consciousness. We utilize an object in order to avoid the sentimentalizing tendency of the heart, or the way we typically imagine the function of the heart.

If, when the rock was an interior image within your heart, the image began to take on autonomous qualities...maybe it began to drift to one side, or maybe it grew wings and started to fly, or maybe you suddenly saw it as the earth floating in space....if these kind of qualities happened, that is an indication that your will-forces that it takes to create the inner image and maintain it there are too weak. You need to gently apply more will in the making and maintaining of the image. You can feel this force of will in your body as you are making the inner image and maintaining it. If you cannot feel these forces in the body, then you are making a mental image only.

If, when the rock was an interior image within your heart, the image simply disappeared, that is an indication that your will forces are too strong…. your will forces, in effect, blew the image away. You need to gently hold back on the will forces creating and maintaining the image in the center of the heart.

It is good to do this meditation periodically to strengthen the capacity to make and hold an image. It is also a good diagnostic tool that can help you make necessary adjustments in heart-imagination.

(4) Forming the Heart Cross: The Horizontal Arm

This meditation involves becoming aware of the heart/soul dimension of your sense experience. Think of it as a way focusing on the border between the sense realm and the heart realm. The meditation will help develop the capacity to be present to the outer world through the region of the heart.

Begin by following out in consciousness, your hearing of a sound…. from your ear to the source of the sound (in this instance, the chime); feel your consciousness ray out toward the sound and then return inward.

Let the chime sound three times and each time let your hearing-consciousness ray out to the sound and then follow the sound current back your ears. (Later, on your own, do the same procedure with sight, and again, later, with touch). You will begin to feel an awareness of the relationship between your inner being and your perception. Now, begin to focus on the awareness of the relationship itself – of the current that runs between the sensory object and the ears, and begin to form inwardly a picture of this awareness, as a clear, glass flask. Then, when you have made this alchemical vessel, take it in to the region of the heart; let your heart be at the center of this alchemical flask.

As the meditation continues, you will find arising quite naturally, images, thoughts, and feelings. In this exercise, do not try to avoid these occurrences; let them develop, and then watch them dissolve. These images arise out of the unconscious. See the images dissolve and come to rest at the bottom of the container as a deep interior darkness.

Hold this image for a few minutes and then erase it and remain in the void as long as you can. Then open your eyes.

(5) Forming the Heart Cross: The Vertical Arm

Always do this meditation above before doing this meditation. Even when you do the meditation above one day, on the next, when you do this one, start with doing the meditation above.

In the inner space of the alchemical flask become conscious of the rhythmic beating of the heart. Allow this perception to grow until the heart is the central and sustained focus of the flask. Then, try to separate the physical-like inner perception of the heart's rhythm and instead become aware of the spiritual essence of the heart.

Begin to picture the heart, in its spiritual essence as at the center of a lemniscate, a figure eight; be aware of the four divisions at the meeting point of the four arms of the lemniscate. Feel a current flowing out and upwards from the heart's center reaching out spiritually to the heights of the cosmos, and feel this current returning back to the center bringing an essence of the cosmic realm with it. Let this cycle of cosmic nourishment form itself into an inner picture of streams of light flowing out and flowing back.

Now, picture the lower part of the lemniscate, how it reaches deep into one's being and carries this cosmic nourishment into the depths of your soul. Feel this nourishment go down and return to the center.

Then, unify this whole picture and experience of the heart, and let the whole cycle circulate. Do this for a few minutes. To conclude the exercise, allow yourself to slip back into the inner physical perception of the rhythm of the heart. Realize that the physical heat is the physical body of the soul heart, the heart center. Then open your eyes.

This meditation takes about 10 minutes.

(6) *Taking Someone into your Heart*

For one month do this meditation, in sequence in relation to the meditations before and after this one only in relation to someone you do not know or do not know well. It is important to get used to the kinds of inner heart currents that accompany this meditation. If you begin this meditation in relation to someone you know well or are close to, there will be confusion in the heart currents. It is extremely important to follow this procedure.

After one month you can try the meditation with someone you know or are close to. If confused feelings arise, go back to the previous part of the meditation.

When you go to the store or are at work or even waking on the street, when you have contact with someone ---saying 'hello' or 'hi' …that kind of contact, immediately, while there with the person, make an inner image of that person and shift that image to the center of the heart and hold the image there for a couple of minutes. Then consciously erase the image.

Try to be aware of the quality of the heart currents as you do this with different people.

(7) Circulating the Heart's Rhythms Through the Spiritual World
Begin by making an inner image of a tiny, clear sphere at the center of your heart. Begin to let this sphere expand. Let it slowly expand out…. It encompasses the heart…. further expanding, it encompasses the body……
As the sphere is expanding, it is important to retain a sense of the center of the heart and at the same time the outer periphery of the sphere as it expands. Your consciousness is at the center of the heart and also at the outer periphery. Let the sphere expand to encompass the room….it is a sphere, so it expands in all directions….. then it encompasses the building you are in…the immediate region…going down into the earth and above into the sky….then the wider region…wider and wider, gradually encompassing the whole earth…then the sphere expands out through the planetary spheres…the moon, mercury, sun, mars, Venus, Jupiter, Saturn, Uranus, Neptune, Pluto….out finally to the fixed stars. Then let the expansion of the sphere stop.

Then, gradually begin to let the sphere, now expanded out to the fixed stars begin to decrease, going back through the regions you just went through….all the planetary spheres in reverse…the earth….the wide region…the region you are in….the building you are in….your body….your heart….down to the very tiny sphere at the center of your heart. Then, open your eyes.

V. Developing Conscious Soul Capacities I - Spiritual Psychology of Dreaming

Along with developing heart consciousness, you can gradually find your way into the kind of imaginal consciousness characteristic of soul life by learning to give attention to your dreams. The spiritual psychology approach to dreams is considerably different than other approaches to dreams. It is a non-interpretive approach based on the notion that dreams, if we attend to them in their activity rather than their content, come as a way of teaching us how to be more awake and aware in the activity of soul life. They teach us how to move closer to conscious soul life, the activity of imaging rather than images already made. We will work with dreams in such a way that your consciousness moves from what is composed to the act of the composing.

A. Freud and dreams – For Freud, dreams are the via regia to the unconscious; dreams have meaning; content of dream images symbolize something from the waking life of the dreamer; related to the personal past; indications of trauma experienced early in life; approaching dreams in this way has influenced dream work for the past one hundred years; approached through method of free association. The central notion of the dream is that dreams are wish fulfillments. That is, dreams express our desires, even those we are not conscious of. The necessary introduction of dream processes; for Freud the dream process consists of a number of ways our desires are disguised so that they can find expression without being censored.

B. Jung and dreams - the content of dreams not only expresses meaning from the personal past; dream figures and events also express mythological patterns; dreams as expression of archetypal events; the gods as determiners of personality; archetypes; meaning deepened from personal events from the past to archetypal meaning; difference between archetypes and archetypal imagination (Hillman). For Jung, the archetypes are unknown and beyond expression. He makes the assumption of archetypes behind the patterns of dreams. Hillman has a different sense. He sticks to the image and speaks only of what the image itself shows. For Hillman, there are no archetypes in themselves but only the given images of dreams which show archetypal characteristics.

C. Spiritual psychology and dreams – dreams are approached, not for what they mean but as a way of coming into connection with the activity of spirit, working into soul, then working into body, and working into waking life; working with dreams, then, is seen as a discipline of gradually learning to sense what the spiritual worlds are like and how they enter into earthly life; learning to sense the creating activity of the spiritual worlds; making spiritual work conscious.

D. Sources; where Steiner works with dreams: <u>The Life of the Soul</u> (pamphlet); "The Psychological Expression of the Unconscious" in <u>Spiritual</u>

Research: Methods and Research (Steinerbooks); The Evolution of Consciousness (Anthroposophic Press).

VI. Dream Pictures

We begin with a consideration of the act of dreaming. What is a dream? Here it is necessary to simply be descriptive. We do not begin with a theory of dreams but with the actual experience of what dreaming is like.

A. Description of the dream; dreams are like images on an empty canvas - but there is no canvas; the dream the canvas, the painter, and the painting, all at once.

B. What dreams picture: a) events directly related to waking life; b) events that resemble perception in the waking world; c) fantastic events and beings - but still presented as if a bodily perception in waking life; dreams resemble perception in the waking world, even when the images are fantastic. For example, if I dream of a purple giant walking on the moon, the dream image appears analogous to perception - this tells us that the body is involved in dreaming because there is a perceptual world that appears; but in addition, a further element is the creating activity of dreaming. Not the dream pictures, but the images as they are coming into being. We need to distinguish dream content and dream activity.

C. The creating activity of psychic/soul life. All psychic/soul life has a creative element. We can arrange soul life along a continuum, starting with the soul activity with the greatest creative element and going to that with the least, in this manner - dream -- fantasy -- memory --- thought --- perception; there is this continuum from the realm of the most free creating activity to most bound creating activity. Working with the creating activity of dreaming can strengthen consciousness of the creating activity going on in other phenomena of soul life and creating can thus work into the world in a more conscious way if we work to strengthen our presence to this creating activity.

D. The content of the dream cannot be taken as an indication of the creating element in dreams, even when the dream content is unusual; dream pictures not related to external events are not necessarily archetypal (e.g. dream of a galloping horse, and I wake up to clicking of the clock); dream content also often pictures bodily processes (e.g. dream of walking by a white picket fence with broken tops - may symbolize aching teeth); dream content also often pictures instinctual level of soul (e.g. slaying of a monster). All forms of dream interpretation confuse the activity of dreaming and the content of dreams; in order to get to the activity, it is necessary to go from the content to the image to the activity. Dream interpretation starts with the content and then tries to understand the meaning of the content. The act of dreaming, the imaging rather than the images, is not attended to. A spiritual psychology of dreaming is most interested in the imaging-activity, and from this viewpoint, dreams do not mean anything – they are a doing, the doing of the creating act coming into the soul.

VI. Dreams as a Border Phenomenon

A. All dreams have both a creative and a perceptual element; if you move toward the creative element then you move toward spirit activity; if you move toward the perceptual element, you move toward understanding of certain aspects of your personal life that you were not aware of, or you move toward certain archetypal aspects of the soul that are coming to consciousness.

B. All dreams are spiritual insofar as spiritual activity – that is something from the spiritual worlds works its way into soul life and shows up as the activity of dreaming. It is not a matter of content; dreams with a specific spiritual content are, from this point of view, no more spiritual than any other dream.

C. Some typical ways of working with dreams
Here is an example of working with a dream: The dream: "I am flying over the city. I feel completely free and unencumbered. Suddenly, I begin to plunge toward a towering skyscraper. I feel tremendous fear that I am going to crash and die. At the very last possible moment I feel lifted by something that is not my own power. I fly over the city and toward the stars."

  a) dream interpretation; by analyst; by oneself; in each case, says more about the interpreter than about the dream.

b) forms of active imagination; based in naive understanding of the soul realm - "soul knows what is best;" ignorance of astral worlds; e.g. astral entities. From the viewpoint of active imagination, it is in all cases good to work with dreams by setting up a dialogue with the figures of our dreams. From a spiritual/psychological approach to dreaming, the figures in dreams are real, imaginally real. There are some dream figures you do not want to set up a dialogue with; they are not about your life; they are intruders and can do harm to you if you let them. Not all dreams are of this sort, and in fact, very few. But it is important to know that such dangers exist.

c) Gestalt psychology; any part of the dream is taken to be part of me; what does that part of the dream feel like; getting in touch with disowned feelings; This approach reduces spirit/soul to empirical ego.

d) mythical interpretation; makes one feel involved in something larger than oneself; collective unconscious; archetypes; psychological form of religion.

VII. Working with Dreams - Toward the Spiritual Worlds

A. What happens when we go to sleep? Our physical body and etheric body, that is our life processes, remain there, lying in bed; soul and spirit - enter into soul and spirit worlds. Consciousness and individuality of consciousness are not present in sleep; these are the activity of soul and spirit consciousness in waking life. In sleep, soul and spirit more of less depart from the body and enter the soul and spirit worlds – these are real worlds, but they do not in any way resemble the physical/earthly world.

B. As we begin to awaken, spirit/soul returns - entering into the "space" between etheric and physical body - a lighting up of the etheric body occurs - this is the dream picture; you can verify that something like this takes place; e.g. those times when you are present to the moment of waking – you experience a feeling of a kind of a rushing in of something, like the wind; also, upon waking, there is always a mood that does not have anything to do with our moods in waking life. This waking mood is a fading impression of the spiritual worlds.

C. Here is a procedure for getting close to the dream activity. First, you must work to get from the dream as you remember it upon waking, the dream story, to the dream image, that is, the dream without the narrative component. The narrative component is what we add to the dream upon waking that makes the dream seem as if it unfolds in linear form, as a story. The dream image does not happen this way. The dream image occurs all at once, all parts of the dream are actually one image. When we write down our dreams, that a memory of a memory; that is, we wake up and recall a dream. Then we write down the dream, which is a memory of that first recall of the dream. When we write down a dream, we always feel that something has been left out, that some part of the dream has escaped. It is this left-out part that is the most important aspect of dreaming for the work of spiritual psychology.

D. In working with dream-activity, we have to find the way from the sequential logic of dream-as-story to the simultaneity of the dream-as-image. Dream logic is different than the sequential logic of a story. It is a when-- then, not a before-after. The first work is to get accustomed to dream as image. Here is an example.

Dream memory: "I am climbing up the side of a steep mountain. As I ascend, the green growth of grass and flowers and trees disappears, and all becomes solid rock. I climb out onto a rock ledge, and the ground behind me falls away, and I am left on a ledge overlooking an abyss with no way to get back. I wake in fear."

Dream image: "When I am climbing, then there is an abyss; when there is an abyss, then I am out on a ledge; when there is no way back, then things have gotten steep and rocky; I feel rocky when ledged and life has disappeared; the greening, growing, flowering disappears when I feel rocky; I am at an abyss when greening disappears; high moving loses greenness; being high is rocky going fear."

Notice what begins to happen internally to you as you begin to work with the dream-as-image. The need to know the meaning of the dream begins to fade. We are taken from meaning into doing.

E. The next step is to move from dream-as-image to dreaming activity. In order to do this, we have to imaginatively "step into" the dream-as-image. The dream image is as if it is before us, all going on at once. We now move from "looking at" the picture to being within the picturing process. Stepping into the image - we do not become another part of the content; when we step into the image, the picture disappears because we are no longer imaginatively looking at an image but are now within the image; but we are everywhere within the image.

> e.g. like a painting; see the painting before you

> to - feeling its action from within; feeling its feeling rather than what I feel about it, or what it makes me feel; move into the realm of pure mobility; feel the rhythm, the tension, the ups and downs, the mood, the flow, the dramatic action, the musicality of the image. Here, there is nothing to interpret; get an actual impression of the activity of the spirit/soul worlds.

F. Then, write what is felt as activity:

> e.g. Climbing overlooks the void
> a ledge of no return
> green, flowering growth, an abyss
> steeped in fear - I am.

G. Notice the difficulty of this work; fear; spiritual courage is required; interpretation is a way of avoiding fear, of avoiding getting close to the spirit/soul realms. Working with dreams in this way is a spiritual exercise; it prepares us to sense the spirit/soul worlds; a moment of real impressions of these worlds. This kind of exercise develops what Steiner calls "presence of mind;" the kind of attentiveness needed to begin to sense that the spiritual worlds are all around us; each dream is different; this form of perceiving cannot become a habit; also shows how spiritual perception is completely individual; sense perception is general - e.g. perceiving a tree; spiritual perception is individual but not subjective; always a "first time" event; a sense of wonder.

VIII. Value of Spiritual work with Dreams

A. All dreams are healthy; There is no such thing as an abnormal dream, no matter how bizarre the content. Working with dreams in this way provides a healthy way of spiritual work. What is meant by healthy – the dream-work repeats the sequence of what naturally happens in waking; a movement from spirit to soul to body.

B. Unhealthy ways of Spiritual Work occur whenever soul is bypassed, and spirit enters directly into the body; either the result of disease or the cause of disease; eg. channeling; trance; hallucinogenic drugs are unhealthy ways of spiritual work and can cause difficulties.

C. The special case of spiritual visions.
People who have spiritual visions go through the experience of spiritual activity entering rather directly into the subtle body and affecting the spiritual body. These people often have physical illnesses because the physical body cannot contain this direct entry of the spirit.

D. Mediumship and Psychic Readings do not belong to the spiritual realm at all. They are not a developed spiritual capacity, but rather subtle sense perception and etheric perception.

IX. Developing Conscious Soul Capacities II - Image-based Meditation Soul Work
A. Meditation in the Context of Life
The way we will approach the question of meditation differs somewhat from the more familiar understandings of meditation. Meditation is not a technique reserved for those following a spiritual path; in our time it may be the only way to preserve a life than can properly be called human. More and more, attentiveness is captured by being submersed in one content or another. We are rapidly becoming more and more passive in our awareness in spite of the fact that our lives are becoming increasingly hectic. We are coming to the point of being ruled by the things that capture our attention. Our attention is no longer our own, and the deepest work of attention - to come into connection with the sacredness of life, is not free and available to develop connection with the sacred. Things are brought to our attention - we do not freely bring our attention to things, and we are rapidly losing the capacity to freely withdraw it.

We cannot approach the world creatively, new and fresh, if attention is continually caught by already created forms - such as required tasks at work, home, church, civic life, entertainment, personal concerns, self-interests, egotism. For example, thinking cannot be creative, it can at the most be innovative, if we think with already formed thoughts learned in the past. We cannot perceive the world as it is constantly coming into being if we approach it through already formed perceptions from the past. We cannot be creative in our speaking if we use words as mere information rather than sensing a connection with the creating source of words. We cannot sense our body or sense the qualities of other human being if we simply rely on the information provided by the senses and do not gradually become conscious in our sensing. We eat rather than experience eating, see rather than experiencing seeing, hear without experiencing the soul aspect of hearing, and so on.

Meditative practices, as we develop them here, are oriented toward becoming aware of the currents of attentiveness themselves. I am well aware that meditation can mean many different things - the mindfulness practices of Buddhism; a way of coming into connection with spirit beings and worlds; a way to increased senses of health and vitality, as in transcendental meditation practices; a way to relaxation; a method for coming to an experience of the self. None of what we will develop opposes these forms of practice. If you are engaged in such practices, I hope what you work with here can illuminate them in a new way. The sources for what we will be doing come from the work of Rudolf Steiner; specifically, the background may be found in his works, How to Know Higher Worlds and Guidance in Esoteric Training I also draw from the work of Georg Kuhlewind; his works include From Normal to Healthy, Stages of Consciousness, and Schooling of Consciousness.

We advise that the meditations suggested here be entered into only after working for a good time on the heart meditations. The reason for this is that the heart meditations help develop the capacity of soul consciousness. If meditations that have a more mental and cognitive component are worked with first, it becomes more difficult to incorporate the soul dimension in an explicit way.

B. Meditation as an act of the Will and the Heart

In any kind of meditation, one begins by concentrating consciousness on something to the exclusion of all else, and holding attention on that one thing, letting nothing else enter. The act of such concentration, as can readily be determined by trying to concentrate on something for a few minutes, is essentially an act of will. But, it is an act of will in which nothing enters consciousness that you do not place there. It is fairly difficult to develop the capacity to concentrate in this way, for there is nothing to support what we are meditating on other than our own will forces.

Meditation involves a second act in addition to the concentration of will forces. I must keep concentration focused on one thing to the exclusion of all else, and at the same time, there must occur a reversed act of will - I must become available to, be completely open and receptive to something that comes into consciousness, something that meets us, so to speak, which is difficult to name, and equally difficult to describe; it is a wordless reality that goes beyond the content of our concentration. This wordless word creates the content of what we are concentrating on. Ordinarily, we are only aware of the content and not what gives rise to it.

We can choose to meditate on a sentence, an image, a sensation, a feeling, and in certain circumstances, even an emotion while we are undergoing the emotion, or a perception; no matter what we choose as matter for meditation, this same method holds; concentration as an act of will, and a reversed act of will - will in order to be willingly engaged in receiving.

C. Meditation on a Sentence

We will begin by meditating on a sentence for about five minutes.

WE ALWAYS LIVE IN THE LIGHT

1. It is important to begin with a sentence that is formally understandable for ordinary consciousness. This is not a mantra; even if we do not fully understand the sentence, it is one which awakens the thinking. The aim is not just to think about this sentence, though such thinking serves as a point of departure. We are concerned with what can develop from ordinary consciousness - what is the next stage of development of consciousness.

2. A meditative sentence such as this "forces" the consciousness to understand the whole sentence at once. We can understand each word with our ordinary consciousness, but we cannot understand the whole sentence. We know what "we" means, what "always" means, what "live" means, what "in" means, what "the" means, and what "light" means. But what do they mean all together? This is not available to ordinary consciousness.

3. In order to meditate on this sentence, we begin by pondering each of the words, or at least some of the words. "We" relates to human beings who know of one another. [Live" in this sentence cannot refer to biological life - the sentence would not make much sense because biological life does not always live in the light. This sentence does not convey information - it is, rather, something to be realized. This realizing is the meditation itself, for which the sentence serves as the theme.

4. In meditating on this sentence, for this sentence to become a realization, it is necessary to sense, to feel each word as a predicate, as active, as a verb rather than a static noun. After you have pondered each word for a few moments, it is helpful to then condense the whole of the sentence into one of the worlds. We can, for example, concentrate on the word "light." Or, one might focus on the word "in" - to be in something, to be inside, spatially, temporally; but also, to be "in the life." beyond space or time; at the same time, to be it completely.

5. If one succeeds in truly experiencing at least one word of the sentence, the other words of the sentence will dissolve into the contemplated word.

6. If one practices contemplating the sentence in the manner suggested, there will come a time when it is possible to condense the sentence to one word, and then, to let go of the one word and to dwell within the wordless reality.

7. In meditating on the above sentence, one thing to avoid is representing the sentence with some kind of mental picture. If we made a mental picture, say, of standing out in a field at dawn, experiencing the first moment of the light, this would be a gesture of past consciousness; that is, we picture something we are familiar with, which of necessity is from the past.

8. If a sentence such as this is taken up daily, spending only five to ten minutes a day, new soul forces are developed - the currents of attentiveness become free. There comes a time in the practice of meditation when we no longer move from one point to another in our meditation; a continuity of consciousness is established; rather than meditating on something, it is as if we become meditated; that is, the inner reality of the sentence becomes something quite tangible, and we experience being seen by this reality.

D. Meditation on an Object

Some additional qualities of meditating can be experienced by choosing to meditate on an object. Meditation on an object should start with a human-made thing rather than a natural object, such as a plant; meditation on nature is more difficult. The object should be uninteresting, and something for which we have no particular attachment. There is no need to look at the object because the practice involves moving from thinking about an object to meditating.

Let us choose A PAPER CLIP as the object for our meditation exercise.

1. First, we form an inner picture of a paper clip and try to hold the image without letting other thoughts or images enter. We then begin to "circle" the object with thoughts about it - the color of the paper clip; the construction, the particular form, the functions. If our thoughts stray to far away from the object, we gently bring them back. For example, if I begin thinking about the tin mine and the rock ore from which the metal comes to make paper clips, we are at the edges, the limits of the meditation if this begins to take us away from initial object of meditation. It is not possible to say in advance that going this far is too far. You can tell in the meditating itself if this is the case. If so, then gently come back to the object of the meditation.

When the exercise is repeated every day, it is important each time the exercise is done to think again, not just to remember what one has thought in previous meditations. The content of the thoughts may be the same, but they must be thought and not just remembered. One can think the same thing every day, without ever noticing that it is the same. That is the ideal.

2. Initially it is helpful to think in short, firmly contoured trains of thought ... "the paper clip is silver. It is curved at both ends. One end of the metal overlaps the metal toward the other end. The metal is firm but flexible. It serves to hold papers together." If distractions occur, try to look through the distractions rather than fight against them.

3. As [circling" the object continues, thinking becomes more intensive. This happens as if by itself. At first, will is required to think about the paper clip. Gradually, "thinking about" becomes "thinking within". This is a new experience of thinking - it begins to live. Thinking begins to "unroll" from within. One no longer wills. One simply does it. Everything becomes natural and unforced. A playful attitude is needed.

4. At first, one thinks verbally. As the thinking intensifies, words and representations fall away and one begins more and more to think the theme itself, not just the words and images. The aim is to gradually come to "think" continuously rather than intermittently. At first, the thinking is likely to be intermittent ... "the paper clip is made of metal. It is silver in color...etc" The slight pause between the intermittent thinking allows distractions to enter. One must attempt to concentrate in a continuous movement.

5. Once thinking begins to unfold on its own and the theme itself becomes clear in meditation, a second phase begins to unfold. We can now begin to produce many possible versions of a paper clip...one made of plastic, one that looks more like a clamp, other objects that might be used to hold papers together. We begin to experience what all of these objects have in common. This is not abstraction, however. And, the focus of the meditation is not on inner perception of various objects, but on the commonality among them. This pure idea becomes the theme of meditation. Idea and picture are one at this stage. It is hard to describe this experience - it is intuition. When the paper clip was invented, for example, someone did not sit down and think - "we need a paper clip". There was an original intuition. Out of this original intuition came the form of the actual object. Our aim is to get back to the original intuition. This original intuition is not a representation - that happens only later. It is a flow, a stream of thinking, like light or music.

6. With this kind of meditation, we begin with an object, but as the meditating progresses, we no longer behold the object as if it were being looked at. We instead, in every moment are creating the idea of the object; our experience is the same as the idea; it is no longer an idea about the object. All thoughts that we might have about the object stem from this original intuition, which is always there, but which we cannot be aware of in ordinary consciousness. It is like fluid that still contains suspended particles which will later crystallize out of this fluid.

This stage of meditation works on the whole soul-life. Gradually, feeling becomes free and the ego no longer needs to assert its existence, but there is not a direct attempt to circumvent ego either.

E. Meditation on an Image

Meditation on a symbolic image is somewhat easier than meditating on a sentence or on an object because such images already embody multiple meanings and spiritual realities. Symbolic images do not represent perceptions, although they consist of perceptual elements. But no one has seen a Ouroboros in the world, nor a Rose-cross, nor any of the images, for example, portrayed in alchemical texts.

As an exercise in meditating with symbolic images, let us work with the image of the

OUROBOROS

The word, Ouroboros is Greek: a snake in the form of a circle, biting its own tail. The meditation consists in "reading" the riddle of the image, becoming aware of its meaning, realizing its meaning, not simply knowing what it means by being told.

1. I will not present a drawing here of the Ouroboros. It is better to make up such a symbolic image. If a drawing were presented, then one would have to remove the remembered picture from consciousness as part of the act of meditation. Starting with a pictorial representation can sometimes be helpful - it can function to develop the initial concentration. I think each of us can make an inner picture of the Ouroboros. To start, it is necessary to be able to "hold" the image without effort and not be pre-occupied with holding it. We then become inwardly silent and allow the image to speak.

2. We imagine a snake which holds the end of its tail between its fangs. A preparatory thought is necessary in order to indicate the direction of the meaning of the image. Such a thought might, for example, be: Where is the reality of this image? No snake is actually doing what this image is showing. The image does not have to do with snakes.

3.Just like meditation on the sentence and on the object, the image is experienced as an activity. One can imagine, for example, that the snake follows its own tail. In the image of the circular form, the snake will never catch its tail; the tail will always be a little bit ahead. In order to reach its tail, the snake's body has to change. Beginning and end of something are touching; beginning and ending even bring each other into existence. If there were no tail there would be no head, and if there were no head there would be no tail. The head, though, cannot be said to be producing the tail and the body, and the body cannot be said to be producing the head. The cause and the caused are one.

4. If one relates the image to consciousness - the consciousness brings something into being, sees it, and that which is brought about is the consciousness. One meaning of the image is consciousness. Self-consciousness stands before us in pictorial form, realizing itself, in its beginning and in essence. This is only one meaning of the image; the image of this snake means infinitely more. (aside - esoteric texts, alchemical texts, many spiritual texts are meditations of this sort. Thus, they cannot be understood out of ordinary consciousness; they are meditations which have been created into word. Thus, in order to understand things of this nature it is necessary to develop meditation capacities; at the same time, reading such material in an attitude of complete openness also develops these capacities.)

F. Perceptual Meditation

Meditation on an object of perception is more difficult than the forms of meditation thus far described. When we meditated on the object of the paper clip, this was not a perceptual meditation because we concentrated first on the inner image of the object, and then on the thoughts surrounding the object. It was not necessary to have the object before us, and in fact it was necessary not to have it before us. It is more difficult to meditate on a perceptual object because many different qualities come together in an object - for example, color, shape, size, weight, place - and these qualities weave together with whatever surrounds the object. It is also difficult because an object, at least an object of the natural world is part of the whole, so it is difficult to determine the theme of meditation - what are the boundaries?

As a start, it is helpful to meditate on one quality of a perceptual object. For example, one can begin with the green color of a plant. One could also begin, say, with the red color of a rose, and then go on to include the blossom, and then the whole plant, and then the plant in its surroundings. It becomes quickly quite complex.

For our exercise, let us choose to meditate on the Green Color of a Plant which we place before us.

1. First we simply concentrate on the plant before us, taking it in and excluding anything else - try to fill our consciousness with the plant that is before us.

2. At first, the green color of the plant is perceived in our ordinary consciousness as being the surface quality of the plant. The first aim is to have the theme - the green color - become a process - i.e. to concentrate on the color, seeing it as "coloring" in the verb sense, rather than an object that has the color green. This can be described as a "lifting -up" of the color from the object, as if we had a mental picture of the object, but now it happens in perceiving.

3. As an analogy, this way of perceiving color is much the way an artist sees color; an artist does not simply apply color to a surface like paint is applied to a wall. The artist "colors" structures the color through the technique of the brush. The inner gesture of the meditation is - what does this color want to tell me? It is not an intellectual question, but an inner attitude, an attitude of silence.

4. In this attitude of silence, in this "staying" in the meditation of the percept, one forgets what the phenomenon is, its name, and what one knows about it. It is as if seeing for the first time. In this attitude of "seeing", the color is actually <u>felt</u>. What does the green color feel like? Not what do I feel about it, but what does it feel like?

Exercises such as this can be tried with any of the senses. Such meditations begin to awaken the senses so that we begin to be conscious in the senses rather than, as we ordinarily are, conscious only of the information brought through the senses.

G. Meditation on Feeling

Attentiveness can also be directed toward feeling and can be a most valuable approach to the healing of feeling. Meditation on feeling, at first, needs to be directed to a feeling in retrospect, that is a feeling that has already occurred rather than on feeling at the moment it is occurring. With present feeling we are too submerged in it, torn by it, it is too self-directed to be able to gain meditative access.

What is usually taken to be feeling is not the feeling itself but the reaction of the ego to the presence of feeling. Feeling itself has more the quality of a dream-like reality. What we usually take to be feeling is also the response of the body to the reality of feeling - feeling always affects the body

- in extreme cases the breathing and the pulse are changed, bodily signs of pain or joy appear. As a preparation for meditating on feeling it is helpful to observe the aspects of feeling just described as they appear to our ordinary consciousness.

The exercises we did prior to this one we are about to do on feeling give a good introduction to feeling, for when we meditate in the ways described the actual experience of meditating is also feeling - but it is not our ego response. Even when doing an exercise in thinking, when the reality itself is allowed to speak that reality reveals itself as a quality of feeling - for example, the feeling one experiences when we have gone from thinking about something to thinking within it is a feeling of "that is it." In the exercise of meditating on a color, the presence of feeling is even more apparent. It should not be thought that meditating is a mental activity.

Another way to orient toward meditating on feeling is that it is more like the kind of feeling that goes with any artistic activity. The artist works in the domain of feeling, but this mode of feeling is not a reaction of the ego; it is coherent with the activity itself, flows along within this activity and directs it.

1. As an exercise in meditating on feeling, remember a situation in which feelings were evoked. Let us choose as our theme of meditation a remembered situation in which you felt anger.

2. In order to meditate on feeling we have to first differentiate it from thinking about a feeling we had in the past. First, in memory we re-experience as best as possible the feeling - in this case the feeling of anger. Then, we try to "back up" the anger just a bit. Try to get to the moment just before the feeling became a reaction, before it became a sensation. Try to experience what that moment was like. Then try to get to even one step earlier in the feeling, to the phenomenon that awakened the feeling in the first place. Do not attach this moment to the person in the presence of whom the anger originated, as if the person were the cause of the anger. We are trying to locate the feeling in the world - in the world of feeling, and not in the feeling as it is "felt" by us, which is the ego's reaction to the feeling world.

It should be pointed out that working with feelings in this meditative way does not diminish the feeling life; we gradually become aware of the substitute feelings we used to be satisfied with and how much richer the world of feeling is.

This concludes this correspondence seminar on the inner methods employed in spiritual psychology. Entering into the exercises described here will help considerably with any further work you do in spiritual psychology. You have a basis in inner experience to work from so that you will approach further material from the immediacy of inner experience, have a sense of conscious soul life and a feeling for the ways in which spirit lights up the life of the soul.

Cultivating Spiritual Imagination

Because our current culture is profoundly informed by mechanistic and "cause and effect" thinking, it's supremely important, even urgent, to become reacquainted with the art of passivity. Moreover, I refer to passivity as an art because it's both immensely creative and a move into a brilliant life that is non-linear. This new approach places us in a creative realm rather than in the worlds described by typical modalities of learning. Spiritual imagination is limitless, not to mention profoundly beautiful. Thus, it will never reveal itself through an accrual of facts; rather, it becomes available in a manner reminiscent of an (artful) courtship.

If Spiritual Imagination is Limitless, where is Its Center?

The answer to this question is both simple and heart-stalling if you thoroughly grasp its import. The center of your new life in spiritual imagination is nowhere and everywhere. It's akin to taking into your very core of being the well-known Biblical quote, "… put off thy shoes from off thy feet, for the place whereon thou standest *is* holy ground." In other words, no matter where you are — or what preparations you take — to begin becoming attentive to spiritual imagination, you are in the right time and place. Every place is, indeed, holy ground if we choose to make it so. All that you need is a willingness to recreate the space in which you currently dwell. It merely requires a shift in attention, a shift in consciousness.

To offer more clarity, a return to the analogy used in the heading may prove helpful. Spiritual imagination begins with the process of cultivating an interior field — one in which we can be resolutely assured that an abundant loveliness will issue. However, the analogy is not completely apt because this revolutionary and metaphorical harvest isn't seasonal; it's perpetual and evolving. If this seems too arcane — or too much for us to attain — we'll soon begin exploring simple techniques that will enable anyone willing to put forth effort to enter this deeply gorgeous way of inhabiting the world. Not only is it possible to begin to limn the "space" of stillness and spiritual imagination, it's inevitable that one's life will subsequently become new, and extraordinary aspects of beauty, virtue and sublimity will emerge.

The Paradox: We are fully ourselves when we give ourselves away.

Once we discover the filial (shared) instant that exists in stillness, it marks a new recognition of the self that bears no resemblance to previous "isms" that have been used to describe our lives, our history or our experience. Instead of fixed ideas and methods, we are granted a vector into sacred moments that usher us into the realm of the spiritual imagination. And the expression of such an imaginal landscape is conjugal in nature, and informed by healing, love, and a oneness with all that is, regardless of time or place. Paradoxically, it is also a place of absence. It allows us to dwell in a place devoid of death, pain, want, or avarice. Additionally, it shows us a terrain free of chatter and notions of "this" versus "that." This oneness is precisely what is alluded to when its "conjugal" aspect is underscored. From this moment forward, you can never again be encroached upon and rendered wholly alone.

Importantly, let us not forget the artfulness of this process of moving toward spiritual imagination. Cultivating stillness and the subsequent (e)motion is a creative act that remakes our interior world while simultaneously renewing and refreshing all that we have encountered throughout every intersection with people, places and things. It's profoundly personal, yet completely devoid of ownership or narrowness. Think of it in the following way: "You can now witness the gate beyond which all you love — and all that loves you — beckons."

So. Let us begin.

(Psychologically) disrobe. Divest yourself of the thought processes that dominate the modern, secular mindset. We've been told that we are accretions of biological, social, physical or even collective, imagistic forces. Note, too, that many well-meaning techniques in therapy operate in similarly unhealthful, yet surreptitious, ways. You need none of these past modes of understanding — nor should you do battle with them. Opposition only allows a means for them to maintain or accrue greater psychic terrain and, of course, this is counterproductive. Instead of thinking, simply allow yourself to begin the most luxurious of excursions: cultivating the passivity and stillness that leads to spiritual imagination.

Initial Step in Cultivating Stillness.

Exercise One.

Refrain from assessing or examining your current cosmology. Let it "drop" — make the effort to momentarily let it fall away. "You" will not be lost. In fact, this is a first step toward discovering the quintessential "you." And that can only occur if you are willing to enter a place that is "no-place." The philosopher/theologian, Henry Corbin, refers to it as the *Mundus Imaginalis*, the imaginative world. Let us approach it in the following way:

Close your eyes and enter into Silence; Draw your attention into the interior of the heart. Pay attention to the qualities of this new inner darkness.

Release all thoughts, images and fantasies until "no-thing" is present. This darkness is already another world.

If you accomplished this, even if only momentarily, you have already made the transitions from "isms" and entered into spiritual imagination.

What to expect in this new world, this new landscape.

Often people describe this spiritual imagination as an "illumined darkness." Moreover, it is not delineated as one might describe the shape of a room. Rather, it may feel round, like the interior of a sphere. There may seem to be currents circulating within this round space. In other words, it's not like looking at a dark screen.

Also, there is no sense of going from "here" to "there" — there is no linear movement and, thus, there is a sense of freedom in this new space. Importantly, do not let notions or "outside" and "inside" intrude into this newly experienced "round space."

Reside in this new and nurturing space for a time — until it no longer feels as if it is naturally sustaining you. Likely, it's "roundness" will become disturbed and you will have the sensation that you are being nudged back into "reality."

Exercise Two.

Imaginal Knowing.

Re-enter the "round world," but, this time, imagine a tree. However, don't just see the tree. You'll soon realize that imagining the tree is not merely seeing it. Instead, it is at one with "feeling" the tree. Thus, this act of feeling-knowing the tree is easily accomplished. We do not "have" ("possess") images that subsequently need interpretation. Interpretation is a reductive process. Thus, feeling is quite different from seeing or fantasizing about the tree. Fantasy is constantly changing and moving; hence, we know this is a very different kind of activity than what we find in the *mundus imaginalis*.

For instance, "imaginal knowing" holds the shape of an image. This is image-cognition versus mental-cognition. Put simply, ordinary consciousness will not be able to apprehend the imaginal world. It "fractures" the form of an image and demands that we revert back to the simplistic understanding of things — which we have erroneously been taught is the best and most thorough of mental processes. This is far from true; in fact, it is antithetical to what is true.

Spiritual Desire — "Mysteries of the Heart"

The heart is the organ of spiritual imagination, and we will soon explore ways to engage it. Thus far, we have relied upon our will to conjure, say, the image of the tree. We can sense the act of "seeing" the tree as a kind of forceful exertion. At this juncture, we will depart from the typical way of "making" mental images. Rather, by dwelling with them, we will come to know them far better than we do by thinking about them. Feeling-thought is profoundly deeper — and far more revelatory — than rational processes.

At this point it is now helpful to turn to the "action" of the heart as desire. This new idea is only new to contemporary culture. In fact, this concept has been described as *"enthymesis."* a Greek word that connotes meditation and conception. The latter, of course, needs little explanation. It implies that actions of the heart incur a perpetually birthing process that is profoundly creative.

Needless to say, this new way of understanding the heart demands that we abandon typical notions of it as merely an organ, a medical, pumping apparatus. With spiritual imagination we can begin to heal the split in typical notions about the heart. It is not a pumping machine, nor is it a simile associated with love, feelings, warmth, etc. that ultimately lack substance.

A New Way to Understand Heart

An imaginal understanding of the heart requires that we acquiesce to it as metaphor rather than mere simile. That is to say, it is simultaneously both a physical organ and a spiritual entity. In fact, it is a bodily area in which etheric space is created. This means blood is drawn into the heart by a non-material force rather than "pumped." What is a far more truthful is: An understanding of the heart as an etheric center of spirit that transforms matter into spirit.

Astonishingly, there is an etheric center of spirit in the heart that transforms blood into etheric substance that is then radiated outward. Moreover, this process of taking something in, transforming it, and radiating its spirit is an ideal way of understanding the path of spiritual imagination. Thus, like all meditative work, we will consistently be taking natural processes and making them more conscious by giving them our careful and meditative (imaginal) attention. Thus, it is not a theory or a system. It's a profound new way of creating the world by vivifying it imaginatively (meditatively).

The Heart as a Bridge Between Matter and Spirit

Let us now turn to the work of Jakob Lorber. He describes a vital nerve close to the center of heart that "receives (a) vital nutrient and stimulates it into becoming life-sustaining substance." He then describes two tiny ventricles corresponding to two larger ventricles that control the life of the heart — as well as the entire body. "The first and most essential ventricle corresponds to what is of the spirit and its life." The second one is "of minor importance but still essential for the natural life, (and) corresponds to matter." Thus, the heart bridges soul and body and, similarly, it also bridges spirit and body.

Lorber continues on by speaking of heart and meditation:
"Everyone who strives for true knowledge of himself and God must
spiritually enter this unpretentious ventricle of the heart in a spirit of
nakedness and submissiveness, and spiritually return the life received from it.

A person who does this widens the ventricle of life, illuminating it
throughout. This animates the entire heart and, through it, the whole being
spiritually, and the result is the human being's cognition of God within. Now
the person is able to see how life out of God flows into our heart, where it
accumulates and forms into a free and independent life. Thus, the actual
Spirit of God operates in this tiny ventricle and, if the human soul enters it
in meekness and love to find the infinite divine love, it achieves its rebirth
in the Spirit from god; and only thus can man become God's image."

Entering into the Interior of the Heart

Heart Alignment Process
Moving from Head to Heart
Placing Attention into the Interior of the Heart

Qualities of the Interior of the Heart

Some cautionary notes are now in order. First, all meditative practice
requires persistence. But what will keep us meditating when oftentimes there
seems to be no result? When working with the heart, we must look for
answers within the meditative work itself. For instance, the qualities of the
heart's "interior space" include the presence of a rhythmic flow of the
illuminated darkness within. In fact, the very presence of tis quality is a way
of knowing you are, indeed, in the interior space of the heart. Additionally,
there are feeling qualities you may experience, such as warmth and a
welcoming sense of protection.

Go daily into the interior space of heart for a few minutes. No more.
This will result in a few things: an exploration of the heart currents and
feelings; a shift in the etheric body; a death of logical (linear) thinking; and
a gradual change in the constitution of the blood (more on this to come).

Changes in Knowing Changes the Knower

Working with the qualities of the interior of the heart brings about changes that gradually allow you increasing access to spiritual imagination. Thus, you will begin to experience less of a desire to "see" than to simply "know." This is an actual transformation, not something that occurs as an act of the will. Thus, you may continue to find it easy to enter the innermost "roundness" of the heart.

Sometimes, however, daily life (collective consciousness) continuously seems to wipe out the "heart-felt" experience? Simply persist. Simply going back into the heart will produce change. And this is far more than a change in your being; it's an act of creative imagination. Amazingly, it creates the presence of spiritual beings. These beings are experienced through creative imagination; however, they are not created by any action. A new form of perception that is subtle and sensitive to the presence of the heart-field is capable of recognizing the presence of spiritual beings. And these beings are inevitably and always benevolent. This is certain because the interior of the heart is inviolable and can never be entered by malevolent beings.

How can we be assured that the "heart presences" are benevolent?

Go back again and again to the interior of the heart. Notice the subtlety of the space that is no-space. You will begin to feel a longing, a kind of actual "tug," and you will begin to feel the physical presence of your heart within your chest and perhaps begin to feel a kind of "tickle."

It takes spiritual courage to enter as fully as you can into this longing, this feeling within the heart. Importantly, be certain you are present to the longings inherent within your heart. This is essential because there is soul-longing versus spirit-longing. They each represent two forms of desire. If the longing issues from the soul, it will push us into the world. On the other hand, the desire of the heart pulls us toward the unknown. The latter is far more subtle and, once it is felt, it is unmistakably quite different from spirit-longing that will propel us back into the things of ego and the world.

Exercise Three: Ardent Desire and the Intensification of Prayer

Heart Alignment
Move into the Interior of the Heart
Etheric Praying Within the Interior of the Heart

Etheric prayer is referred to as "Theophanic Prayer" by Henry Corbin. It marks the release of the soul from its exile, loneliness and abandonment. Prayer, in fact, is the heart's way of knowing its Beloved. This is what the longing heart seeks, and this way of praying is a liturgical act. Thus, this prayer begins with a Remembrance — the Our Father, the Hail Mary, etc. The first words are a sacred initiation and must not be done mechanically. Next, we are ready to explore the Three Acts of the Etheric Prayer of the Heart!

Place yourself in the presence of the spiritual world. This is done through closely praying the Remembrance mentioned above. Second, in the interior of your heart, meet the Being with whom you commune while in prayer. Meet the Being face-to-face; this "meeting" is reciprocal. Recognize that the way this Being appears to you in the imagination is in accord with your ability to be within the interior of your heart. It can assume a wide range of attributes. And it will change as you change. The experience may manifest as a visual metaphor, or simply be evident as a sensitivity to its presence.

The third moment of etheric praying is simply being in the presence of this Being. It is the moment of contemplation. Even if no "communication" seems to occur, stay within the aura, the presence, of this Being. About this experience, Corbin offers the following:

"Thus, the life of prayer... represents the authentic form of a 'Process of Individuation,' (of) releasing the spiritual person from collective norms and ready-made evidences and enabling him to live as a unique individual for and with his unique God."

Note that God is different for each individual, just as each person is unique. Here it is important to note that this difference in presence can happen without concluding that we are making up our God. Instead, God's presence occurs in relation to our own uniqueness.

Now, work closely with Corbin's passage. It offers the way, the only way, through and out of collective consciousness. It is also the only way through the ready-made material available to us via our culture; what preachers say; what others say; and what the Bible (taken literally) says. The Presence, the Being, with you is objective — yet utterly unique and wholly appropriate to you.

Silence as the Matrix of Integral Spiritual Psychology

Profound silence usually comes to us as a gift, opening and revealing the depths of the world for a few moments that feel like forever. No doubt, this gift is being squeezed out of the world, and such moments are becoming rare. If this gift continues to recede, shortly we will forget that there is such an autonomous reality as silence. Once forgotten by humanity, we enter a world completely dominated by greed. As Max Picard has said: "Happiness is to silence as greed is to money." When we don't have something essential to being human, we go looking for it in all the wrong places.

Sacred phenomena, such as the life of the soul or the life of the spirit, in an age of such materialism, undergo a degradation that follows a particular pattern. First, such phenomena are cosmic, and they are world-phenomena and we participate in them because we too belong to the world. Gradually, these world-phenomena become more narrowly conceived and are said to reside within human beings as inner, subjective and invisible elements of some importance. Having stuffed the sacred into the interior of our being, it then becomes possible to deny that they exist at all. In fact, those who do stand in and for the sacred element within their lives can easily be labeled as strange, weird, even insane. The phenomenon of silence has suffered this same debasement. People who exude an aura of inner silence are held suspect in the modern world. Why do they always say these days of the person who goes on some sort of rampage, "Well, we didn't know him very well. He kept to himself and was a very quiet man who seemed very nice." It is as if the quiet is the culprit who is somehow responsible for the atrocities. And, certainly, silence is kept out of the world. You cannot go into a restaurant and eat in quiet. If you manage to make a space of silence around you in a public place, it will be sharply interrupted by someone shouting on a cellphone. So much talking, guitar-playing, and other distractions go on in church that even this sanctuary of silence is endangered. Matthew Fox, who has written so beautifully and so spiritually on so many concerns of the modern world, is at the same time the primary promoter of the rave mass.

Given this situation, where Silence is now endangered, we have to start at the beginning and demonstrate that Silence is a cosmic and a world phenomenon, one that is essential to the very being of the Earth. Then, we can re-imagine our role in this phenomenon. We must save the phenomenon from being taken into the realm of inner subjectivity, refrain in every way possible from psychologizing it, which would be setting it up for elimination altogether.

It seems important, then, to know as much as possible about the conditions under which silence visits in order to discover how to enter into it. When we learn to consciously enter this world rather than accidentally fall into it from time to time, then we can also develop the capacity to perceive the fullness of what is there, to move around in it, explore it, to let it reveal itself to us. We, of course, cannot probe this world as if it were some kind of alien terrain and we were scientific explorers of inner space. It is, rather, a matter of exploring what is already here, all around us and within us; a matter of getting in touch with something that is so close and so intimate and so much a part of everything that we continually bypass it with our excitement-seeking mentality.

I am going to start by suggesting some ways of finding silence. These suggestions are in the way of phenomenological observations, simply drawing attention toward the evident and the subtle, noticing that the instructions for finding the door to silence are written in our own bodily constitution and in the book of the world. The methods I am going to suggest, then, simply elevate the given into consciousness and are by no means clever contrivances devised to try and give you an experience.

One of the residences of silence is in the intervals of our speaking. Narration, speaking about our experience rather than from within our experience, covers over this most natural region of silence. Not only does narrative-speech run one word into another, one sentence into another, eliminating the sense of the interval, this same pattern installs itself into our inner life. When we first go inward all we find is an endless narrative stream of ourselves talking to ourselves about things and experiences. Even our inner presence to images and feelings are mediated by this same narrator, now serving as a kind of inner guide of the galleries and museums of the mind. We have no genuine inner life if it is all filled with everyday content all of the time. A very first entry into silence concerns developing an appreciation for the pause, for the stumbling, for the inarticulate, for the gaps in our speaking. We can feel the presence of silence only when are speaking is accompanied with an act of listening. Then, speaking, rather than telling someone about something, which easily turns into an excretory function, instead becomes a voicing of our listening.

The intervals of speech, those interesting pauses between words, set silence into motion. Silence is certainly not the empty space between the words, not a mere void. When I say a word or a few words, and then pause, not an affected pause, but merely the pause that tries to listen, then the words said set up a rhythm with the silence, a rhythm within which the palpable substance of silence can be felt. In addition, the wave of silence draws to it the next words to be said, and the rhythm of those words, even before said, also enter into the silence as an aspect of its motion.

You can get to the doorway of silence by the following meditation: close your eyes. Say to yourself a phrase, letting pauses enter into the phrase or sentence. Repeat the phrase or sentence varying the pause between words, like this:

I	enter	the s	ilence
Or			
I	enter	the	silence
Or			
I	enter	the	silence

This kind of little word meditation holds secrets. While silence is not something we do but rather a world we enter, we cannot neglect the importance of our part in orienting toward this world. A meditative sentence, such as the one above, sets up a current of silence. However, silence must already be there for this current to take effect. We attract silence to us by a kind of anticipatory act; it gathers through our anticipation of it. In order to enter this meditative sentence, we have to already be oriented toward silence. In terms of the meditative sentence, even before we speak the sentence in an inner way, the sentence already has a silence before it and a silence after it. That is, the sentence is already surrounded by silence when we enter it. If we incline toward this silence before speaking, the silence spreads throughout whatever we say and is evident as the rhythm of speech. Rhythm is the way that silence pervades the spoken word.

With this orienting exercise, we also encounter the presence of silence as a particular quality of our body. It is as if silence comes and envelopes us.

A particular bodily feeling comes. We feel the boundaries of our body because something gently presses up against us. This something, which is palpable silence, is always there; it is as if it holds our body-shape in form and without it we would spill into the world like a burst water-balloon. But, when we attend to silence, we feel this presence more actively. It surrounds our body and stirs the silence within our body. When we attend to this enveloping presence, we notice that it cannot be something cognitively known. It is known through the region of the heart. When silence visits we descend from mind to heart.

This subtle envelope has a shape; silence is not formless. It is as if our body stands within the form of the vesica. The vesica is the form made where two intersecting circles overlap. It is the middle-form, the almond-shaped form between the two intersecting circles. This form is often seen in sacred art. We do not see this form but feel the silence around us as formed in this way. This vesica, however, is three-dimensional, so it is somewhat like a transparent cocoon of silence, as if we are in a vessel, maybe the vessel of the heart itself. Through our heart we enter into some kind of larger heart; our heart is the center of a larger, more encompassing heart-center.

This form is not just an external presence around us. While silence announces itself to us in this form, it is not an emptiness, but rather an extraordinary fullness that makes possible feeling of the interior, the innerness of the body. We feel our body interiorly as a body of wholeness. This experience is characterized by an inner bodily joy, absence of strain, and an immediate presence to a flow of currents from within the body outward, a flow of force from within that maintains but does not produce this transparent vesica of silence.

If, through coming to our heart, we enter into the center of a larger heart, an invisible heart, have found our way to the interior of the world, or more accurately, to the world-as-interior.

We can tell if our orienting meditation works, not by continuing to sit with eyes closed, but by, after a time, opening them and noticing the world. We can then perceive that the inner silence spreads all around us. The transparent vesica-cocoon has the peculiar quality of maintaining its enveloping presence around us, while at the same time, it now becomes the organ through which we are able to perceive Silence in the world.

In silence, the individual things we perceive are surrounded by fringes of a great quiet. Objects are as if filigreed. Silence wraps around them like lace.

This filigree is most apparent with things of nature such as the leaves of a tree, a flying bird, a tree, a boulder, a valley, a stream, a mountain, the sky. Human-made things are also wrapped in Silence, but generally it is harder to perceive with these things. These things – such as buildings, bridges, furniture, and so on, do not typically share their silence and seem to sit in it rather passively rather than glow in it as do the things of nature. And, not only things noticed in their individuality, but groupings of natural things, such as a grove of trees or the relation between a tree and the building next to it and the grass in front of the building can be seen swathed in the glow of silence. It is as if the filigree extends outward, filling the space between things. Or, the space between things is actually not empty space at all but is of the substance of silence that comes up against things and gently touches them, setting off a resonance of silence within them.

The perception of silence is, not strictly speaking, visual. All of the senses are in this moment gathered together into a whole. If we attend closely to this moment, it is even possible to shift our attention around each of the senses and experience the presence of silence gently impressing itself into each sense. We feel the touch of silence, experience it within the inner wholeness of our body, and sense its distinct quality of movement, which is like a swirling gentleness. We also hear the silence, smell it, and taste it. Of course, something is happening in this kind of sensing that differentiates it from ordinary sensing. The sensing of silence is not only subtle sensing; it is also an imaginal sensing. That is to say, our sensing becomes elevated to the level of imagination. It is *as if* we smell the silence, touch it, feel its movement, and so on. However, such sensory experience is not imaginary. We are not experiencing something that is not there, but rather are taken into a different level of what is there. The sense-perceptible world is raised to the level of the imaginal for us the moment we cross the threshold of the noisy world into silence. This imaginal world is neither all image nor all matter.

A further aspect of this world is that there is an intelligence to it. We do not cross into a world of chaotic images. The form of the world maintains, though now we have some perception of its spiritual body. The devotees of Silence in the time of Dante spoke of the silent intelligence of the world as "Madonna Intelligenza", a quality differentiated from the "Goddess of Reason."

The autonomous nature of silence can be missed if we focus only on our own quietude. Thus, if the orienting exercise, for example, is followed by keeping our eyes closed and remaining silent, it is more difficult to experience that silence has an independence from us. It is possible, of course, to experience this autonomy even under these circumstances. The silence felt within is just as autonomous as that in the outer perceptible world; in fact, they are not separate at all. In attending to the silence within, however, we have to notice that, while this silence is experienced within, it is absolutely objective. That something occurs as an inner experience does not make it subjective. It is just a different point of view on the same phenomenon.

Through attending to silence within, we discover a quality that is also present in the perception of silence in the world, where it there mingles with the other perceptible qualities. This quality is depth. Depth, we can say, is the pure innerness of silence.

Let me try and develop a bit of the phenomenology of the depth of silence, for there are many aspects to it. With a phenomenon as subtle as this, what becomes important is to not let a word stand in for the whole of the experience, but to let the word open up. We are forever using words as shorthand ways of expressing experiences, expecting that others understand the word in exactly the way we are meaning it. The word 'depth' has a lot of power to it and it can easily pass as if something has been said when using it, while the particularity of the experience is missed.

There are three qualities to the depth of silence. First, this depth is intimate. Our perception of the things of the world alters in silence from one in which we perceive surfaces and have the impression that there are only things in the world standing side by side, to the perception of something of the utter particularity of each and every thing. There are no 'its' in silence, only the particularity of the 'thou'. Perceiving becomes meeting. Not just any meeting, and it is even something more than an encounter. Meeting through silence can be described as a mutual enveloping, in which the individual things of the world, too, are wrapped in silence, and the first quality of depth is silence meeting silence through inter-enveloping. We are allowed the extraordinary privilege of entering into each other's space of silence. Can you imagine anything more intimate that being together with another in an entwining of hearts?

A peculiar aspect of the intimacy of depth is that there is absolutely no negation anywhere within silence. Now, there are definitely negative silences. Silence can be terrifying, deadly, hurtful, filled with anger, divisive, cruel. In these instances, however, silence is usurped, used in order to convey or do something to others that actually has nothing to do with the silence. We have all experienced these qualities, specifically in our relations with others, and most of all those with whom we are intimate. But silence itself is never negative. I have tried very hard to be sure that I am not sentimentalizing silence by virtue of the fact that there is not a single negative moment that I can find in the phenomenology. There are aspects of silence that can be emotionally difficult – sometimes it is an overwhelming sadness, a grief, but in all instances the quality of positive intimacy is never broken.

Speaking of this intimacy as positive is not to say that it is something personal. The intimacy excludes our ego. We are, in our ego-being outside observers only. The intimacy focuses on the more impersonal aspects of our being and the being of the things of the world. Our body, externally and internally experienced feels in intimate relation with silence. It is also a soul intimacy, and it is definitely a spiritual experience. But it is not an ego experience. This last realization, that the ego is kept away from the substance of silence, accounts for why there is no negative experience of deep silence. Judgment of any sort has no part in this experience. We experience the full range of emotions in silence, but without the accompanying inner evaluating that goes on in ordinary consciousness.

A further quality of the depth of silence can be described as a particular sense of entering into the world as holy. A good, descriptive word for this quality is liturgical silence. A good place to go to experience this quality is a cathedral or a temple where there are great rhythms of liturgical silence, even when a liturgy is not being performed. When we enter silence, we enter a temple, a region where we not only contemplate, but are also being contemplated. The experience of this quality signifies going more deeply into the world of silence, where the initially multiple envelopes of silence surrounding each thing become encompassed or nested within an invisible form that reverberates intimations of a holy source within the particularity of each thing.

A second reason, though, for naming this quality of the depth of silence liturgical, concerns the subtle perception of silence as anything but static and still. The ever-present movement of silence is dramatic in form, and liturgy is always sacred drama. We have dramatic form whenever there is the experience of polarities, opposites, contradictions in motion. The dramatic quality referred to here concerns, for example, the presence of irresolvable opposites in the experience of silence. Opposites such as perception of the utterly particular in tension with perception of the deepest meaning of the things around us. And, the unsolvable tension that silence is mine and not mine at all; of its closeness which is infinitely far; of it being a phenomenon of surfaces and also a phenomenon of depth. We also experience ourselves within and part of an infinite activity that is simultaneously moving and still. Then, there is the dramatic quality of being within a reality while being able to observe it as an objective reality. It is like being within soul and being able to observe it at the same time. And, being able to engage in this kind of observation without splitting off part of oneself to become the observer. There exists a reflective quality to silence. It seems to mirror the dramatic, creating actions of the cosmos, making it a cosmic phenomenon. At the same time, we find ourselves mirrored in silence; we come home to ourselves. But, all of these qualities are present, in motion, without conflict, held together in contrariness.

In silence there is anticipation. This is the third quality of the depth of silence. The anticipation is not ours. What does it involve? An anticipation of what? By whom? Partly, in the experience of silence, the answer to this question is not known. Yet, it is the strongest element of the depth of silence. It is as if silence poises and just about speaks. That is the anticipation felt; something about to be said. The saying goes so far as expressing itself as the things of the world. In silence we have the immediate experience that all of the space within which the things of the world exist is not empty at all. It is as if all the things of the world are being squeezed out of silence; they are the word, the word that is deeper than any one word or all of the words of all the things of the world. Through the silence we feel the unity of the word, and the things of the world as expressions of the word.

You know what it is like when you have something to say, something that comes quite spontaneously and yet has an urgency to be expressed. That moment before it is said, that is the quality of anticipation that characterizes the depth of silence. A preparedness, an about-to, a coming, or as they used to say in the 60's, a happening.

In perceiving the depth of Silence, we come to discover the invisible body of the world, the spiritual flesh within which everything is nurtured into existence every moment. And, we discover ourselves in a new way. We are participants in the great being of Silence. We are not detached observers of an independent phenomenon but exist within what we are observing. This engagement does not make what we can say concerning silence subjective. Typically, we think of ourselves as individual beings, and the world as spreading around us. We take our inner life to be private and subjective. In silence, this relation changes. We no longer exist within the kind of polarity that oscillates between a focus on ourselves one moment and a focus on the outer world the next. The area of Silence is more like an ellipse, within which one focus is the being of silence creating our soul-being while the other focus is the inclining of our soul-being toward and for silence. This picture gives us the beginning of the way to imagine the topography of the spiritual region we are investigating here. Within this vast region what occurs between us and Silence can no longer be thought of in linear terms nor in terms of any kind of causality.

Different laws prevail in this region, laws well known to those who know the ways of the imaginal worlds. I am thinking here in particular of Henry Corbin and his description of the primary law of interaction within the imaginal worlds as being that of *sympathetic union*. The currents of silence set up a resonance within our heart prompting an inclination of the heart toward the great silence. This inclination is something more than a kind of bending toward a silence conceived as already being there, ready and waiting. The inclination is needed for silence to activate. Even through it is already always there – it does not go away; we go away from it – the extent the depth silence can attain depends upon our inclination of soul toward it. Silence's inclination toward us spiritualizes our senses so that the material world becomes perceptibly spiritual. Our inclination toward silence embodies it so that this essentially spiritual realm can be sensually perceptible.

The Fluid Body of Silence

Thus far I have described something of the nature of Silence, how to find it and become oriented toward it. Then, we saw how the fullness of our being is involved and also the fullness of the being of the world, the mutuality of sacredness which together form the phenomenon of silence. And, finally, I tried to give the metaphor of 'depth' , so characteristic of soul, the substantiality it deserves. Depth has many qualities, each of which further describe the body of Silence.

Our phenomenology has taken us to the immaterial body of the world, the whole of the world as interior. This spiritual body of Silence is highly differentiated. We can tell this is so because there are many different qualities of silence, each very individual, while each is also an aspect of the whole of the depth of silence. But, while differentiated, the invisible body of silence is not a body of parts, each existing alongside the others, like the organs of our physical body. The highly fluid body of silence is something better understood as analogous to water than to a body of organs and skeleton. The different qualities of silence are akin to the many differently flowing currents that exit within a living body of water -- such as a stream, lake or ocean. Let me give an example. When we were in Australia, we met one of those rare people that we come across now and then – a person who is completely devoted to the realm of the soul and has arranged the whole of life to stay in touch with soul. This particular individual we met in Australia is an artist, a painter. He has cultivated a highly differentiated presence to silence through his many long walks through the outback. When you first step into the outback, it looks like a vast presence of sameness. This artist said, however, that he would be walking along, maybe for ten or twenty miles, and all of a sudden, he would walk into a completely new region in spite of the fact that there would be no perceptible difference in the terrain. He was speaking of something far more subtle than even the great subtlety of the landscape. He was speaking of suddenly crossing into a different current of silence than one had been riding. Each current of silence had, he said, its very distinct qualities.

Our descriptive effort leads us to the undeniable conclusion that we are within the presence of a vast being. Let us now name this being the angelic body of silence, Silence as the Angel of the Earth. Put aside any notions you have about angels as airy creatures with wings, those go-betweens carrying messages back and forth between us and the spiritual worlds. Forget all the picture of angels you have seen. This angel is far more expansive. We cannot conceive of this Angel of the Earth as traveling back and forth between heaven and earth. This is the Angel of The New Heaven and the New

Earth. This angel, by its presence, extends always between the spiritual realms and the earthly realms. It does not have to go back and forth. We have tamed, sentimentalized, crushed the power of angels with all of the current ways of speaking of angels. If we give this talk any credit at all, the angels we know about are all in the image of the guardian angel, that angel that is closest to us and perhaps closest to our own form. But, this Angel of the Earth is far mightier. She sustains the form of everything; the very soul of existence is due to Angelic Silence singing the world into imaginal form.

Having this initial recognition of the Sacred being of Silence, we now confront the difficulty of orienting ourselves within silence. Without some indications concerning this orientation, the ultimate purpose of silence and the necessity of becoming devoted to it will bypass us. We constantly risk making silence into an enjoyable experience that can refresh and renew us, not realizing that this one sided-orientation – that it is something solely for our benefit -- does nothing at all to sustain this source of creative sustenance. The very fact, shown above, that in entering into our heart we enter into the heart of the being of silence already intimates that we bear a co-responsibility toward each other. This notion of co-responsibility has to be rightly understood, that is, understood within the kind of imaginal topography of the region of silence developed thus far.

By referring to Silence as the Angel of the Earth, I mean to imply that she is our protector. Protector at one and the same time in an individual sense – she protects our individual soul being – and protector of the soul being of the Earth. We have not realized our responsibility when we simply bask in this protection from time to time. We begin to exercise responsibility when we consciously seek out the realm of Silence and commit ourselves to the kind of imaginal, heart-knowing needed to develop an intimacy with the Angel of Earth.

Finding our way around within the intimacy of the heart that is the center of the center of the heart of the being of Silence, begins with developing a closer attention to the filigreed wrappings of silence that can be perceptibly seen through the eye of the heart that I mentioned early on in this paper. We notice, for example, that this filigree is actually quite different for different things. Thus, there are many different qualities of silence. The silence of the mid-day sun is different than the silence of the night. The silence enveloping a bird flying through the air and trailing after it is different than the silence of a majestic tree. The majestic silence of a mountain is very different from that of a desert. And, even within a locale such as a desert, a valley, a town, there are silences within silences. Becoming oriented within the world of silence concerns developing the phenomenology of these different qualities, something that goes beyond simply noticing that Silence is not simply uniform soul substance. It also goes beyond naming the different silences according to the different objects and beings.

We can notice by attending to the silence wrapping any particular being that silence functions as a twin-being of any particular thing. Silence also accompanies us in the form of our fluid twin-being. Perceiving silence in the world and as it accompanies us is analogous to perceiving one of those pictures that shifts from one image to another as you observe it, such as the face-vase picture. Perceiving silence is not visual, though, and the switching back and forth goes between perceiving the physical thing and perceiving the swirling silence wrapping it; or with us, the switching back and forth between being engaged with the world and perceiving the silence of our body. In this analogy, both the figure being perceived, and its twin-silence are equally active.

As a part of the practice of learning to navigate in the world of silence, it is helpful to practice moving our attention back and forth between an object and its silence. This exercise seems to be entirely visual, but it is not. When, for example, I look at a tree with this inclination, this orientation toward silence and silence as inclined toward me, then already the visual experience changes into an imaginal experience. There is more to the tree than the eye sees. I can shift attention from the more visual aspect of the tree to the silence wrapping the tree. Then, after a while, shift back to the figural aspect of the tree. Doing such an exercise over time develops the capacity to perceive both simultaneously. The back and forth perception of tree and silence stops and we perceive a new totality. If we describe what is before us now, it is that this tree no longer stands there as a perceptual object, but we can actually perceive that this tree as held, supported, brought into existence, and is being protected. Something more is happening here than, for example, perceiving figure and ground together. This more concerns moving into perceiving the very soul of the tree because now we are simultaneously present to the tree as object and we are also present to something of the interior life of the tree.

We, the observers, are also taken into this new current. We do not stand outside such a moment as spectators. The field of perception includes our being, which we can also feel shifting from attention focused on the outer part of our being to attention focused inwardly as we practice shifting between figure and silence with a particular being such as a tree. However, there is a subtle and important difference. When you focus attention on the tree in its physical being, you are focused much more on the interior of your own being. And, when you focus on the silence enfolding the tree, you are at that same moment more focused on the outer, physical aspect of your own being. In other words, a crossing occurs. Perceiving outer silence intensifies experiencing our body as part of and belonging to the world process. Perceiving outer form intensifies experiencing the inner being of our body.

The body's experience of silence is of particular importance. If we are lacking in sensitivity to the body dimension of silence, then the whole approach to silence becomes abstract and theoretical. The crossing that I just described is not experienced mentally. The practice of attending to the body side of silence, shifting between being present to the outer form of our body and our body in its interiority, is not experienced, for example, as moving between perceiving the form of our body to a mental thinking about our body. Nor is it experienced as shifting from the outer form of the body to an inner, subjective experience of the body. Nor is it experienced as moving from body to something that might be called soul or from body to something that might be called spirit. In fact, through actually doing this practice, we come to realize that all such distinctions come about only when silence has been eliminated as a fundamental creating form of the existence of all things.

The actual experience of this shifting of attention that only becomes possible with the presence of silence is that our body, when we focus attention on the outer form is experienced as also wrapped in the same silence we perceive in union with the things of the world. Already, at this moment of perception, a crossing has occurred, a crossing in which our body and the body of the world entwine. A quickening of body is felt in which we can actually experience that the life of our body is being generated within the fecundity of silence.

Then, when we shift attention to the interior experience of our body, we feel the quickening of silence radiating through our blood. We can actually experience our blood. The inner volume of our body is felt from within. The inner volume of the body can be felt as filled with silence. We discover that the animation of our body originates in silence. Indeed, we can say that the anima of Aristotle, of Jung, of depth psychology is Silence herself. And, similarly, the anima of the world, the Soul of the World, is Silence. We discover the world as Silence, and we discover ourselves as part of the world process.

Through the practice of shifting between perceiving the form of things and their accompanying angel of silence, and the shifting between experiencing the outer form and inner being of our body, there comes a moment when all this happens together. At the moment, we shift into another world, the imaginal world. It is extremely difficult to stay very long in this imaginal world with full consciousness. We only get glimmers of it. These glimmers are the source of feeling renewed, more creative, more heart-centered and closer to the spiritual realms when we spend time with the silence. These glimmers are also invitations to take up an active and conscious practice which would make it possible to become active participates within the world as imaginal place. In this topography of the imaginal, things are physical and spiritual at the same time. The outer appearances fully entwine with inner soul-being.

Our responsibility to Silence is great. By knowing Her we give her Being. And, She, in knowing us, gives us our soul-being. We are, in the words of Henry Corbin, in *unio sympathetica*, a union of sympathy. The movement of silence in the everyday life of the soul is surprisingly experienced, not as silence, but as the realm of our feelings. In everyday life, however, we take feeling to be our own, and we confuse feeling with emotion. But, having traveled some into the world of Silence, re-consider feeling. With any feeling, we cannot really tell how much of it belongs to us and how much of it is autonomous. We immediately, however, identify with the feeling and take it as something happening to us. We do not actually experience the feeling itself, but only what it seems to be doing to us – giving us pleasure or giving us pain. We then become attached to the pleasure, or attached to the pain or to avoiding the pain and miss, bypass, neglect and abuse the opportunity that comes with feeling – to come into connection with the soul being of others, of the things of the world, of the Soul of the World, the Angel of Silence.

What we usually call feelings are actually our ego-response to the world of Silence. Do, not, however, imagine that Silence makes us feel joy or pleasure or sadness. All those ways of speaking of feeling are our unconscious responses to the highly differentiated movements of silence. When spiritual traditions speak of the importance of the purification of the feeling life in order to be available to the spiritual worlds, they are speaking of the process of entering into the world of Silence, which takes us deeply into the Soul of the World and simultaneously into our own soul. We have to guard against the strong inclination to become interested in Silence because we think it can be personally satisfying. The flow of Silence is immediately disrupted by the interference of our personality. The detailed descriptions I have given of the topography of Silence are intended to be an introduction into its laws and how to follow the laws of the feeling world.

When Silence is eliminated from the world, feeling is eliminated. It becomes replace by sensationalisms of every sort. Silence is already so lost that we cannot tell the difference between emotion, sensation, and feeling. And we cannot distinguish our feelings from the interiority of the spiritual flesh of the world as the very life of feeling, a life that exists wholly independently from us but needing us for its continuing act of inspiring the beauty of the world. The intention of this presentation, then, has not been to learn how to bask in Silence, but how to turn to Silence for the sake of its renewal, and for the sake of the world.

A Fairy Tale of Spiritual Psychology

Introduction

Before 1992--when The School of Spiritual Psychology began—back when I guided the program in phenomenological psychology at the University of Dallas and later taught spiritual psychology at the Dallas Institute of Humanities and Culture, the unfolding of a spiritual psychology was a work in progress rather than an accomplished fact. Even after Cheryl and I established the School, our definition of spiritual psychology was left intentionally fluid, as fluid as life itself.

Since 1992, mainstream psychology still has had limited place for spiritual experience, and what is available consists mainly of importing Eastern spiritual approaches—such as mindfulness—and chakra analysis. The term "spiritual psychology" exists in various contexts but is a quite indefinite term and certainly not a psychology in its own right.

The available soul psychologies also did not satisfy what this inchoate longing for a spiritual psychology sought. C. G. Jung, of course, was very important, and in many ways, I found the archetypal psychology of James Hillman even more relevant, because it included the soul of the world. But archetypal psychology had no place for spirit.

I was close to James Hillman and was instrumental in bringing him to teach at the University of Dallas and at The Dallas Institute of Humanities and Culture. But James consistently rejected spirit in archetypal psychology because he was well aware that the understanding of soul itself was in a precarious position in spite of the extraordinary work of Jung. Hillman's whole work is a defense and elaboration of psyche, or soul, as image. Hillman's work is intensely satisfying because it brings soul and idea (*eidos*) into unity. His work in Dallas consisted primarily in elaborating how soul as image-idea can also illuminate world.

So an unsatisfied longing existed; well, several unsatisfied longings: a deeply felt presence with Earth; and an immediate experience of the presence of spirit, that is, a sense of the origination of the Whole; and how to bring these longings into unity with sensation, imagination, and thinking in a living way. This longing still informs spiritual psychology.

This writing elaborates longings embedded in spiritual psychology that have existed for a very long time, at least since the eighteenth century. The writers expressing such a desire include Friedrich Schiller in his work *The Aesthetic Education of man in a Series of Letters*, and in imaginal form by Johan W. Goethe in his *The Fairy Tale of the Green Snake and the Beautiful Lilly* in 1795. Later, in 1899, the founder of Spiritual Science, Rudolf Steiner, wrote a commentary on this fairy tale, finding within it essential elements of the Rosicrucian spiritual path, and he also found it to be an accurate depiction of the concerns of Spiritual Science. The tale also beautifully expresses all the longings of spiritual psychology, which this writing seeks to express.

Instead, then, of attempting to define spiritual psychology, I want to consider this fairy tale.

Part I
The Fairy Tale of The Green Snake and the Beautiful Lily in its Significance for Spiritual Psychology

First, I present an outline of part of the fairy tale, followed by exploring sections of the tale to relate its images to the forming of a spiritual psychology.

Once upon a time two fluttering flames of light, Will-O-Wisps, came to the bank of a river and demanded to be taken across by the Ferryman. The Ferryman obliged them. As they are about to come to the other side, the fluttering lights shake themselves and gold coins fall into the boat. The Ferryman is very upset because if any of the gold touches the water, huge waves will rise and capsize the boat. He cannot take the gold as payment and tells the Will-O-Wisps that he must be paid with the fruits of the earth - three onions, three cabbages, and three artichokes. The Will-O-Wisps leave without paying and the Ferryman dumps the gold coins in a rocky crag. A Green Snake comes across the coins and eats them. She suddenly becomes glowing all through her body and her light allows her to see the rocks, the trees, the grass, and the sky. She is overjoyed to see what before she could know only through touch. She sees flickering lights in the distance and glides to greet them, for they glow like her. The lights are the Will-O-Wisps, and they ask the Green Snake to take them to the beautiful Lily. Alas, replies the Green Snake. Lily is on the other side of the river where they just came from, and the Ferryman cannot take anyone back. There are only two ways to get back. She can form herself into a bridge over the river and carry them back. However, she can only do this at noontime. The second way they can return is on the shadow of the Great Giant who can also form a bridge over the river. But he can do this only at dawn and at dusk. The two flames are dissatisfied with both possibilities and depart.

Goethe's tale concerns the relationship of three worlds: the place of beautiful Lily (the spirit world), the river between (the soul world), and the land on the other side of the river from Lily (the physical world).

The tale confronts the task of each individual human soul to work through the connection between ordinary everyday life in the world, nourishment and care of the soul, and the awakening of spirit. It is helpful, however, to do as Goethe does in this tale - to imagine soul as a place, a world, and spirit also as a place, the place of beautiful Lily. The individual soul, then, is like an organ for perceiving the soul world, and the individual spirit is like an organ for perceiving the spirit world, just as the senses are the organs for perceiving the physical world.

The Ferryman brings people and all living things from the spirit world across the river but cannot take them back. This image is the reverse of the familiar ferryman figure of many myths and tales who take the dead across the river. This reversal implies that there may be a way back to the spirit world out of our own powers, without death. We are transported here from the spirit world at birth, but it is only with soul work and spirit work that we can in this life find a bridge back before physical death, that is, find the way to reconnect the physical, soul, and spirit worlds. The organs of soul and spirit have to be strengthened, because the capacity to perceive the subtle worlds from the place of the physical world is not given naturally.

We are like the Will-O-Wisps. They are clever and intelligent; they produce gold coins out of themselves, which are the products of human intelligence. Out of the ever-moving nature of thought come concepts that lead to the making of things in the world. All these products of intelligence make us proud of ourselves. Look at all that we can do: science, art, medicine, technology, economics, politics, business, war, corporations, religions.

In the tale, if the gold touches the water, immense waves of turbulence develop. The water of the river is like the soul in its natural state, what depth psychology speaks of as the Anima, but Anima, or the natural soul, is not yet psyche. Inner work is required for Anima to become aware of itself through the power of imagination. When the natural soul receives only the nourishment of intellectual knowledge and its products, such as material comforts, what science and technology offer, even what human services provide of a materialistic nature, then deep disturbances arise in the soul. We might picture such disturbances washing onto the physical world as many of the difficulties of our time such as violence, crime, wars, pollution, climate change, and even modern diseases such as cancer, heart attack and AIDS.

We are not led, however, in feeling the movement of the tale, to stand against the Will-O-Wisps. We are not led to reject what they have to offer, for it provides a kind of illumination of the physical world, a way to get around. The question concerns how knowledge of this sort might be oriented toward making soul rather than material comfort. The more material comfort we have, the more anxiety, depression, mania, and paranoia are possible. Even those who do not enjoy such comforts can suffer from the outlook that sees pleasure or acquisition as primary goals. How can knowledge be oriented toward experiencing the relationships that exist among earth, the human being, and the cosmos? How can such knowledge result in products which foster harmony among these realms? The tale says that the Ferryman demands payment in the form of fruits of the earth. The three plants--onions, cabbages, and artichokes--are plants that live close to the earth. These plants convey a feeling of growth that remains very close to the earth; this means that knowing, in order to be life-giving, ought always to be closely connected with the soul/spirit qualities of Earth. This restraint is not about what can be sought through knowledge but instead suggests that we need to unite closely with Earth in the care of soul.

The Ferryman does not keep the gold coins for himself, nor does he throw them to the wind. He drops them in a rock place, hidden from view. The Green Snake comes upon them, eats them, and becomes luminous and able to see. The Green Snake lies humbly close to the earth. Taking in intellectual knowledge is for her extremely helpful. It makes it possible for her to be more conscious, to see more of the world in an attitude of reverence. Knowledge always has this quality when taken in humbly as the qualities of wisdom rather than for our own purposes without regard to Earth as a living being who unendingly gives and re-gives.

Often, the wisdom contained in knowledge is thrown away. I recall listening to a medical doctor presenting a lecture on human anatomy. I sat awed with the interior picture of the incredible wisdom of the body revealed through this form of intellectual knowledge. The particular lecture concerned the bones and the blood-producing marrow of the bones. There, at the center of the most mineral part of us lies the regeneration of life. I suddenly understood more of the mystery of the Grail. I understood that we are the sacred vessel in which new life is continually born. In the anatomy of the bones lies the secrets of regeneration. The lecture, of course, was not presented in this way. Such possibilities of hearing the voice of Wisdom are cast aside in favor of technical questions and practical concerns.

Let us return now to the tale.

The Green Snake, overjoyed with her new vision, goes to explore an underground cavern. She frequented this place because it was mysterious. She could not previously see what was there, but could feel the shapes of definite figures in the cavern, and now she hoped to see what they were. There she sees four human figures ~ one of gold, one of silver, one of brass, and a fourth which is an irregular mixture of these metals. As she explores these figures, a Peasant Man carrying a lamp enters this sanctuary. The Peasant's lamp has a strange magical property. When it is the only illumination, it changes stone into gold, wood into silver, and animals into precious stone. If there is another light around, then the lamp simply adds to the light. In the presence of the luminous snake, the interior of the cavern becomes all the brighter. The Gold King asks the Peasant Man how many secrets he knows. The man answers "Three", but there are four to be known. The Green Snake then whispers the fourth secret to the old man, and he then speaks out to the four figures -- "The time is at hand."

The Peasant Man returns to his cottage where he finds his wife greatly alarmed. The Will-O-Wisps had visited the cottage and had licked all the gold off the stone walls which the light of the lamp had put there. They had also asked the woman to pay the Ferryman their debt of the three onions, three cabbages, and three artichokes. The Will-O-Wisps had shaken more gold out of themselves and Mops the dog looked at them and died. The Peasant Man shines his lamp on the dead dog, and it turns into beautiful brown and black onyx. He tells his wife to take the fruits to the Ferryman and then to ask the Green Snake to take her across the river at noon and give her the onyx dog. Lily would turn the statue into a living being which would be a companion for her.

In this part of the tale we are again concerned with a natural place; this time it is an underground cavern of the earth. In the interior of the soul, in the dark, and not visible to the outer world, reside four qualities. The Gold King has to do with the soul power of wisdom, natural wisdom. We can imagine wisdom as an instinct of the soul life, closely connected with the body, and thus it is to be found here, pictured in the interior rather than as an aspect of the river. We have lost touch with this instinct. A new mother, for example, who knows nothing about babies has a natural wisdom concerning how to relate to her baby. This wisdom consists of the mother's body knowing what to do for the care of the child. The loss of this kind of natural wisdom results in the multiplication of child-rearing methods, wisdom usurped by knowledge; but today, if we do not have such knowledge, we feel anxiety.

We have such anxiety concerning our inner life. In the realms of soul and spirit, we have grown accustomed to ignoring natural (bodily) ways of paying attention to the inner voice of Wisdom and instead turn to others who tell us what our inner life signifies, whether from a therapist, priest, pastor, self-help books, support groups, lecturers, or other professionals. Although much of what we are told is useful and helpful, much professional soul and spirit work has spawned concepts and language that removes us further from intimate connection with our soul and spirit -- and Earth. Without realizing it, we have begun to live explanations of our inner life rather than an immediate and conscious inner life.

When the Gold King asks the Peasant Man how many secrets he knows and he replies "Three," these secrets must relate to three of the figures - recall that the fourth is not something different, but a mixture. The Peasant Man thus knows the secret of wisdom, the simple part of ourselves already knows what is always right for our soul. New therapies are constantly being devised that obscure this natural power. I suspect that the best therapists are those who do not operate from a system but instead can guide one to the place of recovering inner wisdom.

The second natural power of soul--imaged as a Silver King--has to do with the soul power of beauty. The soul longs for beauty. Right here, we could get into a long intellectual discussion concerning the nature of beauty.

Such discussion shows a loss of immediate soul beauty. The Peasant Mans also knows this secret. What is one's inner beauty? It consists of that natural capacity, which we all feel at times, in which there is perfect conformity and harmony between what is within us and what is around us. It is presence in the moment. We have a natural power of soul to experience with presence. Most often, what goes on within us and what goes on around us occur in two different times. We are more or less dissociated from what is actually going on. For example, if I go to a museum, look at a painting of a landscape, and say that it reminds me of New England, that is dissociation. If someone tells me of their difficulties at home and I tell them what to do, that is disassociation. There are many examples. An essential preparatory work for being a researcher into soul and spirit life consists of developing an ability to be aware of the inherent relation between what is going on within and what is going on around us, both sides of the coin. The beauty of soul consists in its capacity to meet the world and to feel the feelings that the world itself holds, the capacity to encounter the soul of the world through soul. This natural capacity of soul adheres closely to the body, so that when we are present to ourselves through being present in our body, we experience beauty.

The third secret concerns the figure of brass and relates to the soul's natural quality of strength. What is soul strength? We are constantly being pulled into the physical world through our senses. Sense experience is stronger than soul experience in waking life, so we are not usually aware of soul or even the involvement of soul in experiencing the world. The strength of soul shows itself when it is neglected, in the creation of symptoms. Our obsessions, anxieties, fears, hopes, desires, wishes, longings, and how these--when not given attention--turn into addictions, phobias, eating disorders, relationship difficulties, sexual difficulties. All such maladies indicate that the soul indeed has a great strength over which we have no control. When we are beset with some "psychological symptom." it is evidence that soul is not some passive religious concept but an actual force.

The three secrets known by the Peasant Man do not consist merely of his knowledge of the soul qualities of wisdom, beauty, and strength. There is more. The further part of the secret is the recognition of these qualities as distinct. The fourth figure, the one of mixed metals of gold, silver, and brass, indicates not a distinct figure, but one in which there is confusion. **This**

mixture is like someone whose feelings are confused with their thinking, and their thinking is confused with their willing. The fundamental forces of soul need to be distinguished one from the other, and this separation constitutes the essence of the three known secrets. In order to go about the task of uniting soul with spirit and spirit with the world, we begin by learning to clearly separate and experience the difference among soul qualities. Spiritual traditions of the past have always known this starting place, and these three secrets were utilized in inner training to sharpen the experience of the differences. In modern life, we are dominated by the irregular mixture and go through the world in a confusion of soul. Outer forms and structures make it possible to navigate in our confusion, but as these organizational structures of life such as family, religion, law, work, education, are now swiftly changing, it becomes more and more necessary to discover how to live from the immediacy of distinct soul forces.

The fourth secret, which is unknown to the Peasant Man, gives the way of the future, the way to go about the task of living from soul toward spirit in the world in the circumstances of today. Goethe's tale is prophetic; it is a set of instructions for living into the unknown future. The fourth secret, which the Green Snake whispers into the ear of the Old Man with the lamp, belongs to soul and spirit work for this time. She whispers, "I will sacrifice myself rather than be sacrificed."

The presence of this fourth secret suggests that old forms of soul and spirit work may no longer be adequate. We shall see that the practices from the past still have a place. They are nonetheless inadequate now because of the further development of individuality. Soul and spirit practices from the past are established and oriented toward the tribe, the collective, or a community. If one follows certain rituals, certain practices, certain prayers, the forces of soul do develop, and one develops the capacity to traverse into the soul worlds and the spirit worlds. However, these practices do not consider the individuality of the person.

The questions for our time concern how to develop these capacities without relinquishing our particular individuality, and how to engage in making connection with soul and spirit in daily life. If we do not take daily life into account as the place of soul-making and spirit-making, our life in the world with others, our life in the world with all of its problems, challenges, and difficulties; then soul and spirit work has a high probability of egotism because it is sought for our own sake and not for the sake of the world. But, here, I have almost revealed the meaning of the fourth secret. For the moment, consider the possibility than when we become engaged in soul and spirit practices of the past such as American Indian spirituality, Celtic magic, Eastern practices, practices from ancient Indian, China, Greece, Mexico, and all the rest; one may be taken into soul and spirit worlds because these practices contain three powerful elements: working with the powers of wisdom, beauty, and strength. However, such practices can dim what was achieved over a long period of spiritual evolution: the development of the experience of individuality.

The Old Man with the lamp gives a picture of the significance of the soul and spirit practices that come from ancient traditions. His lamp, his light, lights up the whole place. Without the presence of traditions from the past, without the living memory of those who have developed practices that bring about an entry into soul and spirit, we would be, if not in darkness, in the semi-darkness that is provided only by the light of the Green Snake. The light of ancient wisdom brightens the way. If we were not aware but only in some connection with the past, then we would not even be aware that we are needed to discover practices that are suitable to our present circumstances.

Another important detail of the tale is that the Peasant's lamp shines forth only when there is another light present. If this other light is not present, then his lamp turns stone into gold, wood into silver, and animals into precious stone. The spiritual practices of the past have a magical quality, and we tend to turn to them looking for a magical transformation of our own world. While we are off on a weekend Vision Quest, or working with the Medicine Wheel, or waking up our chakras, or chanting, or going through past life regression, this magical feeling quality is indeed often present. But when we re-enter the world the following week, the magic does not last. Perhaps this letdown is related to the need for the accompanying light and secret of the Green Snake.

The home of the Old Man with the lamp has stone walls that have been turned into gold by the lamp. He and his wife life in seclusion in the forest. Here it is possible to retain a sense of magic. But as soon as the forces of intellect enter, the Will-O-Wisps, the magic of the place is devoured by them. When the dog eats the gold coins, he dies. When soul and spirit wisdom from the past is taken in as intellectual knowledge and put out as a product, it does not bring forces of life but forces of death. We live in a highly intellectual culture. The peasant and his wife retain the magical sense of the world since they still live close to the earth - the Peasant Woman is told by the Will-O- Wisps to pay the Ferryman the onions, cabbages, and artichokes, so they must have them. In order to live in the ways of soul and spirit from the past, it would be necessary to remove ourselves from the character of present culture. Is there now any place where this is truly possible?

Let us now enter more deeply into the secret of the Green Snake. The Green Snake speaks a deed not a teaching. She tells what she is resolved to do. "I will sacrifice myself rather than be sacrificed." What could that possibly be saying? It is like declaring that the actions that one takes in the physical world are done on behalf of soul and spirit. Such deeds carry the strength that can build a permanent bridge uniting the physical world, the soul world, and the spirit world.

The secret of the Green Snake concerns that dimension of soul where a truly free decision can be made, a decision to remain closely connected with the physical world of the present--with all of its difficulties of violence, crime, poverty, wars, fanaticisms, diseases, homelessness, pollution, rioting, natural disasters, and all that this world gives as gifts - pleasures, enjoyments, conveniences, achievements. Her resolve is to engage in the world as it is, but with a new orientation toward it - to see it all as holy, which requires faculties for extremely subtle perception, for that is what the word sacrifice means, to make holy.

The Green Snake presents a new kind of contemplative consciousness, a new kind of soul consciousness for the present time. It is consciousness characterized by full engagement in the outer world of earthly activity but without seeking for anything for oneself in this engagement. Nothing is given up, but nothing is held onto. Daily life serving soul and spirit. Initiation no longer requires practices, meditations, or rituals of purification that take place in special and holy places, because now the world itself is the temple of initiation. Here no specific actions must be deemed spiritual or soulful while other are excluded, for everything depends not on what one does but on what one does with what one does. I can engage in the activities of the world in order to further myself personally, financially, socially, or even spiritually; or I can engage in the activities of the world from a contemplative stance that sees, feels, and experiences what I do in the world as of giving to soul and spirit.

Now, to the final part of the fairy tale.

The old woman goes to the river, there to find the Great Giant who takes and eats of each of the onions, cabbages, and artichokes. She sees the Ferryman bringing a young, handsome man across the river and tries to give the Ferryman the remaining fruits, but he will not accept them. He wants his pay in full. He says that he will give her twenty-four hours to bring the remaining fruits if she agrees to put her hand in the river. She does so, and her hand turns black and begins to shrink, though she has full use of her hand. If she does not bring the payment in the allotted time, her hand will completely vanish.

She leaves in haste to go over the river on the back of the Green Snake at noontime, and the handsome man now walks with her. He tells her that he is a brave and noble seeker, but all he ever wanted was to be with Lily. They both go over the bridge and come to Lily. Lily is playing a harp and singing, but she is grieving. Her companion, a canary bird, had flown into her while being chased by a falcon, and as anything that touches Lily dies, the bird now lays dead. Lily transforms the statue of onyx into a living being and happily plays with it. The young man is entranced with beautiful Lily, who cannot be touched by anything. As he watches her play with the dog, his longing for her intensifies. He rushes to her to embrace her, touches her, and dies.

The Green Snake immediately encircles the body of the dead man. The Old Man with the lamp, there through the guidance of the lamp and the falcon, now arrives. The Old Woman looks on, terrified that her hand is about to disappear. This group, including Lily, and the Will-O-Wisps, who had arrived, coming on the shadow of the Great Giant, take the dead man to the river and cross over the bridge of the Green Snake. The Green Snake then crumbles into thousands and thousands of jewels which are gathered and thrown into the river. The rest of the party then goes to the underground cavern, enter and converse with the four kings. The fourth king, the one made of the mixture of gold, silver, and brass, disintegrates. The whole underground cavern now begins to move, rising from the depths of the earth. The Young Man comes to life and is united with Lily. The hand of the Old Woman is restored, and her youth and that of her husband as well are restored. A magnificent permanent bridge appears over the river and thousands of people cross back and forth freely.

We have not looked yet at the two possible ways to cross the river before there is a permanent bridge, by going over the bridge of the Green Snake at noon as does the Peasant Woman, or by going over on the shadow of the Giant at dawn, or at dusk as do the Will-O-Wisps. These ways of passage may serve individual development to a certain degree. One may be carried by another who has had spiritual experiences, as for example, inspiration that may come from certain artists or someone who is clairvoyant; this is the way of being taken over the bridge by the Green Snake. One may also be taken over by certain methods that dim waking consciousness, such as certain rituals, the way of the shadow of the Giant. In our times, these ways of entering experiences of soul and spirit are quite common, but they have the limitation that they are not helpful for anyone except the one being carried. What the Green Snake's deed does is make possible a bridge that may be freely crossed by all.

If the Ferryman is not paid his debt, if what we accomplish in the world through our labor is not given to soul, then the capacity to be human diminishes more and more until it disappears, as the vanishing hand of the Peasant Woman testifies. For a long time, we will appear to be human and do outwardly the things humans do, but the debt must be paid. We are living onward in a kind of grace but will awaken one day to find we have lost our humanity altogether. The Peasant Woman realizes that in a short time her hand will disappear, and that prompts her to seek the beautiful Lily.

The Young Handsome Man who strives to be united with Lily is an earnest seeker, who, however, in his youth seems to lack connection with the natural soul qualities of wisdom, beauty, and strength. His beauty lies in his youthfulness and in his commitment rather than in his ability to stay connected with the moment. He goes his way alone. Many young and eager people today seek for something more than what the materialistic world offers and throw themselves completely into what appears to offer soul and spirit experiences. They do this without having gained any inner freedom, without sufficient self-knowledge. Nonetheless, it is the earnestness of such seeking that gathers together the rest of the community of soul in the tale: the Old Man with the lamp, his wife, the Will-O-Wisps, the Green Snake, and Lily. The youthful seeker within us is necessary, the part that is foolish and risky and will not stop at anything.

We must consider now in more detail the sacrifice of the Green Snake. When the young man falls dead after touching Lily, uniting with the

spiritual world without sufficient worldly and soul experience, the Green
Snake immediately circles the body and protects it. It is as if she prevents
the life forces of the Young Man from dissipating. She in effect supplies the
life of the senses to the Young Man who has lost his; she gives her bodily
vitality to the seeker. And when the assembled group passes back over to the
material world, the Green Snake changes into precious stones which are
taken and thrown into the river. First, we notice that both the Green Snake
and the beautiful Lily are feminine figures. This fact is quite remarkable,
because Goethe clearly intuited that spiritual experience in connection with
soul and also in connection with the physical world, is distinctly feminine.
He also intuited that the kind of spirit and soul work that is oriented toward
the future requires the capacity of serving humbly, a feminine quality
exemplified by the Green Snake. Feminine qualities of soul are not specific
to men or women but are instead a quality within us that works and lives in
humility and service without the need for recognition.

When the group returns to the other side of the river (the physical
world), the Green Snake turns into precious stones that are thrown into the
river. These jewels form into the pillars of the now-permanent bridge that
unites the physical world with the spiritual world through the medium of the
soul world. Jewels and precious stones are images of the heavenly within the
earthly. The Sacrifice of the Green Snake makes precisely what is needed to
bridge the physical world and the spiritual world. A marriage between the
physical world and the spiritual world is affected, firmly grounded in the
"watery" realm of the soul. A jewel can be imagined as fire, as water, and as
earth, all combined. The seeking quality of spirit, the reflecting quality of
soul, and the firm quality of earth are united in the bridge and what it
bridges. Life is restored to the young seeker.

The group then returns to the underground cavern, and the following
occurs; The Young Man faces the three kings. The Gold King says, "Know
the highest." The Silver King says, "Foster my Sheep." And the Brass King
says, "The sword on your left, your right free."

The Kings tell the seeker how to proceed in the world with soul and
spirit, how to live daily life in the world fully connected to higher and
deeper realities. Orient knowing to the spirit world - all knowing is a serving
of spirit. Support beauty in the world is the direction given by the Silver
King. And the Brass King say to know your strength but never have to use it.
The fourth king then crumbles, for it had no real wisdom, beauty, and

strength. A temple now rises from out of the earth and as it does so, the hut of the Ferryman is transformed into a small silver temple, a kind of altar within the larger temple. This temple is the world as the place of soul and spirit. The small silver temple honors the Ferryman and is a memorial to the original spirit of humanity.

What becomes of the Giant? At this final moment of the forming of the bridge, the Great Giant stands upright and points to the heavens. His pointing indicates that his powers come from the realms of the spirit and that they belong also to nature. By pointing to the heavens, he shows that he is a power connected with the elemental powers of nature which—as magicians, alchemists, and occultists are fully aware--have their origin in the cosmos. The ways of soul and spirit as practices of the past have relied on using natural, elemental powers, but now there are new means for soul and spiritual work. Thus, we have a fairy tale for spiritual psychology, an image that can orient us toward what is to follow.

Part II
Spiritual Psychology as Working Toward What We Can Be

Psychologies emphasizing soul seldom concern themselves with the future. The fairy tale concerns the presence of the future now, in the present.

Thousands of people every day go to therapy to do soul work, looking for a sense of the future, only to spend their hour looking back at their individual past or entering into the deep past of ancient stories and myths. Soul implies depth, and depth is typically equated with things from the past (gods and goddesses, the inner child, past trauma, memories, ancient rituals), always trying to recover something. Digging, uncovering, recovering, visioning, restructuring, going over things again; these are current ways of most soul work.

In addition, much soul work by itself has a religious rather than a spiritual concern. The word "religion" means to "relate back to," to find one's way back to tradition, to something that gives value to experience, something to live by as intimate as oneself but larger than oneself. The "spiritual" in the term "spiritual psychology" is not the same as religion or a religious concern. The first aspect of spirit that I wish to draw attention to is something that we all feel quite strongly- an intense longing for what we can be, which is, I believe, a stronger interest than that which pulls us into a concern with what we have been, that which pushes around from the past to do what we do in the world. A time-honored word for this longing is "destiny." Destiny has nothing to do with predestination or anything else that is prefigured. Destiny refers to the experience of feeling drawn by the "not-yet" rather than pushed by the past. This destiny feeling remains for the most part as unconscious as what influences us from the past. Destiny has received little attention from psychology; when it has been addressed, as in Jung, it is still from the viewpoint of the past, what the past is working toward, that Jung calls individuation. The impulse for the actions of the Green Snake in our tale, it seems to me, comes out of a consciousness of the future.

The notion of something coming from the future may be quite new; this is not an invention but a way of imagining. It is not the same as planning ahead or thinking about what might happen to us, but it is a distinct quality of the human spirit. Let me try now to characterize this spirit. **Spirit concerns that unknown human factor that creates the totality of our being, makes consciousness possible, gives a felt sense of destiny, finds expression in creating, engenders the capacity of loving, and seeks connection with soul in order to transform the world.**

This definition of spirit contains all of the elements found in the tale. Spiritual psychology attempts to work with all of these elements. Because of its concern with uniting with soul and with the world, spiritual psychology differs both from traditional spiritual disciplines and traditional psychological disciplines.

By pursuing these questions of the relation of soul, past, world, and future, we clear a path that leads from the depth psychology of soul toward a fully waking consciousness of soul with the creating powers of spirit, enacted in the world. While the religious nature of soul psychology leads downward, inward, past-ward to activate meaning for an individual, spiritual psychology seeks to unite the highest (spirit) with the deepest (soul), views the world as the chalice of this union, and seeks to coordinate the inner life of the individual with the outer life of the world and with Earth, recognizing that individual development is not for one's sake alone but for the world.

The desire to formulate a spiritual psychology does not receive its inspiration from seeking something new. The soul itself shows its face in different ways at different times. The psychology of Freud showed the face of the soul in its intimate relation to instinctive life. The psychology of Jung showed the face of soul in its relation to story, myth, and imagination. The archetypal psychology of James Hillman shows the face of soul as image, metaphor, fantasy, and creativity. Soul in present and future times--until this aspect of the future becomes a central aspect of awareness--shows its intimate relation to spirit and the world. This attempt to formulate the beginning stages of what soul is now showing serves as a preparation for the future. It comes out of listening, hearing time and time again how people are now searching, in sometimes exotic and bizarre ways for spirituality. It comes from hearing constant confusion concerning what belongs to spirit and what belongs to soul. It comes from hearing how people are seeing new ways of relating to the world and Earth. And it comes from the foreboding sense that looking toward the future in terms of ideas of the past no longer works.

The word spirit is fraught with confusion. Our main concern centers on keeping soul and spirit in connection, and this in turn relies on a feeling for spirit. An additional requirement, given by the fairy tale, is that this feeling for the reality of individual spirit be closely connected to the world, to daily life. What can we point to in ordinary human experience that signifies an actual presence of spirit?

In ordinary life, there exists only an inkling of the sense of the spirit, a kind of shadow, usually belief, that can gradually become a fuller experience of ourselves as spiritual beings as well as soul beings. This shadow of our individual spirit is found in experience of ourselves as an "I".

The experience of "I" is quite complex. "I" seem to be here, in the place of my body. But, if you try to recall the first time you became aware of yourself as an "I" as more and other than the "me", much more is revealed. I recall a person telling a story of his discovery in this realm. He was remembering his childhood. One day his mother took him on a walk down a country road. She ran ahead and hid behind a tree, and the child faced the task of crossing the road alone to find her. He said that he did not feel himself in his little body at that moment, but rather felt himself spread out all around, of being spread out over the whole surrounding area. He experienced himself as including the whole width of the road, the surrounding trees, and even there where his mother was hiding. The experience was actually dual. He did experience himself there where his body was. And from that place, he felt fear, of being suddenly left alone in a strange place. At the same time, he experienced himself spread out through the surroundings, and "knew" where his mother was. From that place he did not feel fear, but a kind of playful joy. This story represents a process everyone has undergone in one form or another, an experience not usually remembered.

We are living this dualistic sense of "I" all the time. The dualism expresses itself in the very form of the letter "I". The bottom bar of the letter is like the sense of oneself identified with one's body. The warmth of our body in relation to its surroundings gives us the sense, the feeling, that "I" am here, not over there. In order to be aware of ourselves as a "spirit-I," we, in a sense have to face ourselves facing ourselves. Then we have the experience "I am an I". The top bar of the letter represents that other sense of ourselves, as spread out around us in space. We live in both places at once: here, as the warmth of our body, and also as the living effects of everything we have been told concerning who we are -- and there, not only in the immediate surroundings, but also as far as the eye can see, to the farthest star.

As an entry into becoming researchers into one's own soul and spirit life, we must become familiar with this kind of experience. It is a genuine experience of ourselves as spirit beings who belong at one and the same time to the immediacy of our body and to the world around, and even to the stars. We have to rediscover for our own times and circumstances what ancient wisdom simply took for granted. We live in the same world in which philosophers and initiates explored. Plutarch, for example, said that while there is the part of the spirit which is submerged in the earthly body, the human being has another part hovering outside like a star above one's head. T second part was spoken of as one's daimon in the Greek world; as one's genius in the Roman world; and as one's Guardian Angel in the Christian world. Current psychology sometimes speaks of this kind of experience as our "higher self," but such terminology tends toward abstraction; while conceptually true, such concepts make it difficult for the work of keeping soul in close connection with spirit. Soul needs images and experiences.

Depth psychology has discovered that a lack of connection to soul leads to pathologies, soul suffering. What is the lack of connection to spirit? When 'spirit' is nothing more than an empty concept or the object of faith and belief, it is impossible to find one's spirit. When large numbers of people loose intimate connection with spirit, spirit begins to work in the world independently. Spirit does not just float around but gathers into certain forms in the world in such a way that rather than developing an individual experience of spirit, spirit begins to take possession of us. This externalization of spirit increased during the Industrial Revolution and accelerated after the Second World War, and the form it has taken is science and technology, particularly space exploration and electronic technology, leading to the possibility of artificial intelligence.

Spirit is active in all our machinery, computers, electronics, systems, organizations, institutions, economic and social structures, and business but in such a form that we are not able to gain connection with it in an individual and intimate way.

A second wave of collective spirit pathology is also upon us; it takes the form of violence, terrorism, deception, fundamentalisms, abstract economics, and mass murder. We must free ourselves from the religious notions that spirit is in itself benevolent. Spirit concerns the creating activity in the world, an activity that when unconnected to individuality, soul, and Earth, creates darkness as well as light, more or less indiscriminately. When spirit relates to soul and Earth, it can find its rightly creative place, and we recognize ourselves as light and shadow mixed. The way in which the scientific and technological spirit of the age has led to the development of the collectivity of the earthly aspect of spirit, appears to be a mastery of the world. In fact, we can now begin to see that we are being mastered by indiscriminate spirits.

The memory experience of feeling the dualism of ourselves as spirit beings while rooted to the earth can lead to the conscious effort to find individual spirit again. Such an effort is a prerequisite for the subsequent step of researching the relations between soul, spirit, and world. Prerequisite does not mean that one must accomplish in every moment of adult life what was once briefly experienced as a child. It is quite enough to have moments of a real feeling of being 'more' than we think or believe we are. These days, such a feeling is more a longing than a reality, and there is always the tendency to project the longing into some external reality. The task concerns experiencing us as simultaneously visible and invisible and note the sense of this last term--in-the-visible.

We can sense ourselves and others physically, but we know ourselves and others spiritually. Not to 'know about', but to know in the true meaning of that word: a uniting-with. When I 'know' my friend, there is a uniting as spirit with spirit. The central task of spiritual psychology concerns how to develop the means to do this and how to describe such a meeting with every aspect of the human being, every aspect of the world, and every aspect of Earth.

Sacred Purpose, Sacred Hope

A sense of purpose flowers in youth, and at its beginning is felt as an inner urging to do something significant in life, something that contributes to the well-being of the world and of humanity. An inward beckoning draws, and at first, and for a very long time, we do not know what this call is about or where it comes from. We are eager to obey it. This inherent sense of purpose urges untold numbers of individuals to want to be doctors, lawyers, teachers, ministers, scientists, politicians, artists -- world-workers of every variety imaginable. The challenge lies in not only retaining the inner urgings toward a purposeful existence, but to strengthen this delicate aspect of soul life so that it can sustain any challenge.

In later life, even if we have responded to the call of the purposeful life, we begin to find ourselves living more into the day-to-day dimensions. It is as if the idealism of purpose begins to be whittled down. We confront the things that have to be done, the repetition of work, settling into family, making a home, of worrying, experiencing emotions, being ill, making plans --- with occasional "high" spots where something different occurs – a vacation, a visit from someone dear, meeting someone new, buying a house, getting a new job, going on a trip. The sense of purpose lingers but is easily thwarted by professionalism, or having to make a living, collective norms, and our own ambitions. Few can sustain the original impulse to enter into the unknown. It is of extraordinary interest to inquire into what the inherent sense of purpose is doing with us. Is there some soul of purpose guiding the events that we experience as life or does an idealism of purpose pull us into central life questions and then abandon us there?

Purpose, when we are in our youth, whispers as an intimation of the future. As we get older, that future becomes endangered. The ideals we thought would fulfill the desire to serve become illusive as organization, structure, and demands for performance bring mechanization into what lived previously in us as a spiritual reality.

Purpose first belongs to the soul, to our inner life as a felt ongoing impetus, a sense that something is pulling us toward significance, not for ourselves, really, but for the sake of the world. And, at the same time, the demands of the world are constantly working to drown out that pull.

Now, at this cultural moment, the direction of life is shifting for many people. The sense of the future, of the not-yet, of the possible, is stronger than the push to conform, perform, and succeed according to the standards of material wealth. Purpose is no longer felt to be an ideal toward which we aspire but can't quite get to and is increasingly an immediate feeling of the necessity to offer our lives in service.

Purpose, which belongs to our sense of direction, where we are going, works from within. We feel it all the time. There are many people now who are "future-worlders". They experience the fulfillment of working toward the making of a new, more spiritual culture as the primary purpose of their lives. Their sense of the future is actually much stronger than their desire to support structures that seem to belong to the past and no longer provide meaning.

To respond to the new sense of purpose and develop it, we have to consciously enter soul –time. For the soul, future takes place right now. Future is **now** when we move deep inside and make space for soul qualities to stream through us; qualities such as devotion, selflessness, compassion, courtesy, equanimity, patience, truth, courage, balance, discernment, and love. This process of unfolding a new culture is now going on, but it needs our help. It does not occur automatically, but only through conscious effort.

It is not a particular content of what we do that makes us feel a sense of purpose. We cannot say that if one is a doctor or a social worker, or an activist, then a sense of purpose is guaranteed. Rather, it is the presence within soul life of the particular virtuous qualities just mentioned that run through any content of life, qualities within whatever we are doing, be it large or small, mundane or extraordinary, calling us forth to be more than we know ourselves to be. We often don't know what that "more than" might be. And because, within the experience of purpose, there is an element of not-knowing, there is a strong tendency to dismiss the feeling of urgency to want to be of help in the world. That is, the sense of purpose calls us into awareness that something mysterious operates in our lives, and invites us to follow this unknown dimension, no matter where it takes us, but this invitation requires devoted attention.

Moments of the breaking through of purpose crack the shell of conventionality, bringing us into the world as an open system, of which we are the creative part. The ever-lurking husks of conformity have to be cast off over and over again. We do not have the inner strength to do this by ourselves. A presence within the open future that comes toward us is needed in order to be able to work at staying close to the announcement of an unknown sense of purpose. There are spiritual friends in this open form where we become aware of purpose. A quite extraordinary aspect of the quality of this open space is we do not feel alone there. In the soul-time of possibility, the surface-self is overthrown, and the soul can be felt to be in the midst of spiritual companions. We move out of mindscape into soulscape.

The ordinary mind is bound to the ways of the ordinary ego. Notice how your typical patterns of thinking work. They do not move into the new, into unknown territory. We usually understand something by relating it to what we already know. We have to take on the task of continually un-doing what our mind structures. The awareness of purpose does not come from the mental realm. The sense of purpose requires its own organ for its perception, and this organ is the heart. Heart, not as sentimentality, nor as emotion, but as the organ that lies between our head, the place of abstraction, and our limbs, the place of action. When I speak, then, of the heart as the organ for perceiving a sense of purpose, I am seeking to resolve the one-sided notions of the heart we have had since the fifteenth century. Since that time, humanity has lived with a divided heart. For some, heart is a substance without metaphor. The heart is simply that pump beating in the chest that shoves blood around the body. For others, the heart is a metaphor without substance. The heart is the site of emotion, feeling sentiment, but it has no actual force. But here, I am speaking of the actual organ of the heart, which is at the same time the spiritual organ of our body, heart as simultaneously substance and spiritual vessel.

If we simply move our attention from the head, which we typically experience as the site of consciousness, and place it into the interior of heart, there is an immediate and unmistakable alteration of consciousness. There is a sensation of warmth, of spaciousness, of hospitality, of receptivity, and of losing the sense of knowing-in-advance that so inhibits thoughtful spontaneity.

In our ordinary ego-consciousness, we experience the body as a physical substance. It is a spectator's view of the body that we ordinary live. In moments of being within the heart, we feel the body more as a system of currents, body as subtle mobility. We feel light, and the boundary between ourselves, the world, and others is far less fixed during such meditative moments. Levity overcomes gravity, and the seriousness of mental life yields to the joyousness of meeting what comes to us. This sense of the mobility of the body, can gradually, through practice, be extended so that we begin to experience ourselves, others, and the world, in their primordial spiritual presence.

This picturing of the body as systems of currents is not an abstraction. It reveals that we belong to the cosmos and we belong to the depths of the earth, and these come together at the region of the heart, through which we live, here, in the world, open to the cosmos and the depth of the earth, with the task of expressing these realms in the making of a world-in-process. This picturing of the body helps us see that it is not possible to imagine purpose within the framework of a static world-picture. Human life unfolds as the commingling of the angels of the cosmos and the elemental beings of the deep earth. Each of our lives, the marks of which are our biographies, are the particular and individual ways in which we are participating in this dynamic convergence of beings. The new, emerging identity of human beings is that we are an open, empty place waiting for what we are called to be at any moment. This is where we can experience a sense of purpose that cannot be eradicated by fear, terror, confusion, nor the sleepiness of the collective life.

The open, empty, but pregnant place in the region of the heart is where we meet ourselves as beings of purpose. Purpose is not something added on to our lives as if it were a new wardrobe put on now and then. Purpose is inherent to being human, but we have to find our heart to discover our humanity. It is the place of the self-as-activity, without the burden of self-reflection and self-absorption.

Becoming awake to this place of the self as ever-changing brings a radically different dimension to our relationships with others. From the place of ordinary consciousness, the most basic question that arises is "who am I?" From the center of the sense of purpose, the most basic question that arises is "What is the Matter?" "How can I help?" The people we encounter from this place are destiny-others. Our purpose unfolds in relation to them. We do not feel bound to the others we meet from this place. We here meet spiritual co-workers in the making of a new world.

The peculiar individualistic sense of personal identity that is so modern is unknown to the heart and to the experience of sensing purpose. We discover ourselves each moment; and, we discover ourselves each moment as being-in-communion with others. We are, together with others, creating an ever-further articulated inner realm of the heart. We are giving ourselves over to the central realm of the heart. This is what we are doing together. This is where we function as co-workers. This is what we are working on together.

The perception of others is different from within heart than it is from within the ego or the mind. In the latter, we are spectators to others, and our connections come mainly through emotions, common interests, or common needs. There is an unbridgeable gap that exists between you and I. The heart does not follow this way of perceiving others. We perceive each other as in communion. We do not here work to make some external version of community; community is already present. As the great poet Novalis has stated in one of his aphorisms: "I am You." This is the rule of the perception of others from the heart. The sense of individuality, of the I, is no different than the inner experiencing of heart.

If you begin to imagine writing your biography from the viewpoint of the perception of purpose by the heart, you have to imagine some other form than the ego-narrative. Nearly all biographies assume life as moving from the past to the present and toward the future. Biography from the viewpoint of purpose would not unfold in this way. In preparation for the biography of purpose, one might, for example, begin by making extensive notes of all the destiny experiences, moments of intensely felt purpose, that have occurred. Destiny moments are those times when, by living through the heart, we find our lives moving in unexpected ways. We may be living one way today, and then quite suddenly, something new comes, and if is not resisted, it takes us deeper into our purpose. Then, in such a biography, it would be a matter of finding the way to express the moments of these life-changing occurrences so that the way that they break into life unexpectedly is conveyed, and the way they awaken us to purpose depicted.

What such an approach to our biography would reveal is that we now have to become accustomed to the fact that life lived with a sense of purpose is not continuous. We have to adjust to living in a discontinuous universe. Our lives cannot be told from the viewpoint of purpose as a continuity of events. The significant moments are in the gaps, the silences, the places of unknowing, where we are being informed, usually unconsciously, by higher presences, of what is needed of us next. If we meditatively dwell with the gaps in the unfolding of our lives, it is there that we find the direction of our true unfolding, not in the plans and strategies we make that seem to stake out a direction for life and bring about the illusion of living linearly.

Perceiving a sense of purpose through the heart has the power to change the whole of one's life. It is an interesting phrase we use – "I must change my life"; or, "that was a life-changing experience". Usually, these kinds of experiences mean that from the point of the destiny experience onward, our life is different. However, it goes deeper than that; from the moment a true experience of purpose occurs, the whole of our life is changed. The vortex force of purpose also changes the whole of our past, which can now been seen as a past that always had this future destiny event as part of life.

The reconfiguring of the whole of life through purpose opens the soul to a radical experience of hope. Purpose leads to hope, and in a world of fear, terror, uncertainty, instability, the key to not only surviving but to creating is found in finding the way into hope. This capacity of experiencing possibility in all we encounter is a very particular kind of soul experience, one that is always 'on the edge', and can falter in two directions, the two directions of hopelessness, despair and presumption. By "on the edge" I mean the soul's ability to live in uncertainty is the essential defining quality of active soul life as experienced when the sense of purpose is awakened in us. Hope not only lives in uncertainty, it thrives and dwells in peace in uncertainty. Hope cannot be felt when we are in a state of anxiousness or fear. When we are anxious about something we typically want to get out of that state and may say that we hope the trial will cease. This kind of feeling is not hope. Hope is there, but it does not live in this negative sense. When we say, for example, that we "hope something ends soon", we are, at a deeper level, feeling the presence of hope living in the 'not-yet', which it is always doing. The difficult situation in which we find ourselves allows us to feel the contrasting feeling of hope, which otherwise is so subtle that it is not felt.

Hope, as soul's participation in possibility and purpose, is not there to get us out of the tight situations we may find ourselves in. It is there to remind us that there is always more than what we are capable of perceiving. If hope were the soul's way of getting us out of things, then it would be an escape mechanism. It is not. We do not have to do anything to hope; it is already there, in each and every act, thought, fantasy, and even within our body itself. The next breath is possible because hope resides in the body, making it possible to experience that there is a breath after this one, there is a heartbeat after this one, there is a step after this one. Hope links the now and the not-yet into one unity; seamlessly, giving ongoing inner strength to our sense of purpose. We call that link imagination, but it is not at all necessarily something done consciously. What we have to be concerned about is the all-too-easy tendency to turn against hope not knowing we have done so. Hope does not resist, so the only way of knowing we have turned against hope is through feeling the sense of purpose dimmed.

When the sense of purpose combines with hope, the virtue of magnanimity is born. Magnanimity is the courage to seek what is great and become worthy of it, a seeking, taken up with deep humility. Hope, by itself, can sometimes contract the soul when it is put into conjunction with negative wishes. We can live in the hope that something does not happen or that something bad happens to someone else. Hope, by itself, can be something belittling rather than soul-enlarging. We must desire that hope be a way of becoming more fully human; and we must then become watchful that this takes place. Where does magnanimity come from? Who instills it? I think it is a memory in the soul; the living memory we have of selfless deeds done for others. It is not necessarily a personal memory at all. It is more of an archetypal memory, and through it we remember the magnificence of human beings and that we are called to enlarge the possibilities of being human. This memory can be obscured...through selfishness, greed, self-centeredness. Magnanimity directs hope to its utmost possibilities.

There are levels to the experience of hope and is not the intellectual notion that we usually mean when we say we have hope. It is first experienced as a deep, maybe unending reservoir of spiritual strength that is not coming from our own capacities, but is always there, like an inner, still, wellspring, an unending resource. Hope is felt as a kind of presence, holding open the space of possibility. Hope does not lie behind all our actions but is the silent current within them. Hope does not exist totally on its own. It needs the outside world and others to activate it. When we hope for something -- under the condition that it is true hope and not merely having fantasies for what we wish would happen -- the world responds in mutuality. Hope is not crushed by not being fulfilled. It is never disappointed, and when we feel hopelessness, that is not the disappointment of hope, but an entirely different phenomenon. We do not have a limited reserve of hope that gets used up when thing do not work out over and over again. Hope is the ever-present inner feeling of the presence of purposeful possibility in everything we do. It is the simultaneous ever-present inner feeling of the 'could be' that leads us to the next moment in everything we do. Hope does not consist in its basic forms as a thinking about what could or might or should be. It is the inner sense of possibility within our thoughts, feelings, and actions. It does not come into operation simply when things are seeming to go wrong, as a kind of emergency virtue that makes it possible to go on in spite of the odds being against us. Hope is best experienced when we are attending to the details of things. It is not the fantasies we have of something that could happen that is beyond and better than what is happening. Hope is always in the moment as the sense of the future that is an essential aspect of the present moment. It is the aspect of the moment that gives the inner experience of this moment as 'getting somewhere.' Where the moment is leading is unknown; hope is the inherent capacity to experience the moment as also 'waiting' for the unknown that is to come.

Hope resides both interiorly and exteriorly at the same time. We can tell when we have this kind of contact with the world because these moments are always experienced as "quiet moments" that are nonetheless filled with intensity of anticipation. We are with whatever is happening, fully. Concentration is easy and full. In moments of experiencing hope we feel no barrier between ourselves and the world. While fantasy is counterfeit hope, hope always imagines the possible. It is satisfying and it is pleasurable. It is the fulfillment, the wholeness of purpose.

Spiritual Psychology of Silence and Solitude

"Who will prefer the jingle of jade pendants if he once has heard stone growing in a cliff?" – Chinese Proverb

I. The Experience of Silence
A. Silence as a Positive Phenomenon

There is a strong tendency to imagine silence as the absence of speech or the absence of sound, as merely being quiet. Such a way of imagining silence deprives it of being anything in itself. Such a view makes Silence empty, a mere void. In our time, silence has become more or less a void, something far less that it is as a sacred phenomenon. Thus, we need to recover Silence. While it is not easy to describe silence, that is our main task – to describe it in its many and varied manifestations. We do not want to start with our assumptions, acting like we know what silence is, but rather with a careful description of the world of silence. This starting place will also characterize the whole of our approach to silence; working to get ever closer to its presence and let each of its many veils take us closer and closer to its ineffable core.

Silence is a basic phenomenon, like other basic phenomena such as the soul, the spirit, love, death. In fact, silence may be the most basic of these phenomena, since it envelopes each of these others. It is not a derivative phenomenon. It does not originate from something else; silence does not come from sound as its cessation; if silence were the absence of sound, that would mean that sound is basic, and silence comes out of it. But that is not the way we experience silence. It is experienced as more basic that sound, more primary, and in fact, as the very originating force for sound. All we have to do to verify this is to drop into silence for a moment and feel its presence. It is just there. We do not experience silence starting when we are quiet, but rather, we experience moving into something that is already there. It is all around us, but also everywhere within us; silence is all-pervasive; it is experienced that way when we touch into it.

Exercise 1. a) Enter into silence for several minutes:

Write a description of this experience of Silence
What is silence like?

B. The Value of Silence

Later, we will work with some of the specific values of silence for the individual. The first and larger value, however, is that silence is completely autonomous. It is not something that we do; When we are quiet, the possibility exists for us to enter into silence; we do not necessarily do so; silence is an autonomous world, an invisible, untouchable world that, however, is completely, in every part, connected with this world. The first thing that silence does, then, is to strengthen the autonomy of everything with which it can be felt. For example, when we enter into silence the autonomy of our individuality is strengthened. We feel a renewed soul strength. We also experience something of the deep mystery of the things around us, such as the natural world, or animals, or things – anything which lives closer to the being of Silence; they become more defined when we sense them in the context of their homeland of Silence. And, when the world becomes more noise-filled, the things around us begin to be less perceptible.

For the human being, the experience of silence goes together with the experience of solitude. Solitude can be a condition for silence – going off and being alone; but solitude can also be the result – the capacity to experience our individuality more strongly, which is a kind of living in solitude (don't take either silence or solitude completely literally – have to work to develop the imagination of these states of our being). Whatever exists in silence receives some of the power and strength of silence itself. It is the power of re-creation. In silence, everything appears new again. Solitude as the condition for silence indicates that in order to meet silence, we have to disengage ourselves from our other connections. Literal solitude may help bring about this disengagement, but it is also possible to do so at almost anytime, anyplace. Such disengagement is not dissociation or drifting off or daydreaming or even lack of attention. It is even possible, and actually quite necessary if you are an initiate into the world of silence, to develop a kind of dual attention. It is possible to fully attend to what is going on in the moment in your connections with others and to also fully attend to the world of silence, both at the same time. The real work of entering silence lies here, in making silence an ongoing companion without turning away from our duties and responsibilities in the world.

Silence is available all of the time. It does not go away. We go away from it, go into the world of noise, as if into the vast buzzing of insects, existing as the permanent irritation of sound without silence. Sound without silence is something entirely different than the sound that comes out of silence. The former sound is always derivative; the latter, always original, new, as if showing for the first time, a revelation, a pure and originating, renewing presence.

Silence is something that we can no longer take for granted as a reality. What we think of as silence is not Silence. We think of silence as being quiet, perhaps going inward, getting back in touch with ourselves, disengaging from all of the pressures and tensions of life so that we can know ourselves better; silence as our self-confronting our self. This is actually only a very, very small part and aspect of Silence, the tiniest part imaginable. And, actually, if this is the extent of silence, silence has been taken over into an egotistical interest. That is to say, the interest is not really in the world of Silence, but only in what silence can do for me. There are, of course, results from entering into this lost domain. We feel a new sense of freedom, of a capacity to be ourselves again and of realizing that we did not even know that we lost ourselves. We feel a new attunement to spirit in which spirit, rather than an abstract word and abstract concept is a reality, felt directly and immediately all around. We gain a new perspective, the capacity of reflection, of letting the world and things and others mirror within us rather than just going from one activity to the next. We gain a newfound creativity – insights come, new ideas, new ways of seeing how we have been stuck. But all of these results are byproducts of Silence, and not reasons for becoming interested in the phenomenon. Our interest is drawn to the phenomenon because we feel, not quite consciously, but it is there, that this domain is a necessity to the world. Even more, attention to this phenomenon is needed in order that the realm will not be completely lost. We work toward Silence for the sake of Silence, and what comes to us as the gifts of that realm are purely secondary. The moment we begin to concentrate on the gifts, the phenomenon itself will be lost; it will be given over to a thin imitation of the phenomenon, something that has a certain personal but very temporary benefit. If personal quietude takes the place of the great phenomenon of silence, however, what results is nothing more than self-indulgence that is selfish and irresponsible.

In former times, Silence was the great protector that shielded humanity from soul-friction; by soul-friction I mean all of the irritations of non-soul that can wear down the soul and pulverize it. Silence was there, objectively, like a defending army. Silence was present between things in the world, between ideas, between a too-close contact between people, as the great Mediatrix between our soul and the divine and our soul and the world. You had to push against Silence, not aggressively, but calmly, carefully, in order to move from one idea to another, from one word to another, from one movement to another. This having to push against silence had the effect of an inner strengthening of soul. Notice, it was an effect, something that came about as a result of feeling the Silence. But now, instead of strengthening of soul, we have "development of soul." The domain of the soul has been taken into the territory of the entrepreneur, staking out to develop the soul as if it were a new suburban housing development, or a mall, or an office building.

Because we have lost silence, we have also lost thinking. One has to move deliberately through silence in order to come to an idea. You have to find ideas floating around in the vastness of Silence, where they are being nourished and where they remain true and original. We no longer come to ideas; we no longer think, we have our thinking done for us. Ideas rush at us and swirl around, each vying to be seized upon. When there is a vastness of Silence with ideas being nourished in it, there is not a felt need to know everything, nor to confuse knowing with information.

The only little remaining silence is "an hour of silence", or the "two-minute silence" in remembrance of…. Perhaps silence still exists in the monastic communities, but there, it lives in seclusion, like a wildlife preserve for Silence, to be looked at, admired from afar.

Hear what Petrarch wrote about the importance of silence in his
De Vita Solitaria:

"The busy man, a hapless dweller of the city, awakes in the middle of the night, his sleep interrupted by his cares or the cries of his clients, often even by fear of the light and by terror of nightly visions. No sooner is he up than he settles his body to the miserable bench and applies his mind to falsehood. On treachery his heart is wholly fixed – whether he meditates driving a corrupt bargain, betraying his friend or his ward, assailing with his seductions his neighbor's wife whose only refuge is her chastity, spreading the veil of justice over a litigious quarrel, or whatever other mischief of a public or private character he intends. Now eager with passion and aflame with desire, and now frozen with desperation, like a bad workman, he begins before dawn the web of the daily toil in which he shall involve others with himself."

The quote is of great interest because we clearly see that the absence of Silence is not a modern phenomenon. This description might well be speaking of this very time, now. The description also brings out that without silence there is neither soul nor virtue.

IN MEMORY OF SILENCE
And I have felt
A presence that disturbs me with the joy
Of elevated thoughts: a sense sublime
Of something far more deeply interfused,
Whose dwelling is the light of setting suns,
And the round ocean and the living air,
And the blue sky and in the mind of man:
A motion and a spirit, that impels
All thinking things, all objects of thought,
And rolls through all things.
(from Wordsworth: "Lines Composed a Few Miles Above Tintern Abbey")

C. The Beasts Who Guard Silence

It is easy and every-moment tempting to wax sentimentally about silence. If it were simply this wonderful – the bountiful source of creativity, individuality, renewal, hope, love, and all the rest, then most assuredly we would all be quiet. There is another side to silence, part of the very activity and being of silence and not merely what one has to go through to get to silence. Silence is also anxiety, dread, fear, temptation, distraction, fantasy, reverie, imaginal attack, something enormously fearful. Henri Nouwen (<u>The Way of the Heart</u>) calls silence "the furnace of transformation." We cannot avoid the fire of the furnace and go directly to the bliss of silence. When we try to do so, we find it impossible to find that wonder of silence that the spiritual folk are so fond of taking about. We find instead, the Great Beast.

When we go off to be alone, we do not experience an immediacy of silence and solitude. We experience the beast. Not nearly the beast, though, that the great initiate into silence, St. Anthony, Desert Father, born in 251, died in 356 at age 105, encountered. An initiate is someone who goes through an experience in such a way that it makes it possible for the whole of humanity to now encounter that experience. An initiate is a kind of forerunner, one who makes the way for the rest of humanity. Thus, I think of St. Anthony as one of the great forerunners of Silence, the one who has made the path of silence possible for the rest of humanity. He spent twenty years in complete solitude. But he had to find the way through the guardians of Silence.

The way the Desert Fathers struggled to find Silence can be understood differently than the Church puts forward the story. These blocks to Silence are usually understood as temptations, and, as stated above, the devil. We can, however, also understand these beings as guardians of the threshold of Silence. They are not the same as the Guardian of the threshold as understood by anthroposophy and detailed by Rudolf Steiner, though there is a certain relationship. These guardians preside over a different border than that between the earthly world and the spiritual worlds. They preside over a border between physical experience, which is also the physical body – or it is perhaps more accurate to say the soul's attraction to physical experience and the physical body and the soul's attraction to …..another world, a world which is not yet the spiritual world; it is more like the world that is the archetype of this earthly world. An imagination of this world and, as well, of the guardians of that world are pictured in the Isenheim Altar.

One of the truly great images of St. Anthony is given in Grunewald's Isenheim Altar. I want to look only at two panels of the altar, the two that have to do with picturing what is on the other side of the threshold and the panel showing St. Antony confronting the Beast(s) of Silence. As soon as we get rid of our scaffolding, all that holds us to others in daily life, what we first confront is nothing. We confront the very deep and strong experience of being worth nothing, for we have counted our worth in terms of who we are with others, what we can do, how helpful we can be to others, all of which, in themselves are quite good. But, the beast of silence announces itself as Nothingness.

Then, following upon and deepening the sense of nothingness comes all kind of images, fantasies, confusing ideas, strange associations, assaults, inner voices, attacks, all kinds of feelings of anger, lust, envy, hatred – you know, all those lovely things that we usually see only in others, or in the worlds of politics, or the corporation – wherever projections happen to be taking place these days. In the vestibule of Silence, there they are, all these beasts, assaulting us.

Let us work with the beasts of silence as they are pictured in "The Temptation of St. Anthony." First, let us work to let this image live within us. Observe the painting in an engaged way for several minutes; then, close your eyes, and feel, experience, the presence of this painting within your imagination.

Here is a text from the life of St. Antony, that probably goes with this Scene:

"When it was night-time they made such a crashing noise that the whole place seemed to be shaken by a quake. The demons, as if breaking through the building's four walls, and seeming to enter through them, were changed into the forms of beasts and reptiles. The place immediately was filled with the appearances of lions, bears, leopards, bulls and serpents, asps, scorpions and wolves, and each of these moved in accordance with its form....and altogether the sounds of all the creatures that appeared were terrible, and their ragings were fierce."

From one point of view, the beasts of silence are terrible, horrible, possibly demons, evil. From another point of view, the demons are the guardians of the threshold of silence. We cannot enter into the region of silence without going through these beasts. From a strictly spiritual point of view, the beasts are to be conquered – which cannot be done alone. The beasts only retreat when Christ is present:

"Anyone who wants to fight his demons with his own weapons is a fool. The wisdom of the desert is that the confrontation with our own frightening nothingness forces us to surrender ourselves totally and unconditionally to the Lord Jesus Christ. Alone, we cannot face "the mystery of iniquity" with impunity. Only Christ can overcome the power of evil. Only in and through him can we survive the trials of our solitude."(Henri Nouwen, <u>The Way of the Heart</u>, pg. 28).

From a spiritual/psychological point of view, the demons are ourselves and we do not want to too quickly eliminate ourselves. Rather, we need to get to know these demons intimately. For example:

When St. Anthony went into the desert and was confronted with the demons of silence, one time he had a vision of a beautiful silver bowl, sitting there in the desert. In the biography of St. Anthony, written by Athanasius, we are told that St. Anthony took this vision as the work of the demons. It was a deception: St. Anthony turned toward the demon and said:

"Where could a bowl come from in the desert? There are no traveled ways nearby, no habitation, no bandits that live in this place! This is an artifice of the Demons. You will not hinder my spirit by this means! Let this be with you for your downfall!"

So, one of the reasons we need silence is to determine whether our images are illusions or are real images! Silence teaches us how to look at our fantasy life.

Here is a story of how, in silence, we can be fooled by what we apprehend:

"An old man, Heron, had made of fasting an inflexible and absolute law.... The angel of Satan was received by him as an angel of light, and with great honor (because he was so exhausted from fasting). Eager to obey the angel, Heron threw himself head over heels into a well, the bottom of which the eye could not perceive. In doing this, he placed his trust in the promise that had been made to him that, as a result of his meritorious works and virtues, in the future he would be proof against all danger....Thus, as just the middle of the night arrived, he threw himself to the bottom of the well with the thought of proving his rare merit by coming out in one piece. However, the brothers had great difficulty in pulling him out half dead. He passed away two days later."

We have to learn how to approach silence in the right way, with the right attitude, which is not the attitude that says: look at all the good, all the virtue, all the merit, all the deepening, all the creativity, the peace, the sensitivity, the ability to be more present in the world we will get out of the practice of silence.

We do not enter the region of silence for ourselves, but rather as an honoring, giving attention to, caring for, giving homage to, acknowledging, the sacredness of the region and beings of Silence. Otherwise, our interest in silence is nothing more than ego inflation. The autonomy of Silence must be recognized and honored. We can easily become interested in silence for what we think it can give us. But, in the face of Silence, we are continually humbled, made aware of our inadequacy of being with Silence out of our own ordinary abilities.

The Beasts of silence are certainly not always as pictured in "The Temptation of St. Anthony." Sometimes the Beasts are incredibly reasonable. Here is another encounter of St. Anthony with a Beast of silence:

> "Another time, as I was fasting, the Deceiver appeared to me in the figure of a hermit, who offered bread and then gave me the following advice: "Hold yourself upright, sustain your heart with bread and water, and rest a little from the multitude of your works; for you are a human being, and no matter what pretensions you may have, you are burdened with a body. Be fearful of suffering and unpleasantness." I, however, considered his sympathy and held back my words. I turned in the silence to my steadfast way and began to supplicate my Lord in prayer and said: Lord, make him as nothing, just as throughout all time you have been wont to make him a nothing." And when I have finished these words, he was consumed and vanished like dust and in the manner of smoke."

Exercise 2. What are the demons you meet that keep you from crossing into the region of Silence? (n.b. – develop this into an exercise)

Note how in our time, the Beasts have also become externalized:
As: "my responsibilities"
   "my family"
   Entertainment
   Technology
   Comforts
Allowing the quiet to surround and to penetrate us, pulls us back from our being scattered in the world through our desires and interests and activities, a re-collection. We then become available to feelings, images, loves,

aversion, hopes, fears, inner images, archetypal images. But, first, and for a long time, re-collection takes us to the Beasts.

D. Getting Through the Beasts of Silence

1. Is getting through the beasts of silence a matter of confronting all of the beasts, or is there something else that must be attended to as we enter into the region of silence? The beasts are not conquered, but amidst the clamor of the beasts that assail us, it is first necessary to hear the faraway sounds of silence; it is Silence that first all makes it possible for us to undergo the assailing presence of the beasts. And, back, deep back and within the very heart of Silence there is to be found the Word. Silence is the birthplace of the Word. Not just 'words', ordinary speech, but the capacity of speech originates in the Silence. If we do not or cannot find this originating Word within Silence, then silence will be dominated by the beasts. We never, I think, get rid of the beasts, but they can recede into the background and the background become foreground for a while. The two panels of the Isenheim Altar both show the qualities of this background. It appears in both panels to be the sky, and some majestic being there in the sky; I take this, though, to be an image of going into the unending depths, Silence as infinity, both far away and in-the-finite.

Exercise 3: We are all now going to go into the Silence. Close your eyes, remain alert and awake. Work to quiet everything within you – your thoughts, images, feelings, impulses. See if you can go the place of complete silence. Then, from that place, speak out loud into the center of this group. When you are finished, go back into the silence; then someone else, speak out of the silence you are within. We are interested here in hearing the quality of the word that comes from the silence.

Let us now work with the other panel of the the Isenheim Altar, the one that gives a picture of what is on the other side of the threshold guarded by the Beasts of Silence.

We see in this painting a whole other world that appears through the opening between the trees, behind the figures of St. Antony, and another anchorite, St. Paul. The world on the other side over there, that is the world of Silence. Notice that St. Antony and St. Paul are sitting there on the steps in front of that other world. They are close to Silence, but this painting also shows us that we, in life, can perhaps never enter fully into Silence. And, St. Antony, who lived in complete solitude for twenty years, why, in relation to St. Paul, he still looks like he has too much attachment to the power, the elevation, the substance of the world. He is not as close to nature as is St. Paul, whose very garment is made of the leaves from a palm tree. But, St. Antony has come close enough to Silence to be able to have a lively conversation with one who is even closer to this world.

II. The Substance of Silence
A. Living from the Substance of Silence

1. We want to work now with sensing the silence that is always all around us, the silence from which we have become so separated. Let's begin with a wonderful description of someone living in the substance of silence:

"I saw a man in an old suit that was more than merely a covering for his body; it was part of the man himself; it had suffered with him, it was like a brownish grazed skin. The man was not standing and was not walking; as he walked, he stood still, and as he stood still he move forward a little. His face was gentle and rosy, but from his forehead and cheeks, furrows crowded into his face. He eyes looked out high above everything they met, and yet they were waiting for something to come up to them from near at hand. The left arm was held close to the body, as if the body would not let go of the arm, and yet he held his hand stretched out slightly. I put a note into it, and then I did not know (for I dared not wait to find out) whether the hand went back to the man and whether he put the money in his pocket. Or did the hand move on out to another, seeking for another hand to which he could give money? This man was living in the center between giving and taking, between distance and nearness, between old age and youth. He was living from the silent substance in the central place within, from the meeting place and focus within from which every movement proceeds outward. (Max Picard, <u>The World of Silence</u>, pg. 64-65).

Where we can perhaps most easily begin to feel, to experience the objective presence of silence is in relation to our body.

Exercise: Stand and move, trying to find the presence of silence from which your movement can emerge. Work at being present to the silence and then moving – standing, walking, moving hands, arms, legs, head, eyes, out from this presence of silence.

Then, describe what it is like to move in connection with silence.

When we are present to silence, silence is carried into every movement. You can feel the presence of silence trailing along with the movement, giving a soul and spiritual strength to the movement. Our movements, then, do not jolt, one against the other, but are much more like silence made visible. And, at the same time, the silence makes each movement utterly distinct and individual; our movements are made clear, and we then stand out in our individuality rather than merge into the cacophony of noise, where it is impossible to tell the difference between one thing and another, between an object and a living being. Silence, on the other hand, gives nobility to our movement.

Exercise: As a second part of the exercise above, we now want to move among each other with this same sense of silence as the ground from which we are moving. With this sense of silence, move about in the group, from one person to another. Describe what it is like to move in relation to others in this way.

When we move from the ground of silence in relation to each other, one of the first things we notice is that there is the absence of any kind of feeling of conflict. This is because we do not move directly in relation to each other, but rather we move in relation to the silence. It is the objective presence of silence that makes community possible, that makes being in relation with each other. Relationships that do not occur out of the medium of silence are noisy, conflicted, unsure, fearful, and most of all, isolated. In the absence of the substance of silence, we face noise and are not able to be in relation with each other but are actually caught in a kind of isolation in which we are only in relation with ourselves, thinking we are in connection with others. The ego lives in noise; soul and spirit live in silence. There is kind of silence in ego life, but it is the silence of isolation, it is private solitude, subjective solitude. It is of great importance to be able to distinguish between subjective solitude and silence and objective solitude and silence. When we go seeking silence, often, probably far more often that we think, we are merely seeking an egotistic experience – to get to know ourselves better, to be able to tell where we end and another begins, to find ourselves, to be in better touch with ourselves. All of these kinds of interests are interests in isolated solitude and silence rather than engagement with the objective substance of silence.

B. What Silence Does

Being able to feel the objective presence of Silence has great soul value. Silence orders the life of the soul. Silence mediates the polarities of soul life. Without presence to silence, the polarities of soul life are experienced as in conflict and full of contradiction. Faith is felt as contradicting knowledge; body is felt as contradicting spirit; passion contradicting contemplation; truth contradicting beauty; knowing contradicting feeling. The substance of silence stands between the contradictions and   prevents them from fighting each other. The contradictions meet, not head on and directly, but have to travel over the medium of silence, which graces each of the contradictions; We feel this graced presence as humor.

In relation to soul life, the substance of silence also mediates and holds together all of our talents and abilities with all of our defects. Without the substance of silence, a defect becomes glaring and begins to take over the whole of our soul life; we become more and more captured by the defect. In a similar way, silence is the medium of therapeutic healing because spirit re-creates us through the medium of silence. Without the substance of silence, we cannot free ourselves from all that has affected us from the past. It is an extremely helpful exercise to imagine therapy in the metaphor of being recreated by the silence rather than the noisy way we presently understand therapy as "development."

Contemplate this sentence from Max Picard:
   "Happiness and silence belong together just as do profit and noise."

The objective presence of silence makes possible finding a relation to the machine and technological world. Without silence, the technical world is hostile to our soul nature and eats it up. For example, the prevalence of electronic technology in the East is not injurious to those people as it is to us because the East has a long and honored tradition of silence that still pervades that culture.

We can now put forth another definition of silence as it pervades daily life: Silence is the spiritual observation of the world, oneself, and others through the presence of soul. This kind of observation, in turn, orders the soul. The kind of relief we feel, the ability to breathe, the calm, the peace that comes with silence expresses this ordering of the life of soul according to its own inherent nature; that is, order here is not imposed on the soul but the soul recognizes its own order in the act of spiritual observation.

Silence is the great vessel that gives the soul a sense of order. This order is not the order of structure, rigid and hierarchical, like the military; nor is it fastidious, everything neat and tidy; it is the imaginal order of the soul that is contained in the great vessel. In the imaginal order, everything is held together by being a 'thou' rather than 'it. Personification is essential to imaginal order. We will take up personification shortly, but first it is necessary to work to feel the presence of silence everywhere within the imaginal realms. Let us look at several of these realms in relation to silence, prefaced, though, with a picture of the way in which personifying shows in silence. Hear Thoreau speak of his surroundings:

"*I never met the companion that was an companionable as solitude*.....

.... *the most sweet and tender, the more innocent and encouraging society may be found in any natural object*....

.... *I was suddenly sensible of such sweet and beneficent society in Nature, in the very pattering of the drops, and in every sight and sound around my house, an infinite and unaccountable friendliness all at once like an atmosphere sustaining me*...

...*I was so distinctly made aware of the presence of something kindred to me, even in scenes which we are accustomed to call wild and dreary, and also that the nearest of blood to me and humanest was not a person nor a villager.*

I am not lonelier than the loon in the pond that laughs so loud, or than Walden Pond itself. What company has that lonely lake, I pray? ...I am no lonelier than a single mullein or dandelion in a pasture or a bean leaf, or sorrel, or a horsefly, or a humblebee."

In silence, everything lives within. This does not mean everything becomes a subjective experience; it is more than the 'within-ness' of everything can now be experienced. In our ordinary sensing and perception, everything around us exists as "outside", as "over there", "in front of', "to the side of", "above", "below", "behind"; The perception of silence is different. It is different space. Something can be "over there" and "within" at the same time. For example, in ordinary perception, the tree that sits next to the building that I can see through my window is "over there" As long as it is perceived as simply 'over there', I am not present to the silence. And the tree has no particular significance and my perception of it carries no feeling. In silence, I become aware of the tree in a feeling way; it is not that I have feelings about the tree or feelings for the tree, but rather, perceive the tree through feeling and thus perceive something of the feeling life of the tree. At the very moment that shift occurs, a personifying has occurred. Is this personifying merely a projection of my own psyche, such that what I feel are not the qualities of the tree itself, but rather unconscious qualities of feeling within myself that I am not aware of except insofar as they are projected "over there"?

The feeling-perception of the tree can either be projection or it can be an objective perception of the silence of the tree. This possible and likely confusion was the whole point of the anchorites going off into the desert for years and years – to purify theirperception. For us, who have not gone through that work, we have to be aware of that our perceptions in silence are a mixture – our projections of unconscious soul life, but not only that; also objective perceptions of the things and persons around us in silence.

We can, however, begin to separate out these two forms of perception and, gradually purify our perception of the Silence. We do not have to go out to the desert for the next twenty years. Both forms of perception of Silence are important, and it is probably so that we can come to the second, the objective substance of silence, only by going through personal silence. However, it is quite possible to get stuck with the first form. Here are examples of personal silence, and what might be called archetypal Silence:

"*Standing quietly in the water, feeling the sand shifting away under my toes...I lay back in the floating position that left my face to the sky, and shoved. Off. The sky wheeled over me. For an instant, as I bobbed into the main channel, I had the sensation of sliding down the vast tilted face of the continent. It was then that I felt the cold needles of the alpine springs at my fingertips, and the warmth of the Gulf pulling me southward. Moving with me, leaving its taste upon my mouth and spouting under me in dancing springs of sand, was the immense body of the continent itself, flowing like the river was flowing, grain by grain, mountain by mountain, down to the sea. I was streaming over ancient seabeds thrust aloft where giant reptiles had once sported; I was wearing down the face of time and trundling cloud-wreathed ranges into oblivion...I was streaming alive through the hot and working ferment of the sun, or oozing secretively through shady thickets. I was water.*"

—Loren Eisley

Now a description of Archetypal Silence:

"*In the heat of the summer noon the silence breaks right into space. Time itself seems to stand still, paralyzed by this sudden jolt.*
The vault of the sky is stretched up high, and the sky is like the upper edge of silence.

The earth has sunk down low. Only its edge is visible, the lower edge of silence.

The mountain, the trees, and the scattered houses are like the last things remaining after everything else has been utterly absorbed by the noonday silence. The silence seems calm, as it were coagulated; and it is as though even these last remaining things would vanish as soon as the silence moves.

A bird flies slowly into the sky, and its movements are like dark trails that keep the silence enclosed within itself. It is as though, otherwise, the silence might open

—Max Picard

When we get beyond the personal sense of silence and into her world, we also find that there is not just silence, but different kinds of silence. For example, the silence of the day is not the same as the silence of the night. When we can move beyond the ego's more sentimental engagement with silence, we can then become explores of the worlds of Silence. Hear Max Picard's description of the silence of the night in contract with that of the day:

> In the night, silence moves nearer to the earth. The earth is filled with a silence which seems to penetrate the very surface of the soil. The words of the daytime are dissolved.
>
> A bird suddenly begins to sing in the night. And the song is like the residue of the sounds left over by the day-time, which, taking fright, embrace each other in the birdsong and make the song a hiding place.
>
> A boat travels over the lake and the beat of the oars is like a knocking on the wall of silence.
>
> The trees stretch up high into the night as if they were taking something up with them along their trunks and were going to hand it over to the silence. The next morning the trunks are even straighter than the evening before.
>
> Strangers to themselves and suddenly strangers to the place where they are, things stand in the night as though they had not been here in the daytime but had been set down in the night by silence without noticing it themselves. They seem to have traveled in on the silence as on a ship, secretly.

III. Speech and Silence

A. Speech as the Resonance of Silence

Once we begin to have a sense of, a feeling of, the autonomous world of silence and can move into that autonomous realm, we can begin to experience the thousands of forms of silence; the silence of the natural world in the rising aspiration of the trees, in the silent changing of seasons, in the

moonlight falling onto the Earth; or, the silence of animals; the silence of
the human body, the silence of things, the silence of the human face; the
silence of images, the silence of certain paintings, certain art. There is so
much to silence, so much of silence, so many forms of silence, it is as if it
overflows into speech.

We are here considering the spiritual quality of speech, not just the
acoustic quality. Today, the spiritual quality of speech is nearly absent
because speech no longer comes out of silence, but out of emptiness. We
have to find our way back into silence before it is possible to speak again.

Go into a restaurant. Chances are that there will be loud music, terrible
music playing. In order to speak, you have to match the noise of that music,
and your speech, then, is related to noise, not to silence. That is not the only
kind of noise. Even our words now do not come from the silence, but from
the noise of other words. When we speak with someone, we are not
responding to the silence, but to the words. (Note: in the work of therapy,
one works to respond to the silence, not to the words, knowing that when
silence is addressed, healing will take place).

Exercise: Pair into two's, and have a conversation about the nature of

The substance of silence. When responding to what your partner says,
respond to the silence in what your partner has said as you are able to hear
that silence in what is being said. Do not talk about the silence but be
present to it.

What is the difference between speech that comes out of silence and
speech that moves along the horizontal line of a sentence? When speech
comes out of silence, each word comes from the silence and then moves
again back into the silence; the flow of the sentence is broken by silence.
Verbal noise, on the other hand, has no feeling of interruption, just one
word after another, no silence in the words, no silence between the words.
Here is an example of verbal noise

*"Cityful passing away, other cityful coming, passing away too: other
coming on, passing on. Houses, lines of houses, streets, miles of
pavements, piled up bricks, stones. Changing hands. This owner, that,
Landlord never dies they say. Other steps into his shoes when he gets
notice to quit. They buy the place up with gold and still they have all the
gold. Swindle in it somewhere. Piled up in cities, worn away age after age.*

Pyramids in sand. Built on bread and onions. Slaves. Chinese wall. Babylon. Big stones left. Round towers. Rest rubble, sprawling suburbs, jerrybuilt. Shelter for the night."

—James Joyce

Speech without silence is merely information, material statements of fact. It Is strange indeed, that in our time, this kind of speech is what is valued. Speech with pauses, hesitations, blank spots, speech that works to hold and embrace the unspeakable is not valued at all; it is considered unworthy, soft, suspect, maybe even poetry. Thus, things no longer partake of infinity; we have taken the infinity out of them. Speech has become an empty apparatus, the mechanical conveyance of dead thinking.

Without speech that comes from silence, real listening is not possible. Listening and silence belong together. We do not know how to listen. A listener is far more than a non-speaker. One who hears takes speech and allows it to move into the silence. What is a good listener? We only know how to wait until the other person has stopped speaking so that we can take up where that speaking stopped without so much as a pause which would allow for reflection, which would allow for what was said to be reflected back into the silence and become fructified there. Instead of speaking with each other, we unload onto each other. Speech has become an excretive function.

In the absence of speech connected with silence, we begin to lose the sense of existing at all because we are continually created by the Word, and if the Word has no place, we really do not, in an inner way, know we exist. We exist only as reflections of the noise around us. This noise may be mass media, advertising, propaganda.

The question that we have to face is – how do we go about finding the Word? How can we work to restore silence to speech? First, begin to imagine speaking as music, as singing, because music is closer to silence than the way we now speak. You can tangibly feel the presence of silence when you sing, and it is the reason music is calming to people. We also feel that music is the completion of silence, not its opposite. So, that is a good way to begin to imagine our speaking – as fulfilling silence, not destroying it. Only speech has more the quality of solid blocks emerging from the silence, while music still holds the fluid of silence .When we are able to imagine speech in its proper relation with silence, speech takes on its true quality as being more than silence.

A related image to contemplate: In the spiritual realms, silence and speech are perfectly united, one, a unity. How do we know – well, it is not noisy in the spiritual realms, and yet, it is impossible to conceive of these realms as being silence without connections among the beings and forces there. So, in working daily to bring silence and speech closer together, to imagine them not as contraries, but as contingent on each other, we are engaged in an ongoing, meditative schooling of ourselves oriented toward developing the capacities to experience the spiritual worlds.

What does silence give to words? Sure certainty, intimacy, and beauty. The way that words move also reveal that silence is not static; it is full of movement, and the movement of words imitates the movements that happen in silence. Speech hovers between the silence of its origins, which for each of us individually, is our birth, and the silence to which we are going – death. When our speech resonates these two silences it speaks qualities of depth, originality, simplicity. But at the same time, speech, in its closeness to death is fragile, and it is fleeting, transient. Nonetheless, these two "bookends" of speech give speech refreshment and renewal. When we can feel the presence of birth and of death, then the act of speaking becomes an act of awaiting the moment the creation of language for the first time. We, then, do not live with the assumption, which is actually an illusion, that speech is ready-at-hand, that there is no effort of birth and no awe of death in or effort to speak. The rattling off of words without waiting, labor, and trepidation, can never be creative nor create anything new in the world. This kind of speaking only pollutes the world with more noise.

B. Recovering the Silence of Speech

Exercise to experience the silence that exists before birth and after death in our speaking:

Write a one paragraph monologue, addressing something of vital importance in your life. Remember, in a monologue, you are addressing someone – is not just speaking into the air --- a monologue speaks to Silence; a monologue is a dialogue with Silence.

The special role of poetry in relation to Silence; here language has a special place.

Poetry not only holds a great, vast silence, poetry also produces silence; it creates new silence. Remember, silence is not just the absence of speech, but an autonomous reality. Through the creative act of the word, silence is re-created. Poetry is absolutely necessary for the life of silence. After each verse of a poem, there is an active, audible silence. All poetry, of course, does not create silence. In fact, most poetry now belongs to the world of noise. Poetry that comes out of silence and creates silence, for the most part, cannot be understood today. Some of the poets of silence include: Laotse, Sophocles, Shakespeare, Goethe, Holderlin. Here is an example of a poem coming directly out of Silence and creating Silence:

.But where did my soul go?
Come home, come home.
It traveled far South,
South of the people to the South of us.
Come home, come home.

But where did my soul go?
Come home, come home.
It traveled far East,
East of the peoples to the East of us.
Come home, come home.

But where did my soul go?
Come home, come home.
It traveled far North,
North of the peoples to the North of us.
Come home, come home.

But where did my soul go?
Come home, come home.
It traveled far West,
West of the peoples to the West of us.
Come home, come home."

—Eskimo Song

Notice in this poem, how fragile language is; it is barely able to hover above the silence and is every-moment about to be taken back into the Silence.

Thus, this language repeats itself, trying to find a firm foothold in the world, as if it is trying to learn how to live. There is also a kind of fear in this poem; the poem expresses being thrown out of silence into the world of speech, and the fear attendant upon that, and also the fear of being thrown back into silence and losing the word. In this double position of holy fear, language, speech has its greatest power.

Another place of language that recovers the Silence of language is Fairy Tales. Fairy Tales are so simple that it is as if they could disappear at any moment. The events in fairy stories are always quite simple. Everything is strange and mysterious; nature is mixed up with the spirit world; in fairy stories, we have not quite left the Silence that is the spiritual world, but have left it enough so that the events occur in the world, but the world is filled with magic.

Exercise: Read or tell a fairy tale.

Images and Silence
A. Images as Silent Language

The reality of images reveals to us that we cannot simply oppose silence and language; there is, so to speak, a between-station, a reality that is on the way from silence to language; this is the reality of images. Images, in the form of dreams, but also other forms, such as myths, painting and in particular icons, can keep us close to the worlds of Silence --- under the condition that we do not seek to interpret images.

> "*Each time you say what an image means, you get your face slapped....the dream*
>> *becomes a Koan...if you literalize a meaning, 'interpret' a dream, your are off*
>>> *the track, have lost your Koan. For the dream is the thing, not what it means.*"

> —James Hillman

So, the point of images is to be with them, alertly. Doing so, we develop the capacity to remain aware of the reality of silence. If we bypass images as we come into language and speaking, it is nearly impossible to remember the silence, for when there is the absence of language, we do not have silence, but emptiness. We need images as the connectors that keep us connected with silence on the one hand and language that carries silence on the other. The silent images of things in the soul bring their silence to the words which are the life of the mind; through the silence of images soul and mind are kept in connection. When we speak without images, without a feeling for the presence of the image, then our words have too much freedom. Images are like a centripetal force; They exist as an inward moving force, one that keeps the soul in a motion toward silence. Words, on the other hand are a like a centrifugal force – the move outward, away from the center of silence. This between-realm of images – between silence and speech, is essential to keeping speech in connection with silence. Once we have a sense of the importance of images in relation to silence, we also have access to another way of knowing. With words we have knowledge. The soul, however, existing close to Silence, has something else than knowledge, related to the way in which soul images hold together past, present, and future in a unity. Time collapses in knowledge – this is the way it is, so says knowledge. No time in knowledge But time expands with images, and instead of knowing something we enter into the realm of premonition. Premonition does not only mean a foreboding of the future, it also means a remembering of what has happened, both at once. Images are "time-knowing" not intellect-knowing.

B. Iconostasis

We typically miss the silence of our dreams because the ego is strongly oriented toward capturing the dream, to try and make sure that something is not going on that it is not a part of. If we can work to release this anxiety on the part of the ego to have to know what is going on, we then come into connection with the silence of dreams. Dreams, when sensed without the strong interference of the ego are more like icons. Iconostasis refers to the borderland, the region of images between our world and the invisible world. A dream is a creation coming to us from the spiritual world, clothed usually with the materials with which we are familiar from our lives. To work with the silence of dreams, it is necessary to try and hold the whole of the dream, all at once; it then becomes more like an icon, poised right there between the spiritual world and the earthly world.

When a dream is held in this manner, then, as it gradually fades away from our consciousness during the day, the dew of the silence then flows down, filling our day world with the invisible, creative silence.

Exercise: Contemplate an icon for a few moments. Here, in this icon, as in all icons, Silence is tangible, palpable. Describe your experience of being with this icon.

"The holy icons of the Eastern Church were painted as experiences of the creation of the world; the pencil drew the outlines – this was the manifestation as such; the gold-leaf plated the spaces where the divine should show forth – and light was born; the outlines were now etched in color – and the potential world came into being. Finally the visible world appeared. The icons was the purest, the guaranteed form of Imagination, whereas worldly painting is always in danger of being dragged into mere display of things or of day – dreams – it is always tempted to show things not as creations of light but as being struggling against light with all the might of their shadows." – Emire Zolla, <u>The Uses of Imagination and the Decline of the West</u>).

Examples of Silence in art – The Greek temples; Greek and Egyptian statues; the Pyramids; the Sphinx; The Cathedrals; Chinese Painting; the paintings of the Old Masters.

IV. The World as Personified in Silence and Solitude

A. How Silence and Solitude differs from other "disengaged" experiences
  Silence as different from loneliness, isolation, privacy, alienation; these experiences are more emotional states; Silence is not a specific emotional state, but can include all emotions.
  Loneliness is an emotion – the unpleasant feeling of longing for some kind of human interaction.

Exercise; Remember a time, a specific moment in which you felt lonely. Write a description of that experience of feeling lonely.

Characteristics of loneliness:
    a. unsatisfied desire for someone the world changes in loneliness – becomes
    b. distant, or cold, or irritating a strong sense of oneself as separate; a large gap felt

Silence is not an experience of isolation, but rather, an experience of communion. It is thus, entirely possible to experience silence while being in the midst of others, and when not with others, in Silence, we are not only in communion with the substance of Silence, but also in communion with the spiritual worlds.

B. Silence as the Wholeness of all Emotion

Even though silence is not a particular emotion, it is not emotionless. We might imagine silence as the fullness the completeness of emotion, what emotion is meant to be when it is not invaded by ego consciousness, which takes the wholeness of emotion apart and tries to use pieces of it in order to be able to feel itself. Silence is not happy or sad or angry or filled with longing, or melancholic or joyful. We often speak of this wholeness of emotion as "peace", or calm, which do not quite convey the active qualities of silence.

The word "wholeness" is pretty abstract. It is perhaps better to try and describe the way in which this wholeness operates than leave it with this abstract term. In Silence, everything becomes personified. We begin, quite readily and quite naturally, to speak with the trees, the birds, the sky, with animals and plants, as if they were human. This way of perceiving Silence, as a world of beings, is certainly not projection; we are not attributing human qualities to things that are not human. The personification that occurs when we travel in the worlds of Silence is a special kind of personification – it has to do with the immediate experience of everything, absolutely everything as living, spiritual beings. In Silence, we are in a kind of in-between world – between the earthly world and the spiritual world. We are actually speaking with the spiritual presences that are each of the things of the world.

In Silence, the things of the world – of the natural world, and animals, and even things of the constructed world, reveal themselves as mirrors of some other realm. We do not enter into the spiritual worlds when we enter into silence, but more something like the vestibule of the spiritual worlds. In this vestibule, the spiritual worlds mirror themselves in the things around us. We thus are able, at a certain level of our sensing and our perceiving, to experience the spiritual worlds and beings being mirrored in the things around us. The natural way in which we begin to speak with the surrounding world when in silence is simply the most natural and non-self-conscious way of recognizing that the spiritual worlds are worlds of beings. How do you speak or relate with a spiritual being? Certainly, not as an it, but as a Thou.

What is most striking about silence is that the fullness of the physical world is not left behind and that the spiritual nature of the world around us is immediately experienced. In silence we have immediate evidence of the spiritual worlds. Here we are not trafficking in projection, nor in symbolism. A further aspect of this experience – when we enter into the Silence, we no longer have need for concepts to tell us about the things of the world. The world of Silence has its own laws of knowing; it is not a world devoid of knowing, but rather a world of another, a different way of knowing altogether. It is a world of knowing through interaction, through meeting, being together, very much the way we know another person; through engagement.

Freeing the Soul From Fear

A Course of the School of Spiritual Psychology

I. Introduction

A. Description of the School of Spiritual Psychology

-purpose of the School

The School of Spiritual Psychology has as its aim helping people to develop embodied conscious soul life that is open and receptive to the spiritual worlds. The work is of individual importance, but the individual in this work is never separated from the culture and from the wider world. The purpose of the work of spiritual psychology is to bring the soul life to bear on the challenges and opportunities in the world. We seek to help others bring soul life into the wider world.

- when we began

The School of Spiritual Psychology began in 1992.

- what we do

The School offers seminars throughout the country, soul retreats, correspondence courses, and individual consultation in Spiritual Therapeutics. The School also maintains a website:

http://www.spiritualschool.org

- how the school functions

The programs of the School of Spiritual Psychology are practically oriented. It is not a School per se that we offer, but a Schooling – various practices to help develop embodied, conscious soul life that is open and receptive to the spiritual worlds. The School is not academic in nature, though the work is thoughtful and requires the development of inner discipline.

B. Text for this course:
Freeing the Soul from Fear by Robert Sardello
(The book comes with the Course)

C. Instructions for this Correspondence Course

1. Begin by reading through this booklet. First, simply read through the whole booklet. Do not try to understand everything you read. Just read through it, take it in as a whole. This is an important step because spiritual psychology always works as a whole. So, you want to begin by taking in the whole of what is presented. It will then begin to work on your soul. The booklet looks small, but it is packed.

2. Then, a couple days after you have simply sat down and read the whole document, begin to read this now for understanding, and in relation with the chapters in the book *Freeing the Soul from Fear.* Proceed at a pace that is comfortable for you. When you come to something that is puzzling or seems to be difficult, stop. Try to think of an experience that seems to relate to what is being talked about in the text. When you feel you have an inner image of what is being talked about, proceed. If you have lingering questions, write them down. Send these questions to Robert at;
spiritualschool@embarqmail.com
and you will receive a response.

3. There are two assignments in this course. Send in one assignment a time. Do not do the next one until you hear back from the School with a response to your first assignment.

The first assignment consists of writing your responses to practice **1 through 8.** Exercise 8 occurs at the very end of chapter 3. Send these responses via email to: spiritualheart@embarqmail.com

The second assignment consists of writing your responses to the rest of the practices. Send these responses also on email to the same address. While it is suggested that you keep a journal in which you write your responses to the practices, submit only one to two paragraph length responses to each of the practices.

4. When you do hear back, *it will be in the form of a audio recording sent to you via email,* then, go over the comments made to your work. Then, go back and read the whole of this booklet over again. Then, when you are ready, complete the second assignment and send it to the School. You will receive comments back, again, *in the form of an audio recording*

sent to you via email. When you receive the second set of comments, this will complete this seminar. Send all assignments to:

Expect that it will take a week for your assignment to   reach the School from the time of mailing. The School will take about two weeks to work with your assignment, putting it in line with other assignments that come it. Then, expect another week for the comments to be returned to you.

Send your responses to:

Also, periodically, audio recordings will be sent out to all taking the course.

This course has been constructed to follow the book, ***Freeing the Soul from Fear***, quite closely. After you read a section or two over for the second time, then read the chapter with the same title in the book. Between the two, and more importantly, by doing the suggested assignments, not only an understanding of the soul nature of fear will clarify, you will, more importantly, be able to face multiple fears with an inner strength that is developed through this work.

Chapter One: Stepping into the Perils of Fear

A central spiritual task of our time consists in working in the right way with fear. The wrong way would be to put ourselves in a hothouse; that is, it would be ultimately harmful if we arranged our lives in such a manner that we were completely insulated from fear. Our contemporary culture approaches fear in this manner by acting as if external measures of every sort could get rid of fear. Terrible fears exist in the world. The spiritual work of this time consists of, in the face of fears, developing capacities of inner strength. Rather than try to solve the problem of fear by re-arranging all our external circumstances, the point of view of spiritual psychology begins from the inside and works outward.

Freeing the Soul from Fear works with a number of different kinds of fears. I show how various world-conditions result in ongoing anxiety and fear images that live on in the soul, producing ongoing trepidation. Suggestions are provided for balancing these images of fear with images that strengthen the soul life.

What happens when we live in fear?

1. The sense of threat to one's life; to one's livelihood; or health; or comfort - these are the results of fear, what it produces - but not the actual experience of fear itself; important to be able to imagine the moment of fear.

2. In the actual moment of fear; we experience our very central nature being obliterated, wiped out; we are seen/treated as something completely foreign to anything we know

3. Fear begins to infect soul life when we are pulled from ourselves and become unknown to ourselves; the central core of our being begins to crumble; if, once this happens, we succumb, then, from that moment fear lives in us, even though the initial bodily and emotional reactions subside.

4. Fears - tear us from the fabric of our relations with the body, time, others, the world.

5. Living in fear establishes a different sense of who we are - we become an isolated I (ego) rather than an authentic I; I is not an inner reality, but rather the matrix of all our relations, not just with others, but more importantly, with Earth; fear establishes the illusion of an inner, isolated I, the necessary illusion of a self. If we did not experience a sense of self, well, we would be true mystics or true Buddhist initiates.

(Note for the student. The exercises for the first assignment begin here and include all the exercises from here through page to the end of chapter 3. The first assignment consists of exercises 1-8.

In your writing, indicate the number of the exercise you are describing. The number of the exercise is indicated in a parenthesis at the beginning of each

(1) Write short responses to the following questions.
1. Describe in detail a situation in your life in which you experienced deep fear. Focus on the following; what was the setting?; what was your perception of the world in that moment of fear and how did it change from the time prior to the experience?; how did time change?; what did your body feel like?; how did the experience run its course?; What did you experience when the fear was resolved?

The purpose of this question is to begin developing the capacity to stay with and observe your experience in an engaged but objective way and finding language to express it without theorizing, explaining, or psychologizing about it. Description is a way of coming to the phenomenon itself.

2. Describe a situation in your life when you felt ongoing fear but did not or could not get rid of it. How did you work with this experience? How did it change you?

Chapter Two: The Body in Fear

This chapter describes how fear affects our body. Our body contracts when we become afraid. Blood rushes to the center of the heart. The sympathetic nervous system activates, adrenalin is produced, the heart pounds, the kidneys become active. Our breathing becomes shallow. We feel separated from the world and from others, as if an invisible window stands between us and the rest of the world. When we live in constant fear, this contraction then also goes on in soul life. At first, imagination goes wild and we have all kind of fantasies connected with our fears. Then, after a while, imagination shuts down altogether and we become numb. The senses become dulled and nothing seems alive anymore. And life itself does not seem worth much anymore. It is very important to work in conscious ways to keep the senses open and flexible and help our body to go through fears without shutting down or narrowing the possibilities of experience. The following questions and exercises provide suggestions for retraining a liveliness of bodily life and therefore of soul life.

Try this exercise suggested by Rudolf Steiner and described for developing soul qualities of perception. Go outside on a clear, cloudless day, and concentrate on the blue of the sky, for a long time. Fill yourself completely with the blue of the sky. Exclude as best you can all memories, all thoughts. Feel the presence of the blue. **Become the blue in every fiber of your body and experience. Then, close your eyes and** turn your attention inward. Just be present to the feeling qualities of your interior experience, what exists there, holding your thoughts in abeyance as long as you can. Describe what you experienced in carrying out this exercise - both of the act of concentration and of turning attention inward. See if you can do this exercise three or four times. After doing the exercise several times, did your experience of the world, of the things around you, both natural and human-made, change in any way? Describe how. Describe how your perception of another person changed.

There are four senses, which give us the inner experience of our body - the sense of touch, the life sense, the sense of balance, and the sense of movement. These senses become dulled when we live in fear over a long period of time. These senses, how they are affected by fears and how to keep these senses from dimming are described in this chapter.

You can work on these four senses further, doing the following working with the senses in relation to the natural world. Begin, though, with this orienting practice:

Orienting Practice for being within Earth Presence
   a)   Enter into Silence and place attention in the interior of the heart
   b)   Allow the felt forces of the heart to flow into your legs and feet and into the ground.
   - while you are breathing in, imagine that you are drawing your breath from the depths of the Earth.
   - while you are breathing out, imagine that you are releasing your breath towards the expanse of the cosmos.
   - then, after a while, reverse the process – draw your breath from the cosmos, and while breathing out, let it glide into the Earth. –

   c)   return to attention within the heart; this is your 'cloak of protection' - feel heart-presence move from being within you to you being within the heart.
   d)   stay within the heart; listen to your surroundings – do not start to explore on your own but let the place talk to you as you move around; wait patiently for the place to reveal itself to you in your own way. Notice the emotional/intuitive qualities.
   e) when you come to a place that seems to be drawing you to it; turn your back on the place – try to get clear – emotionally/intuitively about the qualities of the place by 'absorbing' them through the back of the heart.
   f) approach something in that place – a tree, a shrub, branches... whatever pulls you; touch this presence very lightly between your hands; listen to your feelings that may stream through your hands.

Then, do these sensory practices

The sense of touch

Carefully describe the moment of touching something in the natural world in the practice above. What did you feel? How did the experience affect any anxieties you were living with?

The Life Sense

Describe the relaxed walk where you were being pulled toward something. Recall the qualities of the world you experienced through your senses. Our sense experience are the adjectival aspects, the verb aspects, rather than the noun aspects of the world; for example, the flowing of the stream, or the gentle fluttering of the leaves, the billowing of the clouds, the spreading valley.

The sense of movement

Describe your experience of the subtle movements of your body as you were relaxed and letting the natural world move you rather than have the intention of 'going to something'.. the in and out movement of breathing, the movement of your eyes, the small movements of your hands.

The sense of balance

Describe your individual relation with the earth and how you keep in connection with the actual physicality of the earth during your walk. Describe your individual relation with the earth beneath your feet in relation with the sky above. Describe how you keep these two realms of experience connected.

Chapter Three: Terrorism, Time Collapse, and Anger

Chapters three, four, and five work with some of the ways fear now shows up in the world and how to work to keep imagination and soul life active to balance different kinds of fears. It is too abstract to think of fear as a single response to something that threatens us. There are different qualities of fear, related to the different sources of fear in the world. Each kind of fear works to diminish soul life. Each form of fear diminishes some specific capacity of soul life. In order to work with fears in a healthy way, we have to notice which soul capacity is reduced, consciously work to develop that capacity through specific concentration exercises, and then learn to work consciously with that soul capacity in daily life. Something that was previously natural, some soul ability, gets shut down when we live in fear. We do have the power to make sure that the soul capacity is not permanently affected. Only then is it possible to do something to counter the specific fear without creating more fear in the process.

Each of these fears and how to restore the soul's vitality is covered in each of the three chapters. The following exercises amplify what is spoken in those chapters. Some of the exercises are in the book but are stated here in more detail so that they can be done more accurately.

Write a description telling what you were doing when you heard of the terrorist attack on the World Trade Center. What was your response? How has this event affected you? How do you work with the fear brought by this destructive act? Choose another world event of fear that has affected you deeply and work with the same questions.

Include in your description consideration of how this event seems to affect soul life, bodily life, and spiritual life in an ongoing way. What are you doing as an individual to balance the fear inspired by these events?

The kind of soul work that must be done to balance the presence of terrorism in the world is to develop the capacity to experience our body as a living activity. This exercise is in Freeing the Soul from Fear, but now you have the chance to do the exercise more carefully.

1. first, focus on the inner image of your physical being. Feel the force of gravity working in your body and in the weight of your limbs. Remember a time when you were ill and felt the heaviness of your body. Or, remember coming home after a long hike, sitting down and feeling the weight of your body. Experience the crystallizing processes of the body; remember growing up, how flexible your body once was, and how it gradually became more solid.

2. direct your attention to the fluid processes of the body. Picture the force of the blood gushing forth from the heart, flowing outward, slowing down in channels, almost coming to a standstill in the capillaries. Picture your blood collecting again in slow streams, which, with greater and greater speed return to the heart, disappearing in a whirlpool in the right chamber of the heart. Experience the initial surge as well as the standstill in the vortex when re-entering the heart.

- picture the fluids flowing into the stomach and large intestine and being re-absorbed by the large intestine. This motion is like the in and out movement of the tide on a beach.

- picture the lymph slowly flowing through the body, around the cells, quietly merging into the bloodstream.

- picture the cerebral fluid bubbling up into the cerebral cavity, bathing the brain and the spinal cord, and then re-absorbed again down in the spinal column.

- picture the air entering the lungs, dividing into thousands of air sacs, where the movement of air comes to a rest. Then picture the air mixing with the blood and being carried throughout the body, giving new life. Then picture breathing out carbon-dioxide, collected from all over the body. Picture the carbon-dioxide returning to the air, being taken up by plants and trees, and plant life releasing oxygen.

- feel the inner warmth of the body. The highest temperature occurs in the digestive organs, while the coolest part of the body is the skin and limbs. Picture warmth radiating from your body. Picture being enthusiastic and how this converts into bodily warmth; how body warmth lightens the body and overcomes fatigue.

(adapted from Bernard Lievegoed, <u>Man on the Threshold</u>)

The second part of Chapter 3 concerns the fears that now center on our experiences of time....the anxiety that we don't have enough time, or that time is speeding up, or that there doesn't seem to be much time life.

Take a portion of a day and venture into the world. Go to three places in which time is experienced in three different ways.. Describe each of these places briefly; then make an image - in the form of words - of the qualities of each of these places. Finally, describe the time of each place. Does the experience of time speeding up relate in any way to the fears we now have to live with around the presence of terrorism?

The fears around the experience of time have to do with the fact that tempo has come to dominate the experience of time while the experience of duration is being lost. We can consciously restore the experience of duration through any kind of meditation. In relation to the experience of time, it is not the type or the result of meditating that is important, but the fact that it takes us into a different and needed quality of time. The following exercise is described in the chapter. Do the exercise and write description of the meditation as you experienced it and how the meditation changed the experience of time for you.

Make an inner image of a paper clip. Then begin to circle this image with all the ideas that belong to the paper clip: it is made of metal; it is oblong in shape; it holds papers together; it comes in different sizes; it can be used over and over again. Then, you take all of the ideas and try to make them live within one idea. This is like taking a progression of ideas and condensing them so that they all live within one idea. Then, dwell for a time with this one idea.

The intention of this exercise is not to have some sort of spiritual experience, but rather to enter into the experience of duration. At first, our thoughts go from one aspect of the object to another. Then it begins to feel like the whole idea is there all at once. Going from one thought to another has a tempo; gradually this yields to duration.

The third part of this chapter works with the ways in which anger is increasing in the world and the fears anger brings. There is not an exercise in the chapter that works with anger. Here is an exercise. It is somewhat difficult and requires practice; it is an exercise through which we can become aware of the anger that lives within us that instills fear in us and in others and makes possible the healing of anger..in ourselves and in the world.

Remember an incident in which you experienced being angry. Make an inner image of that incident.... what happened, who was there, the course of the experience. Once you have an inner image of that incident, then back up the picture to the moment before the anger occurred. Feel what it was like right before the anger; try to feel the anger as it emerges from that moment right before. Through this exercise you can begin to get a sense how anger is often autonomous; it is as if it has a life of its own. Once you have the presence of mind to sense this autonomous nature of anger you will be less prone to letting anger take you over. As anger decreases in you, so will fear.

Chapter 4: Perennial Fears with a New Sting: Money, Relationships, Suffering, and Death

Our relationship with money is the one of the biggest sources of fear in our lives. We are living in volatile economic times, with many unstable

economic factors, such as:

downsizing

stock market fluctuations

corporate greed

debt
job insecurity
rising prices
decreasing income
recession
depression

Money fears are different now than they have been in the past. Money is now more abstract, and the manipulation of the economy is now the typical practice of the Federal Reserve Bank, the stock market, the precious metals market, and corporations. Many of the economic schemes such as lowering interest rates and giving tax refunds do not seem to produce the desired results. Something seems radically wrong with our economic thinking. For most of us, the fears around money have much to do with the way we are treated in our jobs. Most of us would be happy to earn less money if our jobs were fulfilling and meaningful. And, if the world did not put so much value into money and had more a sense of inner wealth, money fears would lessen. We do not go to work anymore; we go to be worked. The soul sense of doing a work in the world no longer exists, so money becomes the primary motivation for work. We might work on the fears around money better by working to restore a soul and spirit dimension to our work. This chapter begins with this concern. The following exercise begins to restore the sense of our jobs as spiritual work as well as world-work. The exercise is presented in the chapter.

Picture in your imagination a scene that is typical of your daily job. You may, for example, picture writing at a computer, or teaching a class, or preparing a legal document, or laying bricks - whatever your job consists of in its most daily way. Then, when you have this inner picture and have stabilized the image so that it does not disappear or change into something else, dissolve this picture into a ball of light. Then let this light re-form into a figure - the figure of a man or a woman, though it may take other forms, such as a troll or an angel or another sort of being. Then ask this being - What is your work in the world? What does this figure say? Carry on a conversation with the figure about its work. After the conversation is completed, thank the being and let the figure again dissolve into a ball of light and then let the light return to your own image of your job.

Write a description of what you experienced.

Fear, Soul and Re-Imagining Money

We must eradicate from the soul all fear and terror of what comes toward man from the future.

We must acquire serenity in all feelings and sensations about the future.

We must look forward with absolute equanimity to all that may come, and we must think only that whatever comes is given to us by the world direction full of wisdom.

It is part of what we must learn in this age.

Namely, to live out of pure trust, without any security in existence.

Trust in the ever-present help of the spiritual world.

Truly, nothing else will do.

Let us discipline our will and let us seek the awakening from within ourselves, every morning and every evening.

— Rudolf Steiner

We are experiencing a great spiritual moment in the unfolding of human-earth destiny. We can tell that this is indeed a significant spiritual moment because all that we rely on and lean on in the outer world is being removed. New foundations of civilization are being prepared; the past is going, going, gone. We are thus being asked to rely on our soul-being, and the soul's openness to the inner presence of the I AM. This moment may well extend for a long, long time. The inner task of such an evolutionary moment is that of relinquishing the false hope of a recovery from the breaking open of the illusory life, and to also see that the Light comes through the opening.

When what we rely on begins to recede, all fear existing within the sub-conscious surfaces. Those fears, when not faced in healthy ways, get projected onto others and onto our pre-formed ideas of what is going on in the world. Such projections are certainly not harmless. Not only do they separate us from ourselves, from others, from the world, and from the spiritual worlds, they also take on an autonomy and become part of 'world-substance.' We thus find ourselves swimming in a seemingly endless sea of astral fear.

The crack in the wall of money

Autonomous fear can only be dissolved through insight. First, insight, and then a shift of consciousness from the region of mental, binary thinking (i.e. thinking in terms of opposites – good and evil, right and wrong, have or not have, do or not do, etc.) into heart presence and heart-thinking.

It is so interesting that the proposed solutions to the 'financial' crisis are not able to look at the assumptions inherent in the definition of money; rather, money, as currently defined is taken as inviolable, and the way through the crisis is seen as the task of restoring confidence in a definition of money that is **inherently** filled with fear. Money is defined as "a unit of account, a store of value, and a medium of exchange." As soon as money is defined as a 'store of value", fear and greed are introduced into an archetypally feminine reality, shifting it into an archetypally masculine reality concerned with power and control. We have lived within this latter reality for centuries. It has been central to the spiritual initiation of the planet, a first phase, having to do with the practical grappling with fear.

It is not at all essential to money that 'a unit of account and a store of value' be part of its definition. What is essential to the definition is that it is a 'medium of exchange.'

There were two notable times when money was defined as a medium of exchange, and the notion of it being a 'store of value' was deliberately excluded. This occurred for a time, in Egypt, and was associated with reverence to Isis. Another time was the several centuries surrounding the building of Chartres Cathedral, associated with reverence to the Black Madonna, a spiritual evolution of Isis, and also associated with the Templars.

During these times, there were formal regulations that worked against the holding of money. In France, at the time of the building of Chartres Cathedral, which is the living presence of Sophia in the world, her presence as having to do with the future, people were required to turn all their money in to the government every four years. The money was then re-issued, at the same rate. However, the more money one turned in, the less new money was returned. Saving money was discouraged. If one had money, it was put into the infrastructure and into long-term 'money-attractors' such as the Cathedrals – which were not owned by the Church, but by the citizens and the community. When money was defined solely as a 'medium of exchange' *fears surrounding money did not exist.*

Financial fear is thus deliberately constructed and manipulated fear for the sake of power and control, which of course then gets out of control. Further, the fear that is touched off is the already existing sub-conscious fear of being separated from the spiritual worlds, an inherent fear that is born by defining money as a store of value. Our fears concerning money, in their deepest sense, are not about money, but about the separation from the divine brought about with the definition of money as a store of value. Money as a medium of exchange is simply the way the beneficence of the Feminine is circulated in the world. It is a tangible presence of the divine worlds, and thus free of fear.

When money shifted to a store of value as well as a medium of exchange, the archetypal backing of money shifts from the Feminine to instability and control (archetypally represented by Dionysus and Apollo, gods of mania and control). Thus, periodically, quite often in fact, this money system is characterized by periods of financial 'bubbles, panic, and regulation.'

The current financial crisis will seem to be solved by bailouts, economic stimulus packages, and a new "New Deal". It is illusory but can give time for us to inwardly develop new imaginations of working with money.

Here are some suggestions for working with fear in relation to money:

We must develop the awareness of how much we like and live out of fear. No one would admit it; it is subconscious. Fear is necessary to the defining of our egotistical selves. There will be tremendous resistance to looking at our fear, the tendency to escape into mentalness, and projecting onto others. It is helpful to do a personal 'fear inventory' as it will diminish projection.

This is a momentous time of spiritual opportunity, a time when a creative, inner working with the heart can produce a right perception of fear as always giving us something to come up against, which builds inner capacities. Fear is, or can be, a spiritual 'helper'.

It is extremely important to know that much of the present money crisis is the result of greed, power, and manipulation. Most of us know that. What has to be worked with is the anger, disgust, and fear that lurks as an automatic conscious or sub-conscious response to this situation. These responses, when sub-conscious, are felt as anxiety. The right response must be of a spiritual and of a soul nature.

All emotional reactions to money provide the needed opportunity to engage in a soul purification. Our soul life is extraordinarily confused in this time – the doubt, fear, anger, violence, manipulations, lying, cheating, killing, power…. related to money, has entered the astral realm and makes collective and individual soul life filled with concerns of survival rather than the presence of the Light. No one is free of this confusion. It cannot be cleared by any psychological means.

Creative work with clearing fears around money requires developing new inner capacities. Heart presence is central. The interior of the heart (different than the heart chakra) is inviolable to fear. Here is a primary practice for developing the capacities of the heart:

1. Entering into the Silence – Silence is not just 'being quiet'. It is an actual, substantial reality. You can sense it, if, by sitting, relaxing, eyes, closed, you then place your attention at the periphery of the body. Anywhere, at the periphery. You will feel as if you are being lightly touched. Anywhere at the periphery of the body where you place your attention, you will notice this quality. Do not, though, simply think about the periphery of the body; actually place your attention there – as if attention were a kind of 'object'. Then, when you feel this quality of feeling, let your attention go into that place of 'touch', and you will be within the Silence. (See, Robert Sardello, **Silence; The Mystery of Wholeness**, North Atlantic Press)

2. When you have entered the Silence, place attention into the center of the heart. Don't 'think' you are there; place your attention there. There will be a moment when it feels like, rather than being in the heart, the hear space surrounds your body. Practice staying within the heart in contemplation for as long as you comfortably can. If this practice is done regularly, at a given time, even for a short time, daily, the capacities of the heart will develop.

a) Be present to others through an 'empathy of the heart'. It is what Steiner called the "new yoga of light." It's easy. After entering the heart space described above, when you are with others, you listen from the heart. Different than waiting for someone to stop speaking so you can interject the idea you've been trying to get across. Let what is to happen emerge.

Fear and Relationships

A second area where fear has always visited but seems to be doing so with much greater intensity these days is in our relationships. Among the many ways fear shows up in our connections with others are:

harassment

co-dependency

divorce

betrayal

disloyalty

abuse

hatred

anger

revenge

abandonment

Fears enter into relationships particularly when there has not been practice in developing a conscious soul connection in our connections with others. We typically simply expect relationships to work based on initial attraction or mutual need, or mutual interest, or familial ties. Then, when strife comes, fear increases and finds a foothold within the relationship itself. A new form of developing relationships is needed to assure that fear does not so easily insert itself. This new form of relating consists of developing soul empathy for the other person.

Practice this exercise with another individual

One person tells the other person what their most significant fears are and how they work in his or her life. Then, after fifteen minutes, the other person of the pair talks, focusing on the same theme. The full exercise is to be carried out as follows:

The first aspect of this exercise consists of consciously turning our attention toward our partner in an attitude of openness to the existence and destiny of the other person. Speak with each other; introduce yourself, tell each other a bit about yourselves - become interested in each other, but not out of curiosity, or self-interest. Try to be completely interested in the other person. Tell your partner some of your most significant fears and how they work in your life. You must find this capacity to be completely interested in another person within yourself, and identify it clearly; it feels like an open space, but one that you have to find, first by being aware of whatever motives might be present, and, in effect, being aware of them as best as possible, releasing them until this open space can be located. Locating this capacity is a conscious process; it will not be there in the foreground of consciousness, which is going to be filled with all of our self-concerns. Once activated, self-concerns dominate. Thus, there must be an initial, conscious clearing of these interests. This clearing is not a mental process, but one of getting out of usual mental processes and moving into an inner soul region of silence. Look for it and you will find it.

The second aspect of this activity consists of dwelling, for a short time, within the inner qualities of the other person. This phase is the most difficult. It does not consist of our usual way of knowing. The more we want to know, the less possible it becomes to achieve this particular way of meeting the inner qualities of the other person. What can be experienced lies more in the nature of a feeling but does not consist of what I feel about the other person. The feeling quality is more like a mood, a color, a sea of impressions that one dwells within in a purely receptive way, not being concerned about remembering what is experienced.

The third part of the exercise consists of returning home, to the part of ourselves that was left in encountering the other person. An echo or resonance of what was experienced while dwelling in a feeling-knowing way within the interior of the other person remains; this resonance now lives within us as an inner image of the soul of the other person. Such an image can gradually be brought to understanding through contemplation.
Then, reverse the procedure and the listener now becomes the speaker. After completing this part of the exercise, speak with your partner, tell of the soul image you have of him or her.

Write a description of your experience of this exercise.

Chapter 5: The Ecology of Fear

The spiritual significance of fear has to do with the way that fears gradually are entering into the world and will eventually change our outer world, and in fact, already have to a great extent. That fears can enter the outer world and bring about changes there is something quite hard to accept as it requires a different mode of consciousness to see this is so. Rudolf Steiner, a gifted clairvoyant and founder of Anthroposophy, said the following regarding fears:

1. from: Guidance in Esoteric Training, pp. 105-110

"Esoteric life consists to a large extent in learning to interpret correctly the subtle processes in oneself and in one's environment. The old Moon consciousness, also, has not completely vanished: the last vestiges of it remain. Both the old Moon-consciousness and the new Jupiter-consciousness are to be found in the human being of today; the former in feelings of shame, the latter in feelings of fear and anxiety. In feelings of shame, in which the blood is pushed up towards the surface of the body, to its periphery, there live the last vestiges of Moon-consciousness. In feelings of anxiety, in which the blood flows back toward the heart, the Jupiter-consciousness announces itself. Our normal day-consciousness branches out in these two directions."(pg. 106)

"We have seen that the new Jupiter-consciousness is already announcing itself in the capacity for fear and anxiety. But it is always so that when a future condition appears too early it is premature and out of place. You can understand this through an example: a flower which should bloom in August can be 'forced' in a hothouse so that it flowers already in May. In August, the time of its proper flowering, no further blossom can unfold: its strength is exhausted, and it can no longer find its right place within the conditions to which it belongs. In May, also, it will die the moment it is taken out of the hothouse, since it does not belong in the context of that season. It is the same with feelings of anxiety. They have no place today and will have one still less in the future. What occurs when we feel anxious? The blood is driven back into the center of the human being, into the heart, in order to form a firm central point and make the human being strong in opposition to the outer world. It is the inmost power of the 'I' which does this. This power of the 'I', which affects the blood, must become ever stronger and more conscious; on Jupiter the human being will then be able to direct the blood to his central point quite

consciously, so as to make himself strong. What is harmful and unnatural today, however, is the feeling of fear which is connected with this flow of the blood. In the future that must no longer be so; only the powers of the 'I' without any fear must be active." (pg.107)

"Throughout human evolution, the outer world becomes ever more antagonistic towards us. You must learn, increasingly, to set your inner strength against this outer world that presses upon you. But anxiety must vanish. It is very especially necessary for anyone who proceeds with an esoteric training to free himself from all feelings of fear and anxiety. Anxiety only has a certain justification in making us aware that we need to make ourselves strong; but all unnatural feelings of anxiety which torment the human being must disappear altogether. What would happen if the human being should still have feelings of fear and anxiety at the onset of Jupiter-consciousness? The outer world at that stage will be far, far more antagonistic and terrible for the human being than it is so today. Anyone who does not rid himself here of the habit of anxiety will there fall into one dreadful terror after another." (pg. 108)

"Our contemporary culture is itself creating those horrifying monsters which will threaten the human being on Jupiter. You need only look at the huge machines which human technology is today constructing so ingeniously. The human being is creating demons for himself which in the future will rage against him. Everything which he builds today in the way of technical appliances and machines will assume life in the future and oppose him in terrible enmity. Everything which is created for mere utility to satisfy individual or collective egoism, will be the human being's enemy in the future." (pg.108)

Fear is now spreading through the outer world due to the way we thoughtlessly treat the world. Steiner, in the statement above, is not suggesting that we cease creating technological devices. We must, however, become aware that it is necessary to balance in the soul the fear that these device.... some of which are clearly destructive, others which are helpful...bring into the world.

Here are some of the recent world events that have instilled fear now all around us. Even though these events have happened and are finished, the soul effects are permanent and need to be balanced.

World events which picture the spread of fear throughout the physical world:

- the atomic bomb at Hiroshima
- the bomb at Nagasaki
- resumption of nuclear testing by the French
- the landscape of Chernobyl
- the Alaska oil spill
- the smog over Mexico City, Los Angeles, or any large city
- global warming
- floods in California, Oregon
- earthquakes here, Japan
- hurricanes in Florida
- forest fires
- Oil wells burning in Kuwait
- attack on the World Trade Center
- attack on the Pentagon
- attack on the American Embassy in Africa
- release of anthrax
- attack on Afghanistan

Occurrences in the physical world such as these, affect the soul, which then lives with images of fear. This fear, in turn circulates back out into the physical world.

World Events which picture the spread of fear throughout the life world:

- radiation - including radiation employed to preserve vegetables and meats
- chemical pesticides
- chemical fertilizers
- genetic engineering
- cloning
- artificial hormones given to cows to stimulate secretion of milk
- ultraviolet radiation from the hole in the ozone layer
- electromagnetic pollution from electronic appliances, computers, cellular phones, batteries, electric trains, metal refining plants

Fear that circulates now in the natural world due to the things we do to instill fear, can be balanced by exercises which keep the soul's imagination of the natural world awake. Fear dulls this imagination. Here is an exercise that helps keep this vital imaginative capacity central to the life of the soul:

Look at a plant. Then close your eyes and make an exact inner image of that plant. The way to do this is to build up the image. If you look at a plant, close your eyes, and try to make an inner image of the complete plant, it will not be a precise image but either an abstract idea, or a vague memory of what you saw. Instead, close your eyes and build up the stem and one leaf. Then open your eyes and look again. Upon closing your eyes, add the next leaf to the plant. Continue doing this until the complete image has been built up. Naturally, as this is being done, it is necessary to exclude any other images or thoughts that try to intrude. Once the image has been built up, hold the image stable for a few moments. Do not let it fade away or take on other qualities or shift into anything else. Then, in your imagination start removing the plant-image by removing each leaf that has been built up, one by one, starting with the leaf that was added last and proceeding in the reverse order to the building up of the image. When all the leaves have been removed, then remove the stalk. At this point there is an empty void. Hold this void for a few moments, listening into the emptiness.

Write a description of your experience of this exercise.

This kind of exercise strengthens the soul's capacity of receiving the archetypal, creating powers of the plant world. It develops the capacity to sense the creative beings of the natural world. Such soul work also invites those presences back into the life world. Imagination is a real force, not just a subjective, inner state. As we begin to operate more from the conscious capacity of imagination that is connected with the life world, fear also diminishes in the world of life forms because we now take up the responsibility of returning to them what has been taken away. We can tell this addition is indeed taking place because our level of fear and anxiety gradually diminishes.

This exercise, like all of them, but even more so, cannot be done just once. It has to be done on a fairly regular basis for a while ---once a day for a month. After that, do the exercise periodically to check up on whether this aspect of imagination seems awake and capable.

Chapter Six: The Double
Introduction

Fear is usually understood as a bodily response to a threat to our being. It can be a physical threat, but also a threat to our soul. If you become afraid of walking at night because you might be accosted, your body tenses up each time you have to go out at night. That is soul fear. If you are walking at night and are accosted by a thug who pulls a gun and threatens you, that is physical fear you experience. You would feel shock, anger, rapid heartbeat, sweating, and would become faint. We are very familiar with these kinds of fears, and the multitude of reasons we react in fear, but now fear has gone even further. Something is happening in the realm of fear that goes beyond the usual forms.

We are now subjected to what seem to be overwhelming and constant fears from virtually everywhere. Just think of the strength of the presence of fear:

terrorism

economy

suffering/death

relationships

diseases

energy crisis

food contamination

pollution

violence

natural catastrophe's

The content of these and many other fears, you will say, is not much different than what has always brought fear to human beings. Something else, however, is happening. Along with the presence of a continual onslaught of these fears, there is also a collective denial that these fears exist at all. For example, that there is severe climate change has been consistently denied by the government and gosh knows what else is being hidden from us. At the same time, there is a manipulation of fear. We are made to fear when there is nothing apparent to be fearful of. Every mid to large city now has hundreds of video cameras all over town, as if living itself is under threat. Pat Robertson made his 2007 predictions at the beginning of the year and said that God told him that in late 2007 there will be a terrorist attack that will kill thousands. He makes predictions every year and then later says things like: well, the tsunami did not hit in 2006, but the rains in the Eastern part of the U.S. were the fulfilling of what God told me.

We have the seeds in this kind of presence of fear, where fear is present and denied or when there is no fear present and we are made to feel afraid, of a threat not just to our physical being and our soul being, but to our spirit being. It is this last, what might be called Spirit-Filled fear, that I want to introduce and to find right and healthy ways to counter and to balance.

It is a great challenge to try and work with fear without producing more fear in the process. I have the very interesting task of trying to make fear fun. We can do that.

As a kind of symbol, a condensation of what we are going to be working with, the now famous and very great statement by Theodore Roosevelt comes to mind:

" We have nothing to fear but fear itself."

He was saying in an explicit way that people would triumph in that war if they were not afraid. But, the statement, if we pay closer attention to it can be heard as saying:

There are two kinds of fear – the usual sense of fear and now there is a totally new fear in the world, fear itself. Do you see? The usual sense we have of fear is that we fear-something:

I am afraid of dying
I am afraid of losing my job
I am afraid of not having enough money

These senses of fear are very different than FEAR ITSELF. With the overwhelming presence of fear everywhere, fears about everything, coupled with a massive denial of fear brought about principally through excessive materialism. Remember President Busch's way of comforting us when the World Trade Center was hit by terrorists – "Get out and Shop; Go to Disneyland". These words by our leadership express in condensed form the kind of confusion around fear that has the effect of immersing us in FEAR ITSELF because there is total and complete confusion on what to be afraid of.

Usual protective responses to fear are now immobilized. We need only ask, what happens when there is the presence of fear but we have lost the capacity to feel it. It is entirely too easy, and false, to say "well, if you don't feel fear, there is no fear." And, you might further say, "I have not lost the capacity to feel fear. If there is an announcement tomorrow that the bird flu has now actually arrived, that there is a pandemic, I will certainly feel fear." You see, however, that with each presence of fear on this scale, there will be fear, while at the same time there will be something that negates that it is real. We will be told that there is a vaccine, or that it is only the old that are in danger, or that "we thought that it was coming, but it really didn't get here"; or that, as with mad-cow disease, the matter is taken care of --- until the next outbreak." It is true – fear is just below the surface, and that is where it is kept while the rest of the process goes on, the process of keeping it close to the surface where it can eat away at our physical being by producing constant stress, where it can eat away at our soul being by producing an overall contraction of feeling life .... And most of all, where fear itself can produce a particular kind of dimming of the human spirit.

If we could feel the presence of Fear itself, we would live in a decidedly different way. We would not, for example fight against the fear because we would realize that if you fight against this kind of fear it only increases the fear. We have a sense of this with the kind of collective fears we now face. If you fight against terrorism without fully realizing how it is a vehicle for Fear itself, then you increase the presence of fear itself. We have become a version of the terrorists ourselves the way we have approached terrorism. We are watched everywhere, each of us risks being accused of being a terrorist if we happen to carry a pen knife onto a plane. Or, if you have a can of gasoline for your lawnmower, you could be stopped. And, we do not really know how many people have been gathered up, sequestered, questioned, had their phones tapped, been denied rights, have been exported – as counter measures to the fear of terrorism which increase the presence of fear itself.

From a spiritual point of view, the situation of fear in the world is considerably different than we see it from a strictly earthly point of view. In every spiritual practice, for ages, the presence of fear announces the onset of a movement of spiritualizing – either of individuals, or of the world. The evolution of consciousness is not a smooth upward progression. Not by any means. There are gaps and there are regressions. What someone dedicated to spiritual development must above all learn to work with, to meet and encounter and not be taken over by, is fear. Fear can stop all spiritual progress. But it also is the great awakener to the possibility of a huge leap forward into new levels of spiritual awareness. Thus, these times of fear, from a spiritual point of view have to be hailed, and in some ways even welcomed. They signal the possibility, if we can find our way through fear, of the greatest spiritual awakening mankind has yet experienced. This knowledge makes it possible for us to meet whatever comes to us with a quite different sense than cowering and hiding and contracting. It makes us work to find the inner place both of strength and of love to assist in this great moment of shifting into a tremendous expansion of human awareness.

The Doubling Process that produces Autonomous Fear

One of the best pictures we have of the working of fear itself, not fear of this or fear of that, is the way in which the Nazi doctors who experimented on human beings lived. This story is well documented, with a very important understanding by the Yale Psychiatrist Robert J. Lifton, in his book, *The Nazi Doctors*. These doctors functioned under a situation of constant fear for years under Hitler's National Socialism. At the same time, they were constantly told that they were chosen to do research that would undoubtedly save humanity. They lived constantly under this contradiction. They came to a point where they were unable to see anything wrong with the atrocities they performed each day. It was not, however, that these doctors were turned into cruel monsters, or even denied what they were doing. The effect on the doctors of living under constant fear unless they did exactly what they were told, coupled with their understanding of being heroes of humanity, was that two ego's developed in these people, and these two egos existed and functioned alongside each other without any sense of conflict. These doctors' sense of their self, on the one hand was that they were humane physicians, working for the good of the country and for the good of humanity. They also considered themselves good husbands and fathers, were highly cultured in art and music and lived somewhat exemplary lives. Alongside of this sense of ego-life, however, there was the doctor who performed atrocities on a daily basis on people. Torture, operations, infecting people were the order of the day, while dinner, dancing and the opera at night. Without any sense whatsoever of conflict or disparity between the two. Lifton terms the process by which the side-by-side egos develop, the process of **Doubling.**

Doubling, then, occurs when there is constant fear while there are also conditions that not only deny the fear exists, but build up a completely different sense of self than the sense of self under fear. Doubling consists of the forming of a false self alongside the individual self, a self that completely follows outside directions, without, however, knowing that it is doing so. The more that fear intensifies in the world, the greater the possibility that wide-scale doubling will occur without our recognition of it. We do not recognize doubling, first, because it is a spiritual pathology rather than a psychological pathology. The individual spirit is usurped. Second, we do not recognize the syndrome because it is characterized by an increase in cleverness and capacities for lying. Doubling brings about more effectiveness in functional behavior concerned with survival, and the capacity of conscience is completely debilitated. Those who experience doubling do not suffer, but it brings terrible suffering to other individuals, institutions, and culture.

What I want to work to show is that Doubling is in fact the incarnating of Fear itself. That is to say, when people live under a constant ongoing state of fears of every sort, but the constant presence of fear is, on the one hand denied and covered over by an emphasis on every sort of materialism as a way of masking fear, and on the other hand the presence of fear comes out every so often in increasingly strong ways that bring about soul and body contraction --- that if people live under these circumstances they begin to lose the sense of their individual spirit-being. We know of course that when people live under constant fear, they begin to be completely compliant. For example, people who work in sweat shops for terrible wages, and are every moment afraid of being fired and live under constant fear of not having food, clothing, shelter, become compliant and lose individuality. But, the kind of fear I am describing is one step beyond that because Doubling produces a false sense of being perfectly alright. In fact, doubling brings about a sense that one is a very powerful human being. And, doubling usually brings the possibility of having power over others.

We all have a sense of two egos. Typically, in spiritual circles these days, a sense of two egos is spoken of as our lower ego and our higher ego, our lower self and our higher self. And, our spiritual ideal is supposed to be to develop from lower ego to higher ego. In fact, they are both always present.

Our usual sense of ego is our self-identity, who we imagine ourselves to be, which is more a less the accumulation of our history. Thus, when someone asks you to describe yourself, you will usually say something of your history – when and where you were born, where you grew up, went to school, went to college, what you like, and so on. The sense of the higher ego concerns our spiritual being and aspirations and openness to spiritual beings and to the spiritual worlds. Seldom does anyone "leave" the lower ego and live only in the higher sense of ego. We feel both. But we also know the difference. When fear occurs in the manner that I have described, the possibility of becoming aware of and of developing a higher sense of self disappears. It is, in effect, replaced.

It is entirely too abstract to simply speak of the higher self. We need to have a clear understanding and description of what this is. This part of our being, what some speak of as the 'superconscious' is not conscious without the inner effort of development. We are not conscious of our spirit-individuality. Thus, we are very subject to having this central aspect of our being slowly eroded without having much more than a vague sense that something is wrong. We only feel that we have not found our destiny; we do not know what it is, nor how to look for it. We feel a vague, though sometimes sharp feeling of longing for something more in life. And, we have the sense that we want to feel close to spiritual realities, including the spiritual reality of our own being. We feel helped, perhaps, but not fully satisfied with religion as being the source of this inner knowledge and feeling. And, if we are under a state of constant fear, while we might at first seek spiritual help, if the situation of fear does not ease, we begin to lose the sense that there is within us a spiritual center of our being that cannot be touched by any threat at all, no matter how intense or what the source might be. Fear begins to take us over.

If you have had moments of experiencing your higher-self, your true spirit –individuality, it is something quite astounding. It is like entering a vast loving resource that makes itself known to you through immediacy and intimacy of contact. It is not something that you *know about*, because your spirit being is your inner holy sanctum, the holy of holies. Sometimes, church can help bring us to those moments, but without the effort of inner development we cannot stay in touch with this dimension of our being. In the workshop tomorrow we will give some practices that can bring a more vivid and permanent sense of individual spirit-being when practiced regularly over time, since coming to this presence of spiritual love that we are at the very core of our being is the only way that this new kind of fear, fear itself, can be diminished.

It is imperative to recognize the consequences of, first, failing to come to be able to experience the core spirit-individuality that we are, and even more, to have this eroded without our being very aware that this is happening. Doubling is now a rampant spiritual pathology in our culture. It consists of cleverness taking the place of creativity; incredibly cruelty taking the place of selflessness; complete self-centeredness taking the place of community, and force taking the place of true inner power and authority.

We see this kind of spirit pathology taking place with many corporate leaders, politicians, heads of state. When we look at these people, it is easy to see that the person is 'not there', that something has usurped the very core of their being. This pathology cannot be accounted for nor understood by any current psychology because it is not about psychology; it is about the spirit.

With our bodily being we are part of the physical world. With our soul nature we experience inner reality. With our spirit nature, we discover within ourselves the potential for participating consciously in a Divine World. Fear, when it goes unbalanced by other forces, in particular the force of love, erodes the capacity to experience the Divine World. Fear in its psychological dimension has the effect of assuring uniformity. Fear, in its spiritual dimension removes the awareness of being in a world of hope, a world of what Plato called "Potentia".

Potentia is not in some far-off place of archetypes, but is an integral aspect of everything. Potentia, however, is not the same as 'possibility'. What is now possible enters at the next moment into actuality. Potentia does not mean potential, which in the next moment can be the actual. Potentia does not enter into actuality as its cause or prior condition because it is an ongoing aspect of everything. That is, it does not have to enter into actuality for it is more powerful, more effective, more real than the so-called "actual". It is the creative, coming-into-being, coming-into-form of everything. It is the not-yet that shapes how we are oriented to the openness of ourselves, our bodies, others, the world, the cosmos. It is only through potentia that we come into connection with the elementals, the angels, the dead, the spirits – for they are pure potentia and cannot be literally known but only imaginally felt. It is the 'unfinished' of all that exists. Potentia has to do with the unknown, with where we are going, with destiny rather than with fate. It can be experienced, but it cannot be measured. It is the open-endedness of imagination, why imagination can never be a content, but is the not-yet in whatever presents itself, inwardly or outwardly. The experience of potentia is a capacity not a content. It is the capacity of our spirit-individuality. In our spirit-being, we live in the world with the sense of Potentia, of life as full of the unknown, but as constantly unfolding, as constantly feeling ourselves pulled from the future, from what is coming-to-be, rather than being pushed from the past, being fated to do, again, what we have already done.

Carefully write a description of an incident in your life which seem to be an encounter with someone who seems to be doubled. This kind of experience is quite subtle and may be a bit hard to catch hold of. Tell why this experience seem to have the qualities of the appearance of a double and tell how you reacted upon recognizing it, and what was the result of this experience in your life. (It would be well to read over and contemplate the chapter on the double several times before working with this question, not because the material is difficult, but because the phenomenon is not only subtle but also tricky).

The primary protection against doubling in oneself is the strengthening of conscience. Read the chapter on doubling, the section on conscience, to make sure you understand conscience as a soul process rather than moral standards inculcated in us by others. Here is an exercise that will help strengthen the soul process of conscience:

This exercise is called the "Evening Review." In this exercise, the day's events are reviewed in reverse order (starting with the more recent and working backwards), feeling remorse for hurts caused and opportunities missed, and gratitude for help given and received. This requires objective observation and intelligent judgment and evaluation of these events. This exercise should not become a cause of brooding or depression or guilt feelings; the events must be put out of mind after the review has been completed.

The "Evening Review" exercise does the following: a) it trains us to be observant; b) it empties the 'subconscious mind' of fears. Eventually, this exercise can become more of an ongoing conscious process throughout the day, and constitutes a 'prayerfulness' way of living.

Chapter Seven: Love Casts Out Fear
This chapter develops an extensive picture of the many forms of love that
are gifts from the spiritual world to human beings. All love counters fear.
Bodily Love
Emotional Love
Spiritual Love
Creative Love

In the chapter, it is stated that these many modes of love are not
hierarchical; our soul task to experience them all, in depth. Love is One,
whole, but it expresses itself in the world in these multiple ways. There can
be 'gaps' between one mode of love and another mode of love. These 'gaps'
are where bridging forms of love need to be developed and are the most
important forms of love to develop as a counter to fear. Not much is said in
the chapter concerning these bridging forms of love.
Between bodily love and emotional love, the bridging form of love is
self-love.
Between emotional love and spiritual love, the bridging form of love is
friendship.
Between spiritual love and creative love, the bridging form of love is
community.
Do the following heart meditation for three successive days. Write a
description of the inner experience of doing the meditation. How did the
meditation proceed on each of these days? Describe any effects the
meditation produces - bodily, on consciousness, on outlook, on feelings, on
your relationships. The effects might be quite subtle.
Entering the Heart and Emptying
Think of a difficulty or a worry you are currently experiencing in your
life. Make this difficulty into an inner mental image. Then shift this image
from the region of the head into the center of the heart. It disappears there
as a worry or concern, and this is a simple method for shifting into heart
consciousness in a way that you can feel the difference between head
consciousness and heart consciousness.
Then, stay in the heart—keep your consciousness centered in the deep
interior of your heart. Then, with an act of will, empty your heart-
consciousness of any content and apply just enough will-force to keep it

empty. Try to feel the currents that are active in the interior of your heart. Do this exercise for no more than five minutes.

Chapter Eight: Artistic Living

Beauty cannot co-exist with fear. Thus, if we make our lives beautiful, fear has been conquered. This chapter describes how to go about being present in our senses in a soulful way so that we begin to live beauty. Beauty here is not meant to be merely 'aesthetic.' To be able to live in beauty is one of the strongest, most forceful ways to live a conscious soul life. There is nothing sentimental about it.

The exercises suggested in the chapter can seem a bit daunting. I have since realized that some preparation may be needed to step into the world and be present to the beauty of soul-sensing. Here is an exercise that can be done that, when done over time, helps develop the soul's capacity for beauty.

Go to your local florist and buy a single, long - stemmed rose. Take it home and put it in a proper vase. Observe the rose carefully. Then close your eyes and make an inner image of the rose. Do not remember the rose, but make an inner image, one that exactly mirrors the rose you observed. Stabilize and hold the image steady. Try now to be aware of the qualities of the rose image. After a while, try to "step" into the image. Be aware of the qualities now experienced. Then extinguish the rose image and remain as long as possible in the void of silence and listen into the silence. Then, open your eyes, but do not immediately turn to other tasks. Try to be aware of the qualities you now feel.

Write a careful description of what occurred in the exercise. Include in your description the "how" of what you experienced, not just the content of what you experienced. If fear was present as you tried to do the exercise, describe how it worked. Describe in particular, the qualities of the rose that went beyond what you sense and know of the rose.

Chapter Nine: Fear and Consciousness

This chapter describes how fear comes to be installed in the very processes of our consciousness. I do not mean that fear can come to dominate the content of our consciousness - our thinking, our feelings, our motivations - though that can certainly happen. Going through this study guide will go a long way toward eliminating that danger. But, fear can begin to infiltrate the very processes of consciousness as well as content. When, for example, fear has installed itself into the processes of consciousness, memory become dulled, feelings are more or less absent, and thinking becomes more like a string of opinions hanging together rather than the intricate and beautiful movement of the development of thought. The best place to begin working to counter fear entering the processes of consciousness is the realm of thinking because this realm is more conscious to us than the processes of feelings or the processes of motivations or will. Here is an exercise to strengthen the soul process of thinking:

Fear works in the intellect by making us feel we have thought something but have not thought it through to the end. We are always having thoughts, but typically do not think them through to the end. A picture of how this works is given in the Greek myth of Theseus and the Minotaur. Theseus goes into the labyrinth, following the thread of Ariadne. At any point along the way, he may encounter the Minotaur. Following a thought is like following the thread of Ariadne. In the labyrinth of thought, it may seem like we have come to a dead end. At that point we become afraid. The monster may be lurking around the next corner. So, we stop or turn back, refuse to follow the thread.

This exercise consists of following a thought through to its end. In order to concentrate on a thought, we will do so meditatively. Take the following thought:

Perfect Love Casts Out Fear

Follow the thread of this thought through to the end by meditating on the thought and closely following it, step by step. What is "perfect"?; what is "perfect love;" how does "perfect love" have power? What is like to "cast out fear?" Take fifteen minutes and silently meditate this sentence. When you meditate a sentence, first say the sentence in an inner way. Then, let one word of the sentence come to the fore. Like, *perfect* love casts out fear. The whole of the sentence is then considered under the light of this emphasized word. It becomes the link between all of the words in the sentence. Doing an exercise like this periodically strengthens the processes of consciousness so that fear cannot come in and begin to take hold of the processes of consciousness.

Spiritual Psychology and the Laws of Love

The Evolution of Love in the World

Earth as the Planet of Love

The Earth, says Rudolf Steiner, is the Planet of love - but not yet! The whole evolution of the Earth and of consciousness has been oriented toward this end, and yet such a destiny is not an inevitability; it will not necessarily happen. This possibility is destined but not fated. Note, in particular, Steiner does not just say that human beings are here on Earth to love one another, but that Earth herself will, under the proper circumstances, evolve into the Planet of Love - not simply the place where love happens, where love constitutes the dominant mode of activity of humans toward one another and toward the Earth. No, the very substance of this planet can transform eventually into the substance of love. (Steiner speaks of this transformation in a number of places; for example, the lecture entitled "The Origin of Evil," November 22, 1906 and the lecture entitled "The Apocalypse", June 24, 1908) This transformation will certainly not take place in our lifetime - not even in several lifetimes. But, human beings are the instruments of love, and unless we function as proper instruments this transformation cannot take place. Thus, how we form ourselves as instruments of love, right now, in daily life, is decisive for the future of the Earth. If we do not become instruments for the transformation of Earth into the planet of love, Earth will not simply remain as it is; it will instead become more and more dense, so that anything of a soul or a spiritual nature will not be able to express anything of soul or spirit qualities.

Whether this evolutionary course takes place or not depends entirely upon human beings. We are to be the determiners of the destiny of Earth. If this responsibility can be felt in even the smallest way, then a strong motivation to learn about love, about what it is and how it works, arises within us. As conscious beings of the realm of Earth, are we not all called to become scientists of love? Not the kind of scientists that breaks things apart, makes theories, performs experiments, analyzes and develops technologies, but rather filled with the desire to know the intricacies of this force that has been turned over to us to develop this seminar hopes to develop at the least the beginnings of a knowledge of love, a participatory kind of knowing.

There exists, I am quite convinced, a certain resistance to entering into knowing love. Everyone wants to experience love - to be the recipients of it and even to be givers of it - we want to know how to do it, how to be successful practitioners of the art. Such desires are a little like someone wanting to paint without knowing anything about the laws of color. We also feel that knowing love would somehow destroy its mystery. A very large aspect of the attraction of love concerns being taken by an unknown force and hurled into the unknown, hurled into a force over which we have no control, expecting to come through the encounter successfully. To suggest that we can know quite a lot concerning the force of love, however, does not imply that we can control it, for control implies using something for our own designated purposes. Love will never be subject to this kind of control. So, suggesting that it is important to become knowers of love does not imply becoming controllers of it. We do want to know how we can act with the presence of love that makes possible the freeing of love to accomplish it purposes.

The kind of knowledge we are thus seeking could be called functional knowledge, which is quite different than technical know-how. We well may not be able to speak much concerning what love is, but we can say quite a lot concerning how it functions - what it does, where, and how, and in what forms. This kind of knowing can help us to rightly and in healthy ways submit to its reality rather than trying to get it to do what we want it to do. A word of clarification concerning the title of this seminar - "The Laws of Love." The word "laws" is being evoked, not in a legalistic sense, something to be followed or dire consequences will be imposed. Rather, the term is used here more in the sense that science uses the term "laws" for characteristics or properties of something observed that follows regular patterns, as for example the law of gravity, or the laws of quantum dynamics. The term is used to suggest that we begin to be able to be objective concerning the phenomenon of love, though not objective in the same way that natural science is objective. The kind of objectivity involved in the phenomenon of love requires that the observer can observe love only through the capacity of love within the observer.

A second word of introduction is also needed. Love does not appear in the world in only one form, but rather reveals itself in different modes. It reveals itself through the human body, through the soul life, and through the individual spirit, and does so differently in each instance. Then, we will suggest, if we become the vessels in body, soul and spirit, for the force of love, it can begin to enter into the world. Love works through us in body, soul, and spirit as a necessary preparation for entrance into the world. This way of viewing the activity of love constitutes the assumption for what is to follow, an assumption that is quite different from the way we ordinarily imagine love, which we rather naively take to be something of our own doing; while at the very same time, any experience of love at all shows us that it is not something we control. We can, however, work to become that through which love can do its work. Our focus, then, is not on such questions as "how can I love more, or how can I be loved, what are the techniques for bringing love into my life?" Our focus will be on becoming the instruments, in body, soul, and spirit, for the development of love in the world.

The development of love in the world has not always been in the hands of human beings, nor is it completely so even now. But, a gradual process of the handing over of love to us is indeed taking place. By handing love over to us, to emphasize what was said above, I do not mean we become the originators of love, but rather its instrument, and we are responsible for the condition of this instrument. A very long preparation for the event of our becoming the guardians of love has occurred. The first part of this preparation consisted of the evolution of the planet of Earth as a living being functioning according to the laws of Wisdom. Everything in the outer world operates according to laws of Wisdom. In accordance with the laws of Wisdom, for example, nothing exits in isolation, on it own. The current concept for expressing this law of Wisdom is ecology. The cycles of day and night, of the seasons, the breathing of the atmosphere, the wise relation of mineral, plant, and animal kingdoms, the weather, the relation of Earth to the other planets, the functioning of the physical human body - all this and much more belongs to the sphere of Wisdom.

Love is not installed in the outer world, the sphere of Wisdom, but entered the earthly realm in the form of human sexuality. Sexuality of a certain form exists in both the plant and animal world, but there belongs to the sphere of Wisdom, concerned with reproduction. Human sexuality does not centrally concern reproduction. Plato's myth of human sexuality, told in the Symposium gives a picture of the human being as being a comfortable creature, round in form, that happily rolled along in the world, quite self-satisfied, having no needs and no aspirations. Zeus, becoming irritated with the complacency of these creatures split the comfortable spheres in two with a lightning bolt, originating the sexual urge, bringing about sexual desire. In a most physical and bodily way, we each feel incomplete, as if we are but half of the complete beings we are intended to be. This incompleteness expresses itself as an attraction toward other human beings. Such attraction, at this level, is quite impersonal, something very close to instinct. Love first shows itself in the human world and shows itself as the pressing need for bodily intimacy, the need to unite our body with another body.

I am not at all proposing that each time we are aroused from bodily complacency by the unsettling presence of desire that such desire needs to be satisfied. No, it is sufficient for it simply to be there, jolting us into awareness of something surging through our body that, while it reflects itself within the physiology of the body, cannot be reduced to mere physiology. These urgings are more of the nature of a holy force, right there at the center of our bodily being, the presence of love right at the center of bodily existence. If this presence is denied or suppressed or becomes strongly connected with fear or guilt, or understood to be something "only physical," have we not turned away from the most basic way that love has taken to show forth? And, if this force of love within the body is, on the other hand, approached recklessly, not understood as a sacred presence within the body but as nothing more than natural urgings demanding satisfaction, have we not then, in a different way, but with the same result, reduced sexuality, abandoned love's physical presence?

Based upon these few slight observations, let us formulate a first law of love, a law that we can though go on and provide some verification given by some individuals who know a great deal more about love than I.

Love celebrates its entry into the world through a vivifying presence within the human body, announcing itself as human sexuality.

An individual who expressed such an understanding of sexual love is the poet, Rainer Maria Rilke. Rilke was born in 1875 and died in 1926. In his Letters he has this to say concerning sex:

> "*Here, in the love which, with an intolerable mixture of contempt, desire, and curiosity, they call "sensual," here indeed are to be found the worst results of that vilification of earthly life which organized religion has felt obliged to engage in...*"

Before going on further with the quote, let me say that Rilke here, I do not think, is setting himself as opposed to religion, but rather the ways in which religion has sometimes been utilized, fearing that the blissful presence of sex in the world might somehow detract our attention from the divine. Such a view, in fact, expresses a very deep fear of the divine, an inability to see that divine love expresses itself right at the center of our existence."

He goes on: "How we have to creep around about sex and get into it in the end; like burglars and thieves, we get into our own beautiful sex, in which we lose our way and knock ourselves and stumble and finally rush out of it again, like people caught transgressing..."
"Why have they made our sex homeless, instead of making it the place for the festival of our competency?"

"My sex is not directed only toward posterity, it is the secret of my own life - and it is only, it seems, because it may not occupy the central place there, that so many people have thrust it to the edge, and thereby lost their balance." "The terribly untruthfulness and uncertainty of our age has its roots in the refusal to acknowledge the happiness of sex, in this peculiarly mistaken guilt, which constantly increases, separating us from the rest of nature..."

"Physical pleasure is a sensual experience no different from pure seeing or the pure sensation which a fine fruit fills the tongue; it is a great unending experience, which is given us, a knowing of the world, the fullness and the glory of all knowing. And not our acceptance of it is bad; the bad thing is that most people misuse and squander this experience and apply it as a stimulant at the tired spots of their lives and as distraction instead of a rallying toward exalted moments."

The fire of sexual desire is certainly not comfortable. Who does not, at times, wish that this fire would just go away and leave us alone? But, as Rilke so strongly says, it is the mark of fully entering into earthly life, and thus, vilifying sex at the same time condemns earthly life as being of no value, of being only a trial, with the aim of leaving this miserable condition as soon as possible.

Now, in the modern world, sex does seem to occupy the center of life. Everything around us - the media, movies, television, magazines, books, advertising, places sex at the center - but certainly not in the way prompted by Rilke. Having removed sex from the healthy center of life, having pushed it aside, into the closet for so long, it returns to a central place in an unhealthy, a pathological way - our age is obsessed with sex. While, in Rilke's time, the connection of sex with sin and guilt was strong, in our time the opposite error takes place; having set sex free from the restraints of religion, we do not know how to be responsible for this force of love within the human body.

Another poet who has had important insights into sex is Novalis. In his Aphorisms, he says:
"All absolute sensation is religious."
"Art of becoming all powerful. Art of realizing our intentions totally. We must receive the body as the soul in our dominion. The body is the instrument for the formation and modification of the world. We must therefore seek to form our body as a wholly capable organ. Modification of our instrument is modification of the world."
"There is only one temple in the world, and that is the human body. Nothing is holier than this highest Form. One touches heaven, when one touches a human body."

The question of living the presence of love within the body in a healthy way, given to us as our sexuality, does not have anything to do with engaging or not engaging in the act of sex. Sexual desire constitutes a divine force, centered in the body. We are responsible for housing this force, for letting this mighty being live and breathe therein, not to stifle it nor to harness it to our own purposes. Sexual desire is an absolute sensation - and, as Novalis says, our most immediate connection with the spiritual realms. The recognition of the responsibility we bear for giving the force of love a home in the body leads to a second law of love:

The divine force of love, living within the body as sexual desire, submits itself to the care of humanity for its further unfoldment.

The errors surrounding instruction concerning how to go about being proper guardians of the force of love that lives within the body - either the error of labeling sex bad or the error of trying to confine sexual love to propagation or the error of promoting free use of this force for our own pleasure, we should by now have learned, indicates that it is impossible to formulate general directives concerning sex. Because the force of sexual love takes up residence in each individual human body, it is the responsibility of each individual to gradually learn the particular way in which the force of sexual love shapes itself in accordance with the individual. Learning the particularity of how sexual love inhabits one's body takes a long time - a very long time. Here are some observations made by Rilke concerning this matter:

> "*Love is something difficult and it is more difficult than other things.....in the heightening of love the impulse is to give oneself wholly away. But just think, can that be anything beautiful, to give oneself away not as something whole and ordered, but haphazard rather, bit by bit, as it comes? Can such giving away, that looks so like a throwing away and dismemberment, be anything good...? When you give someone flowers, you arrange them before hand, don't you? But young people who love each other fling themselves to each other in the impatience and haste of their passion, and they don't notice at all what a lack of mutual esteem lies in this disordered giving of themselves; they notice it with astonishment and indignation only from the dissension that arises between them out of all this disorder.*"

> "*Sex is difficult; yes. But they are difficult things with which we have been charged; almost everything serious is difficult, and everything is serious. If you only recognize this and manage, out of yourself, out of your own nature and ways, out of your own experience and strength to achieve a relation to sex wholly your own (not influenced by convention and custom), then you need no longer be afraid of losing yourself and becoming unworthy of your best possession.*"

These reflections lead to a third Jaw of love:

Finding the right relation to sexual love is a wholly individual matter, demanding a high degree of inner presence and observation developed over a long period of time. Sexual desire announces itself in the human body before we are fully human beings. It takes a very long time and much inner effort to become a human being. Before we mature into a human being, sexual desire is unruly, impetuous, frustrating, demanding, impatient. Perhaps, though, it is not wanting its release so much as it anxiously waits, pressing us to enter into our humanity.

What signs are we given that we have at least begun the road toward becoming a wholly human being? I suggest that as long as we see a woman or a man as a member of the opposite sex, we have not yet trod very far on this road. Rilke, for example, says:

> "And perhaps the sexes are more related than we think, and the great renewal of the world will perhaps consist in this, that man and woman, freed of all false feelings and reluctances, will seek each other not as opposites but as brother and sister, as neighbors, and will come together as human beings, in order simply, seriously and patiently to bear in common the difficult sex that has been laid upon them."

I am not at all dissolving the differences between men and women, which will have to be considered. But, these differences, while immensely important, are not the difference between the male and female sex but rather precisely differences between man and woman.

Love Between Individuals
Emotional Love

Love between individuals is an essentially different mode of love than sexual love. While sexual love has a strong impersonal component, when love appears between two people, there exists an attraction toward a particular person, taking the form of the heightening of feeling, of emotion toward that person. Emotional love does not derive from sexual love as a kind of evolution to a higher level. It can and does sometimes exist autonomous from sexual love. Great confusions come about through linking these two modes of love too closely together. On the other hand, it is certainly true that sexual attraction between two people can sometimes bring about emotional attraction and emotional attraction can bring about sexual attraction as well. Because these relationships can certainly be complex, that is nonetheless no reason to approach them in a completely confused way. The intent of sexual love is essentially different than the intent of emotional love. The former constitutes a current flowing through the body, while the latter constitutes current flowing through the soul. Great difficulties come about when one current serves as a substitute for the other. Certainly, there are, at times, a confluence of the two currents of bodily and emotional love.

The emotional quality of love signifies that there is work to be done between two souls. The divine force of love here inhabits the soul and indeed encompasses the souls of two individuals, as if both were encircled by the divine being of love. Two people say that they are in love. We are in love together - in this mode, love does not really go back and forth between one individual and the other individual. Even if one says - "I am in love with you" the very language betrays the fact that the love here is not the connection between two separated beings, but rather that this love encompasses them both. This mode of love is of itself beautiful, but to be encompassed in this way by love is extremely painful to the individuals upon whom this love visits. The beauty belongs to the love; the pain derives from two related sources. On the one hand, it is unbearable to imagine that this beauty might be ephemeral, which it is not; changeable, yes, but not ephemeral. On the other hand, what we do not realize, is that we are every moment trying to rid ourselves of this terrible beauty because it seems to be a radical threat to our individual existence. It feels like we could completely lose ourselves.

In emotional love we desire to merge with the other person, which is not the intention of this love. The intention of this love is actually to educate us into our separateness from one another by forcing us to have to discover this separateness as a true inner experience. Alone, we feel lonely and alone, not because we lack a partner, but because we are not at home in ourselves. However, the threat to the total dissolution of our loneliness brought about through being in love is at the same time the urging by this love to discover our separateness. To the extent that we are able to do so, remaining in love, staying in love with someone while remaining a separate, full individual, becomes possible. Only then does it begin to be possible to work out our indebtedness to the other person.

Rilke says the following concerning the difficulties of emotional love:

> "Love is at first not anything that means merging, giving over, and uniting with another (for that would be of something unclarified and unfinished?); it is a high inducement to the individual to ripen, to become something in himself or herself, to become world, to become world for himself or herself for another's sake....Only in this sense, as the task of working at themselves, might people use the love that is given them. Merging and

*surrendering and every kind of communion is not for them, is the
ultimate, is perhaps that for which human lives as yet scarcely suffice."*

Rilke is saying here that it is impossible for two human beings to merge;
our desire to do so collapses that which we must develop, our own selves,
and nothing results except pain and confusion. But, he also suggests that at
another level, not the emotional level, there perhaps can be the union of
two to become one. In spiritual love this is possible, without the loss of
individuality. It seems of great importance to realize that the "urge to merge"
is a calling from the future, of what we might become, but to also realize that
as we are - still struggling with the beauty of sex and the flames of emotion,
we are not yet suited to such a union. For two individuals to attempt to be
completely united as one in sex or in emotion tries to substitute sex or
emotion for an essentially spiritual activity. Rilke goes on to speak of the
purpose of emotional love:

*"To hold this to be the highest task of a bond between two people; that
each should stand guard over the solitude of the other. For, if it lies in the
nature of indifference and of the crowd to recognize no solitude, then love
and friendship are for the purpose of continually providing the opportunity
for solitude. And only those are the true sharings which rhythmically
interrupt periods of deep isolation...."*

*"A togetherness between two people is an impossibility, and where it
seems, nevertheless, to exist, it is a narrowing, a reciprocal agreement
which robs either one party or both of his or her fullest freedom and
development. But, once the realization is accepted that even between the
closest of human beings infinite distances continue to exist, a wonderful
living side by side can grow up, if they succeed in loving the distance
between them that makes it possible for each to see the other whole and
against a wide sky!"*

We can now, perhaps, formulate a law of emotional love:
*Emotional love encompasses two souls in order to drive them out of the
emptiness of their aloneness into the fullness of their separateness.*

*Novalis provides a wonderful aphorism that also expresses the paradox of
the law formulated above: " One is alone with whomever, whatever one
loves*

We can in no way serve the soul of another, work out our karmic debt, if we are enmeshed with the other. The poetess Emily Dickinson gives this aphorism to remind us of the serious duty we have to the soul of another whom we love:

"Whoever disenchants a single human soul by failure of irreverence is guilty of the whole."

Understanding this aphorism in relation to emotional love, Dickinson is here saying that to disrespect the solitude of another, to fail to be its guardian, not only harms the soul of the other person, it brings harm to the whole world. Our little confusions over love have far reaching consequences. To recognize that they do should not be cause for paralysis, waiting to be absolutely sure - she is not being prescriptive, but rather descriptive, telling us to be aware of the larger scope of love and to take it seriously. When we error, which we are bound to do, we can then learn from our errors, and not just go on as if nothing happened.

While emotional love is not ephemeral, it is indeed changeable, in fact ever-changing, ever moving, much like the weather, calm one day, turbulent the next. This form of love does not stay the same forever; it may seem to have completely disappeared and then reappear like a warm breeze through the window, without warning. Given this seemingly erratic character, the worst sort of difficulties stem from trying to cling to this kind of love; it cannot be held steadfast. Thus, we error in expecting happiness as a consequence of being the recipients of emotional love. Eros is not a happy daemon, and in spite of the fact that we romanticize love, calling it beautiful, Eros is not beautiful Socrates, in Plato' Symposium, did not think him beautiful either. Nor does Rilke:

"I saw him just as Socrates had invoked him, lean and hard and always a little out of breath, sleepless, troubled day and night about the two between whom he trod, to and fro, hither and yon, ceaselessly accosted by both: yes, that was Eros. …Ah, he was slender and tanned and covered with the dust of the road, but there was no peace for him amid the two of them."

On the Difference between Men and Women

The love that encompasses two individuals seems to work upon men in a different way than upon women. Common wisdom has it that women are more able to stay in the emotional qualities of love, are more present to the demands of this mode of love, and are more able to let themselves be embraced by the constant variability of emotional love. Men are said to be more tied to the forces of sexual love and not so able to withstand the onslaught of emotion, or even perhaps do not have much of a capacity for feeling emotional love.

The apparent difference between men and women in the sphere of emotional love goes further than the matter of emotions. Women are more complete human beings than men. Such a statement must be taken descriptively, without judgement. Rudolf Steiner points to this difference when he says that men are more tied to the material/physical world; they are more deeply incarnated into earth than women. Women, he says, never become completely detached from the spiritual worlds. Women are more inherently spiritual than men. If we can look upon this difference without prejudice, we can perhaps come to knowing more of the laws of emotional love. That women are more spiritual carries its own difficulties, just as the fact that men are more material carries certain difficulties. First, look at what Rilke has to say concerning these differences. In speaking about how men are more tied by sexual love, he indicates:

"But it seems that this power is not always honest and without pose. Where, as it rushes through his being, it comes to the sexual, it finds not quite so pure a man as it might require. Here is no thoroughly mature and clean sex world, but one that is not sufficiently human, that is only male, is heat, intoxication and restlessness, and laden with the old prejudices and arrogances with which man has disfigured and burdened love. Because he loves as man only, not as human being, for this reason there is in his sexual feeling something narrow, seeming wild, spiteful, time-bound, uneternal."

Love has entered the human world through the body, but love is not bound to the world; it enters into this world in order to bring about the transformation of it, not to be captured by it. Love does not submit itself to this world in order to become our possession. Emotional love can be imagined as a kind of love that treads between the physical and the spiritual. Men, being more tied to the physical, would try to absorb this love into the physical, into sexual love. Men experience the emotional in sexual love and when the pull of sexual love momentarily releases its demands, emotional love may seem to have also left. Perhaps it is not so much that women are more subject to emotional love than men, but that men have a different relation with emotional love. The difficulty in men's relation with the sphere of emotional love is that he easily bypasses the eternal element that is already announcing itself in emotional love.

A further difficulty arises for men due to the tendency to miss the eternal or the spiritual aspect that is a part of emotional love. He can either become oblivious to the unfolding of the mode of love that we will further on describe as spiritual love and become completely tied to the physical, material world, or he may feel the calling of spiritual love and try to let this mode of love have its place in life, but do so bypassing what, to him, seems to be the capriciousness of emotional love.

Now, let us look at what Rilke has to say concerning emotional love in relation to women:

"*Women, in their unfolding, will but in passing be imitators of masculine ways, good and bad, and repeaters of masculine professions. After the uncertainty of such transitions it will become apparent that women were only going through the profusion and the vicissitude (often ridiculous) disguises in order to cleanse their own most characteristic nature of the distorting influences of the other sex.......Someday there will be women whose name will no longer signify merely the opposite of the masculine, but something in itself, something that makes one think, not of any complement and limit, but only of life and existence: the feminine human being.*

This advance will (at first much against the will of the outstripped men) change the love-experience, which is now full of error, will alter it from the ground up, reshape it into a relation that is meant to be of one human being to another, no longer of man to woman. And this more human love will resemble that which we are preparing with struggle and toil, the love that consists in this, that two solitudes protect and border and salute each other."

Women, then are the educators of men into the task of becoming human beings. This task carries its own difficulties. Love in the emotional sphere already announces another mode of love, spiritual love. But women can experience the difficulty of trying to possess emotional love in the same manner than men can experience the difficulty of trying to possess sexual love.

The special difficulties experienced by men and women in the sphere of emotional love lead us to something quite interesting. Women, through their special relation to emotional love are the educators into being full human beings. They can fulfill this responsibility only insofar as they do not yield to imitating the present state of men, who in their incompleteness are more male than human. Men, through their special relation to the physical, keep love related not only to the body but thereby also to the physical world. Women, considered in relation to love, without the relation to men, would tend to fold spiritual love into emotional love. Men, without the relation to women, would be in grave danger of abandoning the spiritual altogether, or through bypassing the transformative powers of emotional love, move to the spiritual in an abstract way. To be good guardians of the force of love as it enters into the human world through the emotional domain, it is necessary to understand the laws by which this love force functions. We might state this functioning through the following law:

Emotional love works through women as a world force for the development of becoming fully human and for developing receptivity to spiritual love; this love works through men to dislodge them from becoming bound to the physical realm or from ascending to spiritual love abstractly.

Spiritual Love
On the Meaning of Spiritual Love

Our concern in this seminar centers on love as a transformative power in the world. We are concerned with how love gets into the world where it functions to change Earth, the planet of wisdom into Earth, the planet of love. Human being are the mediums through which this Earth destiny can take place. In order to understand that we are the mediums of love not the controllers of it, it is necessary to have a perspective in which the ego is relativized. Sexual love and emotional love, felt as strong and powerful forces, thwart the ego's incessant assertion of itself as the controlling center of our consciousness,

Spiritual love constitutes a third mode of the action of love in the world. This mode of love is even more difficult to understand. First, let us focus on the way in which the word "spirit" will be used in what follows. I am using the word spirit as a partiular function of the human being, based on the understanding of the human being as a being of body, soul, and spirit. "Spiritual love" can be a term describing a particular kind of relation to beings of the spiritual worlds - the gods, the angels, the spirits, the dead. It is also a term that can describe a particular kind of relationship to others. This latter sense of the term will be explored first - what is involved in a spiritual relationship to another human being.

In our exploration of spiritual love the stance is taken that this form of love in relation to another can function in a healthy way only if we have matured, at least somewhat, in our sexual being - that in our body we have become vessels of love, capable of neither repressing sexual love nor haphazardly using this form of love as if it were our possession to be used for personal pleasure, though both pleasure and immense frustration are experienced though being recipients of this love. The stance is also taken here that spiritual love can function in a healthy way only to the extent we have matured in our soul life. If we develop the soul capacity of experiencing the emotion of love, letting it flow into emotional life without blocking it nor becoming obsessed by emotion, seeking to have the emotion of love be present every moment, then healthy spiritual love for another can also function.

Spiritual love can only be oriented toward the spiritual nature of another human being. It sees something of the spiritual individuality of the other, but sees this quality shining through the whole of the personality of the other person. The experience of spiritual love in relation to another person is one in which the other person is perceived as someone unknown and unknowable. The other person is perceived as a holy mystery. Novalis says:

"Our spirit is a connecting link to the wholly incomparable."

He also says in one of his aphorisms: "I am you." This means that it is through our own incomparability that we perceive the incomparability of the other and we are alike in our incomparability. "I am you" does not mean that I find myself in you, which would be a terrible distortion of the other person, one that takes place quite often and leads to spiritual co-dependency.

Spiritual co-dependency means that if find myself in you, and you decide that you no longer want to be around me, then I lose any and all sense of myself as a human being. There can also be emotional and physical co-dependency. In the first, 1 rely on the other person in order to have the experience of love. In the latter, I rely on sexual experience with another in order to experience my own sexual being. In our work in this seminar, however, we are not so concerned with these possible thwarting of the various modes of love, though they are extremely important to understand.

The spiritual connection between one individual and another individual that characterizes spiritual love is something for which we have as yet little understanding. Cultivating this form of love lies in the thoughts that we bear concerning the other person. But the thoughts having to do with spiritual love are not the same as the thoughts that may emerge from missing someone or from remembering something about our being together in the past or thinking about what that person might be doing. It is more like thinking the very existence of the other person. Further, and most important, this quality of thinking is not carried out with the head, as it were, separated from the rest of the body. This new kind of thinking that thinks the existence of the other person is a kind of thinking with the whole of our body. Thus, this kind of thinking is not thinking in terms of content. I can never know the spiritual quality of another person through a content of thought. It is not thinking about him or her, for these forms of thinking are for my own purposes. If] call someone I love and say that I am thinking about her, this kind of thinking has an emotional purpose - it makes someone who is absent present; this is fine and good. it can help keep me in connection with emotion. But that is not spiritual love. Do I care, though, about the destiny of the other person; that gets closer to spiritual love. How can I avoid interfering with the destiny of another person? Do I stand for his or her full reality? *Novalis says:*

> "*Clear understanding conjoined with warm imaginations is the true, health-bringing precious food of the soul.*"

Understanding here does not mean fully comprehending the other person, it means standing in every part of my being for the full reality of the other. And if we read the aphorism closely, it says that this standing for the reality of the other person, conjoined with warm imaginations - a healthy emotional love - is precious food - note here, he says of the soul, not for one's own soul. He is saying that this kind of love nourishes the soul of the other person.

When it was stated above that spiritual love concerns thinking the existence of the other person, that statement may seem quite difficult - what is meant by such a statement? This form of love does not have the rhythmic periodicity characteristic of both sexual love and emotional love. It does not come in waves but is ever-present. This love does reflect back into the emotions and into the body, giving these modes of love a new coloring. Spiritual love, reflecting into other modes of love can also be confusing, producing the possibility of taking spiritual love as either sexual love or emotional love. Such confusion can be ameliorated only if one has a sense of the true spiritual nature of thinking. Novalis puts it this way:

> *"The highest duty of education is to take possession of one's transcendental self, to master the ego. For so few, strangely, is there a need for a complete sense of and understanding of another. Apart from complete self-knowledge, one will never truly learn to understand another."*

A law of spiritual love can thus be put forth:

We must know ourselves pretty thoroughly in order to provide the pathway for spiritual love. When such self-knowledge exists, which may not be ever quite so complete as Novalis proposes, enough freedom exists in our thinking to detect that the beloved subtly pervades every corner of conscious life, not as a theme or as a content of thinking, but is there, centered in the very activity of thinking itself. Novalis speaks of this quality of spiritual love in the following way:

> *"Whatever one loves, one finds everywhere, and everywhere sees resemblances and analogies to it. The greater one's love, the vaster and more meaningful is this analogous world. My beloved is the abbreviation of the universe, the universe an elongation, an extrapolation of my beloved. The knowledgeable friend offers all flowers and gifts to his beloved."*

This very beautiful aphorism seems to high and lofty that it may seem that very few of us could possibly achieve spiritual love. Yet, we do so. Why do you bring gifts to your beloved? It may be, on one level to demonstrate your love. But at the more spiritual level, in an analogous way you see your beloved in the gifts you bring. You bring him or her something beautiful because you see his or her beauty. You may write poems expressing your love, and such poems express the world as an analogy to your love. You may find yourself thinking imaginatively in relation to anything - your work, life, the world, and such imaginative thinking is in fact an expression of spiritual love. Such ways of thinking, far from distorting what we may be thinking about, give us our only true pictures of the universe. Think, for example of Dante. The whole of the Divine Comedy is an expression of his love of Beatrice. Through this spiritual love, a true imagination of the whole of the world comes to expression. We come, then, to another law of spiritual love:

Spiritual love expresses itself as imaginative thinking.

Another aspect of spiritual love, one that draws out further what is meant by saying that the medium of spiritual love consists of the quality of our thinking, is that spiritual love expresses itself as thinking that is inspired. Again, Novalis apprehends this aspect of spiritual love when he says:

> *"If a spirit appeared to us, then we ourselves would take possession of that singular spiritual state; we are inspired inasmuch as we and the spirit are together. Apart from inspiration, there is no appearance of spirit. Inspiration is appearance and reflection, appropriation and communication together."*

Spiritual love apprehends the spirit that is the essence of the other. But, apprehending the spirit of the other person places us in conjunction with his or her spirit, and this conjunction is lived as inspiration. Inspiration is the mark of spiritual love, the mark of the spiritual presence of the beloved. Anything that is created in the world comes about through inspiration and expresses something of the spirit of the beloved; and all such creations inspire love in the world. The difference between something new in the world that is a mere invention or something that is the manifestation of spiritual love depends on whether the object, event, or idea inspires love in the world. We thus come to a further law of spiritual love:

Spiritual love inspires the visible presence of love in the world.

Creative Love
The purifying fire of Love

The many difficulties surrounding love have less to do with the deficiencies of our personality than modern psychology and psychotherapy would have us think. Love of any sort is itself a difficulty. It hurts, burns, brings confusion, discomfort, keeps us awake at night, distracts us in the day, and even when it inspires it does so with such intensity that we find ourselves as if chained to a force that will not let loose. It burns a hole in the interior of our body, seems to use everything within the soul for kindling, and intensifies the small flame of the spirit to the point that the fire seems uncontrollable. Our small ego and personality can hardly withstand the conflagration and it seems as if we go to pieces. Indeed, we can be destroyed by the force of love. We are hardly aware that we have been immersed in the fires of purification. Much that goes on these days in the realms of counseling, therapy, self-help practices, acts as if there is something wrong with us if we cannot handle love. Very few therapies know how to guard the flame and instead provide instruction on quenching the fire. These instructions take the form of how to get along with our partner, finding out what men need and what women need, talking it to death, strengthening the ego, putting getting along together ahead of tending the fire. The instructions also involve how to find satisfaction in sex, how to avoid obsession, and even take inspiration to be something pathological. Little do we see that "pathology" is the rule of love. Insofar as the difficulties of love are approached in these ways, the creative force of love is being subdued and instead conventionality of every sort is being fostered.

All attempts to subdue the force of love, to try to get it to behave the way we think it ought to, whether in accordance with our religious notions, our psychological notions, our social notions, are all oriented toward trying to harness love for our own purposes. Human beings are the instruments of love and love itself must form its instrument. It does so through a process of purification - of body, soul, and spirit. The purpose of this purification process is to make possible the entry of love into the world, to transform the world.

Love does not really have a human purpose; its purpose is far larger than that. In the process of carrying forth its purpose, we undergo significant transformations, and if these transformations do not happen, love cannot fulfill its purpose either. But, part of the purification process often seems to us to be the goal of the process. We may think that the highest purpose of love is to love one another. That is one result of the purification process, but not its final end; it is an indication of the working of love, the making of human beings into the vessel of body, soul, and spirit through which love can flow into the world. If love flows between human beings, then it can also flow into the world. But, if the flow of love is restricted to what occurs between human beings, even in its highest, most noble way, we have unwittingly bound love. And, in the process of this binding, what seems to be the highest aspiration of love will then become destructive. If we can imagine that the time arrives where it becomes possible for every human being to love one another, and that is as far as we can imagine, stopping there would actually turn destructive. This most necessary part of the process cannot be bypassed, but it cannot be the end either.

In order to free our imagination from love as being limited to the human sphere of activity, to help us from confusing the instrument with the purpose of love, we are now going to develop some laws of love that begin to show the movement of love into the world. Because we are the instruments of love, we are certainly involved in love executing its purposes; it needs us to do its work. First, though, it is necessary to say something concerning where these laws come from. We have had to sufficiently suffered the fires of love in the body to come to the point of letting love form the instrument of our body where we can feel the surges of love as the living sexuality of our body without trying to either purge them or to use them in a haphazard manner. I am not at all saying that we must become celibate. The mark of having undergone to some degree the fires of sexual love is feeling joy in the body, joy in being sensate, joy in being here on Earth, feeling fully incarnate, feeling joy in the presence of all things of the earthly world. Second, we have had to sufficiently suffered the fires of love burning in the soul. Do we really feel our separateness, feel that this separateness is guarded and protected by those who express love for us? Do we feel inner joy, amazement at the unending depth of our soul, feel called to guard and protect the depth of soul of those that we love? Do we know the soul realm, no longer need to ask that someone give us a definition of what is meant by soul? Then, does the fire of love not only burn through the body and through the soul but also completely transform our thinking so that we no long just think about one thing or another but experience the creative force of love inspiring living thinking? When love has worked through us and transformed us, at least to a certain extent, it begins to be possible to propose how acts of love begin to enter into the world.

The following laws of creative love take the form of paradoxes that are intended to stimulate flashes of insight; they take this form because of the present limitations of language. Outside of the poets, there does not seem to me to be a language adequate to the phenomenon of love. New language is needed, and that language can come about through taking up the ordinary language we speak, and, as it were, utilizing it in sucha way that it breaks open. For example, a first law of creative love might be:

The Law of Quality: The smallest act of love released into the world produces the same result as the largest act of love released into the world.

Let us now explore this law a bit. Love does not exist as a quantity, so, strictly speaking, "large" and "small" do not apply to this phenomenon as long as we are thinking quantitatively. But, there certainly exists qualities that can be termed "large" and "small." Say I am walking down the street and stop for a moment to talk to a friend. In the course of our conversation, in a split second, in the continence of this person there is revealed the inner light of his being. In that moment, love flows through me as the act of recognition of this person as a spiritual being. A small act of love. Now, imagine the daily work of someone like Mother Theresa. Her care for the suffering would definitely be considered a large act of love. Can we say that the small act of love does less than the large act of love? At first, it seems a ridiculous question; it would seem that without question the large act of love does more. That is an intellectual response. Notice whether within you there exists a resistance to this intellectual response, a quality of feeling, one that sides more with the love itself than to the apparent logic. Out of ordinary logic you might say that the love that flows through Mother Theresa affects many more people than this one small moment in which creative love worked. But, in so saying, we have once again reduced quality to quantity. Another argument might say - well, if this law is indeed valid, then why should one work as Mother Theresa does when the same result would come about though our everyday encounters. Well, some are called to love in one way and others in another way. It is exceedingly important to come to know how you are called to love and to be faithful to that way.

What if we focus on the key word "result"? About all we can suggest with regard to this word is that in both instances love flows into the world. But, seeing this perhaps clarifies this law. Creative love moves into the world and does so in such a manner that there is absolutely no expectation that anything be gained for oneself. The very thought of gaining something does not even enter. No bit of selfishness can be detected. Can we say that Mother Theresa is less selfish than the individual who experienced a moment of complete selflessness? Still, it might be said that Mother Theresa makes her selfless love into a discipline and a practice that is done fully consciously, while this individual was perhaps surprised by this momentary gift. However, it is most likely that the individual came to this moment out of a considerable background of preparation or else he would have been oblivious to the moment.

To allow the statement of this law to, as it were, explode into an insight, it is important to pay particular attention to the felt quality of the statement, something that resides within the statement beyond the content. The importance of the law lies in this feeling quality, which if taken up and lived within breaks through old conceptions we might have of what is entailed in living and acting out of our spiritual center. The old concept that we bear within us might well take the form of thinking that one has to be a truly great soul to love as we see someone like Mother Theresa love. Well, she is certainly an extraordinary woman, of that there is no doubt. But she does not have capacities that are beyond the rest of us; rather, she is someone who demonstrates what can become of these capacities when they are put into practice. In our own way, in the forms that are suitable to our particular circumstances, we can also begin to put these new capacities into practice.

Now that you see how these laws work, let's develop a few more of them, shortening the commentary, making possible more conversation concerning how you take up the statement of the law into meditation:

The Law of Intensity: The stronger the intensity of love the greater the increase of love in the world.

As the instruments of love, it is possible for us to increase or decrease the intensity of love by focusing of attention. When attention is focused then love is more intense than when it is not focused. We cannot focus love itself, we can only focus our attention. When we are able to be fully in attention, having nothing before us except what we are attending to - that is, not having other concurrent thinking or feeling going on, and our perception and sensing oriented toward what is before us, and our body at ease and we are fully in our body, then love is able to work with fuller intensity. When our attention is not focused, then love dissipates by virtue of working through an inadequate instrument. When we say that a person loves a little or loves intensely, we are actually speaking of the quality of the person as an instrument of love. Once we have a real feeling for the quality of love as autonomous, that is to say, it is not something that we do out of our own powers, but must rather undergo development in body, soul, and spirit in order for love to function, then our care can shift from the illusory question of whether I love rightly or strongly enough to care for the instrument through which love comes into the world. The question is not what can I do to love better or more fully, but rather what can I do to be a vessel through which love can work?

Let us look at another law of creative love:

The creative power of love derives from the capacity to surrender to love without losing oneself.

This law states something that is impossible for us to do out of the kind of consciousness that we ordinarily live out of, that is, consciousness centered in the psychological ego, the ordinary sense of the I. If we surrender to the force of love and only have the ordinary sense of ourselves but no sense of ourselves in our spiritual dimension, we will lose ourselves. On the other hand, we do not have the ability as human beings to say, "well, I will love out of my spiritual self rather than my ego-self and then J can surrender to love without losing myself." Well, we can say this, but we cannot do it. What we can do is work to disregard our ego, to gradually pay no more attention to it. That is something quite different than deliberately trying to get it out of the way, which would only increase egotism. Many are the times we will lose ourselves in surrendering to love before gradually coming to be able to disregard our ego. But, it is love itself that finds for us our spirit to work through, and thus it is through the force of love that the sense of ourselves as spiritual beings is discovered.

An important aside. Because of this commentary on the ordinary ego, it might seem that love cannot or will not work through the instrument of our ego. This is not correct. For example, if someone has a farm and some cattle and a garden, he or she may come to love these things that are his or her possessions. The person has spread his ego over those possessions in a caring way. That kind of love is egotistical, but it is certainly beneficial for the farm, the animals, the garden. We could have included egotistical love as a separate dimension of love and would have seen that such love can be good. There is nothing that love cannot touch.

Let us go to a further law of creative love: The results of love in the world lie in the realm of the indeterminate. Thus, the practice of love cannot be based in a desire for outcomes.   When love finds its way into the world, we cannot know what it does there, how its transformative effects will work. We cannot direct what will become of love because love is completely free. Even if love works through us toward another person, the effects of that love cannot be known - in advance. We may later see the effects of love - with respect to another person or with respect to the wider world. But these effects cannot be sought without love being turned into manipulation. This law is quite self-evident.

Conclusion
Where to From Here

These very introductory reflections on the function of love in the world can be followed up in a number of ways. Further laws of love can be developed in relation to each form of love. The laws listed under "Creative Love" in particular, can be further developed. What laws can you come in relation to this mode? Another pressing task concerns working through in detail the complex relations among the various modes of love, how they interrelate, of which little has been said.

A further work to be undertaken based upon this introduction would be to begin to work out the laws of love as they might appear in various particular areas of life work. What are the laws of love for education, for medicine, physics, business, technology, law, art, and many other areas? Could we not put love at the center of all of human concerns, build a world based on the premise that the most basic force of the universe is love?

The Laws of Love

Love celebrates its entry into the world through a vivifying presence within the world, announcing itself as human sexuality.

The divine force of love, living with the body as sexual desire, submits itself to the care of humanity for its further unfolding.

Finding the right relation to sexual love is a wholly individual matter, demanding a high degree of inner presence and observation developed over a long period of time.

Emotional love encompasses two souls in order to drive them out of the emptiness of their aloneness into the fullness of their separateness.

Emotional love works through women as a world force for the development of becoming fully human and for developing receptivity to spiritual love; this love works through men to dislodge them from becoming bound to the physical realm or from ascending to spiritual love abstractly.

Spiritual love functions through the medium of relatively complete self-knowledge.

Spiritual love expresses itself as imaginative thinking. Spiritual love creates the visible presence of love in the world.

The smallest act of love released into the world produces the same result as the largest act of love released into the world.

The stronger the intensity of love the greater the increase of love in the world.

The creative power of love derives from the capacity to surrender to love without losing oneself.

The results of love in the world lie in the realm of the indeterminate. Thus, the practice of love cannot be based in a desire for outcomes.

Contemplative Listening

Introduction

The intention of this writing is to increase our capacities of receptivity. The word "listening" refers certainly to being able to listen in new ways to other people, but it also refers to a deeper, more pervading way of being in the world. It refers to developing the capacity of 'inner waiting' to 'hear' what is truly being said at the soul and spirit level of the speaker or the world and developing the capacities to respond to these dimensions of other people, the world, and especially the Earth. When listening matters, matter listens as the speaking-listening goes beyond what occurs only between two or more people and joins the Listening Cosmos.

We live completely within a "pronouncement culture". Little is said or written concerning the receiving side of addressing others and even less to addressing the world and the Earth in such a way that we begin to feel in ongoing relation with what is around us rather than simply using what is around us. Assertion rules – saying without listening. Or, listening and hearing only information.

It is not possible to listen within a wholly pronouncement-oriented universe. Such a cosmology, the current Big Bang Cosmology only expands, there is no back and forth rhythm to this cosmology as there is, for example in Plasma Cosmology. We live, unconsciously but surely decisively, within a pronouncement theory. Such a cosmology shows up in daily live as overly confident intellectuality, exaggerated emotional reaction, and the imposition of will. Within this kind of universe, opinions go back and forth between people, one person pouring forth their pronouncements, intellect, and opinions while the other waits for their turn. – not to respond but to do the same thing to the other person as just happened. If we learn to wait politely or to mirror back to others what they just said, then we imagine we have learned some techniques of listening.

This writing is much deeper than leaning techniques of listening. It is a speaking from within the "Listening Cosmos", we will come to be able to sense that the world all around us is in the deepest state of 'listening', and how the receptivity of listening forms the most foundational of all creative acts. And, if we can come to be listeners as the Spiritual Earth is the receptive, listening heart of the universe, then we can re-orient daily living to be in harmony with the ways of the spiritual presences of Cosmos and Earth.

The Crumbling of the Pronouncement Universe: its degradation into the Lie.

The anonymous "They"

Before describing the process of Listening, it is of some importance to have a sense of how the pronouncement universe now functions as its destructiveness comes to clarity all around and within us.

Pronouncement is the way of present collective consciousness. Our interest is not in political, religious, scientific, educational pronouncing, for all institutions seem equally affected, but rather how we who cannot help but be skeptical of such non-listening, are trapped into a narrow range of response. It is up to us to find the way out of pronouncement, isn't it?

The 'pronouncement universe' is characterized by our own abstract responses concerning the "anonymous "They" – the politicians, the corporations, the church, the educators, and so on. Such a way of being with others – as the "They" against whom we stand and criticize, keeps us isolated as ego-beings, unable to open to spiritual dimensions, and trapped in a kind of addiction to the 'me-me'.

The inability to listen is characterized by a strange quality of a certain kind of exaggerated 'bravado'. Don't let the bravado of pronouncement fool you into thinking that this form of speaking and non-listening is based in genuine confidence. It is, rather, an escape from our most human condition of living in the 'not-knowing'. It is the incapacity to make surrender to being completely human. To even be oriented in that direction requires living inwardly, constantly, with the question --"Why am I here?" Without that question, in whatever situation we are within, we seek only the comfort of sameness, seemingly guaranteed by the 'pronouncement universe'. Further, the incapacity to listen manifests as curiosity, the love to chatter about others with a seeming interest, but it is in fact an ongoing distraction from living within the question --- "Who am I"? It is not hard to locate how these inabilities of the receptive ear have completely invaded not only the individual life, but also our collective life, for example, politics, religion, and all collective forms. When the beings who inspire non-listening take hold of a nation, it is the major announcement of entering the time of the end.

The fact that you are reading this work, interested, deeply, in the concerns mentioned, indicates an engagement in spiritual work that is very demanding of you. You are somewhere within the following phases of what we stumble through in coming to realize that to listen to spirit, and be able to reply, not merely to follow the pronouncements of someone, requires an inner effort of great strength over a long period of time. The phases:

- I feel general dissatisfaction with the roles the present world imposes upon us.
- I then begin to visualize general abstract possibilities leading away from that fated way of life and becomes restless.
- This restlessness within can remain abstract and be drops away as I enter into being anonymous, even to myself.
- If the tension is maintained, the self-dialogue continues, and the possibility becomes clearer and more individually meaningful.
- Tension develops between the old way of life and the new but the unknown, resulting in anxiety.
- If this tension is sustained, specific action gradually becomes clearer. Rather than continue living in complaining, what can arise is the capacity of wanting to listen and hear what both may be 'above' and 'beneath' the distraction of pronouncement.
- If the awakening interest in hearing, in listening, continues through the tension and anxiety, the isolated individual comes to the experience of the I-being, a sense of being an individual embodied spirit/soul being, not, however, imprisoned within this individuality, for it is an 'open' individuality, capable of being in full participation with others.
- However, there is an inner place where a leap is involved. The phases described are not a natural evolution, where, at some point, you will feel the sense of wholeness and inwardly know exactly what that is like. And, when you face this leap into the void, it is not like there is another side as it is a leaping *into* rather than leaping *over*. This gap is surrounded by the presences of fear. It is possible to make this leap

only from the place of the *heart* as the interior of the heart, its very center, is incapable of fear, and thus we transform into heartfulness.

From whence does listening arise?

Listening, true listening cannot come about from what someone else says to us, not unless what is said to us is said out of the Silence. Silence is required for listening, and if what is said has no inherent Silence, we cannot listen. We can take it in and utilize it, such as we do with information, for information has no Silence. But we cannot hear the soul/spirit with this kind of hearing.

The greatest vessel of true Silence, always available, is the Natural World – Earth and all Her creatures. I do not mean that the natural world lacks the capacity of language and is therefore silent. We are not here using the word 'silence' in such a simplistic way. The natural world speaks, but in such a manner that for her, Silence is always in the foreground.

As I listen to the rustling of the leaves of the trees outside my door, the rhythm of the breeze, the soft sounds, the delicate movement of the branches, pulls me into the Silence. It takes very little attention to listen. And, right here, we have before us the demonstration of a very different kind of cosmology than the one we have come to adhere to. It is not at all that the natural world speaks to us, we listen, and then respond, even if that response is no more than a kind of sigh of joy. To think of listening this way puts us right back in the 'pronouncement' universe. We have not really listened. We typically use the Silence of the world and the Earth in this way when She speaks, and the most we take in and feel is a moment of being refreshed. There is so much more to listening to the Natural World.

We can be present with the Natural World in a primordial act of listening because the Natural World herself is a world of Listening! To say it even more truly, though it will thus be more radically – the world of matter is the world of listening!

The Greek word "physis", from which we receive the words "physics", and "physical" originally means "a rising", a "borning" an emerging from the hidden – emerging every moment -- from the Silence. This arising of things from the Silence occurs as a whole, a unity. It is Whole-coming-into-being. Thus, when you enter into The Silence, you feel the active presence of Wholeness. Silence is not divided up into parts, and it is itself not a part but the Wholeness itself. I am not speaking here of the Silence as the absence of noise, it is not that kind of silence. The Silence is the 'place beyond place', all around, within, beyond, below – everywhere, the "land of no-where". It's like that no-space from which all art that is true art emerges, the so-called "negative space".

Right here we enter a different cosmology, one of "giving" and our proper response is "re-giving", not out of demand or command, but the listening—not just to the vocal or written word, but to all that exists, reveals itself only when listened to. The word is the Word, the unity between the mythical and the literal. This truth cannot be known by the intellect, though intellect too can be taught how to listen. Reality is made of listening, so we must listen to understand. Our usual modes of consciousness only hear bits and pieces, not recognizing the presence of the Whole. We presently engage consciousness as it were arrow – going out to strike consciousness, bringing back only this's and that's, forming a certain view of reality 'out there', thinking that is all there is. Consciousness as a vessel has its own precision, but it is not one of capturing parts for examination by the mind. Focusing here primarily on the process of listening between people is only a rhythmic instance of the symphony reality sounding, a vibratory instance of Cosmic-Earth Wholeness undivided.

When we listen, truly listen to someone, we are abiding within our place as Earthly beings, and we are do something very unusual. We are hearing not the word, but rather, through the word we hear the particularity of the Silence as it configures itself to the moment. In order to listen, which has nothing whatsoever to do with the quiet you are in while someone is speaking, something else has to go on --- what I am hearing as content has to every moment be sacrificed, given away, in order to hear how the Silence is addressing us, through what is being said. The 'content' becomes secondary to any particular moment of its reconfiguring into the word. The practices we will be working with all rely on the understanding of listening as the making of something holy, the original meaning of the word – sacrifice.

Practice: Listening to the Natural World

Take a walk. Begin to listen to the Natural World that you are within, and indeed, you are an aspect of the Wholeness, not just an observer of it, capable of enjoying its Wholeness. Attempt to listen to the deep Silence of the physical world – not the given physical world as you typically notice it. Notice that the Silence is very different as you stand and simply gaze at a tree, and then go to a boulder and do the same thing, or to a plant, or anything else of the natural world. Even each particular thing – one tree and next to it another tree of the same kind, speak in the Silence very individually. The things of the Natural World do not speak our language, so we are not interested in trying to put what they say within Silence into our language. Rather, feel the ongoing presence of the physical world within your heart. When it feels time, stop and draw/color the immediacy of the currents of the voice of the world around you. This kind of drawing is not intended to be representational nor symbolic, nor figural. It is a sensing of the arising of the physical world, the ground of listening. The purpose of this drawing is so that what you are listening will reverberate even more strongly within your body. It is not at all necessary that the drawing be 'artistic'. What we are interested in is coming to have a real felt sense that each thing of the natural world is a living gesture.

Contemplative Listening with Others

We are interested in the practice of contemplative listening. Such a practice cannot be a matter of learning a technique. The practices we will be doing are not to develop techniques but rather to develop the capacity of wordless listening. Regardless of what someone may be talking about, it is possible to engage in contemplative listening. In contemplative listening, we hear something of the spiritual quest of the speaker; we hear that quest within the Silence, regardless of the content of the speaking. And, when we listen to the world around us – both the Natural World and the constructed world, we also begin to be present to their questing. Lived questions having to do with the spiritual life are more than personal or psychological questions. They are pre-personal, inter-personal, and trans-personal questions that address both the speaker and the listener. The true questions 'hide' within the most ordinary of conversations. They hide not out of fear, but to attract true listeners who are ready to listen.

People seek others to listen to them because they sense there is a felt question they have not found or asked themselves. When we are nagged or oppressed by a felt question, we do not feel ourselves. We feel the question as being apart from ourselves. Questions of this deep nature are not essentially psychological questions. We are usually present only to our psychological reaction to the unknown questions living within us. These deeper questions cannot be heard by us without cultivating the inner life being present with others who are truly capable of listening without engaging in psychological interpretation. Sometimes, often, the other is not necessarily another person, but something within the world, usually the Natural World that reveals to us our questing.

A central concern of contemplative listening is to learn to listen to felt questions of this spiritual nature. These questions are experienced wordlessly. They are also not what might be called existential questions either – questions about themes such as death, freedom, meaning, values… they are wordless, and are not questions that we have, but rather are questions that have us. We don't have a problem; we are a problem. To enter into this kind of question requires surrender.

You may have noticed as you read the above few paragraphs that you began to feel confused – who is speaker and who is listener? Who bears the spiritual question? When we truly hear a spiritual question within the most ordinary of conversation, it also becomes our question and it is in the place of this spiritual confusion (con-fusion – "with fusion") that the questing can be heard. Such moments of confusion are very, very different than a kind of unhealthy fusing with another. Only from the place of the heart, the heart can join with another person occur without the loss of individuality of both speaker/listener and listener/speaker. In fact, this kind of meeting together with another is of the essence of contemplative listening.

Explain to a friend that you are trying to learn to be more heart-aware and heart-present with others. Ask this person to sit across from you. Explain that you are going to begin by closing your eyes and doing a kind of preparation – you do not need to tell the person the details. Simply say that you are going to go inward and place your attention within the heart for a few minutes, and that when you open your eyes, you are simply going to sit with him or her for a few moments in Silence, but that you will be wholly with this person from the place of the heart. Indicate to the person that you are interested in how he or she experiences your heart-presence and will invite her or him to describe it after you come to an ending.

Then, ask your friend if she or he will go again to the place of the heart with you. This time what you are both going to try and do is to speak aloud with each other while being consciously focused within the heart. This means that while one person is speaking, the other person remains fully within heart-presence while listening, and the same thing occurs when there is the switching of who is talking and who is listening. Do not suggest a theme for the conversation. Let it emerge. Be in a comfortable place.

You are interested in 'listening' to the soul/spirit presence that is your friend. This presence has little to do with the content of what is being said. You can feel the soul/spirit being of your friend by noticing the Silence in the rhythm, the pauses, the tone, the gestures and the whole feeling of the 'atmosphere' you are within. In order to focus on this more invisible dimension, it is important that you do not 'leave' the sense of the content, but rather allow your attention to broaden enough to include this 'invisible' and wordless dimension that is nonetheless present through the speaking and listening that is going on between you.

After speaking with each other for maybe five minutes, then bring that to a close and speak with each other about the experience of being within the heart while speaking and listening in this way.

As a way of helping you broaden your attention to include the soul/spirit dimension, it may be helpful to imagine your friend as if he or she has just arrived on here on Earth.

To help you feel the mood of such a way of listening – it is as if your friend is a newborn child, or even better, a child on the way from the spiritual world, full of yearning to incarnate. Here are two poems that are exactly this mode:

The Vision

In a fair place
Of whin and grass,
I heard feet pass
Where no one was.

I saw a face
Bloom like a flower—
Nay, as the rain-bow shower
Of a tempestuous hour.

It was not man, nor woman:
It was not human:
But, beautiful and wild
Terribly undefiled,
I knew an unborn child.

Fiona Macleod

Chorus of the Unborn

We the unborn:
Already longing starts to work on us,
The shores of blood widen in welcome,
And we sink into love like dew.
Yet time's shadows still lie like questions
Over our secret.

You lovers
And sick with farewell, listen:
It is we who begin to live in your glances,
In your hands that seek in the azure blue;
It is we who bear the fragrance of morning.
Already your breath is drawing us in,
Admitting us into the depths of your slumber,
Into your dreams, our kingdom on earth,
Where our black wet-nurse, the night,
Will let us grow
Until your eyes mirror us,
Until our voices speak in your ears.

Butterfly-like,
We are caught by the clasps of your longing–
And sold to the earth like the singing of birds–
Fragrant with morning,
We are lights that approach to illumine your sadness.

Nelly Sachs
Translated from the German
by Mathew Barton

Before you enter into this listening conversation with your friend, be sure and read these two poems; not just once or twice but read them contemplatively and find your way into them. They are very much the language of the Silence, the language of the sense of what it is like to experience the soul/spirit being of another person. In our soul/spirit being, we are always 'arriving' from the spiritual worlds. It is not something that happened just at the moment we are born. It is happening all the time.

Listening through Wholeness of Body-Soul-Spirit
The Body in Listening

When someone speaks and we are listening not just with our ears but with the whole of our being centered in the heart, the speaking is felt bodily. We usual hear through our ears and listen with our head. Now, we can begin to feel a subtle bodily resonance. This resonance is its own way of knowing, something essentially wordless and thus pre-cognitive. Gradually, this resonance can be brought into harmony with the content we are hearing, and we hear the person or the Natural World as we have never heard it before. The only and best analogy is if you remember what it is like listening to someone speak when there is a strong presence of love between you. There is a difference, though. The kind of listening we are drawing attention to here does not have the reactive, emotional component that is often present with feelings of love. It is intimate listening and is much freer of the egotistical component – as for example, when we listen to someone from the place of emotional love.

With contemplative listening you have to be aware of staying in body, that is, being present to the resonance of the speaking. Some practice is needed to both become aware of what it is like to 'descend' from the head to the heart in listening, and to feeling currents spreading through the body.

You can deliberately make a descent into the soul-body by shifting your attention that is habitually located in the region of the head to the region of the heart. Try this first by simply being present to the Natural World around you. When we simply notice the Natural World, it will be through a visual consciousness located in the region of the head. Once you are aware of that, however, it is then possible to shift attention downward, toward the heart. You immediately notice that you are now sensing the Silence. This practice is very similar to the first practice in this series – of taking a walk in the Natural world and Noticing the body. Here, however, we want to begin to be even more aware of the body in listening.

A second result of shifting sensing to the region of the heart is that we begin to be present to what we are experiencing in its qualities as *gesture*. The mind categorizes so fast that it misses this aspect of what is being sensed, and thus misses allowing what are with to permeate our being.

Gesture is wordless. Nonetheless, it is important to try and approach describing what it is like. If I am sitting on the porch watching the trees – well, that is all the mind registers. Trees – and perhaps an emotional response of relief from anxiousness for a moment, or a sigh of letting go for a moment. And that registering is so strong that the 'silent speaking' of the trees, while present is severely dimmed. When you shift attention to the heart, sense the world, and feel the body resonance, then you may see something like:

> *The rhythmic swaying of a tall tree in the background while those closer are like guardian sentinels of the playful rhythms of what is going on behind them. The sunlight touches a portion of the trees as the shadows reach back and engulf the leaves behind, darkening them into a sense of mystery. Through the thickness of the swaying and the quiet greening, the soft, light blue above, shows through revealing a different reality, a farness that is invited into the play of the rhythm, and indeed, feels as if it is the very source of the swaying green movement.*

When you are present with the world in this way, the listening lingers on bodily long after the experience. You feel altered by the experience of allowing Earth to penetrate you. The nature of this lingering is important. The lingering is bodily felt, and is not just the registering of something that happened, but a process in which the body itself is undergoing change. Such a changing of our own physical nature, because, in our physical nature (which is also a spiritual nature) we are aspects of Earth (which is also the Spiritual Earth), our presence in listening affects the listener – that is, the Natural World.

Listening Deeper from within the Body

In listening while remaining completely open rather than waiting only to give an opinion or feel one inwardly, we become be aware of staying in body – that is, being present within the bodily activity of sensing-as-bodying. If you begin to be 'out of body' while listening, exhaustion results, because it then becomes possible for one person to drain the vital forces of another person without even knowing that is happening.

It is also possible to give out too much of one's vital forces in listening while being open and at the same time still mentally oriented in listening. The way to avoid such a possibility of becoming de-vitalized is to stay in-body, and yet fully open. That is just another way of saying stay in the activity of sensing, alchemically understood, not mentally understood; that is, sensing as the 'between', the field of creating that is every-moment creating the body-as-force-field. Staying in body does not mean concentrating on being in the body for that would be mental, and thus doing exactly the opposite of what is needed. Staying in body, means noticing the currents bodily occurring when listening, while, alongside that, hearing the content. It is a balancing that has to be practiced.

Contemplative listening does not involve going out-of-body, but rather more fully into sensing – in very particular ways. One enters into the vibratory force of another through the vibratory field of one's own body. It is like being in a musical field, where you hear the content of the music while at the same time are completely bodily immersed in it and one with it. And, while one is within this I-Thou field, one has to be doing something else simultaneously in order to truly listen; one has to be releasing trying to grasp everything that one hears, that is, to try and hold onto the content. When this kind of conversing occurs, listening occurs as a form of mutual embodiment as if within a ritual. Ritual is always embodied; it is the embodied way of being in connection with the more encompassing worlds while fully within body.

In listening, there is yet a further dimension of the ritual embodying with another -- the act of complete identification with what the other person is saying. You do not allow any aspect of your consciousness to be outside as an onlooker or "on-hearer".

One more – exceedingly important requirement for contemplative listening. You have to listen with your whole being – body, soul, and spirit, not with your mind. If you listen with your mind only, you will be completely subject to the qualities of the vibratory speaking of the other person which will enter into you as suggestion; in other words, listening then becomes a kind of reverse-hypnotism; you become infected with the suggestions of the speaker; nothing then happens between you and the other person. The other person has effectively persuaded you of what he or she already knows and you simply mirror that back to them.

When I speak of remaining in-body, the term 'body' here means the human being. It is not bodies or brains that see and hear think and feel, walk and talk, breathe and metabolize, but embodied human beings. However, if we go out of body while being with another, we become ethereal spirit trying to be with a human being.

So, by body, I do not mean physical body in our usual understanding of body, but in the extended sense that was introduced earlier – physis as a-arising. It may be helpful to have the sense of being in relation with the body as organism. The word 'organism' derives from the Greek verb *organizein* – to play on a musical instrument. The organism is the musical instrument with which we give form to inner feeling tones, embodying them in muscle and nerve tone, cell and organ tone, our tone of voice and the resonances of our words and deeds. The organism is also the body with which we resonate directly with other human beings in listening. It was Aristotle who first spoke of the human organism as a purposeful and communicative instrument or organon of the soul. The soul is a skilled organist, which forms its organs while playing them.

Find a place where you and sit quietly within the Natural Word. Enter into the heart and into the Silence. Notice when you come to an inner place – just by noticing, where the surrounding world changes in your sensing from being an "it", as happens in mental 'sensing' to be a 'thou', as happens when feeling in the whole being of body.

Sit with each other in Silence; what is the tone that you together are creating like?

After a time, as long as you like, shift out of this attention and sketch the resonant field that exists between you. Do not draw a representation or a symbol of the field but let what your body feels flow into your hands and come out as a sketch.

Do the exact same contemplative exercise with another person, that is, where you are sitting in the Silence with another person rather than with the Natural World. Again, after a time of being in this Presence, sketch the resonant field that you felt happening. After drawing the resonant field, have a conversation with the person you are with, telling him or her what you experienced, and asking that they describe what was experienced.

Wordless Listening: Giving Birth to Speaking

By now you must be realizing that listening is something more than the interval of quiet that takes place as you hear someone else speak and wait for your turn to do so, often not successfully. as you find yourself jumping in before the other person has finished their thought and sentence. We hear the outer human being; we listen to the inner human being. The only access we have to the inner human being is listening. But hearing the content of what someone says, even attentively, is not listening. Listening is a wordless attunement that patiently and meditatively 'gathers' the felt inner sense, resonance, and essence of what has been said.

Listening, as following the inner speaking of the other person, a speaking that in essence, in itself, is wordless, but can be heard, not as the content of words spoken, but THROUGH words spoken, when the speaking is inwardly felt by the listener as a resonating, ongoing, after-effect, or after-image, helps both you and the another person follow new ways of being rather than going along pre-established tracks. Listening is an active form of wordless inner communication through which we can be present to the a-rising of our new self in conjunction with the other person. While you both are bearing this new sense of self, but it has not yet been birthed, you both may feel uncomfortable, but it is an uncomfortable excitement of something about to happen. The discomfort here has nothing to do with psychological matters, with what you or the person has suffered in the past. Adhering to the past in pain, gives the emerging self a place to latch on to when there is absence of the capacity to listen on the part of others.

The emerging new selves have to be called-out through the listening process. Listening is a kind of midwifery. Thinking we understand interferes with the listening. A person knows if your listening is not led by the inner voice of their own being but merely hears along already heard and known tracks. We begin to truly listen when we sense something lacking or questionable in our understanding. To maintain our listening means maintaining this continuous sense of "not-understanding" and relinquishing the urge to understand. To try and make the other person clarify what I do not understand as listener is to shut down the listening. The access to the inner being of the other person is through the not-understood. To try and make the person clarify the not-understood so that I can understand it means that I am making the person speak according to what I already know. This shuts down the emerging new self. To maintain listening to what is not understood is to be aware of a center of absolute Silence within ourselves where we hear nothing. We have to become able to be present to this absolute inner Silence, even while listening. It is by guiding this original Silence that we guide our capacity to respond to what calls to us in this Silence. We learn to hold someone in our "aural gaze", just as you gaze into the eyes of a beloved. You know when you are listening when there is the felt quality of loving what is heard through the voice, through the words the other person speaks.

Practice

By now you should have an 'established' partner. That is, ask the person with whom you have been doing the practices above if she or he would now accompany you in this process. That will require meeting several times together. Do not do all of these listening practices that require a partner in one meeting.

For this practice, you can perhaps begin by reading this short section of the course to your partner so that he or she will have some sense of what is being asked. That is, read from section IV above, to here. Then, together, read the instructions below before doing the practice together.

a) Enter the space of the heart; speak together concerning how you maintain inner silence while not only hearing what someone says, but also while speaking

b) The focus of this practice is on speaking ONLY what wants to be said next, not "What do I want to say."

c) In order to speak and listen in this way, you have to wait for your inner voice to respond.

d) You will not be able to speak in terms of what wants to be said unless you feel the bodily field between you and unless you begin to be aware of the after-effect, the after-image that lives within you as the other person speaks.

e) You may notice that words come slowly or that there are pauses as you learn to listen to your inner voice. You will know when you are done. It is a sense that there is no more to say right now.

The Gift of Contemplative Listening

When we listen, we give someone our attention. That is a remarkable gift, the gift of our spirit-being. Giving someone your attention is an act, a doing that is something very different than paying attention to what the other person is saying. When you simply pay attention, you retain your attention and give a little part of it, as if you were having to hand out money. You guard yourself, making sure that you do not give all you have away. True attention is not like that, so when you pay attention, you are not utilizing attention at all. Rather, you are temporarily, for a moment, restraining your ego, holding it back, waiting to release it once again. Attention is whole. It cannot be divided into parts, hold one part, give another part away.

Giving your attention is listening is the act of holding someone in your attention. You literally hold them. The one speaking feels held. That is the first moment of the gift of attention. What does being held in someone's attention feel like? Attention is not our intellect, nor our understanding, nor is it our feeling. Holding someone in our attention does not mean being sympathetic. In fact, we still want to later work with the inner dimensions of listening when in conflict with someone.

The great mystery of attention. Georg Kuhlewind says, "We are our attention." Attention is not something that we have as one has a couple of quarters in the pocket. Giving attention is not like that. When you give your attention to someone, you give yourself completely, something that can never be a matter of mere technique.

Attention is Silent. So, you cannot give your attention until you find inner Silence. There are different levels of Silence that have to be gradually worked on and felt.

The capacity of listening is a spiritual path. It is not a technique that we can learn and then feel, "I've got it." It is a particular way of the unfolding of the individual spirit in the world. It is what we do with presence in spirit. It is a different way of being-in-the world. If we enter this path, everything changes. It is the way of surrender.

The spiritual path of listening involves stilling the various levels of our being:
The Intellectual Level
The Vital Level
The physical level.

The mental or intellectual level consists of the thoughts, opinions, beliefs, ideas, and values that guide our conscious thinking, conceptualizing, and decision-making processes. The mental level also includes the interfering beings known as Ahrimanic Beings and Luciferic Beings

The Vital level consists of the semi-conscious sensations, urges, desires, feelings, emotions, and attitudes. The vital is where we experience the vital sensation of the central nervous system, our urges, desires, and fears; where we experience emotions and passions of life; it is where the emotions are processed into emotional thought, that is, into the emotions' perceptions of knowledge. The vital level also includes the same interfering beings as well as the currents from the physical body level of the asuras – unconsciousness, death, suffering, and falsehood.

The physical concerns both the physical-etheric and the physical. The physical level consists of the subconscious awareness and impulses of the body; it is that which gives us our material form.

We have to learn to still the mind. Very, very hard. The process of being empty.

The practice

The practice of being empty is not at all the same as being in the Silence. There is not much to describe in terms of doing it:

After doing the heart alignment, placing attention in the center of the heart, and entering into pure body and pure heart awareness, just sit and try to be completely without thought. As you try to do this, at first you will feel great anxiety. That anxiety shows how the beings of thoughts that have already been thought have rushed in and occupy the empty inner space of silence and will do anything not to be evicted. Not only anxiety, you will also find that as you try to remain empty, it feels as if you are suffocating; it feels as if you will die. It takes a long time to still the intellectual level.

It is evident, however, that if stilling the intellectual level does not occur, true listening is not possible because everything that is heard is already interpreted by the world of given thought. The feeling of suffocating comes from the fact that our ordinary thinking is tied into our breathing. Steiner's brain-free thinking is very close to being empty because that kind of thinking occurs, as if 'above' the head. Sri Aurobindo describes how, if in complete stillness, one can be present to a space above the head, there will be the receiving of living beings of thinking.

The primary importance in stilling the mind in listening is so that what you say in response to what resonates inwardly in relation to one who is speaking really comes from that inward resonance and not from the mind. If it comes from the mind it will be suggestion, a form of hypnotism. Suggestion does not at all merely mean "I suggest you try this or that, or I suggest this may be what is going on. That is, of course, suggestion. But, when one is at all open, then it is the force of the reality of thought – thought as force that has an effect and produces something in the other, something that is not coming from his or her own being, but was placed there and makes the other person subject to the person speaking.

Another Practice of Stilling the Mind

It is nearly impossible to be within a stillness of mind for more than a few seconds. A better way is to give consciousness something to be focused on by resting within an image. This will allow you to feel what the body feels like when it is not invaded all the time with our thinking.

Go into the Silence and place attention in the center of the heart. Then, make an image of you lying on your back, floating on a clear, calm, lake. Be within this image – go into it. There will come a moment when you actually feel that you are floating on a clear, calm lake. The body will be floating there. As long as you are present within this sensation of floating on the lake, your mind will be clear and no occupied with thinking. You have given consciousness something to 'do' that is other than thinking. You will be able to notice, 'out of the corner of your consciousness' as you are floating on the clear, calm lake the complete relaxation of the body – and also, what the 'empty mind' feels like.

Do this practice on a rhythmic schedule, the same time every day, for a few minutes, for a month.

Next is the stilling of the vital, emotional level of our being. We may feel that it is quite easy, really, to refrain from reacting to what someone says, to remain emotionally quiet. When we listen, as long as we have not worked directly to still the vital, emotional level, this level still operates, though at a sub-conscious level. The way that the vital, emotional will find its way in, in spite of the fact that we try to withhold it, is curiosity. That is the way you will be able to detect the presence of the interfering vital, emotional. You may also find yourself reacting emotionally but trying to suppress it. Without developing capacities to work very directly with the emotional life (the subject of another course), there is but one way to still the emotional level of the soul: If you find yourself 'jumping' out of the place where you have lost the clear division between yourself and another person or yourself and the Natural World while engaged in contemplative listening, immediately, but gently return attention to the center of the heart. The easiest way to still emotion is to be within the heart.

Stilling of the physical body.
When you are within the space of contemplative listening, the most significant stilling concerns the physical body, but it is the one that may take the longest to develop. Here, it is not a matter of literally coming to body stillness, which implies leaving the body, for as long as you are within body, there will be felt body-currents. Spend time, practice time, just trying to notice that indeed there are such currents. It feels like your body is

'humming', or perhaps, 'vibrating'. These currents are quite subtle. When you are within contemplative listening, at first, there is a meeting between the currents of your body and the subtle currents within the body of who you are with, or the subtle currents of what you are within your attention in the Natural World. There is a difference between the two.

First, in the Silence and from the place of the heart, let your attention be within your body, and notice the quality of the currents there. It is very tempting to speak of 'frequency' here, because it is something like that. This is only an analogy and is not intended to imply there is a 'electrical' frequency.

Once you notice the quality of your own body currents, then place your attention with the bodily-felt currents of who or what you are with. For a moment, you have to let awareness of your own body-currents fade into the background. Then, notice those of the 'other', and notice that it is a different quality, although you are experiencing it within your body. The presence of the soul-body/spirit of who or what you are with is living within you if you are giving them your attention. In order to enter fully into spiritual listening, you have to adjust your body-currents to match the body-current of who are what you are with. To do this, imagine the currents of your body as a 'humming'. Enter fully into this humming. Then, notice the 'humming' quality of who you are with. Move the 'humming' of your body with your attention to match the humming quality of who you are with. The moment you do, you will experience the body as being within contemplative listening. You move the 'humming' of your body by an act of intent, the subtle will moving the currents. It is something quite different than thinking about what is going on in your body and may take a good while to develop this ability.

Working with the Listening Response

An Initial Caution: This section is the most subtle. You will most likely have to read it through several times, even if you think you understand it. The concepts themselves are something very new and it takes time and concentration to find your way into them. It takes even more time for the body to adjust to what we are here pointing to, and in order to be able to experience what will here be spoken of as 'the turn-around'.

We now want to work with paying attention to the turning point of listening; the way of verbally responding to what is felt bodily and is listened to in the Silence and what is felt with the inner being. Where and how does a verbal response come about from within the depths of contemplative listening? That is our question and our quest

1. When we are in the hearing phase of listening, we maintain listening by the continuous sense of 'not-understanding'; being within the quietness of mind and vital, emotional being, and adjusting to the currents of who we are with. Being within such empty-fullness, within body, feeling the field, is something very far from being passive. It is a force that can be felt by the one speaking as welcoming and yet forceful currents, drawing what is unknown by the speaker into speaking. A descriptive term for the felt sense of drawing the unknown by being in open and alert emptiness, is HEARKENING. To hearken is to be aware of a center of absolute stillness within ourselves where we hear nothing.

2. When we, as listeners, receive the sense of the inner being of the speaker within our own inner being, vibrationally, through the felt sense of body, we wait, in patience. We WITH-HOLD, hold-with, allowing what is heard and felt to resonate within our being, where we come, then, into union with the other, something decidedly different than "communication"; we commune in the field "between". We hold the speaking-person within our "aural-gaze." In patience, we allow our response to gather.

3. The TURNING POINT of listening is the point at which our inner listening response to a speaker begins to transform into an outward verbal response. If the turning point is minimalized, then listening shuts down without our realizing that has happened. The physical time interval of the turning point is less important than the psychological time interval that expands during the moment. The turning point has an expansive feeling when you have been listening to the 'between' and not just to what the other person is saying. The way that you can tell if you are in the 'between' is that speaking slows down; it slows down because it is gathering from the 'between' rather than just 'shooting back' pre-known concepts, or using 'listening-techniques' such as "yes, I understand," "Oh, that's certainly interesting", etc. In the gathering, it is the un-said, the un-spoken that is being heard. This is crucial because it is here that interpretation usually enters. And, if one tries to directly speak the unsaid to the speaker, it will be felt as interpretation, or as an authority speaking, or a kind of pronouncement. So, the real art of listening lies in this turning point.

4. The language of the turn-around needs to be open. You may experience yourself speaking 'falteringly', full of pauses, shorter, in sentences not quite 'worked out'. Here, this feeling of 'imperfection', is an indication of being within the 'coming-to-be' of a response rather than slipping back into pre-formed concepts and words that lose the pregnant pauses and turn too quickly into pronouncement and information.

Practices

1. What is the feeling-sense of words coming-into-presence-to-be-spoken? To begin to get at this sense, when you with someone in conversation, let your responding slow down, try to be within the Silence and within the heart, and, when you have bodily felt the 'currents' of the speaking of the other person or of the Natural World, and have adjusted your bodily currents to theirs, then notice, in the Silence, the manner in which a response begins to form out of the Silence. It is like a birthing taking place.

2. Work with your 'listening' friend with this practice. Again, as in a previous practice of contemplative conversation with your friend, begin by having centered yourself, entered into the Silence and the heart, and adjust to feeling your body currents and those of your friend. You do not have to pick a topic to speak about together. Just let the conversation emer. Both of you are speaking and listening; a conversation. As you are listening, notice the qualities of the moment of "Turn-around." And notice the qualities of your speaking from being close to this quality of "Turn-around" within the Silence.

The oscillatory motion between Self and Other

Rudolf Steiner has a great insight about speaking with another. He says that while one person is speaking, the other person is 'asleep'. And then, when the person who was 'asleep' begins to speak, the other person sleeps. This, he says, is the way that ordinary conversation takes place. We put the other person asleep when we speak. Developing capacities of listening begins to open up the space between speaker and listener. If we take Steiner's description and work with it, we can see that the space between speaker and listener is the space of waking-sleeping. We have to begin to get a sense of both of these as the whole of the space. The listening space is one of waking-sleeping, not an alteration between the two as usually happens, but being awake while being asleep – is actually the definition of Contemplation. While we, in our usual consciousness understand sleep to be 'unconscious', that is only because of our restricted range of consciousness. As this range broadens, we close the gap between waking and sleep because sleep is not at all unconscious in itself. It is the mode of consciousness within the spiritual regions.

The last thing said to the other person is the same as the last thought you have before going to sleep. Then, when you speak again, it is like the first thought you have when you wake up. The last thought before sleep reverberates into the spiritual world, and the first thought in the morning is the spiritual response to that last thought. This is the quality of presence we try to bring to contemplative listening.

With this description we have a quite amazing way of working with listening as a contemplative path. And, we are able to recognize that listening can be a path in which two people, together, initiate each other. That is, initiation, or developing the capacity to be present to the spiritual world consciously, while it has always been something that occurs as a result of individual meditative practice, alone, and the spiritual world is taken to be something other than the human world, is now in the process of changing. It has been for a long time – since the Grail stories of the 12th century. Only now, however, is this new form of spirituality becoming something that anyone can participate in. The spiritual world exists between two human Beings.

The moment of catching the sense of the spiritual worlds as 'between' oneself and another person is the moment of turn-around. When someone speaks, hear what is said as a response to your own last thought, resonating now in the spiritual world. The person who is speaking, is at that moment, the initiator – even though that person seems to be the one who is wanting to talk, wanting to be heard, wanting some kind of an answer to a question they are struggling with. What is never given any attention at all, however, is that the person who wants to be listened to is bringing a remarkable gift to the listener, a gift that has only one possible form of reciprocity – that of doing the same for the other person – being the initiator of their spiritual consciousness – in turn, in the turn-around. The turn-around that was practiced earlier, becomes very, very important; it is not just a technique – it is a central aspect of the contemplative listening initiation. However, there is something even more important. The initiation is actually mutual and occurs in the oscillatory movement between Self and Other in speaking and listening, now understood as last-thought, first-thought.

Practicing Contemplative Listening

Again, enlist your friend to engage in a speaking-listening conversation. Nothing new is required in the practice, but it is a deepening of how you have worked before, working to emphasize the contemplative moment of listening by inwardly repeating the last word a person speaks before she/her pauses to listen to what you say. Then, at that moment, be present to the way in which what is spoken by the other person reverberates within you; allow what is spoken to come to a stopping place. Notice the last words but try not to focus on them mentally. Say these last words inwardly, repeating them several times before you respond to the person. For example, if a person says "I am most afraid of not finding my real task in the world", you would repeat "finding my real task in the world." Then, wait, and notice the a-rising of words and be present to the turn-around. Your listening friend does not have to go through this process. Just see how the conversation unfolds when you do.

Distinguishing Contemplative Listening from Psychological Listening

We have been developing the contemplative path of Listening. We are all used to, conditioned to, think of listening as integral to coming to some kind of psychological insight. People go to therapists to be listened to, to be heard, to be understood. Psychology has so invaded all of culture that we automatically imagine that listening will lead to psychological insight. In developing the path of listening, we have carefully stayed clear of using listening for psychological purposes. The kind of listening characteristic of psychotherapy can turn out to be working the contemplative path of listening; when that happens, however, it is something that goes on unconsciously. There is a great deal of interest in what happens between a patient and a therapist. The interaction of psychotherapy is understood to be transference and countertransference. This theory of listening says that what goes on between therapist and patient, the "between" consists of projections by the patient of their felt sense of someone else, such as father or mother, onto the patient; and then later, Freud also discovered that similar projections occur on the part of the therapist. In this model, two people always relate through a third, the third of projection. In Jung's psychology, this model has become more sophisticated and approaches what we have been working with.

The "between" of listening is called the "interactive field". Transference, as well as the interactive field is understood as the field of 'Eros' in the archetypal psychology of James Hillman. In other forms of depth psychology, the field, or the third, can be any archetypal figure. Those individuals who live unconsciously in the interactive field carry the psychological label of "borderline personality". Such individuals lack the capacity to clearly differentiate their own being from that of the 'between'. Such individuals also lack the capacity to retain so-called 'boundaries. In psychology, the 'between' is also said to bring about difficulties of fusing with another personality and thus losing the sense of one's self. Well, if you read all of these kind of things and sink into the depth psychological tradition, listening will probably, if not frighten you, make you feel that you have to undergo deep psychological training in order not to get caught in the psychological pitfalls of listening. You don't, for example want to fall in love with everyone you listen to. And you don't want to be responsible for the confusion of boundaries between yourself and another person. And you don't want to be listening to someone who is "psychologically unstable" as you may be taken into the craziness. And, gosh, you want to avoid the currently popular psychological category of co-dependency.

You will fall into all of these traps if you believe in psychology and if you try to take the work of listening as a strictly psychological process. You will fall into these traps if you listen with curiosity and the desire to try and help others, as if you are the powerful one and the person wanting to be listened to is the weak one. We never, from the start of this course, set up the picture of listening involving one who talks and one who listens. Listening is a non-dual, contemplative, spiritual unfolding that takes place in the between of two individuals. It has to be held, however, as a contemplative spiritual path, but one that is being asked for in the current state of a 'non-listening', world.

If there is ambiguity about this, you will then fall into all of the traps of psychological interpretation.

How do you clearly distinguish contemplative listening from paying psychological attention to what is going on with the other person, or even psychological attention to the interactive field between you and another person? And, there is also the other side of that question. How do you clearly distinguish working the contemplative spiritual path of listening from imposing spiritual pre-conceptions on listening that utilize spiritual rather than psychological interpretation.?

The primary distinction between a psychological and a contemplative approach to listening is this: In a psychological approach, what is always heard is absence, void, and thus longing, need, desire, want, seeking. If you listen in terms of lack, in terms of someone trying to find an answer to something missing within themselves, then you are engaged in psychological listening. In a contemplative approach to listening, what is always heard is fullness. Nothing is lacking or absent. Everything is already here and present and the work is completely oriented toward developing the inner capacity of hearing the fullness of what is present. Psychology, in its therapeutic dimension is always based in the imagination of lack.

The practices of listening are all within a kind of cosmological context, at least within a felt sense of the Whole. If contemplative listening is taken as a set of techniques, the practices can actually become dangerous because they open up certain aspects of our being, for example, one or more of the bodies, without the least sense of what is happening and the long-term result.

I think of practices more like learning to play a new instrument or learning a new language. You have to have a sense of the Whole. The practices, then, are in the realm of synthesis rather than in the realm of analysis. Plus, when a 'practice' is for the purpose of having an experience, the development of a new capacity is not prompted or strengthened. A contemplative practice is not separated out from the whole; and, therefore, it helps you be more present and more within the sense of the whole. A practice that is for the sake of having an experience is more of a 'nerve jangling' than a soul awakening. The two are not so easy to distinguish; and, for people who have not gone through soul awakening, it may take a very long time for a practice to be felt. And, such a contemplative practice that is an aspect of Wholeness has the quality of continuing to deepen. There is no end to it; how could there be, given that it is an aspect and expressing of a Whole. A practice that is to make one have an experience does not deepen us.

The way through the confusions is really simple. The felt decision is to work with listening only as a contemplative path of inner development that occurs in conjunction with another person and with the Natural World. This decision has to be followed through with beginning to form all of your attention toward what is occurring within you as a result of the contemplative path of listening. You begin, for example, to listen to dreams differently. You notice what is happening around you differently. You begin to see that the path of listening is inwardly changing you. Listening then, is not something just for the moments between you and another person but begins to be your very mode of being-in-the-world, central to contemplative living with Earth.

Does the other person have to know that this is what is happening? No. Their spirit awaits this chance, this possibility. If anything, at first, the person may experience a kind of disappointment at the personality level. Disappointment that you are not listening to his or her egoism and falling into it. And, one must be prepared to face the interesting trickery that occurs that will try to pull you into that personality egoism.

Contemplative Listening in Times of Conflict

A wonderful arena to work inwardly as a way of discerning the difference between a psychological approach and a contemplative approach to listening is how to work with listening in the midst of a conflict with someone. Conflict with someone presents the strongest possibility of contemplative listening and it is where this possibility is most often missed because of the fear brought about when there is conflict, fear that results in a contraction of the body so that the realm of the 'between' is lost and one is abandoned to one's own personality and whatever is affecting it and the resulting incapacity to realize that when one tries to speak and listen to another person in the midst of conflict, one is essentially having an unconscious conversation with oneself. For some this unconscious conversation occurs primarily at the mental or intellectual level, which sounds very rational, but is no less isolated and isolating than trying to be in conversation with someone who is locked and isolated with the emotion and reaction of anger.

What would lead us to suggest that conflict provides the greatest possibility of spiritual advance? Because trying to listen in the midst of conflict is a situation of the greatest possible tension. This is the tension of opposites, and this tension produces the strongest field of oscillation. But, only under the circumstance that one or other or both do not fall into separate psychological domains and do so unconsciously. The great tendency in situations of conflict is, even when there is the attempt to listen, to see the other person as figuring into the painfulness of the situation (maybe it is possible, though very difficult to avoid seeing the other person as the cause of the difficulty or the reason for it), think that the painfulness is something to get out of, or that a psychological approach is definitely what is needed.

In order to listen in the midst of conflict, a breather is necessary. Here is a technique. (this is clearly a technique and not a practice):

When conflict with someone begins"
   1. Take a breath: Inhale and identify within you what is upsetting you.
   2. Let go of it as you exhale.
   3. Second breath: Inhale and feel the Silence at the center of your being.
   4. Exhale
   5. Third breath: Inhale and ask yourself inwardly "What's next?" Listen.
Exhale and notice what comes to your mind.

Beyond technique, however, is the question of the spiritual importance of conflict, and how to avoid psychologizing it, and instead, take the situation of conflict into the contemplative practice of listening, not to try and resolve conflicts or learn how to get along better with someone. As such, one has to take a longer-range view. If, in a given situation, the conflict still takes over, then it is more like a contemplation that did not go so well rather than an emotional disaster, and it becomes a matter of research rather than scheming how to win next time.

In order to follow the contemplative path of listening in a situation of conflict, it is absolutely necessary that everything said be extremely specific without any generalizations whatsoever. This requirement is actually one of the main reasons conflict is actually a paradigmatic situation for the contemplative practice of listening. Listening cannot occur when abstractions or generalizations or sentiments or notions taken from somewhere else, or truisms enter.

Another aspect of the contemplative practice of listening-in-conflict is the need to relinquish what will happen in the listening. Since these kinds of situations are charged with wanting to win, one gets a chance to see that 'attack mentality' within oneself, which is simply an intensification of that mentality that is always present but usually hides. Listening as contemplative practice gives the opportunity to see and turn away from that mentality in oneself. Listening has no intention other than the listening itself. It is more like poetry than like discourse. Everything within listening carries its own inherent meaning. There is nothing outside the listening that listening wants. If change comes as a result of listening it is as a result of the grace of being, in listening, in the presence of the spiritual world. The change has nothing to do with what we have tried to have happen because we have relinquished trying to have something happen.

What is the spiritual purpose of conflict? This is the kind of question appropriate contemplative listening. A question that takes the whole phenomenon of conflict out of the realm of emotion and out of the realm of psychological difficulties, and even out of the realm of viewing conflict as something gone wrong. The spiritual purpose of conflict is where we get the chance to see all that interferes with listening and also the opportunity to listen through the difficulties rather than living in a emotional/psychological fantasy that they have to be gotten rid of.

Everything that comes forth in a situation of conflict comes forth in order to be offered to the spiritual worlds. Not for judgment, not for transformation, but because the spiritual world is intensely interested in all of the possibilities that we are as human beings. Not just the aspects that we think are "spiritual". A lot of inner work has to take place to clear old and useless notions of how we think the spiritual world works. Such clearing is even more important for those engaged in spiritual work, for those who think that they have left old religious notions behind. The notion that the spiritual worlds want us a perfect is such an old religious notion. The more of the possibilities that we are that are revealed to the spiritual worlds, the more possibilities that are the spiritual world become available to us. This way of seeing, however, is based on being engaged in an ongoing spiritual work that has achieved a certain level.

In order to engage in contemplative listening in a situation of conflict, only one capacity has to be developed that is in addition to the capacities described thus far.

When speaking with someone with whom you are in conflict, emotion comes out of an unknown place and 'has you' before you even notice that has happened. However, you can begin to be present to a subtle inner reaction to 'being had'. There is a kind of pleasure in it. There is a tendency to go ahead and go into the reaction. If that can be noticed, then there is an inner space of freedom. When that tendency is recognized, then you have to inwardly go back to the instant the emotion emerged and 'catch it there', at its inception. And go through the technique described above. Then, all of the aspects of contemplative listening we have worked with are attempted in this kind of situation.

Contemplative Action

Introduction

Our conversations and practices together concerning contemplative action take us into relatively unknown places of our soul and spirit, the spiritual/ soul realms of the will. We all certainly have an understanding of what it means to act, and we do so all of the time, and we may try to do so in ways that are of service to others, or are in keeping with being a researcher into bringing soul/spirit to action in the world. The striking thing is how inner presence seems to be so strongly divided from outer action. Each of us could, with no trouble, say what we mean by 'contemplative action' – the words themselves seem to tell us that it is 'action', doing something in the world, but doing it while being conscious of the action itself as the presence with the physical world, the soul worlds, and the spiritual worlds all at once. And, perhaps the most central aspect is action that is for the sake of something or someone other than ourselves. The tricky part, perhaps the central beginning, is to be able to notice that when we are doing something that seems to be for someone else, or some other reason – such as doing something for Earth, even stronger egotism can intervene than when we directly and clearly do something only for ourselves – because at least then, we are aware of the focus. But, when we seem to be engaged in doing something for others, we are not so ego-aware, and ego actually is open to having free reign, though in disguised ways.

Meeting Our Ego, The Shadow of Our I.

Through the first three modules of this course, the notion of the ego came up more than once. And, taking 'about' ego begins to feel an abstraction, for our ego is not so good at hearing not so wonderful things about itself. In addition, ego is so close, we are so identified, that we can only get hold of the mental abstraction. So, let's begin this work with contemplative action by meeting exactly Who this ego is. Ego is not the individual you see in the mirror, nor who you as you imagine yourself to be, or who others address when speaking with you. And ego is also not that very deep and subtle and light center of your being, you as an "I". Ego and I are very close, so perhaps it would be good to begin by meeting them both, getting to know them. Then, entering contemplative action is likely to be much easier.

Practice – Meeting Ego

Do the heart alignment. Go to the interior of the heart. Enter the Silence. Enter into pure body-awareness and pure heart-awareness.

Imagine the presence of a being, who looks just like you, sitting with his/ her back to your back. This being is of a subtle nature, so don't literalize the picture. It is both a felt sense of you and it may also have the quality of being as if visual. But, you can picture the being as looking like you. This is your spirit-being, who carries the burden of your unclaimed shadow aspects of the spirit. This presence is something considerably different that the Shadow as described by Jung and worked with in analysis and now in the numerous ways the concept has become popularized. The presence of this figure is your individual spirit holding, carrying you as ego. We begin to get the sense of ego as our spirit acting as it were independent of the spiritual and soul realms.

Sit quietly, in Silence. Then, let this being glide like a breath through your body, so that touches every cell of your body as it is moving from the back to the front. Let it move through you and then "float" in front of you. Look at your spirit-shadow in the eye and admit its presence into your subtle-sensing field – the body-sensitivity that extends beyond the physical body. Be aware of the qualities, gestures, and features of this being, no matter how difficult they might be. Let this being say what it wants to say to you; let it tell you who it is and what it wants. Then, ask for the grace of change, that this presence does not dominate you unconsciously. Take time and let this unfold slowly. If you seem to be 'making up' things, don't be concerned. Just notice.

After this is done, while you are sitting facing each other, feel he way in which both of you together form a rounded space with its midpoint between you.

Lead both figures – the Shadow and the immediate image of your body to this midpoint. Let them both lean slightly inward, into the vortex of the heart. Feel this movement. Be present to the qualities – the power of love that was previously frozen in the Shadow is now freed.

Practice – Meeting "I"

The I is always invisible, is 'no-thing' and can be imagined as the inner sanctuary of who we each are, so this practice has to be understood to be an imaginal practice. It is not an illusion, not by any means, but rather it as if we can meet the I only at a juncture of being clothed by what we already know. It is possible, to feel a sense of the I in its 'trailing clouds of glory.'

a) Make an inner image of your full being (i.e. body, soul, and spirit – but you don't need to think of these dimensions) as an egg-shaped multi-colored mist of light extending outside, around and through your physical body.

a) At the center of this mist is a tiny spark – your usual "I"

b) Your "I Am" is outside this egg. See it as a golden mist reaching down to your multicolored being.

c) Sometimes it reaches the surface of your being; sometimes it withdraws into the universe.

d) See it as a flowing, continual movement like gentle waves kissing the shore. Sometimes the sun glistens in this golden mist making it finer and lighter.

e) Sometimes the sunlit mist shines into your egg-shaped being like through a dark forest – engaging your small I, that tiny spark at the center of your being.

f) The tiny spark starts to flicker within you, and grows, becoming one with the sunlit mist.

The I Am Mantras

To be inwardly, bodily-gesturally said from the place of the central point of the heart:

> *This I Am is a body of Light*
> *I Am a body of Light*

> *This I Am is a body of Silence*
> *I Am a body of Silence*

This I Am is a body of Love
I Am a body of Love

These two practices are essential for being able to enter into contemplative action. They are contemplative practices to be sure, but they are also the kind of practices that need to be done not just once, not just for a while, but periodically – from now on. They keep you honest in contemplative action.

Encountering the Inevitability of Power in Contemplative Action

We want to inquire into the ways that power inserts itself into nearly all acts of contemplative action. Ego inserts itself into action through a doing that inevitably involves a relationship between power and weakness. If this polarity is taken into contemplative acting, however, then we risk acting only in order either to experience or to maintain a sense of power.

Think of even the simplest action that seems to be helpful. Someone tells us of some difficulty. We immediately provide suggestions, or more likely pronouncements on what to do. Or, we do something that in our eyes, and maybe even in the eyes of the other person seems to be helpful. And, perhaps it is helpful in solving the immediate problem. Maybe a friend says that they are about to be shut out of their apartment if they don't pay the rent. We give the person the money, and the problem is solved. This kind of action, contemplatively viewed, maintains a division between the powerful and the weak, and is thus an action of the ego rather than the I. We are not evaluating or judging that action and are interested only in developing an inner clarity concerning the unique nature of contemplative action.

Some Images of Contemplative Action
Rather than beginning with describing the difference and relation between action that maintains one's sense of power and action that is truly contemplative, it may be helpful to look at some images of contemplative action.

A Hasidic Tale
"How can we determine the hour of dawn, when the night ends and the day begins"?

"When from a distance you can distinguish between a dog and a sheep?" suggested one of the students.

"No," was the answer of the rabbi.

"Is it when one can distinguish between a fig tree and a grapevine?" asked a second student.

"No."

"Please tell us the answer then," said the students.

"It is then," said the wise teacher, "when you can look into the face of a human being and you have enough light to recognize in him your brother. Up until then it is night and darkness is still with us."

"The Secret" by Jean Vanier

"The *secret* is…. that we need each other, the weak and the strong. Obviously the weak need the strong. What is less easily understood is that the strong need the week. That is the secret.

Many come to L'Arche (the movement started by Jean Vanier for working with those who are mentally and emotionally in need) to serve the poor, and that is good. But then they will stay in our communities, because they have discovered that they are poor, that we all have a wound, that we are all vulnerable, that there is a broken part in each of us,….that we all have masks and a system of protection, hiding our vulnerability…that inside all of us there is a place where anger hides, and fear, and depression, a capacity to live and lock ourselves up into a world of dreams. That is the *reality* of all of us. We have a handicap. It's all of us…some it's more visible, others its less. But the reality is there. We come to serve the poor. We discover, after a while, that *we* are the poor……

People come to discover the secret, the secret which obviously many do not know, because in many places there is that need to crush the weak. But that secret also is known in many, many places: that those who are powerless have the gift to give to transform our hearts. The secret…. that if we get close to those who are broken, according to our call, according to the gift of our hearts, according to our situation, if we get close to people who are powerless, people in need, people crying out. If we enter into relationship with them, not just….., not just doing something for them, but looking them in the eyes, entering into a relationship where we enter into them. If we do that, certainly we will touch our own pain. We will touch our own fears. That is why we need community, because we can do nothing all alone. We need to belong. We only know ourselves and each other when we live with our weaknesses."

The Greek Myth of Chiron

Chiron was the first Centaur, a being that has the body of a horse and the head of a human. His mother was so disgusted when she saw him at birth, she abandoned him. He was brought up protected by Apollo. Chiron was accidentally wounded in the thigh by Heracles, with an arrow, tipped with the poison from the Hydra. He was the offspring of a god, Kronos. It is told that Kronos, in the shape of a horse mated with Philyra, a daughter of Okeanos.

Chiron was incurably wounded, accidentally shot by an arrow by Achilles. He went and lived in a cave on Mt. Pelion. The back of this cave was an entrance to the *Underworld*. The opening of the cave looked over a great and beautiful valley. In this valley grew all the herbs that could heal any illness. Chiron became learned in the art of healing, though he himself could never be healed. He was the teacher of Asclepius, the god of healing. Finally, Chiron made a deal with Zeus. In return for being healed, Chiron agreed to relinquish his immortality. He agreed to take upon himself the suffering of Prometheus, who was chained to a rock, his liver eaten away each night by an eagle, as punishment for bringing fire to the realm of the humans. Chiron thus took on the suffering and death of Prometheus. When he died, he was elevated to the stars and there shows forth as the Constellation of Sagittarius.

In 1977, it was thought that a new planet was discovered, and this planet was named Chiron. It seems that rather than a planet, this body, is actually a massive comet. Nonetheless, astrologers now work with this body in astrological charts. In one's astrological chart, Chiron's placement indicates where one is wounded, in what sector of one's life, which shows up as the particular house in which Chiron occurs. Whatever kind of wound's one bears are also the source of one's power of healing others.

The Washing of the Feet
From John 13:1-11
"Now before the feast of the Passover, when Jesus knew that his hour had come to depart out of this world to the Father, having loved his own where in the world, he loved them to the end.

And during the supper, when the devil had already put it into the heart of Judas Iscariot, Simon's son, to betray him, Jesus, knowing that the Father had given all things into his hands, and that he had come from God and was going to God, rose from supper, laid aside his garments, and girded himself with a towel. Then he poured water into a basin, and began to wash the disciples' feet, and to wipe them with the towel which he had tied around him.

He came to Simon Peter who said to him, "Lord are you going to wash my feet." Jesus answered: "You do not know now what I am doing, but later you will understand." Peter said to him: "You shall never wash my feet." Jesus answered: "Unless I wash you, you will have no share with me."

…. "When he had washed their feet, and taken his garments and resumed his place, he said to them: " Do you know what I have done to you? You call me Teacher and Lord; and you are right, for so I am. If I then, your Lord and Teacher, have washed your feet, you also ought to wash one another's feet. For I have given you an example, that you also should do as I have done to you. Truly, truly, I say to you, a servant is not greater than his master; nor is he who is sent greater than he who sent him. If you know these things, blessed are you if you do them."

Working Imaginally with the Stories

Each story gives a somewhat different picturing of contemplative action. To just read the stories, though, and figure out how contemplative action seems to work, does not do much. We must go deeper than this, for you can then discover the clue to what is asked for in developing an inner life capable of contemplative action.

Begin by asking yourself, with each story … how is it possible to do what is done in each of these stories… and in such a way that there is never a separation between the contemplative act and the actual doing. That is the central question. If we work with the stories in any other way, they easily slide into kind of sentimentality where if we try to act as the characters in each of these stories, we will be captured immediately by ego forces.

Practices

To prepare for working with each story imaginally, do the heart alignment, enter into the Silence, place attention in the center of the heart, and enter into pure body-awareness and pure heart-awareness.

1. With the first story, inwardly make an image of meeting an individual with whom you have an ongoing difficulty and have come to live with anger, hurt, and evaluation of that individual. Do not attempt to 'solve' these ways or resolve them. Simply do as is done in the story; meet the person imaginally, enter into the image of sitting, looking into each other's eyes; let unfold whatever wants to unfold.

2. With the second story, what vulnerability that you bear has given rise to a desire to engage contemplative action? How does it motivate you to do contemplative action right now? (This will change as a result of this work.)

3. With the third story, the key in this Chiron myth is that his healing power is given in the image of his home – the cave that looks out over the valley of every healing herb; while the back of the cave is the entrance to the Underworld. It is the connection with the Underworld that is the source of the contemplative action. We will work extensively with coming into conscious connection with the Underworld. For now, though, what are some of your own images of the "Underworld"? What do they have to do with contemplative action? The interest here is in coming into connection with collective notions of anything like an Underworld, which is in religious imagination connected with notions of 'hell'. Or, it is someplace deemed dangerous and a place to stay away from, even imaginally. Are such collective images valid?

4. With the fourth story, once you recognize how power is involved in your contemplative action, how do you go about releasing that power?

Re-Imagining Soul in relation to Contemplative Action

A. The word "psyche", from which we get "psychology", the study of the psyche, was not originally the center of the self, the center of personality. In the Iliad of Homer, for example, Psyche (psukhe) meant "breath"; it does not mean literal 'breath', but rather, being able to be wholly receptive to the gods, and here, receptivity is a very active stance, it does not imply passivity. Homer also used this term to refer to life, and to soul. The psukhe was the soul gradually received into and sustained by the life and love of others, by parents, family, tribe, and by those for whom the psukhe was to be in relation with, ultimately by the Spirit of the universe. This sense of the psyche is understood by Jung's psychology and its later developments as life, or soul, being breathed into human beings by the gods. But, the early usage went further than this and included other persons. Psukhe was a gift from others, the 'active-receptivity' that others engage in when with us, not just when together at a given time and place, as psukhe is not bound by time and space. Only later did the psyche come to mean the center of the private personality. This meaning of the soul as being generated by others and the soul of others being generated by receptivity to others, as well as to Earth herself, is central to the deepest sense of contemplative action. It is my spirit-soul and your spirit-soul, when truly receptive to the other person, that breathes the life of soul into the other person. And it the active-receptivity of spirit-soul of the other person that breathes the life of soul into me.

B. Soul, understood in this new way (which is actually the very old way, not only historically old, but old meaning first, primary, original), means that contemplative action originates at the level of the soul. A great deal of our doing, even so-called altruistic doing is not done from the level of the soul, not in an explicit way. Our actions in the service of helpfulness are typically mixed. We serve others as a way of gaining some degree of ego satisfaction, and the serving of others also, at the same time goes on in this deeper sense of generating the soul of the other who generates my soul. The nature of contemplative action is thus always paradoxical. Our serving is always the paradox of doing something that gives us a sense of one of a variety of kinds of power and self-identity, and at the same time, there is this deeper level where we are responsible for the other person. Even further, we are, at the level of soul, not only responsible for the other person, but also responsible for their responsibility. We do not, however do this act in a self-generative way; it is always occurring as a communion, in which the other person is also doing this very same thing for me.

Contemplative action entails being much more aware of this basic situation; this awareness constitutes a first meaning that differentiates contemplative action from other forms of altruistically oriented action.

C. Ego is our center of power, the sense we have of an identity, of practical knowledge, of the capacity to be someone and do something. The soul is our center of weakness because soul is not self-generated; we, each of us, rely completely upon the divine worlds, the spirits, the dead and most significantly, others, for soul, whether we realize this or not. A person in need, any kind of need, at that moment does not have a strong sense of power in the way that I am using the word power here; a strong ego. But, typically, they are not consciously present within soul either, for then they would be fully prepared to be in contemplative action.

A person who has the capability of being of help to one who has a weakened sense of power, has power. Here is the central difficulty of service that must be worked through to come to healthy ways of contemplative action. There are actually two parts to the difficulty; first, acting to be of help can easily become a matter of the powerful serving the weak in order to have, retain, and experience their own sense of power. This can and does happen, no matter how idealistic and pure the notion of help might be. The second part of the difficulty lies in the fact that when helping becomes a matter of a relation of the powerful to the weak, when we serve out of our power, we also run the risk of losing altogether the sense of our soul, our own center of weakness.

D. A further understanding of soul which derives from what was just stated is:

The psyche is the Other in me (Other meaning the presence of the divine worlds, the archetypal worlds, the spirits, the dead --- and of particular importance for contemplative action, the other person, in the soul dimension). From the viewpoint of ego consciousness, the reality is quite different. The other person is, for our ego, a kind of object "over there", someone who can satisfy or frustrate my needs and desires. From the viewpoint of the ego, if I help someone, it is for my own satisfaction; it may be, for example, out of pity, or out of imagining the world would be a better place if there were not homeless people, or because helping makes me feel good, or because I imagine that helping others is something good to do. Whatever the reasons we are of service to others, considered from the viewpoint of ego consciousness, none of them are to be evaluated as less than worthwhile. I am not saying that doing things out of ego consciousness is not serving. I do want to put forth the view that this kind of serving is different than contemplative action. In addition, the view of acting for the sake of someone else from ego consciousness isolates the self from the other;

in this view we are completely separated from each other, so my acts of serving, rather than coming from a deeper meaning of responsibility, come from what I think is my generosity, my goodness, my virtue, my responsibility--- thought of, though, as if it were self-generated responsibility.

Still, these distinctions have to be taken lightly. Serving, it seems, is almost always mixed, involving both the psyche and the ego. Entering consciously into contemplative action, though, begins to alter the center toward conscious soul/spirit presence of the other.

E. In this mix, the work, it seems, is to be present to the level of the psyche. At the level of the psyche, we are together with the other person, but in a very particular way. If extreme individualism characterizes the functioning of ego consciousness, that does not mean that collectivism characterizes the functioning of the soul. It does suggest that the soul can be radically altruistic (I say, 'can be' because this is so only when experienced from within the purity of heart), is not interested in anything like private wants, and by its very nature is responsible to the other person. There is a true individuality to the soul; we are who we are by virtue of our responsibility toward the other person. The individual identity of the soul is its responsibility for the other. Responsibility here, however, has a completely different meaning that the usual sense of responsibility, which is a learned ego characteristic. Here, we mean 'response-ability'.

F. A picture of moving from ego-centered service toward the direction of contemplative action: A volunteer at a day shelter for the homeless:

"When I walked in I was hit with a bad odor. I looked around and everyone seemed the same. They were all shabby and mostly alone. Many were asleep hunched over on chairs or curled up on pads on the floor. At first, they were all the same: they were poor; they were simply poor…After a while I got to talking to a man near the coffee counter. He told me about his tough luck as a family man…Another man joined us and told me he hadn't seen his daughter in twelve years….After a while, they weren't all the same. I went in there expecting and seeing stereotypes. I met guys who blew my stereotypes apart. Each one had a story that was both like and not like everyone else's. Each on had more to his life than being unlucky and therefore poor. "

We do not create goodness from out of ourselves; we find goodness, outside of ourselves, in the other, goodness appearing in the guise of needing help, for otherwise we would not be able to recognize the presence of goodness, but only our known concepts of it. The individual above went into the situation with a notion of doing something good for others. A shift was made when he found the goodness that was there. The goodness that is there, then, draws out the goodness I am:

"People who are powerless and vulnerable attract what is most beautiful and most luminous in those who are stronger; they call them to be compassionate, to love intelligently, and not only in a sentimental way. Those who are weak help those who are more capable to discover their humanity and to leave the world of competition in order to put those energies at the service of love, justice, and peace. The weak teach the strong to accept and integrate the weakness and brokenness of their own lives which they often hide behind masks." (Jean Vanier, <u>The Scandal of Service</u>)

Meeting the Other

Totality and Infinity

One of the more important ways of imagining the complex relation of soul and ego consciousness in serving comes from the contemporary Jewish philosopher, Emmanuel Levinas. His primary work is entitled <u>Totality and Infinity</u>. While his philosophy is quite difficult to understand, he approaches the question of soul much in the way it has been presented here. He introduces two concepts – totality and infinity. In the description above, when the volunteer first enter the homeless shelter his attitude is one of totalizing. His experience, at first, is nothing-more-than what his pre-judging categories made of it. The men in the shelter were nothing-more-than-poor. The stereotype helps the perceiver to make sense of what is experienced. Ego consciousness functions in this totalizing way.

The concept of infinity, on the other hand, is the soul's breathing into the other and our being breathed into soul by the other. From this point of view, the other person is always-more-than what I know. But, this "always-more-than" is an actual experience, not just a lofty thought.

Noticing how these two levels of experience occur in our relationships with others can be extremely helpful. What is of great importance is how the other person virtually always pulls us out of our totalizing consciousness. We are bopping along, doing our work, comprehending our situation, feeling in control, and then, someone else enters and makes a request, or asks a question, or gives another point of view. All of a sudden my totalizing attitude gets tilted, disturbed, and even shocked. We become irritated that our clear categories of understanding and functioning are brought up short. The inherent autonomy of the other person will not be totalized. I am, instead, confronted with infinity. The idea of totality is produced in the experience of things needed, grasped, comprehended, controlled, and consumed. I can, indeed, treat people this way, even when I think that I am serving them.

The idea of infinity is produced in the experience of the other person as essentially *uncomprehendable, uncontrollable, and unconsumable.* Out of the concept of totality, I may move toward helping someone, but it is totally out of my categorizing them as "needy", "poor", "wanting". Out of the concept of infinity, *I am called to respond to the soul, somewhat visible through weakness of ego, and not at all a center of power, but of receptivity.* Here, the other person is outside my grasp. The other person is recognized in his or her inherent worth and dignity; it is not derived from my needs nor from my evaluation and judgment of the other person. The other person, as infinitely Other, commands dignity, and this dignity is revealed to my immediate experience.

Practice
The work done with practices of Heart Initiation are an important preparation for encountering the receptivity of another person through your active receptivity. Now, though, the practice room is the world. Each day for the next week, without pre-planning it, see if, when you meet someone, if you can be in the heart immediately and perceive, sense, be present to the utter boundlessness of that being. What is that like? And what is it like to do so in full clarity of consciousness, not a kind of semi-dreamlike state; but also not a mental consciousness either.

Further Clarification of Contemplative Action
A. Why everything above is no more than getting to the Portal

1. If you have faithfully read to this point – perhaps several times, and have tried the practices, which have to be done a number of times so that they begin to be capacities rather than inner self-instruction, you have come a very long way toward contemplative action. Still, it is almost certain that there is an expectation that your actions in this mode will produce visible results, results as you have come to expect doing something producing not only something tangible, but recognizable as connected with your doing – as a kind of cause-effect sequence.

2. Contemplative action does not work in this way at all. There is a further developing involved. Contemplative action is the doing of something in complete absence of expectations of outcome, while at the same time, being alert and aware and capable of noticing – first that the contemplation is the doing, and that the contemplation in rest and inner Silence is one aspect of the action-awareness, while what shows up synchronistically in the world is the second aspect of the action-awareness.

You may have to read the above paragraph several times because it is a picturing, an image from within a different mode of consciousness than we are used to.

In contemplative action, having seriously engaged the clearing and clarifying of ego and power, we then enter into a contemplation of the heart, hold a particular person, or an event, or a situation, or a condition going on somewhere, within our heart – that is half of the contemplative action. The other half is then waiting, alertly, but without expecting anything in particular, noticing, being within a sensing-awareness, and something will show up in the world that very, very clearly is like a completing of the half of the contemplation you were aware of doing.

3. Contemplative action is a 'non-doing-doing'. It is entirely 'unspecialized', and it does not matter whether your life engagement is with some outer from of activism or action or helping or serving, or not. If you are engaged in some outer action of this sort, it is something different that contemplative action and can be carried on as usual with all the difficulties and joys entailed – though now you will be much more aware of how power works. And, if the power of power is curtailed, it may be possible, in an entirely silent and even 'secret' manner, to engage also in contemplative action. It is an open secret, of course. There is nothing 'occult' in what we are suggesting here; only a kind of wisdom that cautiously understands that those around you are not likely to understand nor value contemplative action, even if it is the most profound of all action possible.

Practice

The first half of a contemplative action:
Do the heart alignment, enter into the Silence, place attention in the center of the heart, enter into pure body-awareness and pure heart-awareness. This aspect is more than preparatory, it is essential because the shifting of language from concept into language-as-action which occurs when within pure heart-awareness is employed as central to the practice.

Once within pure-heart awareness, be inwardly present with who or what situation or event that you are working with. The difficult part from here on is to be able to relinquish, completely, any desire or need to want to change the person or the event or situation. It is, further, not simply a matter of trying to negate a desire to want to have something change, for that negation would be merely the negative desire to want something to change. Rather, it is necessary, once within the contemplation, just to be with, and to have that person or situation or event, in its imaginal being, present within you.

Inwardly gesture the name of the person or the situation or event. Bodily feel the currents of this naming, an indication that the name is no longer a concept but rather a soul/spirit presence.

Inwardly gesture the word 'heal' and bodily feel the currents. (Note – the word 'heal' here is not, within the heart, intended to be a command or a wish or a desire, and in fact does not, as gesture, indicate anything like we now understand healing. We understand healing in a causal fashion – something is wrong, a treatment or something 'magical' is administered or happens, and the ill or wounded or unbalance person or event is restored.) When the word 'heal' is gestured, there is the presence of the wholeness of the person, the event, or the situation. Nothing has to be done because there is nothing wrong. The contemplative action, this part of it, is simply seeing a wholeness that we are unable to otherwise see. Nothing has 'changed' as far as the soul/spirit of the person or event, for nothing was missing.

The Second Part of the Contemplative Action:

The second aspect involves now noticing – almost certainly it will not show up immediately, but within three days of the first part of the contemplative action – you will see the action aspect of the contemplation within the world. It will appear as a synchronicity. That is, something will occur within the world, usually the Natural World, that is unmistakably the presence of what you engaged in contemplation, though in a very different form. The content of the what is noticed is not the primary quality that informs you of this presence being at-one with the contemplation. It will be a strong, subtle response of recognition. You will feel a distinct quality of being 'befriended' by a presence – this may be a bird, a stone, something in the landscape, or something occurring – an action. In itself, it will not seem related to the contemplation, but you will know, without question that it is. This is the action-dimension of the contemplative action.

If this practice is done many times, there comes a time when it becomes possible to begin noticing the whole of the world around you being this kind of action – always.

The question perhaps now occurs – yes, but does the person, situation, or event change? This inevitable question slips back into a mode of consciousness that does not apply, not in the way the question is asked, which bears within it the notion of something moving from imperfection toward perfection., as if it could indeed be produced. Medicine, for example, constantly puts forth this kind of notion of changing from illness to health. When there is the appearance of this kind of change, it is never due to the pharmaceutical action, which can only alter the surface. And, such a question also guides all sorts of service. We fall out of a contemplative stance with such a question.

The intention of contemplative action is to be able to bodily, in soul, and in spirit, be completely with the wholeness and completeness of another person, doing so in such a way that this dimension is actually experienced. Such an experience comes in 'halves' as it were because of the bodily attunement necessary for the perception of wholeness. We are not able to control this kind of perception. The reason why so-called synchronistic events occur is not because of anything spiritually special about the events, which we are actually immersed in all the time. But only when there are moments of being completely within body, open, and at the same time fully within world-attention, able to forget ourselves, do experiences of wholeness occur.

Such experiences are not private, nor subjective. They are world occurrences, perceivable from within the "I" of the heart and are healing of the division between ourselves and the spiritual substance of the world. The further we can deepen into such awareness, the more evident this healing becomes.

The Imagination of the Heart
Imaginal Reality

1. Imagination, which we rely on so much in these courses, is often taken as something 'not real', as what we make up or fantasy, something private and subjective, or something belonging to the arts, and the arts more and more reduced to 'self-expression'. The concern of being able to 'prove' that imagination is a doing, is something we have to develop further.

2. The sense of our imaginal experience as existing on its own, even though it is intimately entwined with us becomes more apparent as the imagining takes place through the power of the heart. If I imagine someone's presence within the heart, there is a mirroring of that presence as it exists both in the spiritual world and within the earthly world – combined. The person appears through the mirror of imagination but is not in the mirror. When image-feelings occur through the heart, they are very different than imagining from the mind, for when done through the mind, mental image have a strong subjective component. There are mysterious *powers* of the heart which allow the symbolizing – the creative 'putting together into one' the spiritual presence with the inner presence of what we hold in imagination.

3. What are these mysterious powers of the heart that make contemplative action possible? We can name them, but we, much more importantly, have to try and have the sense that all these powers are simultaneous, blended into heart-power, and heart power is action, a doing, the completely open doing of active-receptivity.

The heart is a power of focus, being able to be completely with something or someone, not to the exclusion of everything else as is required, for example in concentration of the mind, but focus by total inclusion. Whatever is the focus of heart-imagination is done so by the heart by including the individualized sense of the whole within the focus.

The heart does not just hold something or someone within, in focus, but does so by creating what is being held. Heart is a birthing of what is being imagined. Heart is inherently a creating capacity. It does not create 'out of nothing', it is not a 'making-up', but for there to be anything or anyone with the heart, there has to be the 'making' quality. This is easy to verify. If you hold someone within your heart, you will notice that this holding is accompanied by the act of attention doing the holding. The act of attention is the creative act of the heart itself.

The heart 'images'. "Image" does not mean that what or who we hold within the heart exists there as a picture, as something 'visual-like'. The word 'image' comes from 'imago' and is very connected with the word 'magic', as in "i-mage". When we say the heart 'images', we mean that there is the 'magical' presence within the heart of whatever is imagined. This power of the heart is one of the reasons imagination is excluded from the present world except in its fantasy form. It is too powerful, and there is a mystery to imagination that cannot be controlled by rationality.

The heart 'projects'. This power of the heart is the power that is central to contemplative action, and in fact is the power of contemplative action itself. Whatever heart imagines, under certain conditions, endows what is being imagined with existence in the world. The action of the heart is not private. We will now go further into this heart-power in our exploring of contemplative action.

The Ardor of the Heart

When we enter into the Silence and the place attention within the heart and stay there, we notice, after a while, that while we began with the sense of placing our attention 'inside', when we are 'within' the heart, the heart is actually experienced as being 'around us'. Rather than heart being within us, we are within the heart. We do not have to do anything to have this happen except notice that it happens; it is not of our doing but is of the nature of heart experience.

The quality of heart-imagining as being 'world-imagining' – in the sense described above, can be intensified and amplified, and doing so is the central aspect of contemplative action. However, the other central aspect of the work is consistent confrontation with questions of power, for heart-imaging as action cannot function as long as there are overt or hidden power dimensions operating. As we now proceed, it will become very clear how the interference of usual senses of ego-oriented power form the greatest hindrance. We say this without in any way suggesting one has somehow to become 'egoless'; that is not the direction. One has to become heart-capable.

Becoming heart-capable involves strengthening ardor of heart, the inherent love-action of the heart. Any time we enter the heart contemplatively this quality is felt. What usually occurs, though, is that the feeling is experienced, and along with it a sense of joy that would guide one toward more constant heart-presence. A further intensification is required for the action of the heart to become autonomous world action. The heart projects whatever is reflected within it. This is the ardor of the heart. What is heart-imagined produces changes in the world, it becomes external to us. Right here is where power immediately want so seize and convert this reality to something utilitarian. If that happens, a different kind of projection occurs, psychic projection, which is illusion. The work 'projection' used in relation to the heart is used in the alchemical sense of the word. When alchemists came to a certain point of the alchemical operations, it then became possible to 'project' the stone into the world. That is, alchemical transformation entered the world and became world transformation.

Heart-produced world action is always spiritual action, it is action in the world that occurs in a spiritual manner, that is, the action occurs in accordance of the laws of the spiritual world, not according to the needs and wants as we conceive of them with the mind.

Practice – Orienting Toward Ardor of the Heart

The first entry into the world-process of the heart is being able to experience the ever-present ardor of the heart in a way that does not immediately become something for oneself. The best, most favorable place to practice sensing ardor is in relation to the Natural World. There is a infinite infinity between the heart and the Natural World, though that can be harder to detect for those, for example who are involved in some sort of environmental activism – simply because such activism has an agenda. This recognition does not imply that environmental activism should be dropped if one is interested in the work of the heart.

Select a place to do this practice outside, a place that you want to experience not only within the heart, but with a sense of the ardor of the heart. Do the heart alignment, enter into the Silence. Then open your eyes and be present to the Natural World. With attention, focus on something, while at the same time, allowing your peripheral vision to be wide. After a few minutes, close your eyes and be present to the manner in which what you were within the Natural World now lives within the place of the heart.

While present with that inner imagining of the Natural World, have attention focused in the heart and in an act of active-receptivity, allow the feeling within the heart flow into the inner imagining. With a very, very gentle act of the will, increase the intensity of that heart feeling flowing into the inner imagining. This heart-feeling is not an emotion; it is a very strongly felt 'urgency' within the heart, as if there is a very strong, unending force within the heart that is autonomous from you, though also the most intimate aspect of you. This unending force desires union.

Notice what begins to occur. When the inner imagining is approached in love in this manner, what is present responds. You will begin to experience that the inner imagining is now experienced as autonomous, as a Who, facing you. You are still intimately engaged – this other is within imaginal space and is not 'objective' in the way that in ordinary sensing the things of the outer world seem 'objective'. It is also very clear that the image is not of your doing.

The Time of Contemplative Action

The False Split between the Spiritual World and the Earthly World

For centuries and centuries, long before Christianity (we don't blame this problem on Christianity) – as far back as the century following the Indian Vedas (1400 BC – 1900 BC), for the division is not yet in the Vedas, humankind has divided the earthly world from the spiritual world; a division between time and the timeless; between the Transcendent and the Earthly.

The work of contemplative action belongs to a whole set of actions that does much to dissolve this division. We are not questioning the division, but suggesting that we are now entering a time when the boundary is dissolving; by now, though, I mean for a very long time; there is evidence of the dissolving occurring in the 12 and 13th century; much of the developing here of spiritual imagination comes from the esoteric Sufism of Ibn Arabi. In the realm of spiritual imagination, the sharp division of the transcendent and the earthly does not exist. However, later, with the advent of rank materialism, the split again occurs, much sharper than ever before.

The spiritual worlds (below called 'the transcendent) are always characterized as:
unmoving
imperishable
indivisible

The earthly is always in motion, and thus has a beginning and an ending implied; there is death, that is, all that is earthly is perishable; and everything of the earth is divisible.

There is a huge glitch in this way of dividing the Whole. If the transcendent is INDIVISIBLE, then there cannot be anything outside of it, for then there would be a division. If the transcendent is indivisible, then there cannot be a division between the transcendent and the earthly, for then there is something outside the indivisible. Very simple. Living the wholeness, though, is not nearly as simple, particularly after 6000 years of living as if the spiritual and the earthly were disconnected. But, for now, let's follow this picture through as it will/can totally re-arrange your furniture.

Since the timeless is indivisible, the timeless cannot be disconnected from time; and imperishability must contain within it what is created and destroyed.

The division – time vs. the timeless is due to a limitation our equipment; the limitation of the mind, which functions in a binary way and can only comprehend in terms of dualities, separations, divisions, one thing as different than another, etc.; the limitation of binary thinking.

Here is another way of imagining; once we have a sense of this, we will be able to both understand and feel how spiritual imagination, the union of the spiritual and the earthly, functions in the world through THE FORCE OF IMAGINATION, WHICH IS LOVE.

The transcendent, in its act of becoming manifest, is reduced to an active seed, the interior realm of the heart.

Time is the driver, the propeller of this seed for the <u>expression</u> of the fullest attributes of the transcendent; so that the Absolute can know him/herself and enjoy him/herself.

Time's function is to draw the compact elements held in the seed to fruition. Time urges the manifestation of the transcendent to completion; sensing/feeling, intuiting this process, we have a sense of how unity and multiplicity are simultaneous.

The Centrality of Love in the Unfolding of the Timeless in Time

The continual act of manifestation from the unmanifest is held in equilibrium by love. Thus, to experience this ongoing process requires that we center our being in the heart and that we become practitioners of love (more on this in a moment). LOVE IS AN EQUAL FORCE IN THE UNMANIFEST AND THE MANIFEST. The force of love keeps the process from dissolving back into the unmanifest, or of a complete forgetfulness of the unmanifest within the manifest.

To be within the process requires that we begin to be aware of the constant double-longing of love.

Practice
Do the exact same practice as the one above – "Orienting toward Ardor of the Heart" with another person.

The Escapism of (most) Spirituality.

Not looking at religion here. Exoteric Christianity has the view that there is only heaven, purgatory, or hell after that.

In eastern and most western spirituality, the notion is that you spiritually develop in earth life, die, reincarnate, and over many lives, get to the point of perfection where you no longer have to return. Or, within one life, you work and develop inwardly to the point of illumination; ecstasy. It is based on a notion that this earthly realm is the realm of suffering and imperfection, and the goal is to get out of here – now.

The interior of the heart, however, is the seed which, through us, the manifestation of the unmanifest unfolds. In the heart, the unmanifest and the manifest are a unity. So, we need to look further into spiritual imagination, the heart, and love.

The mutuality of Spiritual Love and Earth Love as Contemplative Action

Our excursion into Time and Timelessness will help us enter into the relation between spiritual and earth love.

Loving others is always a double-longing – a longing for the divine good that longs for us, and a longing for the good of someone or something other than us, that also longs for us but does not know that it does. The spiritual practice, one that fully realizes that earth is not a temporary place of suffering and being tested, but is crucial in the unfolding of the All, becomes the practice of holding the dynamic, active equilibrium between spiritual and earth love.

Clarification of the equilibrium that is needed for spiritual imagination's action in the world:

Love is a WHO, and the nature of the WHO is that there is no distinction between this who and the act of Loving. We do not need and do not want to slide into religion here, and the moment we do, we will lose the capacity to simply track the experience. Within the imaginal realm, there are only Who's, no 'its', no 'floating abstractions'. We are interested here in sensing that the longing of the heart, when entered with attention, is felt as a Presence. If this longing is felt only as a kind of force, then we have not yet completely left usual awareness, or slide from heart awareness into usual awareness.

We cannot even get started with this capacity unless we realize the real lover within the heart as a Who, without reducing this Who to a 'known', either monotheistically or polytheistically. Both are notions that stop the unfolding. The unfolding of realizing the heart is a Who. A Who whose 'Wholeness" is wholly the action of love. We love, only because that is what our heart is. Heart is both love and the medium of love. As medium of love, heart is the open receptivity to the presence of love everywhere, present to the action of everything, nothing excluded, as having and being a holy unfolding. When we find our way into this reality, just a step in, then we are within contemplative action.

The inner space of the heart is the organ of love. Love occurs through the organ of the heart, and this is felt as a longing that is also a being longed for. Whenever we are within heart we are within this complexity of longing It is very interesting indeed to try and feel this seeming complex, but at the same time completely unified complexity of the heart.

Practice

Place attention in the interior of the heart. Be present to the felt senses of longing within the heart. At first, just be present to this 'general' felt sense. Then, yield into this longing and feel how this longing is a Presence. Gesture a name of this Presence. In order to do this, you have to stay in and with the longing, sense that it is a Who, and let the name come rather than imposing a name. Whatever name does come, it is a naming of something or someone in the world, here, an Earth Presence, even if the name that comes is of a spiritual presence. This is the point of this practice; to begin to be free of the false division of a 'here' that is 'Earth' and a 'there' that is the spiritual World. Feel the resonating force spread through the body. The 'here' is far, far more than we can imagine.

In your inner 'waiting', if you find that you begin to skip around from name to name, that is an indication that you have left the heart for the mind.

This practice must be extending into another that is not really separate from it.

The practice is divided into two parts only for purposes of your initially being able to engage the practice without slipping into just mentally doing it, and also so that we can concentrate for a moment on the significance of this second part of the practice.

If we did only the practice above, and get to the point of it being an actual capacity, we would inadvertently go into a kind of personal religion, because what is given above does not yet stay completely within the imaginal space of the heart, and thus the enactment of contemplative action as the same as imaginal action would be lost. We would slip into a 'religious literalizing'.

The additional aspect of the contemplation has already been introduced; here it is as the crucial part of this one:

Once the name of the longing Presence has arrived, then allow the ardor of the heart to pour into the inner Presence. You will find that this Presence responds. The Presence becomes inwardly 'more vividly present', there is a much stronger sense that what you are inwardly facing now faces you. It is as if this Presence now trusts that you have been able to leave your own self-interested-self and can be totally with another person without degrading the other into being something literally 'objective' and 'over there', nor simply 'subjective' and 'in here'.

Practically, that is, in terms of experience, what happens with the above practice is that you immediately feel a huge relief in relation with whoever and whatever 'you' love. You are released immediately from any possessiveness. Love-feeling intensifies. The action of love intensifies. The experiences of syncronicity where you see the response of imaginal love appearing in the world multiplies. We find that love for someone or something is not the love for a possession or a potential possession, for the beloved is ever changing when held in the equilibrium of love and is uncontrollable and not able to be possessed, not even in imagination.

Social Action, Activism, Environmental Action, Protesting, 'Serving', 'Changing the World' as Doubles of Contemplative Action.

As you move into the heart and begin to function more from that center, you will feel the hurts and sorrows of all that is around you, the sorrows of the world, even the animals and the elements. What we typically speak of as feeling is the feeling of the false self – sentimentality, concern that wants something or wants to do something. But, we live not only within a materialistic culture but also, now, within a culture in which every good action of the heart cannot find heart-action, but only direct and literal action that can only work laterally – that is, can only work at the same level of the problem itself, so that good action is captured and does not know that it is captured.

Further, as you move more to the place of the heart, it is like globs of parasites begin to fall off the heart center itself and love intensifies, but it is not sentimental love, not the love-as-only-feeling. This love desires serving the world without, however, knowing what this is or how it is to be done. But the desire itself moves out into the world, and then, rhythmically, something comes back; this something is light. You experience this happening with any of the heart exercises. When we open our eyes and are present to the world again, it is as if the world is on the one hand more intense and color-filled, and at the same time it is more transparent. So, what flows from the heart goes out, adds and awakens the soul element of the world, and returns to us multiplied.

A further thing happens as we live more consciously from the will of the heart. Our heads will tell us that this is all pretty ridiculous, that what we are experiencing is not real. This is the presence of the Double, a sense of ourselves that looks, feels, acts as ourselves, takes up causes, and feels they are absolutely literally real, and moves us to do something. We can tell that Doubling has taken hold, because it takes up primary residence in the region of the head. Thus, the fantasies that occur to us are the work of the Double putting all kinds of head -imaginations there, none of which are real, but are in the imagination of being the real 'problems.

They, the notions that we have the ability to know what is needed in the world , come from quite narrow views of what 'world' consists of, and, from the viewpoint of unified spiritual/earth reality are all illusions, but we do not know they are illusions. We do not know they are illusions because these kind of imaginations tell us that we have to do something directly in the world to counter what is going in the wrong direction, and they tell us that it is foolish to just feel the sorrow of the world, that we have to get out there and act, and they delude us into thinking we can know what to do to stop the terrible things we see in the world. It all feels right and is even experienced as kind of images that might seem to be soul images. But it is all false. These kinds of imaginations are doubles of true imaginations. The fantasies are actually beings working in conjunction with beings that are doubles. Rudolf Steiner says this concerning the doubles:

"These beings spend their lives making use of human beings in order to be present in the domain they wish to be present. (that is, the earthly domain – my comment) They possess an extraordinarily high intelligence and a very remarkable will, but no feeling heart, not what is called human heart and soul."

Notice, in particular, the mentioned connection between these double beings and the will, which implies the importance of developing the will of the heart, for the will alone is the domain of doubling. Also, notice that in order to be present to the earthly domain, doubles, which when more specified include particularly those who have died having lived a completely materialistic existence, have to make use of human beings. They want only to be back in this world of hyper-materialism. Often, what looks like will, determination, ability to get things done in the world, is the work of this doubling. In fact, most of what we call will is the action of doubling working through us to accomplish what they want in the world, which is adherence to the earthly world so strongly that we first begin to doubt there is a spiritual world, then we begin to disbelieve there is one, and then we even forget there is a spiritual world. Or, more likely, we return to the false split between this world and 'heaven'.

Through the heart exercises described above it is possible to remain free of the double of will. However, there is a particular tendency to back away from the world when working through the heart. The rhythm of the heart moves out in expansion and back in contraction, and if we are within fear, the felt sense of contraction becomes stronger than expansion. The practices all restore the fullness of heart rhythm at an etheric level.

Entering consciously into this rhythm frees the will from its paralysis. The double of will works in the world because the human will is paralyzed, crippled, lame, cannot move, cannot walk. This is the experience we have when we see the huge movements of the double of will operating in the world. We feel, "What can we possibly do to counter the multi-national corporations who build empires, have the power to paralyze us by downsizing at will, price gouging, devastating the environment. Social activism against these forces, oppositional force, because they are a lateral move of consciousness rather than a movement into a different kind of consciousness, actually feeds the double. Working through the heart makes it possible to breathe again.

But a further capacity has to be developed. It is necessary to see the will of the double at work, and it is also necessary to recognize our own stubbornness, which is the form the paralysis of will takes. We have to confront our own selfishness that wants to have things our own way. The will of the heart can be open and yet the movement of will into the world can still be paralyzed. We experience and feel and participate in the sorrow and also the beauty of the world, but we feel, well, nothing can be done. In order to be released of that feeling, which is not of the heart but the false presence of the double, it is necessary to forgive what we see operating in the world as the double of the will. If we do not enter into forgiveness, then we are still functioning within an oppositional mode but are simply softening our tactics of opposition by working through the heart. Our true will thus remains paralyzed. People who cannot forgive are driven by a fallen will, a double of the will. They move in the world almost automatically, and coldly.

The theme of forgiveness and how the heart forgives, always, inherently, is a very large theme that will be taken up in a further course. Still, here, it is important to recognize and practice a sense of forgiveness – which is not something that we can spiritually do – we can do so at a certain level of our emotional being and our usual consciousness. Spiritually we can only orient toward forgiveness and try to feel its presence as a real force

The action of the true will in the world, the will connected with the heart, is action of virtue. This is the way that the great American teacher, Emerson speaks of will in the world; *"All goes to show that the soul in man is not an organ, but animates and exercises all the organs; is not a function, like the power of memory, or calculation, of comparison, but uses these as hands and feet; is not a faculty, but a light; is not the intellect or will, but the master of the intellect and the will; is the background of our being, in which they lie; -- an immensity not possesses and that cannot be possessed. From with or from behind, a light shines through us upon things and makes us aware that we are nothing, but the light is all. A man is the façade of a temple wherein all wisdom and all good abide. What we commonly call man, does not, as we know him, represent himself, but misrepresents himself. Him we do not respect, but the soul, whose organ he is, would he let it appear through his action, would make our knees bend. When it breathes through his intellect, it is genius; when it breathes through his will, it is virtue; when it flows through his feelings, it is love."* (Essays, "The Oversoul)

Contemplative Action: The Way of Weakness

We come to soul, not by going inward, but by being faced by spiritual Otherness. We are *inspired* by mysterious, spiritual Otherness, most clearly visible as the Natural World, but available everywhere. There is a quite perceptible experience of this happening, noticeable at a very subtle level; you will notice it increasingly as you do the practices. The presence of the spiritual Other, drawing us to responsibility, is not power, but the *soul authority* of the other person. The first way in which this authority speaks to us is as a silent command, "Do not do violence to me." In the way of weakness, we do not so much determine to serve, or how to serve; we are called to service by the other person. The other person calls us to serving in very particular ways:

At the level of knowing, spiritual Otherness inspires *simplicity*. When we read the words of those who were/are the great contemplatives of action of the world, such as Jean Vanier, or St. Francis, or Mother Theresa, what is always most striking is the simplicity with which they speak of their action. They do not engage in complex philosophical, theological, or psychological thought to try to explain what makes them act. They speak simply. This simplicity is not something given as a gift to these individuals; it is earned.

When we truly encounter spiritual Otherness, what goes on between us has this kind of pure simplicity; we know each other. I don't engage in a lot of trying to figure out the other person. And, while this simplicity is earned, it is not something that I achieve on my own; we do not come to this though the efforts of the ego. Rather, facing the unknowability of spiritual Otherness, I become receptive, a residing in the desire to know rather than having a fund of knowledge that I bring to bear. I sense that my usual ways of knowing are defenses designed to keep me away from the full presence of the other and of being called-out by the other.

At the level of feeling, the other person inspires *patience*. The word "patience" is from the Latin "patiens", from the present participle "pati", meaning "to suffer". I allow the presence of spiritual Otherness to work through me. This is a suffering. This suffering, this allowing, is not suffering for the sake of suffering; it is a suffering for others, which redeems suffering. Suffering for the sake of suffering is useless. Also, suffering here does not mean 'pity', which is a mixture of sorrow and disgust. Suffering 'with' another, means that our tendencies toward self-satisfaction, are held in check, not by an act of the violent will, but simply by being within the heart. Patience is a kind of forgetfulness of ourselves, an inattentiveness to our own needs because our attention is riveted by spiritual Otherness.

At the level of doing, spiritual Otherness inspires *humility*. I am able to hear the needs of the other, able to be touched by the needs of the other and freely choose to remain engaged without needing to know what will happen. Humility is disinterested commitment to work for others, stripped of self-interest. I do not achieve humility on my own; it is not self-generated. It is called out of me by the presence of spiritual Otherness.

The person in need, the Earth in need, the World in need receives power when met with the simplicity, patience, and humility of the heart. In facing spiritual Othernes in these ways, we discover and can become free of our obsessions, compulsive habits, and addictions. This is the power we receive from spiritual Otherness. We receive freedom.

All of this is Just too Idealistic

Not Idealism

We have tried to present a whole view of contemplative action, to include the ego as well as the soul, and the heart as intimately world-engaged. The descriptions may seem idealistic; they might also seem as if they belong to the actions characteristic of, say, the religious person, but do not apply to us in our everyday lives. In fact, it might seem that the kind of soul serving described can be enacted only by one who is a saint.

Whenever we turn to the other person and put aside as much as we can our own ideas, private feelings, and will, and at the same time enter into the dimensions of the heart, we find ourselves in contemplative action. Contemplative action does not have to be understood in a completely literal fashion, and in fact, this way of imagining will most certainly issue only from the ego's point of view. Describing the soul of serving is not intended to say that we are to go out and devote our lives to this kind of action in some specialized way. Rather, the intention is to change our focus and begin to see that life itself can be contemplative action. Contemplative action does not exhort us to do good; it asks us to open our eyes, be touched by the face of others; that is all.

Second, contemplative action as described here is not a moralist stance. We are too skilled as a culture in achieving our own success and meeting our own needs to be turned from this by moral exhortation. Everything developed in this course is at the level of description rather than prescription. Contemplative intends to be much more of a description of attention that is inwardly free and thus is able to notice what is happening when that attention focus within the heart and simultaneously within the world with others.

Spiritual Psychology and Dante's
Divine Comedy

The Divine Comedy is one of the great poems of all times. It has shaped our world, and yet it is strangely inaccessible to us, or at least, it seems inaccessible to the ordinary, intelligent reader. The form of the Divine Comedy is likely to be misconstrued. It is likely to be thought moralistic, over-intellectual, solely for Catholics, and thus parochial in its intent. Its universality is the issue in question. Does this poem speak of the depths and heights of human experience, saying something that is applicable to all? We will indeed see that this great poem is of universal significance; it speaks of the journey of the human soul to its fulfillment in God. Dante may use the material of his day, including theology and philosophy, to construct his poem, but the poem is not about theology or philosophy, or history, or politics, or the city of Florence - though all of these concerns enter as the substances with which Dante works.

The very beginning of the Divine Comedy, the very first lines of the Inferno, tell us that the poem concerns the journey of life (inferno, Canto I, line 1 on). The action of the poem is this journey; it is not about the soul after death; this poem uses that metaphor, but the poem concerns the journey of life and the movement of the soul toward God. Further, the poem is not just the journey of life - it is our life. So, Dante speaks of an interior journey. He says, right at the beginning "I came to myself." He discovered that he had lost the way, and now he comes to his senses. But just waking up is not enough. This is just the beginning of the labor. Now, what is this dark wood? It is the fallen world into which we are born, and in which we come to our senses. We wake up to that wood when we lose our innocence.

How, then do we get the vision of the Divine Comedy? How do we grasp it? We start out by reading it, reading it through without being concerned about the whole structure and with knowing where we are going. We get the images in it. We are better off if we do not begin by trying to understand the whole structure, but rather reading it through, even without fully understanding what we are reading. We take in sufficient images that the poem begins to come to life for us. We let the personages that we encounter along the way come to life for us. We step back enough that we can remember those images that have made a particularly deep impression. We remember, for example, Francesca (Hell, Canto V). We remember Pier deile Vigne (Hell, Canto XII), he who, when you break a branch, issues words and blood out of a branch, as Dante says, the way a burnt branch of wood will ooze sap and steam at the same time. Now, if you let yourself picture that image and at the same time remember Pier delle Vigne, and remember that he is still telling us "I am not guilty of infidelity. I was loyal to Frederick of Sicily. I was accused unjustly. People talked against me and turned him against me, but I was innocent. And, somehow, he does not notice that he is not placed in the realm of the traitors, but rather in the realm of the suicides because he killed himself out of despair, since he had been spoken about unjustly. When we take in images such as these and dwell with them, we gradually begin to understand, not just intellectually, but in a deeply feeling way, that the whole realm of Hell is characterized by the lack of self-knowledge. This is the point that Dante would have us see through these characters in Hell. They have no self-knowledge. They never had any sense of freedom. They think that fate has been unkind to them, that they have simply been treated unjustly. They do not learn anything from their suffering.

We are going to see a very different attitude in the Purgatorio, and of course, in the Paradiso. But, in the Inferno everyone is plausible and self-explanatory. Many in this realm speak of the "sweet life", because, for them, their idea of heaven was the world they had been in - this world. So, they say to Dante things like - "when you are back in that sweet world, clear my reputation. Tell others what you have seen." When we get to the Purgatorio we find that the people there do not speak of the former world as the "sweet world". They simply call it "back yonder." They remember it, but they no longer think that it is the supreme point of reference. Begin to be familiar with these characters in the Inferno - with the proud Ferinata (Hell, Canto V1), with Brunetto Latini (Hell, Canto XV), Dante's teacher, who still is teaching Dante when he meets him there in hell. Brunetto Latini is there in the realm of the Sodomites - but that never crosses his mind. He is not interested in that; he is interested in how his pupil is doing. His pupil had so much promise; if he would just continue to read my book, then he would accomplish a great deal; that is the attitude of Brunetto Latini. You remember the last image we have of Brunetto Latini - Dante sees him, with great regret, and says that he turns and runs as one who wins and not looses the prize. That great nobility of the teacher, that great dignity of the teacher, is something that we must examine; what really is missing from Brunetto Latini as a teacher is this dignity.

Now, what is the Divine Comedy about? It's about a journey, a spiritual pilgrimage. It is a movement of spirit from one state to another. Now, that is the hardest thing to write about, because it deals, really with the invisible, interior life of the soul. Dante's whole poem is about that inner journey, that we could simply call learning. This poem, in fact, could be read as the great paradigm of education - of how you learn, of how you move from ignorance to knowledge.

There is a temptation in reading The Divine Comedy to want to know about it, to have that kind of knowledge which is simply knowledge about rather than an intimate knowledge of. We ought not concentrate on what can be known about it - history, what was going on at that time in Italy, the background of the characters. We need only a touch of such knowledge, and maybe not even that. We need to confront the poem itself. Dante's poem gathers up all of the knowledge of the middle ages - theology, science, philosophy, ethics. We do not need that knowledge to learn from this poem, to have it change us.

The poet is a mediator between the inner recesses of the heart and the human community. He speaks to the larger human community of which we are all a part, and through his imagination, he finds the way to gather up the past and prophesy the future. He writes always of the nature and destiny of humankind. He makes an artifact, a work of art that re-enacts a spiritual movement. He makes something subjective into something objective. The making of the work of art is an imitation of that insight that the artist has into the heart of the human community. He has to dress his poem in the garb of his day; he has to embody his insight with whatever is at hand. We make a mistake then if we take the accidents of the poem for the substance of the poem. I do not mean that the two are inseparable. The poet does not have an idea in the abstract; rather, his insight grows out of his observations of the things of his day. However, we as readers are likely to turn the poem into an antique if we simply think of it in terms of its own time.

Dante uses a large metaphor - he sees life as a pilgrimage. He takes the mystical journey of the soul to God as his vehicle that is his carrier for his subject. He is not necessarily himself the mystic that makes this journey. He is the poet who sees in images the significance of that journey. Dante has watched and thought about and admired and pondered the mystical journey, and he has made of it something that is universal. Dante has made the mystical journey something that we can all participate in because he has made it into the form of image. Every soul feels within itself the necessity for transformation. Every soul feels the necessity for some kind of spiritual progress. I think this is why the poem remains as important as it is and why it is still read today and is not simply thought of as a period piece.

Dante's images and his deep understanding of them had to come from faith. Dante experienced this journey of the soul imaginatively. He had to see it, to live with it, until gradually he knew its truth. We ourselves do not have to agree with Dante's specific judgments in order to "get" this poem. My whole attitude, for example, toward pagans would be different than those expressed in this poem, if I took the poem only literally. But, Dante's poem is based on the insight that reveals the total inadequacy of humans to reach the highest good without grace. This is what his poem is saying. All these goods that we have pursued are not sufficient. And, if we understand what Dante's underworld is, we realize that he is not simply being vindictive and relegating someone to hell. He is attempting to say - how far does a particular quality take us in that perfection of the soul which is possible for the human person.

The journey to hell is Dante's great metaphor for one's journey in life when one is lost in a dark wood (Hell, Canto I), when one has lost the true path. This is one of those threshold experiences that marks a turning point in our lives. We do not have too many of them. Occasionally we are bereft of everything; everything we thought we were certain of; everything which seemed to point to the right path to us. It is almost as though we have lost a world rather than ourselves because it has fallen away from us and we do not know where we are or how to proceed, Dante portrays being lost in this way as being in a dark wood. Three beasts cut him off from any path that he would take. So, he is in that condition of stasis, and he combines that moment of stasis with the vision of the underworld. A visit to the dark wood necessitates this journey to the underworld. In the very first words of the first canto Dante tells that it is our life he is telling us about, not just his. We come to a point in our lives when we have gone as far as we can under our own impetus. This point is the point that Dante calls the "middle of one's life." It does not literally mean the middle. It is that point where we do not know where to go next. He comes to his senses in a dark forest, having lost the straight path. Then he says that even to think of it again renews his fear. Notice that this is a retrospective poem. Dante the poet is writing this about Dante the pilgrim. So, we have a very complicated situation of having two Dantes; one who knows how the whole thing turns out because he took the journey and came back and wrote the poem. The other one is ignorant, naive and has to learn the most rudimentary things. He has to be taught all along the way. He has to be scolded when he finally encounters Beatrice, when he finally looks into those eyes that he has been searching for, that he has been yearning for. When he finally sees her face, she talks to him as a teacher. She scolds him for not having done the right thing, and he must weep.

The lady, Beatrice, is the governing presence in this poem. What she says is right. She is wise and intelligent and concerned. So, the feminine is very important, as she always is in comedy. Incidentally, this work is a comedy because, as always with this genre, we have life beginning in turbulence and ending in tranquility. This is the mark of comedy - not whether a work is funny. At the same time, this work is really a comic-epic.

Return now to the dark wood. The poem says: "How I got into it I cannot say, Because I was so heavy and full of sleep when first I stumbled from the narrow way." This is characteristic then of despair, losing the way, what we these days call burn-out. All of a sudden, we wake up and things are meaningless. The things we were doing with such purpose no longer have any purpose. We cannot tell how we entered it; it seemed to have occurred step by step, invisibly somehow.

For Dante, abandoning the way had something to do with his work. We might pay attention to that. It is not that he had lost his faith in God. That is not mentioned. Rather, he had not served his vocation, poetry. He had turned more to philosophy. He had been following the path of Lady Philosophy instead of following Beatrice. Beatrice is like the muse of his poetry; she is like the subject of his poetry. She is the lovely revelation of the glory of creation. He has deserted Beatrice.

We have to look at this image and see it analogically. When we do not do that for which we are intended, we find ourselves in a dark wood. The path to our transformation, the path to the divine depends upon our finding our true way. The way is different for every person. Dante's way was to serve

Beatrice and to follow her guidance. And, since her death he had not been true to her. So, she has sent for him, Virgil, a poet, a poet who is dearest to him, the one he most admires, the one he has studied, the one from whom he has learned.

Dante puzzles about why Virgil has come to him (Hell, Canto I, 31). Both Aeneas and Paul have been to the other world, to the underworld. Dante says that he is neither one of these individuals. He says that he is not that important. Virgil then reveals to him how it comes about that he is called to take this journey of soul searching, a journey in which he must search the depths of his soul.

We see then that Mary, the Great Mother, the Queen of Heaven, has turned to Lucia, the patroness of clear-sightedness, who has turned to Beatrice, who has a redemptive love for Dante, who has turned to Virgil, who has turned to Dante. With that chain of command, one could hardly say no. So, Dante agrees to go. But notice that he must petition, he must ask and accept and indicate his willingness. It is not going to be done for him against his will. So, it is not going to be simply inspiration. Dante is going to be led, but he has to be willing.

This dark wood, where Dante is surrounded by the three beasts is thus that moment of stasis in which one has been absolutely stopped. He can proceed no further, Dante then is giving us a picture of that divine grace that saves one in spite of oneself. This grace is a kind of aid that requires one to be guided. If a person is to understand the virtues and the vices, as Dante must do in this self-examination, then he must see them out of time. In the actual drama of human life, nothing is fixed. Everything is in action; there is a dynamism to life; everything is subject to change. Someone who has done some terrible thing in life may change and do something splendid; this is why we cannot judge others; we cannot know enough. We cannot see. And how we would like to be able to think that our enemies, those who do those perfectly terrible things, would remain terrible and give us that satisfaction of being able to judge them. And yet we know that something may change them, and that we cannot see the whole story. Life is change. This is not to say that certain actions in themselves cannot be evaluated. They can. If we do not believe that actions can be evaluated, then we lost contact with the whole course of civilization. Murder is wrong. Stealing is wrong, as is envy, jealousy, lying, pride, sloth, avarice, gluttony, lechery. We do know that those wrongs are wrongs in themselves. We do not know when and under what conditions. What are the motives? What are the reactions of those who do these wrongs? What prompted the actions?

In the underworld that Dante goes through, the following levels of learning are displayed: Dante speaks with Virgil and Beatrice and other guides. He finds out facts concerning various persons that he knew. These facts are related to the persons lives on earth, before death. The facts are put into a context. The qualities of human behavior are discerned and are morally evaluated. Human behavior is related to the ultimate destiny of the human race, in terms of the good. There is some mysterious progress in the action of the good that is going on. We learn what our actions should be and something of the larger plan that our actions serve.

This underworld, we must remember, is a poetic creation. Dante made up this world, It is a world that has theology in it because that was part of the material he used in creating this world. But, do not confuse this work with theology. The church, for example, does not teach this view that we read in Dante. Similarly, this world has philosophy in it, but this work is not a treatise on philosophy either. This underworld, we must also remember is not Dante's autobiography. If we see it this way, we would have to see him as vindictive, putting his enemies in hell. The poem is not about Dante's personal life; nor is it about history. It is about the universal condition of humankind, given form.

Let us read the Francesca episode (Hell, Canto V) to show how Dante must learn. You remember that the vestibule of hell is full of those who were for themselves, the lukewarm, and they are the most despicable people in the whole universe. Heaven will not have them, and hell casts them out. And so, they go forever carrying banners, meaningless banners, following causes, but not ever really being or daring to exist. Now this is a terrifying picture. Then we have the limbo for the pagans, the virtuous pagans. They are not strictly speaking in hell. They are as happy as they can imagine being. They had no notion of heaven; they had no notion of being gathered up in love. They had a notion of the good, the true, and the beautiful, and so they have this in the afterlife. Those who yearn for a consummation, those who yearn for that unification, the burning of love, are those who must make their way higher than the place of the virtuous pagans - or lower, if they reject reaching for the higher.

When we look at Francesca, she is in the circle of lust. Notice that the lustful are higher up in hell than those who become progressively more malicious and more violent. Lust is not so horrible and ugly as pride and envy and wrath. Pride and envy are almost considered virtues in our society today. They are invisible, and we don't think of them necessarily as damnable.

Dante calls Francesca and Paolo, her lover, over to him: (read - Canto V, 88 - 142). In this very brief story, one of the most economical in all of literature, Dante is saying is that we are fooled just as Dante is fooled into pitying Francesca. If we look at her speech very closely we see that she has never accepted any kind of blame for wrongdoing. She blames God, in a way, when she says that "if the King of the universe were friendly to us, I would pray to him for you — but he is not friendly to us." There is the implication that somehow this is unjust. She also blames love, courtly love. But, the ideals of courtly love were always spiritual. Here, she depicts it as sensual. And, she blames a book, the story of Lancelot.

Well, though we do feel sorry for her and we do see the pity of it, nevertheless I think we are meant to see that Dante has not yet learned to separate the act from the person. You can feel sorry for Francesca, but you have to see clearly that the act was wrong - at least within this poem. She has not learned from it. That kind of evaluation is the kind we have over and over in this poem and Dante will begin to learn, but as yet he is still tender- hearted toward the sin itself and does not make a distinction between the sin and the sinner.

The many characters of the Divine Comedy are not to be understood as abstractions that have been given the garb of persons. Virgil, for example, is not to be equated with the abstract notion of "reason" as some literary critics have done. The characters are real, embodied persons who are symbolic. Now, that is not an odd way for us to think. It is not an odd way for a poet to proceed. What is implied in this phrase - 'symbolic personages' is that these characters in Dante's poem are public personages, known in the world that Dante inhabited. They are not mythical and legendary figures. Now, there are some mythical and legendary figures in the poem, but the characters that we encounter along the way are historic persons. They are not simply his personal friends, though many of them are. We are not given a glimpse of private and unknown people whose inner thoughts Dante is familiar with. It is as if we took, say, Elizabeth Taylor, or Hitler, Elvis Presley, Ronald Reagan, or Marilyn Monroe as characters in a poem that we were attempting to write. Where would we place them on our scale of virtue if we consider only what we know of them publicly? If we undertook such a task of constructing a hierarchy of virtues and a descending scale of vices, our task would be to place each character within such a scale and our placement would not be a judgment of that person's immortal soul. What we would be doing is taking what Marilyn Monroe seemed like in her actions, not pretending to know the interior of her motives, but from her actions, going ahead to depict her in such a way that our depiction would represent her faithfully. This is what Dante is doing with these people whom his society knew and whom he knew. It is their action he is concerned with, and he is concerned with evaluating those actions in a very interested and complex way. This is repellent, of course, to the modern mentality. We don't like evaluating vices and virtues. It is thus difficult for us to enter into Dante's spirit and not simply to think that he is vindictive, or that he is putting his friends in heaven and his enemies in hell.

Dante brings us the whole complex question of the life of the soul as it balances various goods and must choose among them. The virtues Dante is concerned about are not something tacked on; they are not rules or obligations. There is no outward semblance of virtue that one can assume Dante shows us. Only an inner habitation, a habit of the soul that has been long cultivated. Look now at the story of Guido da Montefeltro (Hell, Canto XXXVI, pg. 240).

Guido had been a military leader who was foxlike. He had outwitted, tricked his adversaries, As he grows older and sees that he is facing death, he decides that he will join the Franciscan Order so that he might die in the Franciscan habit. There was the belief that if you died in the Franciscan habit, St. Francis himself would come for you at death and take you to the good place rather than to the bad place. So, he is ready now to die as a good man. Then the pope, Boniface the VIII, which Dante saw as a villain, comes to him and asks him how to get rid of some of his enemies, an influential family that never accepted him as pope; they still believed that Celestine V was the rightful pope. Guido da Montelfeltro tells him "I have gotten out of that business of giving counsel to people about how to outwit their enemies." The pope says in effect, "Have you forgotten who I am? I have the keys to the kingdom, so do not let your heart mistrust right now. I absolve you." Guido knows what he is being asked to do, but since he is already absolved of it, he goes ahead; "Father, since you wash away the sin in which I now engage, long promise with short fulfillment will make you triumph on your lofty feet." This is just the account of the general intent. He must have told him much more than that. What actually happened was that Boniface promised the Cologna family sanctuary, amnesty, and as soon as they had yielded, he destroyed their house and took away all their property, and this destroyed them.

Now, "when I was dead", Guido says, "Francis came for me. But one of the black cherubim said to me "Don't take him, don't wrong me. He must come down among my minions because he gave the fraudulent advice. Since one who does not repent cannot be absolved, nor can repenting and willing go together because the contradiction does not allow it. Ah, wretched me, how I shuddered when he sees me. The devil says: "Perhaps you didn't know I was a logician." It is impossible to repent a sin and to commit it at the same time, or to be absolved before you committed it, no matter if the pope said it. It is simply not true. Now, what this reveals to us about Guido is that his whole life has been based on such trickery. This is not that he was just caught at this one time. this reveals his whole life and how he has set his own trap. It shows us that he was not sincere in his conversion, that he had joined the Franciscan Order out of desire to conform to a winning system. Now that he faces death, you like to be sure about it. It shows us that he never allowed virtue to shape his mind and heart.

We encounter Guido's son, Buonconte, in the Purgatorio. Dante will put him there as an obverse image of his father. His son, Buonconte(Purgatorio, Canto V, pg. 103) is a notorious sinner, a sinner who has been so open in his misdeeds that he has been excommunicated by the Church. He received a mortal wound, his eyes already blind, his throat cut, he calls upon Mary to help. After he is dead, two angels come for him, one white and the other dark. The white angel is busy taking him and the dark angel protests and says: "Why would you cheat me of my prize for one little tear." And it turns out that the one little tear is sufficient.

So, these two little vignettes are worth pondering. The one man who planned his salvation and who intended then to die a good death, and who is now in hell, burning, and who speaks through a flame that comes up through this whole shelf of flame that comes up, and the sound is like the sound of the bronze bull that someone invented for a tyrant in Sicily and then had to test it for the tyrant by being the first victim. When you put someone in this bronze bull and roasted him, the sounds that came out of him in his agony were like the sounds of a bull. We are made to see this terrible and grotesque image in this burning Guido de Montefeltro is doing in hell.

Guido is so proud that he would not tell his story except that he knows that the person to whom he is speaking is in hell too. And so, he says: "If thought these words were addressed to someone who would return to the world, this flame would shake no more. But since I know no one ever came here that can return, then without fear of infamy I speak to you." The souls in the Inferno are tremendously concerned with fame, reputation, glory. What they ask of the two poets that go through the inferno is that when they go back that they would clear their names.

The journey through the Inferno concerns the necessity of developing self-knowledge. That is what the individuals in the Inferno lack. They are not there just for what they have done; rather, it is because they have no insight into what they have done.

The journey to the Inferno is fraught with dangers. We see something of the danger when Virgil and Dante come upon the Medusa (Hell, Canto IX). You do not go through the journey of self-knowledge unscathed. It is not a free trip. Unless you are willing to go on, then there are certain points at which Dante tells us, "you'd better turn back." Your little boat might not be able to sail in these waters. You might be turned to stone by the Medusa. All along the way it is necessary not to take this literally. To take this story, this journey, literally, is to take the Medusa in such a way that you are reduced to stone. All of these stories require interpretation; they require that you work with them in imagination. The Medusa is that despair which can accost us when we are just partly on the way. We start on a task, and then we can be overcome by despair and turn to stone. The frightening thing about that is that we are worse off than if we had not undertaken the journey.

The literal level of Dante's stories is the state of souls after death. The allegorical level would be their relation to human history in life. The moral level of the stories is their relation to good and evil and to human happiness. The anagogical meaning would be the implications of their actions in the light of divine love. This is the way Dante's imagination works to get at the hidden meaning of events. We have to read The Divine Comedy with this kind of imagination. Otherwise, we will get bogged down, or stopped by the Medusa.

Additional Images to Consider

A. The leopard, the lion, the wolf

B. Virgil

C. Beatrice

D. Circles of the lustful, the gluttonous, the avaricious, the wrathful

E. The Minotaur

F. The Circles of the violent - blasphemers, sodomites, usurers

G. Geryon - "The unclean image of fraud itself"

H. The Circle of fraud - panderers and seducers, flatterers, simoniacs, sorcerers, barraters, hypocrites, thieves, counselors of fraud, sowers of discord, falsifiers L The Circle of Treachery J. Cocytus K. Satan (XXXIV, 23-25 and 52-56)

I. Judas, Brutus and Cassius

The Purgatorio

Preliminary consideration: comparison between hell and purgatory; example, lust in hell and lust in purgatory. In purgatory the redeemed souls walk in the fierce heat of the fire, whereas in hell, Francesco and Paola were mercilessly blown by the cold wind, Lust, which remains unconscious is ultimately cold. Desire is hot. Lust in purgatory - free acceptance of the terrible burning of the desire itself with the full realization of its redemptive meaning.

Another example: wrath in hell and wrath in purgatory. The wrathful in hell lie choking and sputtering in sticky black mud; the wrathful in purgatory are blinded by a thick and gritty smoke. Anger is never a bringer of light; anger is essentially cold and blinding. But in hell, one is stuck; in purgatory it is possible to move.

We can approach Dante's Purgatorio through two large metaphors - disease and curing as one metaphor and consuming and fasting as the other large metaphor. Certainly, Purgatory has a medical analogy. Disease, Dante wants to suggest, tells us of our sins, while repentance draws our cure. Repentance is therapy for the sick soul, something necessary for that soul to be able to establish in mind and heart a habit of loving according to a right order of being. To extend the metaphor, for Dante, that would be health. The penance the souls are engaged in is therapy. It is a regimen for the sick soul, and is essentially the establishment of a habitus, a habit of loving, which is a cure for the pathology of sin. The incarnation is a cure for the virus of the first sin; the Purgatorio is a working out of that first sin, the first virus, the first pathology of the body. Healing takes place by means of a contrary action or through similar things.

The second actions of the body that Dante explores through Purgatory are those of eating, drinking, and fasting. We will focus more on these than on the former, disease and cure, but the former is as prevalent. What we gain from Dante's exploration of Purgatory is a fuller understanding of the finite, the concrete, and the limited ways we have of inhabiting the world, as well as the connection of the finite to divinity, to sin, and to salvation. Dante's poem poeticizes the human body to reveal this level of human habitation.

We are going to explore the arena of the body - of flesh, appetite, disease, cure, and proper nourishment. All of the images of the body point us, analogically, to the way that justice reveals a right ordering of the will. One might consider the world of the Inferno the world of disease; the world of Purgatory, the world of cure, and the world of Paradise that realm of reward and perfection. The other element is love. Love, in its most general form is appetite. All sin is a result of appetite. Virgil will tell us this in Purgatory. Sin is a result of loving which is excessive, diminished, or perverted.

Purgation, then is the proportioning of individual love to the will of God. Dante offers two important images of the body in the Purgatorio. We have the fleshy, breathing body of Dante the pilgrim, the one who takes the journey, and then we have the less substantial, or we might say, imaginal bodies of those in Purgatory, the shades, seeking purification. The body of the pilgrim amazes the souls in this region because it can block the sun and cast a shadow and also because it breathes.

The imaginal bodies of the souls seeking beatification are quite different than this. The action of Purgatorio, of the three regions of hell, purgatory, and paradise, most closely corresponds to our own earthly region. Since purgatory is so close to the earthly region, there is this interest and preoccupation in this middle region of purgatory with the body. Purgatory has its own time, its own space and movement. The actions of the souls in purgatory illustrate the role of appetite and desire, purgation, and levity.

What then can we learn of love and will, of love and grace, of desire and satisfaction, of time and eternity through the kinds of bodies journeying through the region of purgatory? It would seem that part of our answer resides in the poet's rendering of the relation of body to soul. Dante's imagination allows us to see inner realities in terms of their reflection in concrete realities. The shades in purgatory are in fact images of the soul, but they are images given in the form of bodies, less substantial that the body of Dante the pilgrim.

There exists a mutual wonder between Dante the pilgrim and the souls in purgatory as Virgil guides his student up Mount Purgatory. Dante wonders as the likeness of the bodies of the shades. He feels not a little disconcerted when he tries several times to embrace one of them only to find himself hugging himself (Purgatorio, Canto II, line 67 on). At times, the shades are more intrigued with Dante's shadow than with the pilgrim himself (Purgatorio, Canto V, line 1 on). Dante's is a body of matter, whereas the other bodies in Purgatory are in the likeness of a human figure but lack substance. What both kinds of bodies share, however, are the seven sins which weigh the body down, burden it, indeed even bend it over. As contrition is satisfied, the sins are removed one at a time. Dante's body and those of the shades grow lighter and rise higher with more swiftness up Mount Purgatory. Such action is accelerated because all are fasting.

G.K. Chesterton, in his work, Orthodoxy, makes this distinction between saints and satan: "A characteristic of the great saints is their power of levitation and levity. Angels can fly because they can take themselves lightly." It is easy to be heavy, hard to be light. Satan fell by the force of gravity. Satan's demise was the overbearing weight of the sin of pride. Dante has already revealed his final condition, frozen in ice, immobile in the depths of Dis.

The images of the body created by Dante the poet, both substantial and imaginal reveal two dimensions of humanity. They express the distinction given in the Old Testament between image and likeness of God given in Genesis. God said, "Let us make man in our own image, in the likeness of ourselves and let them be masters of the fish of the sea, the birds of heaven, the cattle, all the wild beasts and all the reptiles that crawl upon the earth." The New Testament shows the fulfillment of both image and likeness in the figure of Christ, the Word of God made flesh.

We need to distinguish between image and likeness. As the human being was created in the image of God, which is a gift, without any effort on our part, we are, as a consequence of this gift, called to realize our likeness to God through action. Image is a gift, a given condition. Likeness is a task, an effort, a struggle, which one must will and then do. Dante, placing his pilgrim (Dante) in the state of souls after death, nevertheless, wants to realize the unity of image and likeness in the state of souls on earth prior to death. The substantial body is in the image of God. The shades, which through their efforts of purgation, move toward the Paradiso, are in God's likeness. God's likeness is given in the last Canto of the Paradiso (Paradiso, Canto XXXII, line 127 on).

Dante, true to being a poet, is less interested in realizing Gods' essence than he is in imagining God's likeness. He do not wish to know what God consists of: he wants to be able to imagine Him. Christ is the embodiment of God's image, who through his actions attains God's likeness.

The likeness of God is realized by effort and sacrifice, in love. That is what the souls in Purgatory work at. This likeness is fulfilled by grace, but not without the freedom of human choice. At the end of the Purgatorio, Virgil leaves Dante, saying to him that he (Dante) has reached the point of freedom and no longer needs him.

Hungering, thirsting, eating, drinking, are involved in acquiring wisdom and salvation. Love becomes in Purgatory, appetite. Understanding is that nourishment which appeases hunger (Purgatorio, Canto XV, line 49 on).

Words in the Purgatorio are also equated with food (Purgatorio,Canto XXV, line 27 on). Sight, in the Purgatorio, become seeking truth, is associated with drink (Purgatorio, Canto XX, line 1 on; line 33).

Sight, then, is associated with drink; wisdom, truth, and hope are liquids which lessen thirst; sin becomes a brand of moral gluttony caused by a constant excessive taking in of the world. Only by joining and adhering to a strict regimen of dieting can a shade hope to enter into a community of the blessed where desire for food and drink is no longer existent. The desire for things worldly must give way to the desire to approach God's likeness.

Dante's own appetite for knowing God sharpens as he journeys up the mountain. Images of eating and drinking pepper the landscape as Dante's body and the bodies of the shades grow thinner and thereby move more swiftly. The body is the vehicle through which the soul may be saved. Hope for salvation is always embodied. Hope is at the heart of purgation. For example, Dante confronts the serpent, which reminds him of the serpent which gave Eve the food (Purgatorio, Canto VHI, line 93 on). Here he recalls how the fall of the human being came about through an excess of appetite. In Canto [X (Purgatorio, Canto IX, line 4 on). Here, the flesh of Adam causes Dante to fall asleep.

Early in the process of penance, the imaginal bodies, the souls in purgatory, walk bent over, but with their thoughts straight, oriented toward beatification. Dante walks straight, but with his thoughts bent over (Purgatorio, Canto XII, line 1 on). The corporeal substance of Dante's body is mirroring the souls of the shades. Thus, what is invisible, Dante's thoughts, assume a visible reality for the shades. Their spiritual disposition manifests itself through their imaginal bodies as Dante's fully human body leaves invisible his own spiritual disposition (Purgatorio, Canto XII, line 116 on). Here Dante describes the sensation of having pride, the heaviest of burdens removed from the body. His experience is credible, though, only because the soul's themselves have bodies. As Dante is absolved from each of the sins, his hunger and thirst for new knowledge of human love quickens. That is going to happen until he meets Beatrice. His appetite grows keener, but it is not an enhanced desire for the things of the world, but for those more intangible, invisible qualities which are beyond the world. To remain desirous of the things of the world is to retain a body bent towards the earth, heavy and weighty with desire. The bodies of those shades which have not shed the appetites for the fruits of the world are bent toward the world. The body is the physical image of the soul's disposition.

While formerly, feeding on earthly desires brought spiritual starvation, now, feeding on the knowledge of God though hope, their bodies grow thinner and more mobile. Both kinds of appetite, one directed toward earth, the other toward paradise, show us that love is indeed a transformation of appetite. Dante's poem implies that love is not only at the source of appetite but also the foundation of all sin. Sin may be understood as actions of disproportionate love; purgation, a form of fasting in which the sins melt away under the act of sacrifice, is a way of coming to love in proportion. A wonderful picture of proportion is given in Canto XXIV (Purgatorio, Canto XXIV, line 144 on).

The souls in purgatory are in movement between the fruit tree from which Adam and Eve ate and the tree of the cross on which Christ, wasted and emaciated, hangs, spilling, first blood, then water. Here are the polarities of excess and emptiness. The body of Christ, which is the image of God, and the action of Christ, which is the likeness to God, offer the final nutrition in the Word of Christ, which is the Essence of God. Image and likeness, body and soul, are only made visible by the two kinds of bodies that climb Mount Purgatory.

Additional Images to Consider

A. The Mountain of Purgatory (see Dorothy Sayers description, Pg. 17-18)

B. Anti-Purgatory

C. The Excommunicate, the indolent, the unshriven, the preoccupied

D. The three steps at the gate of Purgatory

E. Images of opposites at each level of Purgatory; eg. The proud - are bowed down under heavy stones; the envious sit with sealed eyes; the slothful run without pause

F. Sloth

G. The poet, Statius CCXI, 58-66) H. Dante's dream of Leah and Rachel (XX VII, 91 on)

H. The appearance of Beatrice (XXX, 22-39; 55-57;73-75)

The Paradiso

It is much more difficult to understand the Paradiso than it is to understand either the Inferno or the Purgatorio. It is more difficult for us to see it as a poem. Why? First of all, it is bright light. As we progress in the Paradiso, things get brighter and brighter and brighter. That seems to be the main action in it. A second reason for the difficulty is that heaven is really not very interesting. We miss evil and we miss the action. We don't think adoration is a very interesting thing to read about. A third reason for the difficulty is that is it so filled with philosophical discourse. It is so purely intellectual. Its open espousal of learning, its didacticism, the questioning, the correction of errors, makes it seem too philosophical. Then, there is the question of belief. A change in the conception of the universe occurs. It is difficult for us to accept this universe, this cosmos. We separate science and theology. Here, it is all mixed in together. And then, another difficulty is differing religious beliefs. Many people, even Christians do not believe the way Dante did. So, how do we approach a poem that seems so didactic, theological, intellectual, sermonizing?

Remember, the whole of the Divine Comedy is a poem. Dante is not trying to convert us. He is trying to make us see. He is giving us a universal experience. It is very hard to express what those universals are. But we can say that he is describing the growth of the human spirit toward its ultimate --- he uses the word "transhumanizing." We have to go beyond the human to be human. If we just live the limits of our carnal life, our fleshly life, we have not achieved the fully human.

So Dante's Divine Comedy is a large, comprehensive symbol. Dante knows medieval society. He knows the Church; he knows Rome and he has all the knowledge of the high period of the middle ages in which all the cathedrals were built, universities were developed, all of that beautiful flowering of 13th and 14th century. But that is not what Dante is writing about. We make a mistake if we think that this is what he is doing. He is using the only symbol he knows. If Dante lived in our time, he would use something else. He has to use physical things because the good poet is concerned with the flesh, the time, the state, mortality, what we are. So, don't let the carrier of this poem throw you off. The Paradiso is really quite simply an allegory of the mind's uplifting to God.

Dante renounces any attempt to depict deity. He depicts divine light and love in the same way he has shown the other two realms, the inferno and the purgatorio - not by description, but by showing their effects. And this is what makes Dante such a great poet. He makes use of the simple thing - to show, not to tell. He also makes use of the dialogical imagination - there is a great deal of dialogue. For example, Dante asks Beatrice why there are spots on the moon. He says that it is due to there being different thickness of the surface of the moon. She says that is not it. Some say it is because some parts of the moon are older than others, that they are farther away in a cave. Beatrice says that if you take three mirrors at different distances you will see that the one furthest away is just as bright as the nearest. Dante had studied with scientists of his day, and so he did not separate science and poetry as we do today. The dialogue goes on constantly. Beatrice ends by saying that some things are better receptors of light than others. God's light shines on all, but some things are better receptors than others. That is why we see the spots on the moon. We have that kind of dialogue going on throughout the Divine Comedy. Dante uses ideas as well as feelings and impressions to make us see. There are not very many writers in the world that can do this. Most writers do not deal with ideas. They deal with feelings and images and impression. So that is one of the big differences in Dante.

The imagination of the Paradiso is one of spiritual growth that is applicable to our lives because he speaks in terms of universals, Let's look at the very beginning of the Paradiso. Dante gives us a warning (Paradiso, Canto II, 1 and on). He warns us that this is a dangerous mission that we are on. You who are going for curiosity, you who are going for historical information, you who are going for some private reason of your own that does not have to do with truth, then your little boat may be upset. You will find yourself worse than you were when you started.

There are places throughout this whole poem where Dante warns us in this way. Remember the passage in the Inferno, where the Medusa will turn you into stone if you are not careful. If we approach learning for the wrong reasons, it can harm us. So, there has to be the right spiritual attitude for us to go on this terrible journey.

Dante is not pretending to know what happens to souls after death. That is his metaphor. He knows that we know that he is talking about this life. He is showing us attitudes, attitudes about ourselves primarily.

We have to be willing to enter into that fluid medium, like Glaucus (line 67). Glaucus was a fisherman. He caught a great number of fish and had hung them to dry. They somehow fell to the grass, and Glaucus noticed that they all came back to life. He then ate some of the grass and began to feel a tremendous longing for the sea. He then returned to the sea and became a kind of sea-god. We have to be willing to enter the fluid medium.

What is that fluid medium here? It is something that keeps us from being separated from the great sea of being. We lose our ego's; we lose our selfish selves.

There is another image that is important, an image of Narcissus. This is in Canto three (Paradiso, Canto III, line 9 and on). If we make the error, when confronted with the great ocean of being, of which we are a part, of thinking that all that is out there is part of ourselves, then we miss the reality. In this great ocean of being we are within the fullness of being, like fish in the water. If we let ourselves be "transhumanized", we are at home in this spiritual medium, where we can commune with each other. If we think that all that reality we see is just a reflection of our own selves, then we have missed the reality of those souls, those presences that are there.

The mirror image is another image that is very important in this poem. God is the great light that animates the universe. Everything in the universe is like a mirror. Medieval theologians spoke of this as the analogical mirror. Every single thing is an analogy of God. Dante would have us see that the light is the truth. Every single thing reflects the light that is God. Notice how this is different than pantheism, which says that God is in everything; no, says Dante, everything reflects God. So, when we see love in anyone that love is divine. There isn't any other love. We misuse it; we spend it on the wrong things; we try to keep it for ourselves. But, the love itself is that light that is the pure Light. So, any kind of love, even the most perverted, terrible love comes from that light, which in itself is the Light of God. Our task is to learn how to use it properly.

A second image Dante gives us in the Paradiso is the image of the seal in the wax. All through the Purgatorio and all through the Paradiso we find that seal in the wax image. Everything in creation is like wax. It is unformed. Ged has placed a seal on the wax, like a seal on the wax on a letter. We have here the whole idea of impressing a form on raw material. Dante, we know, bore the impression of Beatrice. She was the seal; he was the wax. The whole universe is patterned on the wax. This is what we call archetypes.

When Dante comes to the first level of the Paradiso, the lowest level of the heavens, that of the moon, the level of the inconstant nuns, he encounters the woman Piccarda, the sister of his friend. Here, in this section we find the most famous line in all of the Divine Comedy (Paradiso, Canto III, line 85 and on). Dante wants to know if it is hard to be farthest from God in heaven, as is Piccarda. She is perfectly content, perfectly happy. We learn that this distance doesn't mean anything, that everyone is great in that magnificent figure of the rose. The rose is the supreme image of God's relation to his creatures. (Paradiso, Canto XXX, line 96 on).

God is the center of the rose. He is that yellow, brilliant light, which is the center of the rose. All of the blessed, those who have made their way to heaven, and the angels, are present in the rose, so that it is in the image of a city. Beatrice points to the rose and says: "See our city." So, this is probably the most satisfactory image of God and of his relationship to His creation that we have. It is better than the mirror image, and better than the seal in the wax. Everyone in heaven, including Piccarda, has a place in that rose. And angels are going in and out, like inebriated bees. Joy is here so intense that we have to change our whole consciousness to read this work, it is so far beyond what we encounter in any kind of literature.

So, in this heavenly city, everyone is equidistant from God because God is a point with no circumference. He is everywhere, and everywhere all at once. Time and space have been abolished. This is that beatific presence that we intuit in life. We have such an experience from time to time. We have it in lovemaking. We have it in a marriage. We have it in a friendship. We glimpse the abolition of space and time when we are totally present to a situation, totally present to another.

Piccarda is where she is because she broke her vows. She was stolen away as a nun and made to marry. She never got back to the convent. And though she is not blamed for what happened, nevertheless, as Beatrice points out to her, if will were constant, nothing could have stopped her. Those who stole her away would not have been able to keep her, if her will were such that it were absolute. Piccarda's will was not constant, but she is blessed, so she must have been graced to be where she is in heaven. So, we are going to see degrees, even in heaven. It is not that Dante is telling us that it is going to be like this in heaven. He is trying to get us to see degrees of virtue and degrees of love, and degrees of commitment.

One of the marvelous things about the Paradiso is that in it we are involved in a world of excess. Now, hell was also a world of excess, but it was an excess of ego. Purgatory is a world of gentleness and restraint and humility; it is the way we should live most of the time. But, these souls in heaven balance the one's in hell. Dante actually finishes out some of the things he began in the Inferno. Cunizza (Paradiso, Canto IX, line 25 on) is a kind of completion of Francesca in the Inferno. Cunizza is in the planet of Venus and lived a passionate and immoral life on earth. Cunizza was a notorious woman in Florence. She had many lovers. She had four husbands. She was noted for her inordinate love-life. She lived, however, to be in her 80's and she did good deeds for the city. So, here she is in heaven. She has moved through suffering, and is the beautiful portrayal of romantic love, while Francesca is the selfish portrayal of romantic love, for she blames everyone else for what happened.

Cunizza, in her life, expressed the passionate giving of oneself, of her spirit; it is an expression that is like Mary Madeleine. Her passion is really an expression of the love of God that keeps searching for its object.

We learn in the Purgatorio not to dwell on our shortcomings, not to dwell on our sins. It is not true contrition to stay and grovel and feel guilty. Guilt is the most self-centered stance you can take. Now, here, in these moments of blessedness, which we intuit even in our lives, we see those acts which were not the best things we did in our lives as important in getting us to where we are. We see it all as providential. This is what the Paradiso gives us that glimpse of.

If we see Paradiso as balancing Inferno, then another contrast is that of Brunetto Lattini in the Inferno with Cacciaguida in heaven (Paradiso, Canto XV). Here are two teachers, two elders. "O branch of mine, I was your root", he says. Cacciaguida regrets the state of Florence but compare these with the bitterness of Brunetto Lattini. Brunetto Lattini is like the college professor who writes a book and castigates the young. He looks at everything as if it is going downhill. And then, this professor says what he thinks things ought to be like. Brunetto Lattin ends, remember, by saying "read my book." Cacciaguida says to Dante: "write your book." So, we have a real balance. And so, we have The Divine Comedy.

We move on to Cacciaguida and come closer and closer to the time when Beatrice must go. Dante makes a tribute to Beatrice (Paradiso, Canto XXXI, line 79 on).
Beatrice fulfills that pattern of love that we all ought to practice; or at least know about. It is a kind of leading and stepping aside. See how Beatrice is very different from the image of a goddess figure. A goddess figure takes whatever adoration comes to her. Beatrice, in contrast, must leave, so that Dante can see beyond.

The ending of the Paradiso is magnificent and difficult. Dante is blinded by a flash of light and he has a vision of the blessed as they will be after judgment day. Dante asks - after judgment day, how will your bodies stand all this bright light? Won't the brilliance burn you up when you get your body? They say, "our organs will be strong enough for whatever happens. Let's turn to the very ending of the Paradiso (Paradiso, Canto XXXII, line 112 on). "but in my vision which gained strength, as I looked the single appearance, through a change in me, was transformed." That is a terribly important stanza. This says: you learn to see by seeing. There is not another way of learning to see except by doing what you want them to do.

The Paradiso ends with an image of the Trinity. It is an image of intense action. Here is the relation he has been worried about. What is our relation to God? Here, in this last few words he has his answer. We are in there. We are related to the Trinity. It is related to God the Son. It is in that circle of God the Son that our image appears. But, if we try to think this out, there is no way to do it.

Dorothy Sayers says that this poem is about the "en-godding" of the human being. At one moment, in a flash, after having gone through hell, purgatory, and heaven, for just a moment Dante sees, has a flash of the place of the human in relation to God.

Additional Images to Consider
A. The Moon (iI, 31-36)
B. Mercury and Venus
C. The SunD. Mars, Jupiter, Saturn

Dying Awake: Preparing Soul for the Great Life: Spiritual Psychology of the Metanoia Process

Introduction

Last Moment Preparations as Insufficient

There seems to be a quiet revolution taking place in the world concerning how people die. Many wonderful enterprises now exist for caring for the dying in ways that help the person cross the threshold with ease and, hopefully, consciously. These efforts take many and varied forms and are carried out from many different points of view – Buddhist, Anthroposophical, Christian, as well as the Hospice movement and medical care. These efforts are all oriented toward caring for the person after the announcement has been made to the person that he or she is dying. Then the preparation begins. These concerns are a great advance on meeting death face to face and dispelling fear. At the same time, there is the perpetuation of the notion that death is a terminus, even though it might now be imagined as a transition to the Great Life. Death is nonetheless imagined as the end of earthly life; it is, but it is an ending that is happening each and every moment. What does it mean that death is not felt as happening each and every moment? Can we actually prepare for death only once it has been pronounced on us by someone else? Where is there available in culture an understanding of how to live with our constant dying. Rudolf Steiner has said that only human beings die. He was obviously not talking about the mere cessation of life. He was talking about what most essentially defines the human being as a being of body, soul, and spirit – the capacity to be with our dying in a conscious way all through our lives.

In past times, there were constant ways in which people were able to live with their dying. Death had not yet been made invisible. People died at home. People even often knew when they were going to die, way before there was any illness; they had a sense that it was happening. But that was when people died of their death and not of a disease or illness that was pronounced on them. Death also took place publicly as many diseases and plagues made hiding death impossible And, most importantly, there were contemplative practices concerned with meditating on one's death. We feel enormously grateful for the advances in medicine so that we do not have the constant presence of death looming before us. However, the true meaning of this advance may have gotten lost. It means that we now have the freedom to be with our death or to lull ourselves into self-forgetfulness. The presence of death is not forced upon us, not unless we have not opted for this inner freedom and instead act as if we were not going to die. In spite of the fact that we all intellectually know that we will one day die, we do not live within this experience. Our first question will be why this is so. What is it that makes us forgetful of the ongoing inner experience of dying, makes us so forgetful that it is quite doubtful that any of us could describe what it is like to be dying every moment? We cannot do so because we have not developed the capacity to be present to ourselves in this way.

Egotism as the Veil Concealing Dying Awake
Egotism, Evil, and Death
Those of us who are engaged with the work of Rudolf Steiner can take a too-easy comfort in Steiner's statements concerning the fact that in this time the main spiritual work that humanity is to be involved with concerns the nature of evil and how to overcome it. In the past age, according to Steiner, the primary spiritual concern for humanity was the concern of death. Not only is it apparent that we still have a great, great deal to do yet to come to a true understanding of the very great mystery of death, we are also way behind where Steiner had hoped humanity would be. Further, there is the additional difficulty of how death and evil hold hands with each other. This handholding must be addressed. While, in previous times, death was considered evil, now, in our time, we must look at the ways in which evil make it appear that death is but a transition rather than an every-moment actuality of living.

On Egotism
While it is true that we live in the age of evil, it is of central importance to be able to describe how evil gets hold of how we approach death. Egotism is the form taken to obscure the true working of death in our lives and what keeps us asleep to the reality of dying each and every moment.

When one reads and works to take in the enormous contributions made by Rudolf Steiner to understanding the nature of evil, there is one dimension of what he develops that requires a great deal of meditation. <u>The source of all human evil</u>, he says, <u>is egotism.</u> (Here are a couple of quotations from his lecture titled "Evil Illumined Through Science of the Spirit":

> *"So, we can see that our very first steps of ascent into the world of spirit are accompanied by an experience of evil and imperfection....Why is this? If we look closer, we can recognize in this fact a fundamental trait of all human evil....The common trait of all evil is nothing other than egotism........Basically, all human evil proceeds from what we call egotism. In the whole scope and range of 'wrong', whether from the smallest oversight to the most serious crime, whether the imperfection or evil originates more in the body, or in the soul, egotism is the fundamental trait which underlies it all."*

Egotism is something far more than mere self-centeredness. We have to look more deeply and ask what is the process involved in being self-centered; what is the soul and the spirit process involved? We seem just to do it, as if it is something that belongs to human nature and that must be worked against. But, working against our propensities for self-centeredness will produce no result if we cannot see deeply into what brings egotism about in a spiritual/ psychological sense. Egotism concerns attributing capacities to ourselves in our strictly earthly aspect, that is, as beings of the world, that actually originate and belong with the spiritual worlds. For example, whatever power I seem to have is in fact not mine. And, holding this power as if it were mine is a form of egotism. Power as such belongs to the spiritual worlds. If we experience power it is coming from the spiritual worlds, not us. Egotism is a process of consolidating the soul into a kind of center that we speak of as "I", as "me". Egotism is actually an indication of strength of soul. Understood in this fashion, egotism concerns receiving capacities from the spiritual worlds and holding them as our own.

It is most important to be able to see that we are approaching egotism here completely non-evaluatively. I am not judging egotism, merely trying to describe how it functions. And, if Steiner says that egotism is the source of evil, he does not at all mean that we should run from evil, or even that evil is bad. Evil, in its rightful place, is extremely important and necessary.

Whenever we say, think, feel, act out of a sense of "I am….this, or that, or "I have….this or that, we are being egotistical. Some quality of soul has been captured and it then makes us feel we are real; egotism is a matter of needing the quality of self-feeling in order to know that we exist (See: Georg Kuhlewind, From Normal to Healthy). When we become more or less removed from others and removed from the world, then a great deal of anxiety arises. We may not in fact exist… that is the anxiety felt. Egotism gives us a feeling of belonging to something when in fact we only in such instances belong to ourselves. And, actually it is an illusion that we belong to ourselves. Egotism is the illusion of belonging to ourselves.

The soul and spiritual work centered around the difficulty of egotism is to give of ourselves. That is the way through egotism. But this has to be done in a non-egotistical way. An amazing paradox. We have to be egotistical in order to try to do things non-egotistically. What is this way out of this paradox? The only way through this is to develop the capacity of being aware of being egotistical. The way through this difficulty is consciousness. We cannot get through the difficulty by trying to act non-egotistically in a direct way. The notion "I am going to not be egotistical" is highly egotistical.

On Egotism and Dying Awake

The spiritual psychology of egotism is a large domain to explore. We do such an exploration in another course, "The Spiritual Psychology of the Gospel of St. John." Here we want to concentrate on the relation of egotism and being present to our ongoing dying. Egotism makes this awareness as something more than an intellectual thought impossible. We do not in fact feel that we are dying every moment. There is an inner quality that we experience that goes very contrary to the experience of dying every moment. We actually feel immortal, though none of us would quite be able to admit to that. It is, though, a perfectly normal and understandable feeling. We are, after all, in our egotism, living off the gifts of the spiritual worlds, acting as if they were ours, and accompanying that illusion is the further illusion that we are as if gods. Only the corruptibility of the body from time to time reminds us that we are not gods. Modern medicine works assiduously to try and take away from this one great Memento Mori, this one ongoing memory of dying. And, we may be on the verge of believing in this illusion of medicine, the notion that with technical progress, death will be overcome. Death has been overcome, but not by technology. And, the overcoming of death does not mean that we will not die, but rather that we have the capacity to be fully conscious of dying, though this is not possible from the stance of the ego, not without spiritual psychological working through egotism and its relation to evil.

Egotism is not bad. It is, in fact, inevitable and unavoidable. In order to understand how it works, a distinction in experience has to be gained, the distinction between the ego and the I. There is a strong tendency in spiritual circles to distinguish between the "lower I" and the "higher I', or the self and the Self, or the "lower ego" and the "higher ego". Along with drawing the distinction in this way comes the notion and the feeling that what is higher is better and that we ought to be working to get rid of the lower and find our way to the higher. Drawing the distinction in this way comes mainly in the language of New Age philosophy, but it occurs wherever there is the notion that to be spiritual we have to get rid of the ego. In order not to fall into this kind of division which mostly leads to a kind of groundlessness, and even more important, to be phenomenologically accurate, the I and the ego are one and the same. They both express the individuality of our spiritual being. The I is the spiritual you. The I is the spiritual you as it is in the process of coming into being every moment from the spiritual worlds. The ego is simply the other side of the I. It is the I-experiences we have that then goes on to be considered as accumulations. The ego is the I experience as it recedes into the past and then become a kind of fund through which we experience the world and others in habitual ways.

The Archetypal I and the Ego Processes as Veiling the presence of Death A consideration of Rudolf Steiner's sculpture, "The Representative of Man" as picturing the Archetypal I.

When we have not gone through developing a strength of I-being, we are really not able to tell when we are present to what is real and when we are in a fantasy. There are these two unconscious dimensions of ego life – represented by the archetypal Lucifer on the one hand and archetypal Ahriman on the other hand. And, there, in the middle, is the spiritual I, which does not reject the two polarities, but sacrifices some of its own autonomy in order to embrace these two other aspects. What this embrace means, however, is that we cannot tell very readily when we are in a fantasy because it has the characteristics of I-consciousness. The fantasy seems like a real experience that I am experiencing. And, the same is true with the other polarity. I cannot really tell when I have lost a true sense of the spiritual and have fallen into a materialistic consciousness because this too seems like real experience that I am experiencing. The way in which the Archetypal I functions shows us why we are not able to experience the way in which death is with us in an ongoing way all of the time. We are blind to this most essential defining aspect of being human unless we work to develop it.

Due to the presence of the Luciferic and the Ahrimanic aspects of ego experience, we are unable, without inner work, to imagine death. On the one hand, we inwardly refuse to acknowledge as an actual living experience that we are dying. We really don't know what that means nor what it is like to live with that inward awareness. We live day to day feeling that we are not dying. That is the Luciferic side of our situation that keeps us asleep to the possibility of dying awake. Along with this comes notions such as death is but a transition. True, but dying is not. The Ahrimanic side is that we intellectually grasp that we are dying, but then there is no process available to work this through. Along with this comes the cynicism that says, I know I am dying and there is nothing to do about it, so forget about it. So, we act as if we know we are dying on the one hand but live in an ongoing fantasy that we are not dying. **The first aspect of developing the capacity of dying awake is thus the work of developing a true imagination of death. The task of imagination is to imagine the real.** It is perhaps more accurate to say that the work we are confronted with it to develop a soul presence to the reality of death.

There are two ways to go about developing a soul presence to the reality of death. Each of these ways is not exclusive of the other, and they most likely are both required. We can work our way through the egotism keeping us from dying awake by working with the dying. Such work is a pretty good antidote or balance to Luciferic egotism, or one would think so. However, I have seen many people who work with the dying but who come to no inner sense of their ongoing dying, none at all. This situation is not out of the ordinary but is in fact what usually occurs if such work is not accompanied by an inner work of imagining death. This work, that of imagining death is the second way of developing a soul presence to the reality of death, and the one that we will work with here.

Imagining Death

Soul and Death

We cannot imagine the ongoing participation of soul in dying each and every moment directly. The structure of the archetypal I obscures such a possibility. There are ways in which we can enter into a partial imagination of death. We have to provide an access to finding our way to the soul's ongoing concern with death. Once we find that access, then it becomes possible to work with the process of dying awake in a manner that keeps connection and intimacy with soul life. This is what spiritual psychology has to contribute – the development of a conscious soul life of the activity of dying every moment. Access to a partial imagination of dying is through the imaginal act of reverie. Reverie is a kind of memory that begins to take on a life of its own and becomes an experience of imagination. Let me give an example of reverie that is oriented toward our life in the past. Then we will do an exercise to enter this kind of reverie and see how it helps us find the soul's doorway to the ongoing act of dying:

"It is around three o'clock in the afternoon on a late Spring day of my life as I walk the streets of Woodhaven, New York. These streets are not like any other streets. They are special streets; they are the streets I used to roam when I was a boy growing up. These streets which once seemed so large and immense now seem small and, in a way,, confining. Suddenly, I am carried back to that time when the streets were so large and immense. I become aware of the many late Spring days I used to spend playing in those streets. I see a little boy playing ball, running in the streets and having fun with his friends; I see a boy in a snowball fight against the older kids; I see him climbing a tree on a dare. Then he is older and walking up these streets to serve Mass. It is the same boy again who is on his way to grammar school graduation. Then, out of the blue, a car whizzes by and the streets become small and confining once more, and I stand with a feeling of melancholy and sadness." (From: Robert Sardello, "Death and the Imagination", *Humanitas vol. X*)

This description is more than a memory of childhood. Memory passes over into reverie as the person becomes identified with his boyhood. He re-enters his life on the streets of this town but re-enters it at various stages of his life. As the person above stands on that street corner and sees himself as a child again there is a hint of sadness in his heart. Here he moves out of the reverie into a realization of the impossibility of becoming that child again. His embodiment has changed. He will never be that way again. At this moment when we become aware of the changing of our embodiment – not just a recognition that this is so, but something that comes from an act of imagining and is therefore connected with the soul life – we confront a deep feeling of vulnerability. We realize within our soul, which is something deeper than an intellectual recognition, that we are not permanent in our embodiment. There is the unfulfillable longing to become that child again, but we cannot – ever.

The confrontation with vulnerability became an art in the Middle Ages, the art of learning to die. For example, Thomas Occleve's "Lerne to Dye" can be condensed as follows: the best of the arts is to learn to die so that a man need not be surprised by death. A person who is not ready for death when it come in compassed by the sorrows of hell. Spiritually, he has won nothing from life. The hopeless man is in the snares of death and he fears that he postponed amendment too long. Let us keep ourselves always as though we were to die today, or tomorrow, or this week at the furthest. Remember death in time! (see, B. P. Kurtz, "The Relation of Occleve's "Lerne to Dye" to its Sources, *Publications of the Modern Language Association, XL, pp. 252-275*)

The Middle Ages cultivated a contemplation of stories and woodcuts of death. (See, for example, Joan Evans, *The Flowering of the Middle Ages, 1966*) People were constantly reminded that their beauty would pass and that worms would soon be crawling out their eye sockets. Woodcuts depicted three young men on a journey suddenly coming upon three coffins with bodies in various stages of decomposition. The three young travelers step back in horror only to realize that they were looking at themselves. Now these woodcuts were not meant to evoke a fear of death so much as to prepare the contemplator for submission, for the giving up of bodily control and ableness.

Dying Awake

Metanoia

The Greek term "metanoia" means "turn around" and refers to the "turn around of soul life that comes with the inner, imaginal realization of death. We must, however, be clear about what this realization of death means in or time, as it is something different than the medieval contemplation of death.

The soul work is not to contemplate death but rather to daily release the imagination of things that we are attached to. This act of dying to something every day then opens the soul to be concerned with other qualities, qualities that come when the soul is open to the spiritual worlds. We will say something of these qualities below. However, dying to something everyday would produce no soul result if we attempt to do so out of our ordinary consciousness without having gone through the process of realizing, in an inner way, the nature of the archetypal I. As we do go through this process, it is then possible to enter into the process of dying to something every day.

An exercise on what it is like to die to something every day: On ten small sheets of paper, write on each sheet, one thing that is very important to you in life. It can be a relationship, a material thing, something you do, and it can also be something of a more subtle nature, for example, daily meditation. We are then going to give one of these written pages away at a time, putting them in the center of the circle. Then we will write a description of what it is like to give this thing or experience or connection away and how that give-away opens the soul.

Working with the Exercise

What occurs in an inner way as we work through this exercise opens up the actual experience of dying awake. Thus, a careful phenomenological description of the process is important to do. First, the exercise works in its fullness when we are able to be present to each thing that is to be taken away in an inner image. If we just write down the items in a non-contemplative way, not much will happen. If we have an inner image of something that is not just an external attachment but also has become, in a certain way, a very part of our soul life, then a specific experience occurs when we release the item. When an experience has entered us so deeply that it more or less becomes a part of us – in that it now lives within as an inner image, we do not realize it, but that experience obscures, so to speak, the soul's orientation toward the spiritual worlds.

It is extremely important to realize that because an experience that lives on in soul life obscures being present to the spiritual worlds, there is nothing at all that is bad or wrong about this. It is inevitable as long as soul life is connected with earthly life. Further, this obscuring of the soul's connection with an experience of the spiritual worlds occurs precisely so that we can do the work necessary to become conscious of the presence of the spiritual worlds from within soul life. That is, a conscious effort of releasing the matters with which our soul is daily engaged is needed if the experience of the spiritual worlds is to be other than illusion.

Two experiences occur when we release something from its internal engagement with the soul life. First, there is an experience of deep sorrow. And, along with the experience of deep sorrow, there is the feeling of the opening of a hollow space deep within the region of our chest, in the region of the heart. This is the first experience. Then, if we are perceptive in an inner way, a second experience occurs which is related to this first one. There is an inner image that accompanies the first experience. It is an image of light. This image may take a number of different forms. But it is an inner light, a light that is actual and real and unmistakable. This light typically lasts only a fraction of a second. It is not experienced as an image of light, but as an actual inner light. The experience, though, is so strong that the memory of it lasts as this inner image of light.

What may occur in doing this exercise is that when something is released, we feel the sorrow so strongly that this feeling overwhelms the light. This sorrow is felt in a very strong manner, for example, when we imagine releasing from the soul the presence of someone we love. It is very important to realize that we do not release the love, but only the inner image of the person. The image carries with it a lot of emotion; this emotion is not the love. The emotional tone of an image is also not 'wrong'.

Doing the work of dying awake is not to be confused with notions such as detachment, nor other notions from religious traditions, such as becoming 'egoless' or something of that sort. It is a spiritual/psychological work in which we have to become researchers into our own soul life in order to 'see' what is happening and learn how to follow it carefully ever deeper into the experience. We will find that there are connections to the practices of religious traditions, particularly to the mystical tradition, but our interest and concern is with developing practices that are suitable to the current conditions of soul life and that can be carried out in daily living.

Dying Awake and Awakening to the Inner Light

It is somewhat unfortunate that the New Age movement quickly crystallizes certain experiences into jargon language and then makes these experiences into programs to be followed. One such unfortunate example is this experience of light. The New Age Movement is filled with the language of 'light'. There are 'workers of light', 'temples of light', going toward the light.... all sorts of references and programs and directions concerning coming into the light. The inner light of the soul that initiates the experience of dying awake has nothing to do with any of these programs and promptings.

At this point, we could find ourselves in a big hole. This first glimpse of the inner light has to be kept open. We need to keep going, keep experiencing. It is quite important not to come to any conclusion. Let us not call the inner light God or say that this direction is the same as what the mystics were doing, or that this fits into one system or another. The inner work then involves returning again and again to this light; perhaps find ways to strengthen this light; and, most important, to gradually begin to see that this inner light has many, many different layers. Dying awake then becomes a process that we enter into and is not just a matter of stepping over a threshold. All kinds of light are to be discerned. There are layers and layers and layers within layers of light. The ongoing process of dying awake concerns gradually coming to discern the different soul qualities that awaken as we die to something each day.

A first quality that we can discern within the experience of what we are here calling light is that it is actually an experience of time. The inner images of those things, events, experiences that we have taken into the depths of soul life has the effect of slowing. It is as if in ordinary, everyday consciousness, soul is caught in something not of its own nature. The image-contents we carry in soul life keep us more or less caught. I here mean the content of the images. When we release something in the deep manner described above, there is also a release of time. It is as if, suddenly, there is an opening in time. Time opens up into something else. Time shortens. We call this something else 'light'. It should be apparent from this that 'light' is not a content that replaces the image content that was released. In a way, this light is the experience of no-thingness. There is no-thing there. But this no-thingness is not oppressive; rather, it is bright, luminous, and open. In the brief opening of light there is an overcoming of time. But it is not permanent.

One question that comes is why this inner experience of light is so slight and so momentary. It is immediately filled in, not only by our ongoing experiences in the world, but also by all that still lives within us from our past actions and experiences, and also by desires. The opening can be strengthened only by the conscious act of dying to something each day. Another way of saying this is that we are captives of time. Think of time here as a certain kind of being – time as the Lords of Limitation. The first little momentary experience of inner light reveals that dying awake involves being released from time. We cannot live in the world and be released from time. However, we can become conscious of being captives of time, and that consciousness is itself a release, an entry into the process of dying awake.

When we do, in a serious manner, an exercise such as this and take up the task of dying to something everyday, we can expect that other things will happen than just the opening to the light. Various forms of interference will interpose themselves. We may find that our lives are shaken up in numerous ways. A descent may be initiated. What this is about; there are forces and powers that are enraged with what we are doing. We may find ourselves in the darkness rather than in the light. We have to make an inner effort to be oriented toward the light. We will feel powerless, though, to do this out of our own efforts. We feel that no-one can hear our inner cries for help. What we can find in this darkness is not a capacity of our own will. We cannot remain oriented toward the light by a mere act of will. We keep oriented by an inner act of *soul faith*. Faith is the act of being with something that is not present. If I have faith in someone, it means that I am able to be with them completely in a soul manner even in times when that person is not here or when that person seems to be totally disconnected from me. To have faith is to have confidence in what I cannot see or cannot experience. We could also say that having faith is to have trust in what we cannot know. Faith is the intuitive perception of the underlying reality. This perception does not last. The task is to sustain trust in the original perception that we had. When we do the exercises above, we are required to have a presence of mind that perceives very subtle matters. Then, if we do perceive something, it will not last. We have to have trust in what we experienced. We have to want to trust. Without this act of will of wanting-to-trust, there is no faith. This act of will is not something done by the ego – it is not willfulness. It is the act of the deepest aspect of the psyche. Without this act, we lost confidence in the original perception we had. In order to trust the perception, we have to trust ourselves. There is a tendency to abandon our perception because it is safer to remain comfortable. Reasoning also enters – reasoning out alternatives to the truth of the perception. We have to put the intellect away and not argue against the perception we had. Instead, we need to find all things that will keep the intuitive perception alive.

This situation is an expression of a universal predicament. The soul is cut-off from the spiritual worlds, is dominated and overshadowed by what we hold in soul images as image-content. This content keeps the inner life in a state of chaos. Once we get a glimpse that the soul is trapped in the region of chaos, we also realize that our ego has created its own cosmos which we have held to be reality. Once we have glimpsed the inner light, we begin to say no to the world, no to the world as what we have all along taken to be what is real. But, then, an automatic, unconscious rage will raise up. It is not our rage. It is the world trying to get back in as it was before. When we begin to say no to the world, the world moves in ever more strongly. We face then a crisis. We no longer feel we belong to the world, world understood in a literal way. And yet, the world presses in more strongly than ever; we long intensely for the kind of experiences we have released. This longing is experienced as all kind of distractions. These distractions take the form of being pulled into doing things unconsciously. Being attached to the inner images of the events and experiences we go through means that we are not conscious of being affected by those things. The work here is not to release anything in a literal way, but rather to bring the power of consciousness to bear on what we experience. Then we are not captured by those things.

Here we enter into a further and deeper understanding of this inner light. This light is consciousness. Dying awake is to be conscious. What we usually call consciousness is not consciousness at all. As long as I am bound to what I am supposedly conscious of, then I am not conscious. We are half-conscious; consciousness is mixed with darkness. We also have to distinguish consciousness from knowing.

Dying Awake as Climbing the Ladder of Light.
We have to lose our mind, lose our bearings, lose our senses in order to enter into the light of consciousness. We are thrown into chaos when we glimpse the light in order to be rid of our arrogance. We do not willingly go into the

chaos We are thrown into it, and we are thrown into it by the initial act of turning to the light. Then, in the darkness, when we hit rock-bottom of the darkness, only then can there be a turning around. We die before we can die awake. Being thrown into chaos is a eucatastrophe, which means – a happy tragedy. But it is felt as alienation and aloneness. We strongly feel that we do not belong to the world as it is. We, however, do not have a feeling of belonging elsewhere. At this phase of dying awake, we can easily get caught in trying to reform the world into what we think it ought to be. We can become involved in all kinds of projects that try to do this. The inner work, however, is to be able to stay with and in this no-place.

The turn-around is experienced as desire, desire for the light above the light. This way of speaking of the light helps us to refraining from making light into an image-content. This desire, however, is a different kind of desire than our other desires. It is not just a different desire-content. It is not as if instead of experiencing desire for a big house, I now desire the light. Rather, desire is turned inside out. We experienced being desired, though it is certainly something quite different than feeling desired by, for example, another person. To be more accurate in describing this experience, we are pulled toward desire, an autonomous desire belonging to a mysterious Other. The whole situation is reversed. The river now flows backwards. We can feel ourselves being undone. This is the process of dying awake – the process of being undone, a re-organization of existing psychic functions. We undergo the experience of dispersion; reason, logic, sanity is abandoned. This process has to be undertaken, then, with a great deal of care. If we are not particularly stable to begin with, then this undoing can be dangerous. The practical aspect of recognizing the danger of this process of dying awake is that it needs to be undertaken according to strictly individual capacities. No one can tell us how it should be done. It has to be done with the timing that goes with our individual character. Only we alone can intuitively know this timing.

A further entry into the light is through exalting the light. To exalt means to 'heighten'. This little experience that comes from releasing the inner images that we hold onto, is to be seen as a holy experience. That is to exalt. The inner light is holy light.

The experience of the light is also experienced as a return to our authentic and real self. The light that is 'there' is the light that is 'here.' Here, in order to experience that this light is returning to ourselves, we have to be able to admit to the fact that we are in our usual consciousness alienated from ourselves. We have to be able to admit to that; that is a central aspect of dying awake -- to suffer our separation.

Another aspect of the experience of the light is to feel forgiven. As we release the image-contents from the soul, a capacity for deep joy also gradually arises. Whatever we hold onto brings with it a quite subconscious feeling of guilt. We certainly don't necessarily go around feeling guilty, but it is there. We come to recognize it only as the image-contents of the soul are released. We feel quite mysteriously lighter, even though dying to something everyday may be experienced as sorrow. Right behind the sorrow follows the lightening. We may even feel physically lighter.

Another quality of the light is that it is experienced as good. That is a quality of the light itself. It is inherent within the light that the light is good. Since this light is the light within which is also the light without, the light above the light, we feel goodness. We do not have to do anything to merit this. The light is generous light. We begin, then, to be able to abandon ourselves to this light. There is a principle of goodness, of beneficence, something that desires our well-being, that wants us to be uplifted. We can now cooperate with this goodness. This goodness is also the source of any goodness that we have, any soul-generosity that we have, the source of the capacity of serving from the place of the soul. Any other kind of serving is based in egotism; it is not that serving from the stance of egotism is thereby not helpful. It is. There is, however, this other kind of serving, sacred serving.

Strengthening the Capacity of Dying Awake
Feeling the anguish of the heart that we are separated from the qualities mentioned above forms a central and highly important aspect of strengthening the capacity of dying awake. The qualities described above are all very subtle and momentary. It takes quite a bit of soul strength not only to perceive them, but to remember them once we have had the momentary experience. In between such experiences, the heart undergoes a deep feeling of anguish. We may try to locate the source of this anguish with all sorts of things because there seems to be no knowable reason or cause for such anguish. Being present to this anguish, realizing that it is due to separation of soul life from the light, strengthens the soul capacity of dying awake.

Connected with feeling this anguish is the realization that all of our actions in life are actually a search for this inner light, even when what we do does not at all seem to be related to this search. Our search may be misguided and misunderstood, but it is nevertheless oriented toward the light. This realization helps to avoid thinking that the actions that we do in daily living, all that we do out of ordinary consciousness is not spiritual. It is. We can thus come to look upon daily life in a different light. A new consciousness is brought to everyday life.

The experience of anguish of the heart also is a constant inner indication that we, out of our own forces, cannot keep ourselves in connection with the inner light. We are bound to ego life and only in moments when there is a break-through to soul is there an opening to the light. Here, it is important to realize that the ego has light, that the ego is light, but it is a different light. It is light that is invaded with arrogance. If we did not experience heart anguish, we would quick and repeatedly confuse our ego light with soul light. Heart anguish breaks the arrogance of the ordinary ego without doing away with the ordinary ego.

When we are able to be present to the anguish of the heart, a particular kind of soul strength comes. A small voice of inner recognition comes, and it is a still small voice of compassion. This inner strength does not come as a large and overpowering force. It is not the inner voice of the conquering hero that would come to defeat the ego. A further work of dying awake concerns learning to hear this small inner voice in the midst of ordinary ego consciousness, which, so to speaks, hides right in the middle of our usual ego consciousness. This inner voice is a kind of hermetic presence, hidden, secret, working behind the scenes.

The presence of this inner voice of the soul-light will be, of course, detected by the ego. Our ordinary ego then asserts its power in even a stronger manner. The strengthening of the soul-light that has been taking place has been a preparation for this. From within conscious soul life, it is not possible to stand against the ego, not in a defiant way, not in a war-like way, but in the sense of now being able to clearly discern the difference between our ego-consciousness and soul-consciousness. The light is not taken from soul. Rather, light begins to be taken from ego. We experience this as a kind of weakening of ego consciousness. We may, for example, begin to lose the sense that we know anything. We may also begin to lose our usual sense of memory. But, these loses are not accompanied by fear.

We cannot expect slow, unimpeded progress in developing the practice of dying awake. The process includes the break-out of a good deal of pandemonium. There is every step of the way an impulse toward going back to sleep. The more important the things are going on, the more the upset comes. We need to rid ourselves of a false understanding that awakening is a once and for all work, that once done is done. We have the imagination that there is a kind of a threshold and that when we cross that threshold, then we are awake and on the other side and can thereafter be conscious in soul life. We have to be prepared for those around us saying that what we are doing is nonsense, that it will get us nowhere, that it is not practical. These kinds of responses are forms of mockery, not really mockery from other people per se, but from the regions and legions of ego.

There is thus the danger of losing our ideals, of descending again into sleepiness; this danger belongs to the process of dying awake. Compromise is always looming. Immobilization is always a possibility. The most important counter to such compromise is to avoid the feeling of guilt. Guilt is the way that we fall back asleep. Recognize that guilt is egotistical.

Guilt is countered by the capacity of praise. We can keep a connection with the qualities of inner light by an attitude of praise. When we can feel this inner, ongoing act of praise, then the soul-light has strengthened to the point that it will not and cannot be taken away. Praise, the capacity of holy praise of everything is the indication to us that soul-consciousness has strengthened.

Further qualities of the light of the soul now unfolds – grace is one such quality. Grace, Charis, has no specific form. It manifests in graciousness. Graciousness is not the same as being nice or being friendly. Graciousness is very difficult to describe. It is a particular quality of soul, the quality of being able to give forth in the world with the qualities of soul. Our actions in the inner world now carry an inner quality. If, for example, we are to work with the dying, then it has to be out of this quality of soul. Dying awake has to proceed at least to this level as a preparation for working with the dying. Grace concerns the capacity of allowing the spiritual worlds to work through our soul and into the world. Our work in the world then becomes holy work. Grace is thus the consciousness of holy work in the world.

The evidence of grace is to be found in the body. The body becomes luminous. This term 'luminous', is not to be taken literally. The body does not glow with light, not in a literal way, but it does have an inner luminosity.

We are aware when we come upon individuals through whom the action of grace works; they have this kind of 'glow'. This grace comes from the capacity we now have to 'harvest' the light, the consciousness from our experiences. An important part of dying awake concerns what must be retrieved from the image-contents that we release. We release the content but retrieve the light; that is to say, we retrieve soul- meaning from the experiences we go through in the world.

The ego, which is not a dragon to be slain or an illusion to be dispelled but is the lesser light which refuses to acknowledge the greater light does not just settle down. This ego, our individual ego, links into mass consciousness. When, for example, the notion of death as a transition becomes a matter of mass consciousness, when it becomes a general belief which people adopt without coming to that realization through the inner work of dying awake, this is one of the ways in which ego reasserts itself, now in the guise of a spiritual revelation. The collective ego says, "Do what everyone else does." As death and dying enter into collective consciousness, we have to be aware that the individual work of dying awake cannot be bypassed. This is the place we began this workshop. We have been trying to examine the un-reflected notion that it is a spiritual good to help people die by bringing something of a spiritual nature to care for the dying.

Preparing for Heart Initiation
Welcoming "Not-Knowing"
l. The result of dying to something every day is that we lose a great deal of the fund of accumulated ways that make life habitual, and easier, though lacking presence to the truly creative dimensions of life. The 'cost' for presence of the inner, living quality of engaging in actual creation is that we enter into 'not-knowing'. (In the next module, we will see that 'not-knowing' can evolve into 'eros-knowing'.) This 'not-knowing' now exists within as a kind of presence alongside of a certain fund of 'already-knowing' that is used to 'get around' in the given world. Another way of speaking of the presence of 'not-knowing', is that we have stepped into destiny experience. The ongoing sense is that, as we remain inwardly open, we feel that we are being pulled toward something rather than "pushed from behind" into life according to what has happened to us in the past. We move into the realm of 'potential'; what was more beautifully termed in

classical philosophy 'potentia.' We move into coming-into-being, rather than living one variation after another of what has already happened.

Rudolf Steiner has a beautiful way of speaking of destiny – he simply says that destiny is the same as life! Destiny is not some particular content that we are supposed to find and then do. It is life as open expectation, as spontaneity, as courage to stay within the unknown, life as unfolding rather than as programmed.

The essential quality of the destiny experience is that it is not the content of the experience that makes it a destiny experience. Rather, it is a particular perceivable quality of any content, a quality that feels like something is calling us forth. By this moment of destiny experience, we are being called... to what? We don't know. And because, within the experience itself we do not know, there is a strong tendency to dismiss the experience, or to quickly put the content of the experience back into the categories of experience we are used to. Thus, it is of great importance to be able to characterize the qualities of the destiny experience. In our usual, ordinary day-consciousness, we are awake. Supposedly. The moment of a destiny experience is characterized, however, by a change in this experience; we are, at least for a moment, awake-awareness. That is, we are awake to being aware that something mysterious operates in our lives, something that embeds itself within the most ordinary content. The particular content of this awake-awareness is not important. The quality of the experience is; the quality that within everything we know and feel in control of has a more significant dimension of holding the 'unknown'. When we feel such moments the soul steps beyond personal history into the future-to-be-created.

When we are able to stay in this opening of the future, a different way of witnessing our life begins to emerge. When we live in the time-line from the past, we are caught in an identity structure that needs approval, recognition, and position, and power. These things to hold on to, give us the sense of who we are. Further, these markers of our identity effectively have enough power to block the not-yet-known from getting through. The other characteristic of these markers is that they are hardened structures. Destiny moments crack the shell of the ego, bring in an open world, and we become very sensitive, bodily sensitive. If we are not aware of the meaning of such sensitivities, they feel like symptoms rather than gifts.

The impeding husks of the past have to be cast off over and over again. We do not have the inner strength to do this by ourselves. A felt Presence within the open future that comes toward us is needed in order to be able to work at staying closer to the future time current. In earlier times, this Presence was called the guardian angel. There are spiritual friends in the open space of the future where we become awake-aware. They need to be noticed and addressed. A quite extraordinary aspect of the quality of this open space of the future is that when we enter that open soul space, we do not feel alone. Separation belongs to the time-line from the past and its accompanying ego-structure. In the soul-time of the future, the surface-self is overthrown and the soul can be felt to be in the midst of companions of her own kind.

Method: Presence of Mind

While it may seem that being present to the destiny stream is something very unusual, we in fact are doing so all of the time. It is just that the memory stream from the past has been adhered to for so long that it is a habit for us to only be aware of time as moving in the 'forward' direction and being formed from the past. What is unusual, then, is the developing awareness of the time-current from the future. We have to develop a presence of mind that can be aware of this current. In order to be able to do this, we have to begin to be more aware of our habitual ways of living ego-consciousness at the same time as we become more aware of the subtlety of this new dimension.

Typical ego-consciousness lives in a rhythm of looking at itself and thinking about itself. Consequently, ordinary consciousness is inevitably completely self-interested, isolated, separated, and fearful. When we are engaged for example, in work, or with others, this isolation is not so strongly experienced, but it is still present and is simply a collective isolation. It is not possible, on our own, to simply decide to move away from this kind of self-interest. It is not bad, just limiting. The only way through it is to be attentive enough to, at destiny moments of our lives, feel a pull into the not-yet. When we have gone through the awareness of the "dying awake" process, destiny begins to break in, and break in more often. Destiny is like a vortex force that characterizes the time current from the future. As it comes toward us, it also pulls consciousness into it. The inner work is to keep these moments open and empty. They are easily pre-empted, and in our ego-world are called 'opportunities'.

The soul-work concerns coming to have a presence of mind that can detect the various qualities of the kind of force that pulls us into it from the not-knowing, from the not-yet. Notice, we have to speak here of qualities of consciousness, not content. One of the primary qualities is that we move out of mindscape into soulscape. This time-current is a complicated 'road' that is curved, bent, goes down and up, goes way inside, loses itself far outside, keeps shifting. A lot of concentration and rigorous presence is necessary to stay with it.

In destiny moments, when you get a first-glimpse of this 'road', you will notice that if you try to stay within this not-knowing but highly aware-consciousness, you cannot do so; there is not enough strength of consciousness and quite immediately you fall back into habitual ego-consciousness. Whereas, for a moment, you had a sense of destiny, you most likely do not have the inner strength to stay with it. The work of the heart, to come next in the course, will help this a lot.

Some people have a more or less inherent capacity to stay in the not-knowing, but for the most part a strength has to be built-up. One way of building this strength is to return again and again, in imagination, to a destiny moment in life, locate the vortex quality of the force that comes in this destiny moment, and re-enter that vortex through the power of imagination. In this way, you can learn to launch yourself into the time-current from the future, into not-knowing, but being fully aware. Then, notice, over and over again, the qualities of experience that characterize being in this current. When we are there, for example, we are open, permeable, and transparent. What is this like?

Living Two Tracks

It is of importance to point out that as the opening to the destiny current begins to be felt in more of an ongoing way, in these transitional times, we need to develop the intensive discipline of living on two separate tracks. Most people have been doing this, but have not been aware of what they are doing. We have also had an inaccurate language for this. We have called it the 'inner life' and the 'outer life'. This language is inaccurate because the fact of keeping hidden our experiences of the time-current from the future was then put into a spatial metaphor and we lost the time-sense of these experiences.

We lost the sense that the time-current from the future belongs to life and to time, and to the world. Once placed 'inside', these experiences of 'potentia' were either labeled as madness or glorified as mystical. They are neither; they are the right of every human being. In order to pass for normal, those people who inherently could track with the time-current from the future had to keep this hidden and had to develop strong ego-identity structures to do so. The resulting experience is that a lot of people go around feeling that they are betraying what they came here to do, but cannot locate why they feel this way. Now, however, the 'membrane' between past-oriented ego-consciousness, and future-oriented soul-consciousness is becoming thinner; we are approaching the time when these two worlds are coming together. They have been doing so for a long time, so that it is now possible to look at our biographies and detect the many times in our lives when there were transition places. Looking at our biographies in this manner will help a great deal in being present in right and healthy ways to entering consciously into the time-current from the future.

Don't take Mind Seriously

The ordinary mind is bound to the ways of the ordinary ego. Notice how your thinking works. It does not move into the new, into unknown territory. It always understands something by relating it to what it already knows. We cannot get hold of the time current from the future with our mind. We have to take on the task of continually un-doing what our mind structures. The awareness of the destiny-current from the future does not come from the mental realm. It comes from the heart and belly and deeper down. The vortex force of this time current is felt in the heart. That is where you have to go to experience the wave of the future. For this reason, in our biographies, destiny experiences are very often connected with falling in love or being in love. It is quite incorrect, however, to rely upon such experiences to throw us into the not-knowing. Such experiences indeed are destiny moments in life. They are only one form, and a minor form at that, of such experiences. We would be better off, for example, by forming close connections with those who have died as a way into the time current from the future than falling in love. There is much to clear away from the love experience that comes completely and solely from the past. In other words, the love experience, while often pulling us into the future, also is, for everyone, greatly contaminated by the past – by needs, by personal history, by cultural expectations, societal expectations, and most of all, by conventionality.

The Body as Vortex

Ordinary ego-consciousness experiences the body as a physical substance. It is a spectator's view of the body that we ordinary live. In destiny moments, we usually feel the body more as a system of forces. We feel like we are floating, feel light, and the boundary between ourselves, the world, and others is far less fixed during destiny moments. It is helpful to imagine the body in moments of destiny experience as being like a convergence of vortexes. There is a vortex that moves down from above, to the center of the heart; and there is another vortex, moving up, from the interior of the earth, also coming to the center of the heart. There is another vortex moving horizontally toward us, and another one from behind; and one from the left, and another from the right. (You might try to draw this system of vortexes and then try to imagine the body as this dynamic system).

This picturing of the body as systems of forces is not an abstraction. It reveals that we belong to the cosmos and we belong to the depths of the earth, and these come together at the region of the heart, through which we live, here, on the earth, in the world, open to the cosmos and the depth of the earth, with the task of expressing these realms in the making of a world. All our individual destinies take place within this great human destiny. This picturing of the body thus can help us to see that perhaps, we have, up to this point, been trying to imagine destiny within the framework of a static world-picture. That is, we have been trying to imagine the time-current from the future within a framework within which it is impossible to make an accurate picture.

Human life unfolds as the commingling of the angels of the cosmos and the elemental beings, also angels, of the deep earth. Each of our lives, the marks of which are our biographies, are the particular and individual ways in which we are participating in this dynamic convergence of beings. The vortex is but a sketch, a highly schematic sketch, of living from within soul life rather than living as spectators to the world and even to ourselves.

When you look at the diagram of forces you have drawn, it is a picture of a vortex you are looking at. The convergence of vortexes which we are, is thus, not experienced as if looking at vortexes. We live this experience from within. The vortex is an imagination of activity, of pure activity and force. It is not to be imagined as a content, like a whirlwind or a tornado. It is living our lives as a convergence of spiritual beings and earth spirits. It is a re-imagination of the destiny of the human being; human being as the place where these forces converge, where the crafters of the world meet.

What then, are the two vortexes as experiences? The vortex that is the forming of the human body from the cosmos to the region of the center of the heart, is lived as the experience of the call to awaken, the call to experience the boundlessness of our being. The vortex that is the forming of the human from the rootedness of the earth to the center of the heart. is lived as the experience of dreaming, not just night dreaming, but every kind of dreaming – imagination, reverie, visionary. The two vortexes together are thus experienced as dreaming awake. It is consciousness-as-imagination-of-the-heart. If we have an identity as human beings, it is that we are an open, empty place in the center of the center, waiting for what we are called to be at any moment. This is where we can experience our destiny. We dream into the roots; we awaken into the cosmos.

The Other as Future-Being

The open, empty but pregnant place in the region of the heart is where we encounter ourselves without being bound up with ourselves. It is the place of the self-as-activity without the burden of self-reflection and self-protection. From this place, what is the reason for being together with others? And, what, from this place, is it like to be with others? The people we encounter from this place are destiny-others. We do not feel bound to the others we meet from this place. Mainly, we here meet spiritual co-workers. And the main work of being with others from this place is to be clear enough about who they are so that the intensity of the meetings does not get thrown into forms that belong to the ways of consciousness from the past.

The description of others as 'spiritual co-workers' raises the question: co-workers in what? What are we doing together? In order to be able to answer this question, it is necessary to be able to describe what it is like to meet someone with whom you have a deep connection, but who does not fit at all into any of the known categories of relationships with others: not lover, not friend, not superior, not inferior, not any of the kinds of relationships you already know.

In describing a relationship of destiny, a relationship from the time-stream of the future rather than the time-stream from the past, we have to be sure we are doing the description from the time-stream from the future, or at least as much as we can. The relationships in the time-stream from the past are karmic relationships. We all still have these kinds of relationships, too. Entering into the time-stream from the future does not cancel out having to also live from the time-stream from the past. In the time-stream from the future, the I is different every moment. That peculiar individualistic sense of personal identity that is so modern is unknown to the future time stream. We discover ourselves each moment; and, we discover ourselves each moment in communion with others. And, what we do we do together? From the time-stream from the future, we are together creating. What are we creating?: an ever-further articulated inner realm of the heart. We are giving ourselves over to the central realm of the heart. This is what we are doing together. This is where we function as spiritual co-workers. This is what we are working on together. It is very possible to feel that this is going on.

The perception of others is different from within the time current from the future than it is from the time current from the past. In the former, we are spectators to the other, and our connections come mainly through emotions, common interests, or common needs. There is an unbridgeable gap that exists between you and I. The time current from the future does not follow this way of perception. We perceive each other as in community. We do not here work to make some external version of community; community is already there. As the great poet Novalis has stated in one of his aphorisms: "I am You." This is the rule of the perception of others from the time current from the future. The life-stream that we are in, this life stream from the future is a community-based, mutuality-generated life-stream. All questions around community, when viewed from the time current from the future do not have to do with how community is made, but only with how the community that we are comes to be expressed in the world.

We need to be careful to not delude ourselves into imagining that the whole world suddenly is living in this time current for the future ---- or even that, at some point, everyone will step over that line into the future time current. The world will most likely be splitting right down the middle. Old models of external phenomena will persist and even become more structured and rigid. We will be required to be able to endure this split. The invisible sense of community will make this possible.

Soul Perception of the Soul of the World

Our perception is always of the past. It takes four seconds from the time we sense something for the thing sensed to be registered as something. Thus, we, in our ordinary perception are always living in the past. We do not know this is the case because our past perceptions become the concepts through which we perceive the present. What we know determines what we perceive.

What is the experience of the soul like when we live under the rubric "I am You"? Take, for example, noticing the surrounding hills. We feel our being so connected with these hills that when a wind blows through them and stirs up dust, this is also happening through me. We are alive to the very pulse of those hills. But, it does not feel ecstatic or agonizing, nor does it feel ordinary or basic. The hills come from the same inner substance as we do. We are here together. Their nature and our substance-nature belong together. The hills, though, as well as all of nature, seemed to have gone asleep. They seemed for so long to just be inert. The magical tradition speaks of what happened to the natural world as "enchantment". The natural world was caught in enchantment. It is asleep. When we become awake-awareness, the natural world begins to be awakened from its enchantment and can then convey its mysteries to those of us who also begin to come out of our enchantment.

Entering into the time current from the future results in a new relation to the natural world. We do not suddenly switch into this new relation, however, Part of our biography, the biography of each person, now consists of a kind of call to the natural world. We still romanticize this call and feel that it is a call to return to nature, to go back to a previous time. It is actually a call from the future. It is extremely important to be able to experience this call of the natural world as a pulling from the future and begin to learn how to attend to this pull without immediately putting it into a notion of getting away from the world. We need very particular efforts of description that reveal the qualities of the time current from the future operating in the world. While it is one thing to talk and to theorize and to romanticize about the Soul of the World, the actual perception of the Soul of the World remains, for most, still closed.

Some Notes on Blind Craving
and the Foundations of Egotism

There is within the very fabric of flesh a blind craving that turns both inward and outward and is in continual restlessness

This craving does not want 'this' or 'that'; the restlessness is restlessness to be satiated and filled; it desires Life, but lives, always, in confusion concerning what/where/who is Life.

This restlessness separates us from everything else – even from ourselves, for it sets up an illusory notion that there is a 'self' in the first place and establishes this illusion of a self as mid-point, center-point, and peripheral point, excluding all else.

Egotism gathers itself into itself, but then goes forth from itself without ever leaving itself, into the manifoldness of life; it is a perpetual restlessness.

This restless mess and torture can only be quieted and subdued (never gotten rid of) when:
Wisdom
Freedom
Love
Light …. Descend into it.

Love cannot exist without a powerful egoism (note, not quite the same as egotism, which is egoism that takes itself seriously and literally), **which surrenders itself to Love.**

Without the contracting force of egoism become egotism, surrendering to the power of Love would lead to absorption in and fusion with the All.

Without the element of egotism, (surrendered to love) the gentleness of love would degenerate into sentimentalism.

Egotism continues to exist – even if we seem to have vanquished it. It easily flares up. When this fire goes into conflagration, disorder is introduced into resonance with the whole, which spreads into the whole of soul life, penetrating intellectual and spiritual constitution and also bodily constitution.

We, however, must have a 'healthy' ego that willingly allows itself to be vanquished (what foolish ego would do that?).

When ego does not exist strongly and surrender itself strongly, it sets itself up as independent; this is a pause and a stoppage of the heart:
- instead of creating as a mode of being, there is a repetitious sameness
- repetitious sameness darkens and becomes anguish
- the anguish, which is intended to be a dynamic moment now becomes chronic – a constant birth pang without the birth-ing

Some Second notes on Egotism

Ego is a contracting of Whole-awareness (awareness of the whole is an egotism; whole-awareness is just that – awareness, that is conscious but not spectatorial).

The feeling of separateness, of being a spectator to the particularities, rather than, through particularities being able to bodily sense wholeness, is a manifesting of inherent fear – but it tricks the witnessing aspect that exists within wholeness (the inherent consciousness that is Love) to feel it is complete within itself; an illusion at the heart of our being that is not possible to eliminate, but it is possible to always reveal that the emperor has no clothes. Thus, egotism seems to completely overlap with self-love, so it is a necessary illusion and an important one – if one is able to laugh at it, that is take it imaginally rather than seriously and literally.

When we notice – out of the corner of our ego-focus, that is when we are a bit diffuse – what/who governs the illusion of self-completeness (which, by the way, includes the illusion that others are part of our self-completeness), that is, an intuition that the ego is not I, but a kind of shadow-I, then ego relaxes, though does not disappear.

Ego that acts as if separate from Love maintains itself in the illusion of power. It feels good in that power and that makes us feel good. Ego substitutes drama for imagination, and theatrically asserts itself to maintain power. Often, this illusion of power tries to strengthen itself by forming itself into a group ego.

The illusion of separateness maintains itself by acting as if it only had an outside, and exterior and no interiority – when we constantly say I, I, I, it is all exteriorized. The inner, spiritual I, is wordless. And not a content. It is world worlding.

The moment the experience of true interiority is allowed (a stumbling, perhaps, into heart), the restoration of ego to interior I, which is world worlding itself begins.

Towards Cultural Imagination:
Jung, Spiritual Psychology, and the Coming Age

C. G. Jung has given us remarkable guidance into a postmodern worldview founded in the reality of the soul. His own explorations focused on the inner life of soul of individuals. Nonetheless, I believe that his work offers more than an individual psychology, and that in fact we have the task of taking up his guidance and following it into the world. The central question that I want to explore with you is how we can actually face the world with soul. So, my question is not so much about defining what is meant by the term 'postmodern' but concerns the practice of living with soul in the world, living 'postmodernly.'

Jung spoke of living a symbolic life, by which he meant developing the capacity of fully conscious imagination. Does this mean paying attention to our own dream life, keeping a journal, going to weekend workshops, reading the Jungians, and watching Joseph Campbell re-runs on television? Does it mean to live a secret symbolic life on the one hand while on the other hand living in the modern materialistic world seeking comfort, material gain, and economic survival? Most of us who are involved with the life of soul and of imagination do live this kind of split existence, and it seems to me this needs to be examined. This way of having one foot in the modern world and one foot in postmodern world indicates that the forces of the soul are not yet strong enough to actually live in the world. The forces of the soul are not strong enough to create a new social life. Unless those forces can be developed, pursuit of the soul will become a cult activity while the world spirals downward toward destruction.

How can this situation be helped? It can be helped to a certain extent by taking up the task of clarifying over and over the assumptions of modern thought. But this situation can be helped to an even greater extent by hearing stories of someone who actually does live the symbolic life. One such story is Jung's own autobiography, <u>Memories, Dreams and Reflections</u>. That story, however, does not take us into the social world, but rather away from it. In order to try and balance this work as the most valuable precursor to living in the world with soul, I would like to point to the symbolic life of Vaclav Havel, who, as you know, was the President of Czechoslovakia.

Havel is by no means a Jungian. However, Jung was never interested in furthering "Jungianism", but rather with drawing intense attention to the centrality of soul. I believe that he was able to focus attention here as a way of preparing the world for this same focus. Jung gave us the capacity to detect the public appearance of soul in the world when it would begin to show up. Without this background we would not be able to recognize soul. If we look upon the work of Jung as just a psychological theory or practice, or at the most, a mystical path, then the world significance of his contribution would be lost.

I begin with a speech given by Vaclav Havel on February 4, 1992, given to the World Economic Forum in Davos Switzerland. The speech begins:

"The end of Communism is, first and foremost, a message to the human race. It is a message we have not yet fully deciphered and comprehended. In its deepest sense, the end of Communism has brought an end not just to the 19th and 20th centuries, but to the modern age as a whole."

This beginning statement establishes Havel as a witness to the fact that a radical alteration in the evolution of consciousness is in process. Communism, as our own shadow, as the shadow of Democracy, is thus deeply involved in this evolution, and we are witnessing something far more than a change of political system. Havel then goes on to describe what is being left behind:

"The modern era has been dominated by the culminating belief, expressed in different forms, that the world – and Being as such – is a whole knowable system governed by a finite number of universal laws that man can grasp and rationally direct for his own benefit. This era, beginning in the Renaissance and developing from the Enlightenment to Socialism, from positivism to scientism, from the industrial revolution to the information revolution, was characterized by rapid advance in rational, cognitive thinking.

This in turn, gave rise to the proud belief that man, as the pinnacle of everything that exists, was capable of objectively describing, explaining and controlling everything that exists, and of possessing the one and only truth about the world. It was an era in which there was a cult of depersonalized objectivity, an era in which objective knowledge was amassed and technically exploited, an era of belief in automatic progress brokered by the scientific method. It was an era of systems, institutions, mechanisms and statistical averages. It was an era of ideologies, doctrines, interpretations of reality, an era in which the goal was to find a universal theory of the world, and thus a key to unlock its prosperity --- the fall of Communism can be regarded as a sign that modern thought – has come to a final crisis."

Havel sees with amazing clarity that the modern mind-set is finished – it is over! Now, if Havel stopped here, he would be where the majority of postmodern thinkers are – even though he says it better than most of them do. Havel is far beyond this. He has brought the symbolic life into full public view. And, insofar as he is the leader of a country, he has brought the symbolic life to public reality. Here is what he says:

> "It is my profound conviction that we have to release from the sphere of private whim such forces as: a natural, unique and unrepeatable experience of the world, an elementary sense of justice, the ability to see things as others do, a sense of responsibility, archetypal wisdom, good taste, courage, compassion, and faith in the importance of particular measures that do not aspire to be a universal key to salvation...
>
> Soul, individual spirituality, first hand personal insight into things; the courage to be himself and to go the way his conscience points, humility in the face of the mysterious order of Being, confidence in its natural direction and, above all, trust in his own subjectivity as his principal link with the subjectivity of the world – these are qualities that politicians of the future should have."

With Havel, the bridge has been made and crossed; soul is now in the world. After reading this recent speech, as you can well imagine, I went in search of finding more about this individual, for he provides a way to research living in an age of uncertainty.

The first surprise, deep shock, came upon finding a letter written by Havel in 1976 to the then General Secretary of the Czechoslovak Communist Party, Dr. Gustav Husak. This letter is shocking because as Havel carefully described the situation in Communist Czechoslovakia at that time, I found it nearly impossible to tell the difference between that country then and the present situation in America. Havel speaks in this letter of the loss of soul, a loss not occasioned by overt oppression and military power, but from a fourfold process. First, there is the imposition of a political ideology that is so pervasive that contact with reality is lost and in its place is substituted an intellectual abstraction, such as "a totally united society giving total support to its government." The loss of contact with reality produces in everyone a deep and enduring anxiety, but with no way to confront the source of the anxiety. The presence of such anxiety, to be endurable, brings about a state of indifference, finally, this state of indifference leads to people seeking more and more material comfort; they fill their homes with all kinds of equipment and pretty things, try to raise housing standards, get better cars, have more material things.

We can talk forever about postmodern consciousness and it will do no good, it cannot be experienced as real, because the modern, technological, ideological, "scientistic" world keeps coming in the back door, offering the promise of comfort, a comfort contingent upon yielding first to indifference. We see exactly those forces in the present political campaigns for the Presidency of the United States. When Clinton is confronted with one impropriety after another, does he become uncomfortable, uneasy? No, he meets the charges with indifference – and it works! And are not the valid complaints about George Bush doing nothing just another way of saying that he has yielded to indifference? In the meantime, this constant exposure to the indifference of leadership pushes us more and more to seek comfort. If postmodern consciousness is our reality, it does not follow that modern consciousness just disappears. Living with soul in the world, is first and foremost a task of not allowing oneself, in one way or another, to be bribed by comfort. I am not saying that it is necessary to seek pain; the task is simply to avoid being bribed by comfort. As the patients treated by Jung were led to soul through pain, Havel first felt in an entirely intimate and personal way the pain of his country, and his own entry into bringing soul into the world followed upon his imprisonment.

Vaclav Havel, while not a Jungian, is very aware of Jung and knows exactly the next step necessary to bring the private symbolic life into public symbolic life. He addresses this necessary step in an essay entitled <u>Thriller</u>, a title that comes from Michael Jackson's video in which Jackson dresses as a vampire. What Havel sees is that the mythic world, far from being dead and of the past, is fully active and running rampant in this world. He points out that the value of Jung was not simply in the rediscovery of myth, but rather of the discovery of the necessary containment of myth by the forces of the individual soul. What now must be sought and made clear are these qualities of soul that can be consciously developed that can serve as a vessel for the

rampaging mythic forces that are loosed in the world. Look at the daily
newspaper and there you will find myth displayed. Havel says:

> *"It is nine o'clock in the evening and I run on the radio. The announcer, a
> woman, is reading the news in a dry, matter of fact voice: Mrs. Indira
> Ghandi had been shot by two Sikhs in her personal bodyguard…
> International aid is being organized for Ethiopia where a famine is
> threatening the lives of million, while the Ethiopian regime is spending
> almost a quarter of a billion dollars to celebrate its tenth anniversary.
> American scientists have developed plans for a manned observatory on the
> moon and for manned exploration to Mars. In California, a little girl has
> received a transplant from a baboon; various animal welfare societies have
> protested."*

The mythic world has been set loose, but pretends to be twentieth
century man acting out of an assumed authority of science or out of an
assumed sense of being instruments of providence; the mythic universe has
moved from the interior psyche into the world, something that Jung did not
anticipate – or did he?

Our question them become – what are the qualities of soul that can be
developed which have enough strength to serve as the containment of
mythic forces set loose by the very fact that they have been ignored as the
abstract forces of modern intellectualism set about doing business on their
own? In order to approach such a question, it is most helpful to look upon
the outer events of the world and to really see that we – all of us - are on an
underworld journey. Every underworld journey is fraught with one danger
after another, each arranged to develop and out to the rest some particular
capacity of soul. This journey in which we are involved, however, is not the
hero's trio to the underworld; its aim is not to conquer by fighting what is
encountered, but to bring about a strengthening of the forces of the soul. So
that, gradually, soul consciousness becomes fully awake, so that we gradually
developed the capacity of a new picture-consciousness. I shall try to describe
a series of particular events, mythic events, and the kinds of soul qualities
necessary for navigating the coming age.

The Entry into the Underworld.

The explosion of the Hiroshima bomb, and then later the explosion of the hydrogen bomb on Eniwetok-Atole, Marshall Islands in the Pacific on March 1, 1954, and the explosion of an even more powerful hydrogen bomb by the Soviet Union on November 22, 1955 are mythic events that opened the crust of the earth and brought about an entry into the underworld for all of humanity. The anxiety provoked by these events has brought about in the world the fourfold process described earlier that Havel saw so acutely in his own country – separation from spiritual meaning, anxiety, indifference, and seeking of comfort. This fourfold process occurs when the attempt is to continue acting as if the event of the bomb is simply an occurrence in the world and not a mythical action. Once it is perceived as mythic, then the soul quality needed can be perceived. What is this soul quality? It is the quality of stillness. The soul must become completely still, completely quiet, for it has entered into darkness, entered into the realm of sleep and death, there to begin the task of learning how to be awake and conscious. It is a test. The aim of the test is to see whether, when cut off from the day-world, can the force of love be born out of the soul itself? Can love arise where there is nothing to love? It is a test that provokes us into seeking that what we usually speak of as love is actually self-love, a rapture of the soul in which, in the presence of another person an illusion is enacted. The illusion is that while we seem to loving someone, we are actually engaged in self-love. This test is concerned with the development of a new form of knowledge, knowing the world through love, which is nothing less than re-creating the world out of this force.

Grieving

A second source of deep anxiety is the radioactivity released into the world, not only from the bombs, but from the deadly radiation released through the accidents at nuclear power plants. Again, this threat needs to be seen as a mythic event to be met with by the development of particular forces of the soul. There was a recent PBS film showing the present conditions in the area of Chernobyl, the thousands of people who still live in the contaminated region. Their animals all have tumors. The people eat the potatoes grown in radioactive ground, and the cancer rate is exceedingly

high. What does the soul do when presented with such images? The soul
mourns. It mourns when seeing that life, as it once was, is no longer possible.
What is there at Chernobyl in intensified form is present throughout the
world – the unmistakable feeling that no one wants to face – life as it once
was is no longer possible. The modern world has come to an end. The
required response is grieving. In the absence of grieving, the kind of world
that has come to an end continues to assert itself in destructive ways, like a
ghost who refuses to leave until properly acknowledged and honored.

Just as the pain of the soul in waiting and listening in darkness and
silence is actually a strengthening of soul, when we experience grieving for
what is now dead, a strengthening also occurs. In the deep sobbing of grief,
there comes moments in which a deep breath enters unto us. It is like
something is being born within; it is the manner in which inspiration takes
place, not from the outside, but like the first breath of a newborn being
within. It is the activation of the soul life.

Developing the Force of Imagination

We are witnessing the outpouring of false imagination into the world.
False imagination produces sensations, which are opposite to the character
of the actual images. For example, a repellent image is viewed as attractive;
one need only look at television or movies to that that this is happening. A
completely repellent film such as the 'Silence of the Lambs' swept the
Academy Awards. Another example of false imagination is the artificial
imagination induced by hallucinogenic drugs – marijuana hashish, mescaline
and LSD. These drugs bring about a false clairvoyance, an imagination
without the conscious effort to develop this capacity out of one's own soul
forces. The response of modern consciousness is to actually strengthen false
imagination by imposing moral censorship or legal restriction. These
reactions, by suppressing the force of imagination, increase the force without
providing expression, furthering explosiveness. Postmodern soul
consciousness sees what is crucial in these false expressions is that all
imagination is a <u>force</u> and when this force is not consciously developed it
expresses itself as violent forms of sensations.

Sensation is the opposite of what the force of imagination concerns,
imagination is a spiritual force. Active, conscious soul activity awakens the
capacity to perceive the subtle worlds in conjunction with the physical

world. The force of imagination is the fiery potentiality of the heart serving as the bridge between worlds. What, then, does the soul do when it sees the explosion of false imaginations in the world? It sees that the force of imagination is seeking to develop and that this force finds expression in world in the form of service. The force of soul seeks serve.

The Labor of Soul

I am looking at prevalent world events as mythic occurrences seeking qualities of soul. The aim is not to counter such events by suggesting that what is needed is private concentration on soul development while the public world continues in a decidedly different direction. The mythic magnitude of world events calls for soul engagement with the world. The prevalence of terrorism, the rise of violent crime, and the rise of usage of a drug such as heroin, together indicate another domain of deep anxiety.

The human body is losing its subtle sensitivity. In a recent episode of the news program 20/20, members of several Los Angeles gangs spoke of their sense of fate. One gang member said that he knew that every encounter with another gang was a real threat to his life. His response was simply that we all have to die; if it is our time, it will happen; if it is not our time it will not happen. This fatalism speaks like ancient mythic engagement with Fate. Then, later, this same gang member said that there is also a second person within him. This second person within felt very differently – he saw the possibility of adding to the world, the possibility of bringing good into the world. It was quiet interesting that this person spoke so clearly of the presence of another person within. What is this? It is the striving characteristic of soul. The soul strives, and this quality indicates a time direction. There is a current of time that comes from the future into the present. The current of time is real and substantial but can begin to be felt only when the time current from the past has become frozen, crystallized. When one acts only out of the past when the past is dead, destruction results. The past no longer directs us toward the future; the future now comes to meet us, experienced as the soul quality of striving. Soul must now consciously labor. Labor for what? For infinity, for the expression of the spiritual worlds in the finite, physical world. Infinity is in the finite.

Developing Instantaneous Soul Perception

There is now universal recognition that ordinary time is speeding up. Everything is moving faster, happening quicker, no one, however, seems to know what to do with this recognition – perhaps because it passes by so quickly. The speeding up of the world brings about many illnesses. Cancer is the acceleration of the growth of body cells such that the organism as a whole suggests imbalance. AIDS concerns the acceleration of opportunistic diseases overtaking the body. Cocaine is a drug which accelerates mental activity to such an extent that the capacity of thought outruns the body. Similarly, the growth of the calculative capacity through the computerization of the world is an expression of this process of speed. The modern response to speed is nostalgia for past times in which life occurred at a different pace. Nostalgia for the past, it seems to me, is not a soul response but a false romanticism. There is a deeper ground to nostalgia, the longing of the soul for its own environment, the realm of spiritual realities.

The speeding up of time is actually the modern attempt to cross a threshold into instantaneous perception by means of ordinary consciousness, which cannot be done because of the limits of the body. The activity of soul, however, is instantaneous. Take, for example, dreams. Do dreams images occur over time, or is it not that the recall of dreams puts them into a temporal flow that does not characterize their occurrence? A dream happens all at once. Thus, as soul activity begins to be more conscious, the imagistic quality of events is experienced in a split second. I suggest that the speeding up of ordinary consciousness is the futile attempt of modern consciousness to function as a double or a substitute for post-modern soul consciousness. Living in the world with soul does not mean acceleration, but rather learning to trust the qualities of instantaneous, imaginal perception.

Developing Soul Conscience

A sixth realm of mythic world events that is seeking the containment of soul concerns the flaming up of human passions. This conflagration is expressed in the continual outbreak of wars, which is closely connected to the pollution of the world. The release of untold tons of pollution by the burning fires of the oil wells of Kuwait is an image showing the intimate connection between war and pollution.

One of the most significant contributions of Jung is his insistence that the individual's relationship to imagination must have a moral quality to be effective. By this he meant that the pictures spontaneously created by the soul in dreams and in active imagination require active engagement; one must act toward the figures of imagination as if they are real, because they are. Imagination is real, imaginally real within the region of consciousness between usual consciousness and either 'super-consciousness' or 'sub-consciousness.

As the soul activity of imagination becomes more conscious in waking life, the instantaneous soul-pictures we have of the world demand the same kind of engagement. This engagement signals the awakening of a new conscience. Conscience here simply means that we respond to what the image presents, we become engaged with the images presented by the world. Havel alluded to this capacity in the speech I quoted earlier when he said that politicians of the future must, above all, "trust in his own subjectivity as his principal link with the subjectivity of the world." This is an amazing sentence because it recognizes and gives primary importance to the level of the individual soul in active relationship with the soul of the world. The halting of wars and pollution is not for our survival; soul conscience immediately sees that it is the world that is in suffering.

Developing Meditative Consciousness

When we look at the manner in which what is going on in the world is reflected back to us – politically, economically, culturally – we already find that nothing that is presented can be trusted. What is bad is presented as good, and what is good presented as bad. For example, right after the war in Iraq, there was public debate concerning whether the United States should sell military weapons to other countries. By the time the debate was finished, something clearly wrong was presented as right. The argument went along these lines – if we do not sell arms then our economy will be severely affected; further, if we do not sell arms, then the market is opened up for other countries to sell them, which they will do. This kind of presentation is now characteristic on all spheres of life. What quality of soul does this reversal inspire? One might think – well, just take the opposite of what is said to be the truth! However, we should not underestimate the cleverness of the calculative intellect. It is easy to see the many ways in which things can be manipulated. The soul is not clever, but it is always clear in regard to spiritual matters. Thus, the confusion of values brings about the necessity of developing a meditative mode of consciousness, the capacity to see things in terms of their soul value.

Developing Soul Relationships

The difficulty in taking up the contributions of Jung in exactly the manner he presented them, particularly with regard to myth, is that we are left with the inclination to see mythic consciousness as invaluable without any indication of what myth we are presently within. Consequently, some followers of Jung have tried to persuade us that the soul lives primarily in Greek myth, and we go about seeking the gods and goddesses within. Other followers of Jung have emphasized other myths – of ancient India, or Mexico, or Eastern myths. What goes unrecognized is that humanity is under the guidance of the present myth. We live mythically now as humans always have, but the encompassing myth of the present age – which will last until about the year 3575, is the myth of love. Not any of the kinds of love we are aware of, but love itself as the pervasive mode of consciousness, best characterized as 'sacrifice into joy', something like that. Love concerns being fully and completely present for the other, both toward another individual, but also to the world, doing what we do for the sake of the world, certainly of Earth. It is a sacrifice, surely, but carries no sense whatsoever of deprivation toward oneself.

The myth of love needs conscious recognition and work. In the absence of such recognition, strife and disharmony increases alarmingly throughout the world. Strife and disharmony can be met with the conscious effort to develop soul-to-soul relationships. Central to this development is a clear understanding and work on self-love because self-love is continuously confused with love of others. All relationship problems stem from this confusion.

Self-love is the central form of self-consciousness and it is the primary instrument for development of self-knowledge or wisdom. In order to know oneself it is necessary to love oneself. But there is a particular discipline needed to develop self-knowledge through self-love in order that it does not become egotism. One must be able to look upon oneself as a stranger and gradually come to see that there is a hidden life of soul within that cannot be readily perceived any more than we can see the soul within someone else without effort. One gradually learns to know oneself through this kind of self-love, and through this process to become more and more conscious, not of the self, but in the self, and one then strives toward becoming an independent being. This process is what Jung saw as individuating.

But this knowing is not the kind of knowing with which we are familiar. As we get to know ourselves through healthy self-love, it is not as if there were some fixed object in space that can be perceived. In developing the capacity to know oneself through love, there occurs the creating of that which we are knowing. Further, this act of knowing is one in which what is being created is a creating being who creates through love. On this basis, we can begin to see that a relationship of one soul to another soul, one individual with another, is a relationship in which we are, in part, involved in the creating of the soul of another and they are involved in creating our soul.

Developing Steadfastness of Soul

The last quality of postmodern soul consciousness that I wish to consider is based on the observation that the kind of consciousness I have been describing will not develop without great opposition. The modern world is still going to be with us for a very long time. I can well imagine the inner opposition many of you have been feeling hearing this presentation. This vision may seem dark, unpractical, difficult, elusive, and abstract, not in connection with the real world, just pain weird. The response of soul to such opposition is a strengthening of the quality of steadfastness of soul. I have worked to develop a feeling for the kind of sensibility involved in steadfastness of soul, which might be the work of virtue.

An Archetypal Imagining of the Destiny of America

In applying archetypal psychology to imagining "City and Soul", the inherent 'Pathologizing' described by James Hillman stands as the crucial dimension needing attention. In cities, the tendency is to try and 'build' the pathological dimension out, which inevitably hides it and results in literalizing City and Soul according to what one hopes for the city rather than soul appearing within and as city.

I am going to outline an archetypal imagination of the destiny of America. It is an inherently pathologized destiny. You will see how this destiny shapes the way cities are built. Hopefully, we can see, through bringing the soul of the city into relation with the soul of the nation, some aspects revealing how cities might meet their unfolding in ways that bring awareness into the deep destiny of this country while also altering the imagination of cities.

One archetypal revelation of the spiritual destiny of America, begins with two unusual legends. An elaboration of the significance of these legends follows.

The Legend of Amesis

When Jesus was born, the youngest of the three Magi, whose name was Amesis, looked into the eyes of this child and saw the possible future of the human being. He saw that it is possible that every human being could live in complete harmony with the earth and with the cosmos and with each other. This reality was inherent in the eyes of the child. Amesis saw that the future of the human being had to do with the destiny of the land of America.

Amesis came to what is now America, traveling by way of Alaska. He came to a region now known as High Tor, in New York, a place located right above what is now the Tappan Zee bridge, outside New York City. You can see Manhattan from this high place.

Amesis knew that the destiny of America involved soul's encounter with the spirits of greed. The indigenous people of this region had 'handled' the presence of these beings by prisoning them within the earth.

Amesis came to this place where this imprisonment occurred. He knew that we would have to encounter these spirits and hoped to transform them into spirits of good. He set up an altar and stayed there for a very long time. He married an Indian woman, and daily did ritual at this altar. One day, the spirits emerged, but were far, far more powerful than could be imagined. A huge explosion occurred, creating the Hudson Valley and the Hudson river. The spirits of greed were released for the first time.

A hint of what we are now still required to confront within the soul as we build this country into its cities can be heard in two images of the Hudson. The Hudson river originates in a very small, very pristine lake high in the Adirondacks. The name of this lake is 'Tear of the Cloud" lake. Then, the Hudson river itself is a huge estuary. This means that the salty water of the sea comes up the river to meet the tears coming down. The sea flows up as far as Troy, New York, a distance of 150 miles. We can imagine the Hudson as a river of tears – originating from the Tears of the highest cosmos and the deepest ocean.

The Legend of the Salamander

A second legend can be found in the book, Legends of Rockland County, NY, which is the location of High Tor. It is called the "Legend of the Salamander."

Several centuries ago, a group of Rosicrucian alchemists come to High Tor, under the leadership of Hugo – a name that means 'bright of mind'. They too come to transform the spirits of greed. They set up a forge for purifying iron at the site. High Tor is a region plentiful in iron. Much of the iron that built early Manhattan came from this region. The tailings of the mines can still be found there.

Iron is made into steel by purification and by re-heating. Iron itself is brittle. The re-heating strengthens it, that is, placing this metal into human hands imbues it with purely earthly human will, now combined with the archetypal power of iron, Mars. The iron from this region, coming from deep within the earth is also imbued with the spirits of greed.

The tale is long and complex, so I have to present only the barest of outlines.

The group of alchemists set up a forge and begins purifying iron. Two workers constantly watch the fire. The forge has to be shut down for a while every seven years; otherwise, there is danger that the salamander, the elemental being of fire will be released. Hugo's son is one of the watcher's, and he is so driven by this alchemical task that he refuses to shut the forge down. As they look deep into the earth-fire, they see what seem to be gemstones lining the depths of the earth, and at the very bottom of the fire, there is a large salamander, with a golden triangle on its back and within the triangle is a code. They are inwardly told that anyone who can read the code will have all the wealth that they could ever imagine, and thus these watcher alchemists lose the purity of their intention, as does the father Hugo.

The father, Hugo, also has a daughter, Mary. She is exceptionally pure of heart, extremely sensitive, barely able to engage in the will needed for earthly existence.

One day, when the time for closing the forge had long gone by, son Hugo's attention is entirely captured by the salamander. He is trying to speak the code word on the back of the salamander. Hugo's father comes to the forge and is equally enthralled. The fire gets dangerously hot. The elder Hugo's wife comes and sprinkles water on the forge, hoping to drown out the fire. There is an explosion, and she and the son Hugo are killed in the explosion.

The elder Hugo goes wandering, seemingly crazed by what has happened. The daughter, Mary, is left to live alone. Then, one day, a beautiful young man comes by. She and the young man fall in love. It is a completely pure love that goes unconsummated as it is a pure spiritual love.

One day, the elder Hugo comes back. He sees his daughter, Mary, with the young man, and in his delirium, he thinks that the young man is responsible for all the tragedy that has occurred here, and he grabs him to throw him into the fire. As he is about to descend, the young man, due to the purity of love he holds for his beloved, instead ascends. This young man, who is the salamander, is also a 'good' fallen archangel who had been given the task of bringing some capacities to earth for the sake of people. He became entranced with the earthly realm, and in attempting to unite with it, did not complete his spiritual task. We cannot help but feel that this fallen archangel was to bring the capacity to deal in the right way with greed. Instead, the forces of archetypal greed are released into the world. Further, this legend connects greed with the iron forces made into steel that makes the city of New York, particularly Manhattan.

These two legends both take place in that region that overlooks Manhattan. **The next upheaval of the spirits of greed into the world is the Manhattan Project.**

During the Manhattan Project, Manhattan becomes the scene for the preparation of the atomic bomb. The scientific research takes place at Columbia University. Buildings all over Manhattan become the secret headquarters for working out the details. The Kress skyscraper becomes the command headquarters. Stockpiles of uranium are kept on Staten Island. And, Manhattan is where Robert Oppenheimer grew up in a family of great wealth. His home was filled with art and his mother hoped Robert would be an artist. He became the physicist of the atomic bomb.

The atomic bomb, the culmination of the Manhattan Project was exploded on July 16, 1945, at a place with the code name of "Trinity", near Socorro, New Mexico. IThe bomb as an 'anti-Trinity'. And one that releases even deeper forces that assist the spirits of greed. You recall that at the moment of the explosion of the bomb, Robert Oppenheimer says: "Now I become Death, destroyer of worlds". That is, the ego, which is the potential of the I AM of Life turns into the I AM of death. Our very identity as human beings now serves the forces of death.

The explosion turned a square mile of the New Mexico landscape into an eerie kind of green glass, now named Trinitinite. No life takes place there. It is a vast 'black hole' that sucks in the true destiny of America so that the forces of greed become stronger and stronger.

Archetypally, this explosion reaches deep down into the Underworld, there in New Mexico, touching into and joining with the forces of the Aztec gods. The explosion touches into that archetypal impulse of removing the heart from the human being, that is, removing the capacity of creative imagination to make a world; without the imaginal heart, greed meets no resistance.

The religious authorities in Aztec life saw the human being as in a continuous state of debt toward the gods. The sun that sheds his light for the good of the human beings is that very same sun that requires their lives in order to exist, The Aztecs made evil supreme by devising a dualistic worldview and painting evil as the good to be attained. This reversal of good and evil is enacted now in our world by placing materialism as the supreme good to be attained. This goal, emerging since the days of the occurrences at High Tor, requires the dualistic separation of good from evil, and then reversing which is which.

The fourth and most recent upheaval showing the unfolding of the union of the spirits of greed with the spirits of darkness is 9/11. Here we see the forces of greed taking advantage of this reversal of the forces of good and evil. In the aftershock of terrible grief, we were told to continue living, to go out and shop, to go to Disneyland. It is the moment of the unleashing of the forces of greed full force into the world, because now we are convinced in soul that greed is good.

There is much to be imaged with 9/11. Mystery and controversy still surround this tragedy and thankfully keep the imaginal aspect alive. It is not a simple and uncontested fact that America was attacked by terrorists. The heat from the explosion was intense, and the iron remained molten for weeks, when, if the collapse of the buildings were due to the implosion, the heat would have subsided in days. Many engineers have said that the collapse of the buildings and the fires could not have been due to the impact of the airplanes.

There is also a fault line that runs in the region of the twin towers, and an earthquake of magnitude 4.5 occurred in New York City in 2000. That fault line runs up toward High Tor. These imaginal pictures reveal the continued unfolding of the legend of the destiny of America. We can imagine the 9/11 event as an upheaval, very direct, of the spirits of evil, and only secondarily a literal attack.

Perhaps the most important archetypal image is the explosion of greed that has occurred since 9/11. The stock market continues to soar. So does corruption in the realm of finances, spilling over into the government. The division between greed and grief, an archetypal image that is one, not two, is nearly completed, and shows up as divided cities of steel skyscrapers and financial centers, and wealth, and incredible corruption, which everyone sees and cannot stop, divided from our grief, which unmet, becomes violence in the world. We cannot stop the greed because it now lives autonomously divided from its regions of unrecognized grieving, which is the formula for untold violence, for violence is untended grieving.

There is another region that is also called High Tor. It is in upstate New York, north of Rochester, at the edge of Lake Ontario. This is the region where Hiawatha brought peace to the five warring tribes, bringing about the Iroquois Nation. The region is called "Mannahata", from which the name "Manhattan" is derived. The name means something like …"the point of land at the region of the tumultuous waters of the beings of destruction."

The great initiate, Dekanawida, born of a virgin, crosses Lake Ontario and comes to America in a white granite boat. The boat is an image of going through the Underworld. He assigns Hiawatha, who at the time is among the warring tribes, and is a cannibal, to bring peace to the five warring nations. Hiawatha – a name meaning 'he who combs snakes out of the hair' – an image of bringing 'clarity of seeing' into the world, undergoes incredible grieving as he travels from tribe to tribe to try and convince them to live in peace. His wife is killed by a tribe, and his three daughters are brutally killed, and one of the daughters is with child.

As Hiawatha wanders in deep grief, somewhat comforted by the life and beauty of nature, he walks by a lake filled with ducks. The ducks all of a sudden take to flight, and all of the water of the lake is taken up with them. He walks through the bed of the lake and sees the many empty shells and picks them up and makes them into strings of beads…which become 'wampum'. Wampum is never used by Indians as a form of money or trade, never. A group of Dutch immigrants began to introduce this practice on Long Island, right across from Manhattan.

As Hiawatha continues to speak with the warring tribes, he now sits with them, and they share stories of grieving, and Hiawatha gives each person who shares their grief a string of beads, beads holding the archetypal powers of unification.

The two High Tor stories bring back into original archetypal union what remains separated, keeping the destiny of the nation confused and the future of the soul of the city uncertain. Greed forms a tandem, a sygyzy, with grief. The split colors every archetypal pattern imaginable with greed – spiritual greed, greed for power, money greed, and most of all ego-greed, the fantasy that every archetypal presence is about us, the idealism of the city turned into rampant me-ilism – my power, my money, my possessions, my grief … and all the rest. Archetypal presence creates individual character and make character beyond anything personal, and therefore potentially creative.

Suppose we grieve our money-greed. It is not a matter of rejecting or imagining money as 'evil'. Instead, we grieve money, become present to the inner knowing that money is not energy as is currently imagined, but rather the blocking of energy when we hold to the notion that it is ours and is something we must have to exist and that money is held in the imagination of scarcity because an archetypal reality has become someone's ego-possession. Money-greed enslaves humanity. Separating greed from grief in the realm of money closes possibilities, forms the fear of 'not enough, never enough', and separates one person from another.

Grieving money awakens the true imagination that money is not necessary for life. Without money the value of everyone is equal and we can imagine the city as being made according to the unique contribution of everyone and according to the needs of everyone. The same creativity of imagination opens up when the greed – of everything – opens to the archetypal presence of grieving – -- grieving power, grieving knowledge, grieving helping, grieving anything that catches us in the imagination of possessing. Then, we can begin to see that the city concerns people, we might say archetypally free people because the fullest range of imagination is free to work through us, where visions become reality, where people are recognized for whatever contribution they are able to make to the community. The city of Contributionism.

What if we begin, then, living in the imaginal space between greed and grieving in relation to everything, not just money? The archetype itself clarifies and is not confused by still thinking in terms of two realities – greed and grieving. We begin to live the imaginal space of the city as the simultaneous presence of plentitude and emptiness. The archetypal image exists and is all around and within us; we have just not noticed it.

The poet, Norman MacCraig gives us this poem, "Presents":

Presents

"I give you emptiness,
I give you plenitude,
Unwrap them carefully.
-one's as fragile as the other-
And when you thank me

I'll pretend not to notice
The doubt in your voice
When you say
They are just what you wanted
Put them on the table by your bed
When you wake in the morning
They'll have gone through the door of sleep
Into your head. [heart.]
Where ever you go
They'll go with you,
And wherever you are you'll wonder, smiling,
About the fullness you can't add to, and the emptiness you *can fill."

—Norman MacCraig

It is not money, which has become institutionalized greed, that can make the city of people, but grieving --- shared, ongoing grieving as a soul capacity, not the momentary rituals we now enact. Through sharing grieving, the forms of the larger community, of the city emerge.

Encountering the spiritual destiny of this nation and of its cities requires holding the imaginal syzygy of greed-grief and soul's inherent imagining together.

When is done, we notice more clearly how greed now colors every possible archetypal pattern – greed is not just about money – it is also spiritual greed, soul greed, ego greed, power greed, and greed of every sort, and reveals the attempt, rather than to live in harmony with archetypal forces, letting them flow through us in imaginal recognition --- to, instead, harness and use any kind of archetypal force for our own purposes of greed, the attempt to turn archetypal forces into servants of greed.

We, for example, can de-literalize money, a chief manifestation of greed, by grieving our money, by feeling the inherent greed with the very notion of money. We do not have to 'make ourselves feel this grief; we need only notice that its presence. Grieving goes together with money, and because it does, money has become literalized, torn from its archetypal matrix, and used primarily to keep grief at bay.

These days, one of the common definitions of money is that money is energy. It makes things possible. That is false; money narrows possibilities, making them possible only to the few, while the rest live, separately, in soul grief. It belongs to every human being to feel the full and glorious presence of every archetypal pattern and possibility. Money captures energy and funnels it in narrowed ways. Money is the enslavement of humanity.

Money is not necessary to life – a statement almost sure to be met with extreme skepticism but allow your imagination to open. Money is necessary to life only when we are enslaved by it. Without money, the value of everyone is equal. I may be a janitor, and the person next to me a professor, and we are completely equal in value, and in power. This imagination is no fantasy – it existed for thousands of years, and is documented by the research of Michael Tellinger in his fascinating book, "Ubuntu: Contributionism: A Blueprint for Human Prosperity."

Tellinger documents how, for thousands of years, the people of South Africa lived without any form of money. No coins, no barter. This was some 200,000 years ago, further back than the archeology we can imagine. The research is quite astounding, and forms the background of the political movement in South Africa known as "Ubuntu".

Once we can imagine a world without money, we are no longer possessed by the archetypal presences of the spirits of greed. That freedom makes it possible for the polarized division of money and greed into a unified tandem that has the effect of dissolving the ego's fantasy of holding power over archetypal powers, which does not get rid of these powers, but causes them to be projected into the world as the many forms of violence we now experience.

The Power of the Virtues

I. On the Meaning of Virtue
Virtue as the Way of Service

The virtues are inherently practical because they are concerned with the good and it is never sufficient to simply think about the good or to feel it; it must be practiced. For Plato, the True, the Beautiful, and the Good, exist as three transcendent archetypal realms and are grand imaginations toward which we aspire as human beings. We orient our thinking to the True, our feeling toward the Beautiful, and our actions, our willing, toward the Good. In such striving, we seek to unite our merely human ways with the ways of the spiritual worlds. The Good is the object of willing, that which our actions attempt to achieve when we act out of a harmony of body, soul, and spirit.

Aristotle had a more empirical approach to virtue, but echoes Plato in many respects. In the Nichomachean Ethics he seeks to discover the good, and comes to define the good as what it is we are aiming at in life, what we are here to do.

But, as there are many ways of doing the good, there must be one chief good, with which all the rest we can imagine are connected. This chief good, Aristotle calls Eudaimonia, which is best translated with a quite beautiful word - flourishing. The chief good is the flourishing of the harmonious life of body, soul, and spirit. That insight, it seems, is worth holding onto.

What sort of human life is most flourishing? Aristotle holds that a virtuous life is most flourishing; the best human life is one of excellent human activity. In book three of the Ethics, he turns to the question of what constitutes virtuous activity.

Virtues, first, are aspects of "soul", those aspects primarily concerned with mediating our emotional life. For example, anger is lived in a virtuous manner when we feel it neither too violently nor too weakly. Virtue concerns expression and action in the realm of emotion that finds the mean between extremes. The doing of virtue does not so much concern what is done as how it is done. He does not say that we are not virtuous if we become angry; on the contrary, we may not be virtuous if we do not express anger. Thus, we see right at the outset that virtue is not a matter of making a list of what counts as good and one that counts as bad and focusing only on the one, trying to exclude the other. We see that there exists a dynamism of soul that is not subject to simple rules and regulations.

II. Virtue as Artistic Living
A. The Art of Virtue

Living the virtues can be imagined as developing the art of the soul. You have to get the knack of it by doing it. Aristotle's view is that the virtues are acquired by doing; we are not born with them, and we do not acquire them in any other way than by exercising them. An artistic skill is required in exercising virtue. Still, there must be an inner quality of soul that recognizes a virtue when it sees one, and if seen clearly enough, becomes inclined toward that virtue. Otherwise we become involved in a rather impossible regress. If virtues come wholly from the outside, then who determines what counts as virtue and what does not? That is to say, if virtue comes completely from the outside, then this realm would be simply a matter of what is socially or culturally conditioned. Here we have to thread a careful path. The way we take up and live virtue must indeed be sensitive to context. The acts themselves, no matter what the content might be, are not virtuous. A genuinely fair action, for example, is not one that can be determined in an abstract way. It must be an action that a person knows to be fair in a given situation, chooses to do for its own sake, and done in such a way that it expresses the soul character of the person.

B. Virtue, Ethics, and Values

In order to avoid confusion in all of what follows, we need to make a clearing for the consideration of virtue by differentiating virtue from ethics on the one hand and from values on the other. The primary difference centers in the concern with the soul, which we shall be following in an explicit way. When doing the good issues from the inner life of the soul, there is active enjoyment in what one does. We take pleasure in our virtuous activity; it is not a matter of duty or obligation, following a moral code, or doing what one is told to do. Ethics is a code of conduct based upon moral duties and obligations which indicate how one should behave. Values are core beliefs or desires that guide or motivate attitudes and actions. Values are not necessarily ethical.

Look, for example, at the act of treating other people fairly. Fairness can be a value, a characteristic of social life that is held in affective regard. One then acts in fairness toward others because that is what is valued by the group or society; there may or may not be pleasure involved in such action. Fairness can also be an ethic, a matter of moral duty and obligation, connected with the perception of what is right. For fairness to be a virtue, it must express the inner soul life of the person acting in a fair way, and therefore carry a particular quality characteristic of that individual; the individual must also choose to act in this way, and in so doing experiences pleasure, not from what may come from acting in this way, but in the act itself.

C. The Soul Pleasure of Virtue

If virtuous action brings pleasure to the soul, then it is necessary to know how soul pleasure is experienced. It is not the same as sensory pleasure, emotional pleasure, nor the kind of satisfaction we might experience by doing something that brings the approval of others, nor even that which accompanies doing something well. Try to remember a time when you did a courageous act simply because that was what the situation called for. You did not do this act in order to be praised, or because it was expected that you do it; in fact, you did not even consider whether you would benefit. The quality of pleasure involved in this action can be described as feeling free, as if an existing inner barrier had been removed and you were acting in perfect accord with who you are. In such a moment, in fact, you discover more of who you are as a spiritual being than you had known before. While the pleasure connected with each of the virtues has its own particular quality, and we shall try to describe these qualities in detail, the inner quality of freedom characterizes them all.

III. The Soul Gesture of Virtue
A. Virtue as the Medium of Spiritual Relationships with Others

These days, spiritual development may mean learning to concentrate on the chakras, do various forms of meditation, searching for one's higher self, engage in shamanic work, image work, dream work, and a myriad of other possible practices. Very little attention is given to inner moral development, in spite of the fact that absolutely every spiritual tradition places priority on the importance of moral goodness and very little on the kinds of experiences many present day spiritual practices seek. It is certainly the case that working to develop and deepen in the virtues has as one of its effects the gradual opening to kinds of experiences not available to ordinary consciousness. It is not at all the case, however, that working to develop capacities of out-of-the ordinary kinds of experience alone results in being a person who seeks and does the good.

Spiritual development can and often is sought for questionable reasons. Having out-of-body experiences, journeying to other worlds, becoming clairvoyant, developing healing capacities, finding a connection to a higher self - all such matters are considered to be of little importance to spiritual development in the great religious and spiritual traditions. In fact, developing such capacities is seen in these traditions to present great challenges. One must learn to look beyond them and never become enamored. In other words, one must actually learn to overlook the capacities that develop in order to continue deepening morally. This caution toward seeking spiritual experiences indicates that spiritual work, as understood for thousands of years is never sought for oneself and that spiritual work is always for the good of the whole community.

The present context in which every person can develop in the qualities of the virtues is our daily life, in the midst of our connections, trials, difficulties, and joys with others. Another way of seeing the virtues would be that they are the medium of our spiritual relationships with others. The virtues constitute the way of sacred service in the world, for they are the means through which we serve the soul and spirit of other human beings. Only by serving in this manner can a whole community flourish. However, serving the soul and spirit of others has to be distinguished from serving another person or serving the outer needs of another. Further, such serving must be freely chosen and not based upon power or authority or position.

In daily life we are constantly in situations in which a kind of serving of others is demanded. These demands occur in family life, in work, in intimate partnerships, in social situations. We typically respond to overt or covert demands either out of love for the other person, duty, obligation, or fear. None of these ways of responding, in themselves, can be considered a practice of virtue. These situations, however, can be the place of labor, the laboratory for the practice of the virtues. What is being asked for in all of these contexts, seen from a soul/spiritual point of view, is that a demand be transformed by us into an act of virtue toward the person making the demand. This transformation requires that the demand not be attended to directly but rather seen through. By seeing through I mean an act of imagination in which the suffering soul and spirit of the individual making the demand - whether the demand be overt or concealed - can be perceived and responded to.

A quite radical shift in the orientation of soul/spirit work was indicated above, one that I want to emphasize. Virtue as it will be developed here does not concern solely oneself, either in the dimension of going inward toward soul development or going upward toward spiritual development. Virtue concerns the soul/spirit gifts we give to others. Further, these gifts are not something that we already have at hand, ready to give. The other person gives us the gift of having to develop them to give. All of the virtues thus have a polarity about them. We have to, for example, develop in the virtue of patience and patience is also our spiritual gift to others. Or, we have to develop in the virtue of balance and balance is also a spiritual gift to others. Then, a further aspect centers on the fact that virtue as a way of acting toward others is to be oriented toward the soul/spirit levels of the other person and not to their personality needs. Thus, the transaction of virtue may well remain a quite invisible process. The effects of such transactions do show up in the visible world in the form of the gradual shifting of relationships to more refined levels.

The term "more refined levels" certainly requires clarification. I want to find a way to express the fact that virtue does not operate simplistically; it is not a matter of my treating someone nicely results in the other person transforming their view of me and quite suddenly treating me nicely in return. The difficulty with this way of thinking about the matter, and more to the point, of operating in relation to others in terms of this kind of imagination of virtue, is that it quickly turns into a power strategy, oriented toward achieving the results one wishes to achieve. Virtue does not work in this manner, which would turn soul/spirit relationships into materialistic cause-effect relationships. We cannot simply insert virtues into our lives, remaining at the same level of consciousness as before. Once we enter into the task of developing in virtue, we enter into an alchemical process of transforming the gross into the refined.

The alchemy of virtue, becoming engaged in a process of soul refinement, does not shift things piecemeal but rather shifts, or refines always the functioning of the whole. Suppose, for example, in a particular relationship with another person at work, it becomes apparent that the situation asks that I develop in the capacity of faithfulness. Development of the virtue here would mean that I cease moving around my views and opinions and ways of operating according to what serves me best at the moment and that I develop the ability to stand firm in soul and spirit toward the other person. This would mean that I have to deepen in mindfulness of this other person and be able to have a sense of reverence for the soul of this other person. As that ability develops, the character of the whole community of work slightly shifts. My individual relationship with this person may not appear to be any different. At least, I must be prepared to find that it does not seem to be different.

Virtue does not work in piecemeal ways. The circle of the zodiac is a whole, with every virtue being in connection with every other virtue. If you change one you change the whole. So, we have to begin to be able to have a more comprehensive perception of situations and also different aims for what we do. The communal intention of virtue concerns shifting from wholly horizontal relationships to vertical relationships carried out in this, the horizontal world of everyday life. Horizontal relationships are concerned only with what we can get out of changing our behavior, while vertical relationships are concerned with giving attention to the soul and spirit level of our connections with others.

IV. The Twelve Virtues
A. A Background to the Communal Virtues

How are we to approach to question of what specific virtues to consider? There are the three theological virtues of faith, hope, and love, and there are the four cardinal virtues of prudence, justice, fortitude, and temperance; these will not be the ones we shall focus on because it seems important to widen our consideration beyond the classical, Christian understanding, as noble and deep this tradition may be. We shall not leave this tradition wholly behind as much of what will be developed will encompass what these great virtues are about.

The number of virtues varies, from perhaps the single virtue of love to as many as 545 in one religion of India. My method of determining what to focus on is based upon three considerations. The first consideration comes from the meaning of the word 'virtue' itself. The word 'virtue' means: "The power or operative influence inherent in a supernatural or divine being"; or, "an embodiment of such power, especially one of the orders of the celestial hierarchy"; or, "the act of a divine being". These initial Oxford English Dictionary definitions precede the more common definitions of virtue as acts of conduct carried out by human beings. Re-visioning virtue first requires going to this source meaning, recognizing that the more common meanings have now become deadened by being immersed in the dogma of one or another religion. I am interested in developing the spiritual rather than the religious way of attending to the life of virtue because this way invites each individual to find the particular way of expressing their soul life rather than doing so according to arranged practices. At the same time, the interest here is how the universally human is in each particular instance embodied.

A second consideration follows: we most likely cannot directly perceive the acts of spiritual beings but do have evidence of their being in the archetypal patterns of the universe. We can take an archetypal approach to virtue, seeking the imaginal and spiritual background to our practice of particular virtues as human beings in the work of the divine arrangements of the cosmos. A specific relation, for example, exists between the twelve constellations of the Zodiac and twelve virtues. This relation has been alluded to by various individuals, but not yet developed. H.P. Blavatsky spoke of such a relation in The Secret Doctrine. Herbert Witzenmann wrote a brief book of meditations of the virtues, The Virtues - The Seasons of the Soul, based on the indications of Blavatsky and also of Rudolf Steiner. Recently, an astrologer, Paul Platt, has attempted to phenomenologically verify the relation of twelve different virtues to the twelve constellations in his work, The Qualities of Time. Each of these contributions provide no more than indications. For our purposes, it is not a literal connection of virtue with the Zodiac that is of importance; rather, it is to have a cosmological imagination in relation to virtue. Such an imagination will help us feel we are in harmony with the larger world when we act out of virtue and prevent virtue from becoming a code of ethics to follow.

The third consideration in approaching the virtues through an archetypal imagination of the Zodiac concerns the mobility of such an imagination. The year is an archetype of becoming; we move from one month to the next, from one season to the next. The virtues, then, are not fixed ways of acting but a path of inner development that we go over again and again, deepening and expanding our experience of these attributes of the soul. The Zodiac, for us, is an imagination within which we can place this work and not a system that in any way predicts, for example, that someone born under a certain sign will be characterized by a certain virtue. Nor does this imagination provide a new system for astrological reading. We can think of the virtues as twelve stages of development, but these twelve stages repeat because we are not engaged in learning something conceptual; if we were, then once we got the concept, we would have clarity. Virtue educates emotions and feelings. Our emotions have a quality that is much like the realm of dreams. You may have a most vivid and moving dream, only to forget it within a few hours. We experience emotional life in a similar way. While we are in the midst of a particular emotion, it dominates our consciousness totally. Yet, after the emotion passes, we usually have trouble describing exactly what we experienced. Thus, emotional life does not develop in the way that, say, intellectual life develops. The virtues are not intellectual concepts but rather purity of emotion; for this reason, it is perhaps not to the theologian or to the philosopher of ethics that we should look for guidance in practice of virtue, but rather to a depth psychology bearing a spiritual orientation, that is, to spiritual psychology.

The correlation between the zodiac constellations and the virtues that have been proposed are the following:

Region	Virtue	Time Period
Aries	Devotion	March 21 - April 21
Taurus	Balance	April 21 - May 21
Gemini	Faithfulness	May 21 - June 21
Cancer	Selflessness	June 21 - July 21
Leo	Compassion	July 21 - August 21
Virgo	Courtesy	Aug. 21 - Sept. 21
Libra	Equanimity	Sept. 21 - Oct. 21

Scorpio	Patience	Oct. 21 - Nov. 21
Sagittarius	Truth	Nov. 21 - Dec. 21
Capricorn	Courage	Dec. 21 - Jan. 21
Aquarius	Discretion	Jan. 21 - Feb. 21
Pisces	Love	Feb. 21 - March 21

B. Describing the Virtues

The procedure we will follow consists of giving an initial description of the twelve virtues listed above. The challenge of these descriptions will be to find the most adequate way of finding language that is a language of the emotions, since, as was stated above, virtue concerns the education of the emotions.

When we imagine the circle of the zodiac as a whole, while at the same time try to imagine one region as belonging to that whole, then it is possible to feel that one virtue is not separated off from the rest. A further feeling arises; that this particular approach to the virtues can be named, just as the virtues of faith, hope and love are named the theological virtues because they are those soul qualities needed to approach the divine. Similarly, the virtues of prudence, justice, temperance, and fortitude are named the cardinal virtues because they are the principle spiritual ways to develop one's individual emotional life. The twelve virtues listed above, seen through the imagination of the zodiac, it seems, could be named the communal virtues. Thus, as we proceed to describe the twelve qualities of the whole, we will do so bearing in mind a concern for what constitutes a flourishing community.

Devotion
We have to move into the image of each virtue gradually, being careful not to drown out the feeling-voice of the virtue itself by trying to know it rather than feel it first. An image is not a static picture but rather the activity of the soul in the act of creating picture. Devotion itself cannot be pictured because it stands there as a static word, a word that perhaps can be defined but not easily imaged. As an aid to developing an image, begin by noticing that in the zodiac circle, devotion stands between love and balance. Love precedes devotion and balance follows from devotion. Devotion builds on a basis of love and anticipates balance. Devotion concerns a steadiness of the

depth of love. To practice devotion concerns developing the ability to deeply love what one does in a steady, ongoing, balanced manner rather than, say, sporadically. In devotion, we approach whatever we are doing, or attend to who is with us as if the task, the event, the person were sacred and holy. The practice of this virtue requires a certain specific kind of attention, of focus, of concentration - the concentration of love.

Every virtue can also be looked at in terms of its excess and its lack. These two qualities are the shadow of every virtue, and we must look at these excesses and lacks in ourselves quite closely. Such qualities are not to be denied, turned away from as if they are not there, for then they return as obsessions. On the other hand, we have to be able to look at these adverse qualities in ourselves without identifying ourselves with these qualities. For example, the shadow of devotion on the side of excess is malice. The shadow of this virtue on the side of lack would be the incapacity to sustain a concentration of love toward a single goal. If we do not recognize our own malice, then devotion can have no real, embodied strength. If we do not recognize our own shallowness, then our devotion will have no breadth.

Balance

In order to experience the virtue of balance we have to be moving toward a future in a soul or spiritual way. Even in the realm of physical life, it is when we go to take the 'next step' that balance comes into play. In the spiritual realm, a good image for the point of balance is the crossing point of a lemniscate. This is the point of concentration between two spiritual factors - the effort that comes from us in our attempts at spiritual development, and the presence of spiritual reality, which opens itself to us according to its own laws, not according to how hard we work to attain authentic spiritual experience. The virtue of balance concerns the capacity to concentrate, without effort, at the crossing point. Our own personal efforts toward spiritual development must be in perfect balance with the grace offered or not offered by the spiritual realms.

The virtue of balance is also reflected in everyday practical life and concerns the relation of the efforts we bring to a situation in order to influence it, and what the situation itself requires in order to be true to its own internal, and often mysterious order. The disorders of balance often show up here either as an attempt to impose our understanding and/or desires onto the situation or as an inability to act at all, a kind of apathy or inertia. Such unbalance in the horizontal direction of our work in the world, I suspect, reflects an unbalance in the vertical direction; that is, lack of balance in spiritual work precedes lack of balance in everyday life.

Developing the virtue of balance entails moving from the constant oscillations of the mental life into the rhythmic movement of the feeling life, centered in the realm of the heart. This development also entails discovering the exact relationship between matters of the mind and matters of the heart. While balance can only be found in the rhythm of the heart, moving into this rhythmic domain does not mean abandoning thought, but more one of switching which takes precedence. The location of balance in the zodiac circle as between devotion and faithfulness gives an image of the work entailed here. Balance relies on the devotion of the heart and requires the development of faithfulness, that is adherence to the ways of the heart.

Faithfulness
The virtue of faithfulness concerns, before all else, faithfulness to our soul and spiritual life. For, quite often, we may lose the actual experience of the soul and of the spirit. Faithfulness truly exists only when it defies absence. When, for example, I speak of an individual as a faithful friend, I mean this person is someone who does not fail me, someone who stands up to whatever the circumstances may bring, someone we find there when we confront difficulty. Such a friend is truly faithful, though, when his or her presence is not forced, not a matter of duty or felt obligation. Now, with respect to our soul and spirit, the virtue of faithfulness means that we stand in and for these realms, regardless of the times in which we do not actually experience them. Further, to be faithful means that we are present to and for the realms of soul and spirit, that it is something we do for them, not for our own sake. It may seem somewhat strange to suggest that the worlds of soul and spirit rely upon our active attention

Selflessness
The virtue of selflessness lies between the excess of self-abandonment and the lack of self-centeredness. A total loss of boundaries occurs with self-abandonment, which leads to the possibility of being taken over by the needs and desires of others, while the one taken over feels he or she is actual being of service. After a time, one who has served others in this manner becomes completely confused and feels an inner emptiness. On the other

hand, placing oneself at the center of whatever one does, making sure that personal benefit of one sort or another results, leave the person or institution being 'served' in this manner empty. The virtue of selflessness is not easy to come to. Much of what we do for others tends to be either self-serving, or done out of the need to be approved of by others; both are forms of egotism. The way through these two difficulties that lie in the way on the path to selflessness does not involve trying to become egoless. Rather, the ego needs to be given a sacred task. Our ego so voraciously grabs at whatever it can get for itself because, typically, it does not have what it needs, which is connection with something holy. Not having this connection, our ego tries to get hold of anything - power, position, status, material things - and since none of these objects are satisfying, our ego becomes involved in repeatedly trying more of the same.

Development of the virtue of selflessness perhaps begins with orienting our ego toward our self, ourselves in our spirit aspect. For example, when someone takes up a practice of meditation, this is an example of the ego becoming oriented toward the self. Once given this sacred task, which takes repetition and discipline, then the self is able to do its work in the world, to fulfill its desire, which is to serve.

The position of selflessness in the zodiac circle as occurring after faithfulness and before compassion shows us more about this virtue. Selflessness must be based upon the capacity to creatively be oriented toward others and must also partake of the capacity of entering into the experience of others as if it were one's own.

Compassion

As a virtue, compassion has a more restricted meaning than it has as a central aspect of the practice of Buddhism. I have already alluded to this more restricted meaning by giving the ego an important place in the development of virtue. Thus, compassion here does not rely upon taking the ego as illusion as it does in this great religious tradition. Compassion does require that one live and work in relation with others and with the world more out of the center of the heart than out of the mind. The mind, or thinking, is certainly not excluded, but rather becomes a feeling-thinking. We can see that the virtue of selflessness is a kind of prerequisite to compassion; the ego, occupied with the sacred task of keeping connection with our spirit, leaves thinking free to enter into intimate relation with the heart.

Compassion concerns feeling the thoughts, feelings, joys and sufferings of others, and of the things of the world as if they were our own. I want to extend compassion beyond a relationship with other human beings and also include the animal world, the plant world, and even the physical world; in doing so, I stand in the tradition of the Anima Mundi, the tradition going back as early as Plato, and certainly before that, of seeing everything in the world as having soul. Further, when this virtue is developed in a further installment, I will show that it is really not possible to have compassion for another human being without this larger, more inclusive sense of compassion.

A further aspect of compassion to be developed concerns how this virtue is active, that it not simply something that one has for others, but something one does for others, an activity of radical receptivity that has real effects in the world. And, while we can readily understand how feeling the suffering of others may indeed be a virtuous act, we will have to show how this act must be extended to those who do not appear to be suffering at all. Can we have compassion for the tyrant, or for the person at work who seems completely occupied with their own advancement, or for those around us who seem to have no feelings whatsoever toward us, or perhaps even hostile feelings?

Courtesy

The virtue of courtesy concerns holding back one's own emotions - not repressing or denying them - but holding them in order to give a place for the soul life of the other person to be expressed. Certainly, the word 'courtesy' is related to the word "to court", which is to honor the presence of another, to outwardly acknowledge the person as a being of soul and spirit substance. In some ways this virtue may seem to be minor, but that mistake is due to courtesy falling into outward manners with little inner feeling. The virtue must be related to the tradition of courtly love, the troubadour poets, the right restraint in the expression of love.

Courtesy recognizes beauty as being at the very center of human life. Further, this virtue shows that beauty is not simply something to be looked at, to be admired, but that it can be a practice, a discipline. Interestingly, the word 'courtesy' is also related to the word 'courtesan', which on the one hand means the guardian of the court, guardian of the royalty of soul and spirit, and on the other hand means a prostitute. If we restrain judgment, the prostitute serves the bodily needs of a person. This helps us see that courtesy is a very bodily act, one honoring the soul and spirit in body. Of course, this kind of honoring of the body can become a perversion when the sense of soul and spirit is excluded; prostitution has all sorts of different forms.

We cannot bypass the fact that courtesy honors the feminine face of the world. Thus, we can ponder how this virtue can become more extensive, where we can see manners as having to do with the manner of relating. Because courtesy is a matter of the heart, how we do something is as important as what we do, in fact, perhaps even more so. Courtesy makes our act sensuous, full of body, erotic - every act an act of making love. Without courtesy, our compassion, becomes sentimentalized, and without courtesy we cannot find the way to equanimity. Instead, we fall into carelessness - we could care less - which is a lack of courtesy.

Equanimity

Equanimity may be the primary virtue needed for the development of communal relationships. In the zodiac circle, this virtue lies opposite to devotion. Oppositions in the zodiac do not signify conflict but rather show a particular sort of helping relation that goes on between polarities. For example, if the planet Pluto happens to be in the seventh house, the house of relationships, and is in opposition to the sun in the first house, then a person can expect that a transformation (Pluto) will occur in the individual (Sun) through relationships. In terms of the virtue of equanimity, we could say that equanimity is brought about by devotion and devotion is brought about by the practice of equanimity. For example, a saying that beautifully expresses the relation of devotion and equanimity can be found in the Bhagavad-Gita:

> "He who holds equal blame and praise, who is restrained in speech, content with anything that comes, who has no fixed abode and is firm in mind - that man is devoted and dear to me." (12:20)

I introduce here the notion of looking at the opposite of each virtue as another help in understanding the nature of the virtues, a practice that can be applied to all the virtues, not just to equanimity.

Equanimity concerns the capacity to be even in emotional life, neither swinging into highs nor dipping into lows. It does not mean detachment from emotion, but does indicate the ability to see, to observe one's emotions while they are happening and thus prevent being completely taken over by the emotion occurring at the moment. All emotions are held with equal honor. Through equanimity a refinement of our emotional life occurs, and without this virtue emotions remain crude. On the other hand, over-refinement leads to superficiality.

Equanimity is of extreme importance because through this virtue we are able to develop a realistic imagination of our faults together with our virtues, and thus the practice of virtue does not fly off into an impossible and even destructive direction. For example, if I experience strong anger, the virtue of equanimity makes it possible to be fully present to this anger without however being taken wholly over by it. In this manner, the anger itself can be taken over into the practice of virtue.

Patience
Patience is the virtue that shows us that the time of the soul and the time of the spirit is different than everyday time. Patience is required to be in healthy connection with soul and spirit. Patience concerns a particular form or way of waiting; it is one filled with expectation. One waits patiently, expecting something to happen. The virtue requires living in such expectation without hastily seeking after the completion of the expectation. When we do break the tension of patience and try to make something happen, then the soul and spirit involved in the expectation is left behind. Patience is the virtue that holds together the outer events of our lives with the inner workings of soul and spirit so that both occur together with the right timing.

While patience involves waiting with expectation, it is necessary that the expectation not be filled with any content; it is rather a kind of plentiful void. If that plentiful void becomes filled with our imaginations of what should or might happen, or with what we wish to happen, then we are living in illusion. The difficulty with such illusion is that it obscures the possibility of seeing what lies right in front of us now.

The lesson of patience is patience; that is to say, this virtue is unending. We are not patient just until something happens. Rather, patience is an enduring state of the soul that, if it has a purpose at all, is to deepen our receptive capacities. Patience is strained by the fact that things do happen and that makes us impatient and anxious for something to be always happening. The events of our lives, however, are always - always - less than the life of possibilities experienced by the soul. Patience shows us in fact, in a very gradual way, that soul life consists of the imagination, which is the activity of living in the possible and not any particular content. There is always a kind of surplus to any event that we experience, something that goes beyond the content of what has happened. It is this surplus that is the effective agent in bringing about transformation in ourselves, others, and in the world. The impatience of efficiency tries with technical means of every sort to get rid of this surplus, and thus, the world completely lacks patience.

Truth

As a virtue, truth does not concern having knowledge of what is right and correct and knowledge of what is false. The virtue of truth is more connected with emotion; it concerns the ongoing development of the capacity of a feeling for truth. It is more like taste than, say seeing. One has to acquire a subtlety for differences and nuances rather than have something presented before you clearly and complete. We tend to confuse truth with judgment, taking our judgment of what we say to be true as truth. Such judgments reveal more about the individual than they do about the reality being judged.

The need for the virtue of truth shows in its deviations of gossip, slander, moralizing, and subjectivity of opinion. All of these deviations reveal the rather universal attempt to possess the truth. We do not ever have the truth because truth has its own autonomy; it exists independently of what we may think or judge. Nonetheless, its power can reveal itself only insofar as we practice the virtue of striving for truth. We reach for the truth, try to feel it, come close to it, get acquainted with it, befriend it.

When we attempt to have the truth, to know it complete, we are actually trying to seize not truth but the power that lies within truth. At that moment, when we think we have it, the truth we think we have turns into subjective judgment, gossip, slander, or moralizing. Metaphorically, the seeker of truth has to be a person without a place, always on the road, peripatetic, and if the seeker wants instead to take up residence, to feel secure, then the truth turns into lies.

The development of a feeling for the truth intensifies, strengthens, and brings into form our powers of attention, focus, and concentration. These capacities do not involve just the mind, but the feelings and the will as well.

We seek truth with our whole being, not just with our mind. We may find that the greater the concentration the more we find ourselves also practicing silence, and that those great deviations from truth all involved the violation of silence.

Courage

We can begin to sense courage as a virtue to be exercised daily rather than imagining it as expressed only in acts of heroism by picturing the other sides of courage - ambition and timidity. Ambition looks much like courage except that it moves too quickly and too self-consciously. Ambition has too much self-will attached to it, so that strong, decisive action, which may indeed look courageous, serves only the one doing the action and not those who it may seem to serve. Timidity also relates to courage; it is courage that gets blocked by coming to rest in consciousness rather than flowing over into action. The timid person often sees events and situations quite clearly, but is content with being conscious, abdicating giving inner shape to what is seen and taking responsibility for acting according to what one sees needs to be done.

Genuine acts of courage really do not happen on the spur of the moment and spontaneously; they may look that way, but that is because we do not have access or knowledge of the development and inner life of the person who acts courageously. Such as person has had to develop and now lives more from the center of the heart, but not in a sentimental way. Perception, however, cannot be at a distance the way it is for many people; it is, for the courageous person, an engaged perception, fully conscious, but not over-balanced in the direction of self-consciousness. The heart can be conscious in this way, whereas the mind cannot because it is forever self-reflective of itself. With courage we have a perfect harmony of bodily experience, centered in the heart, with the experience of soul and spirit. For this reason, the courageous person has the greatest range of imagination, and is able to move comfortably from the depths to the heights.

Courage, as a way of being, reveals itself in thought and feeling as well as physical action. One's whole life can be an act of courage. It is not at all necessary to face some seemingly insurmountable obstacle to engage this virtue. The person who moves along in life with clear aims and clear values, moving toward these step by step can certainly be called courageous, provided the way is accompanied by the embodied experience of soul and spirit. Ambition seeks the top but cannot see that the high summit really belongs to the spirit, and instead courage is thwarted into having authority over others rather than recognizing the authority of the spiritual worlds.

Discernment

We typically think of discernment as the ability to make choices based on trying to be clear concerning the difference between choices, particularly when we find ourselves attracted to more than one thing at the same time. As a virtue, discernment is not quite so easy as this sounds because of two factors. The first factor concerns the nature of desire, and the second concerns the fact that the objects of choice do not involve things easily apprehended. Thus, the process of discernment must take place in two ways at the same time; we have to be able to feel the often subtle differences in desire, and we have to be able to tell the difference between objects that often have the substance of something like air, such as ideas, destiny path, a future outcome, or the effects of what we do on the lives of others.

Where do we find the inner resource capable of the virtue of discernment? First, a different way of thinking has to be practiced than we are accustomed. We have to learn to be present to the activity of ideas, their coming into being, their process. When we 'have' an idea, it is already thinking crystallized, no longer fluid and part of the creative process. Such solidified ideas, which comprise the material of typical thought, occur too late in the thinking process for discernment of a soul and spirit nature to take place.

A similar kind of presence, presence to the activity rather than to the momentary result of inner activity, is required in the realm of feeling in order to be able to practice discernment. We have to develop the discipline of being present to the inception of feeling more so than feeling those we already have.

The virtue of discernment can be imagined as the way we ride the current of our soul and spirit destiny, and thus concerns the way that we move from where we are in our lives into what is coming to meet us from the future. Without discernment we are in fact always living in the past - in past ideas, in past emotions and feelings, in habits from the past.

Discernment does not enter as something we even recognize as important unless we actually experience the reality of the freedom of our spirit. While freedom of spirit sounds perhaps wonderful, it involves living in the regions of not-knowing and having to learn to navigate these regions. We can do so only by seeking to harmonize the various elements of our inner life - our thinking with our feeling, with our perception, with our desires, with our intent. If one of these elements becomes too strong, then discerning where we are in process becomes confused. The primary discipline in the development of the virtue of discernment is thus inner stillness and listening.

Love
Love constitutes a huge topic unto itself, so we must try to be clear that here were are interested in the virtue of love, something slightly different than the whole realm of the activity of love. The practical question, the question of virtue, is how love is actually practiced. How do we do it? We could begin by saying that as long as we are feeling love we are not doing it. Love feelings, of course are most important, but they also indicate we are trying to hold onto something whose nature is wholly that of being given away; that is to say, the nature of the virtue of love is to give it away.

Since love is not an object, a thing, what does it mean to give love? To experience this virtue, it is necessary to become intimately acquainted with our need to receive love, because this need is perhaps the source of holding onto the love that wants to be free to circulate in the world. Thus, self-love confuses the virtue of love, and yet self-love is certainly necessary, and is in fact a prerequisite for the virtue of love. Self -love consists of the endeavor to be ourselves rather than who someone else might want us to be. Love cannot be given unless it is given freely out of our own individuality; otherwise, the acts of love that we engage in are really for ourselves and not for others and for the world. Self-love makes it possible to choose to give rather than to hold onto love.

I do not want to try to define love, but we must try to characterize it so that it is not confused with certain kinds of feeling states or, alternately, too quickly spiritualized. Perhaps we could say that love consists of universal friendliness fraught with beneficence to all creatures. Given such a broad characterization, we can see the wisdom of love standing in the zodiac circle between discernment and devotion. Discernment is needed for the practice of love in order that love may be universally specific. And, because love does take us into the whole of creation, as well as the whole of the soul and spirit realms, it must look forward to being practiced in very specific ways, an anticipation of devotion.

Developing the Capacities of the Heart

Body-Awareness and the Entry into Heart-Awareness

Shifting into Heart-Dimensional Space-Time

Our ordinary consciousness keeps us distant from the immediacy of Being. We are spectators to the world and spectators to our own bodies; and our feeling life, our life of action, and even our thinking is scripted. Both world and body are considered objective realities, existing totally independently of our consciousness of them and also existing devoid of any qualities of consciousness. None of us here hold to that kind of epistemology, but we nevertheless exist within it because it characterizes the epoch within which we live. And, given that view --- imaginal, poetic, artistic, and religious views of the heart also lose effectiveness, becoming completely marginalized.

We all live an implicit assumption, unexamined, of two hearts. We live a split imagination of the heart. The heart is considered either a substance without metaphor, a mere physical pump that shoves blood around in the body, or it is considered a metaphor without substance – the joyous, passionate, creative, feeling, romantic senses of the heart, a heart that increasingly has no substantial reality.

This course heals split heart-consciousness; we shall work on imagining the heart as substantial metaphor and metaphorical substance; not one and then the other, but both, simultaneously.

From Awareness of the Heart to Heart-Awareness

In order to work on healing the split-consciousness of the heart, we begin with clarifying the new stance from which this healing can occur. We begin with a distinction between physical phenomena on the one hand and primordial phenomena on the other. The word "phenomenon" is rooted in the Greek word "phainesthai"---- to 'shine forth' or 'come to light'; the word "phantasie" is rooted in the word "phenomenon". Thus, when Jung said, that "Psyche is image", he meant "fantasy.' The whole of Spiritual Psychology, stands on this ground meaning of "phenomenon." We will be working with the heart as a primordial phenomenon.

Understood as a primordial phenomenon, the heart is not that physical organ of the heart, but rather is own organizing field-pattern of awareness. The physical heart is the outwardly perceived form of the organ. But the human heart is not simply that organ as we are aware of it from within; that would be awareness of the heart, but not heart-awareness. The primordial heart consists of patterned tones and intensities, densities and textures of awareness – feeling tones, in short. We are interested in developing the capacity to be present to the felt sense of the heart.

Because we are entering a primordial dimension – we have to engage practices each step of the way; not only engage them once, but many, many times, in order to develop the strength of soul to be able to be within the awareness of this primordial heart dimension within the world that is only just coming gradually into this dimension.

A Note on Practices

This course is filled with practices. It has to be. Each practice has been developed from within the experience of the phenomenon of the heart itself. That is, none of the practices have been 'mentally' concocted. They are practices which take what is present, but out of usual awareness and bring them into presence.

As you work though this course and come to a practice, do not go on reading without doing the practice. For now, while going through the course, doing them once or twice, for the purpose of understanding the course, will be enough. When you come to the next section of the course, the practices will be given again – in audio and written again, with suggestions on how and how often to work with them.

Practice: A first Entry into Heart Presence

(Adapted from the work of the Heartmath research group)

Think of a difficulty or a worry you are currently experiencing in your life. Make this difficulty into an inner mental image. Then shift this image from the region of the head into the center of the heart. It disappears there as a worry or concern, and this is a simple method for shifting into heart consciousness in a way that you can feel the difference between head consciousness and heart consciousness.

Then, stay in the heart—keep your consciousness centered in the deep interior of your heart. Then, with an act of will, empty your heart-consciousness of any content and apply just enough will-force to keep it empty. Try to feel the currents that are active in the interior of your heart. Do this exercise for no more than five minutes.

The felt sense of the heart is not any particular feeling, not in the usual sense of the world "feeling", which typically means some specifc subjective state, as when we say, "I feel sad,", or I feel depressed', or "I feel elated." All specific feelings of this sort are cognized ways of expressing the felt sense of the body, but are not themselves the immediately felt sense itself. The moment the felt sense of body is cognized, we lose touch with the living process. Depth psychotherapists are well aware of this difficulty, or should be. If a patient, for example, is encouraged to "talk about" his depression, that is a way of trapping the inherently deepening felt-sense of the process of depression, making it into an object for spectator consciousness. We do not want to make that kind of mistake in speaking of the heart. We attempt to avoid it by seeking to develop the capacities of the heart.

Developing the Capacity of Sustained Heart-Presence

We are going to avoid using the term 'consciousness' because of the mental connotations of this word. The word 'consciousness was introduced by the empirical philosopher, Locke, and was defined as the mental reflection of outer events. The term has broadened considerable since then. Still, it is not suitable for what occurs when we enter into sustained heart-awareness because, when there, there is the clear sense that we have entered a region of soul-spirit Presence. We shall see and you will discover that the qualities of heart-Presence are more like being within and simultaneously aware of a kind of natural, holy Presence than in a region as neutral-sounding as consciousness.

In order to begin to develop a sustained capacity of heart-Presence, it is necessary to come into a kind of alignment. We are typically scattered – the bodily sense of our self may be located at different bodily regions at different times; we may be thinking one thing, while our fantasy is in a completely different place, feeling in another place, and willing in yet another place. Soul multi-tasking. Much more concentration – though not mental concentration is required for heart-Presence.

Practice: Heart Alignment

This is a basic practice that becomes the practice that is always entered into before entering into the heart. Always. Over time, you will find that what occurs with this practices deepens and develops in very amazing ways. It is in itself a contemplative work, while nonetheless it is the most central of all the heart practices.

Heart Alignment Exercise

(Adapted from Guidance in Esoteric Training by Rudolf Steiner)
Always begin any of the heart meditations with this heart-alignment exercise:

Focus your consciousness at the center of your forehead, near the bridge of the nose, at the interior there. As your consciousness is focused there, say, in an interior way, "I am."

Move your consciousness, now centered at the center of your forehead and dwelling in the experience of the words "I am" down to the center of the throat area, again at the interior there. As your consciousness is focused there, say, in an interior way, "It thinks."

Move your consciousness back to the center of your forehead and focus there and inwardly say "I am.". Then move your consciousness down through the throat region and inwardly say "It thinks." Then, move your consciousness to the region of your heart. As your consciousness is focused there, say, in an interior way, "She feels."

Move your consciousness back to the center of your forehead, focus there and inwardly say "I am". Then move your consciousness down through the throat region and inwardly say "It thinks"; and through the region of the heart and inwardly say "She feels". Then, move your consciousness to the region of your solar plexus. As your consciousness if focused there, say, in an interior way, "He wills."

Let your consciousness be within these four areas for a few minutes. Then open your eyes.

The whole exercise does not take any longer than about seven minutes. As any spiritual practice, at first it is rather 'clunky' because you are doing something inward based on outer instructions. After a while, when you no longer have to think of the instructions and sort of self-instruct yourself to do them and just do them, the sense of time changes radically. They are now done from within a different awareness and a different time. The suggested 'seven minutes or so' no longer holds.

It is important to point out that when Rudolf Steiner introduces this practice (though in a somewhat different way than describe here as it has been adapted to the work of heart Presence), he says little about it – other than we should not try to understand the words spoken. Here, in this practice, they are what he speaks of as "power words", rather than words carrying the usual mental content we would ascribe to them. "Power words" are a 'doing', and together, these power words, spoken inwardly in this way, align our subtle bodies.

With this practice you will feel much more 'here', as if all of your bodies are now in alignment and you realize that there was no awareness whatsoever of how scattered you were – and usually are.

It is also both possible and valuable to spend inner time at each of the 'places' of the alignment as each 'place' is a particular kind of subtle-body experience. The "I am" gradually opens a sense of your deepest presence. After a good long while of practice, the dynamic currents of this region begin to be felt. And, after even a longer time of doing this practice over and over, those currents can be felt streaming downward through the whole interior of the body. This is a most important experience for it is a new kind of 'bodying' – where we feel the qualities of the spiritual substance of the body.

The "It Thinks" at the place of the throat – can be, over time, felt as either currents emanating from that region of the body outward in multiple directions simultaneously, or equally, currents entering this region of the body from the wide spiritual expanses. The resonance of this area gradually develops the sense that it is not us who think, but rather thinking thinks through us.

The "She Feels" at the place of the heart opens up a very deep feeling of receptivity that is not at all passive, but rather reaches out beyond the physical body, without being an out-of-body experience – to embrace whatever is noticed.

The "He Wills" at the place of the solar plexus is the region most people find most difficult to feel and it may take some time to come to feel that when these words are spoken, a current goes from there radiating simultaneously upward and downward, extending the sense of embodiment to include the Earth.

Silence as a necessary prerequisite to Entering Heart Presence

Entering the Silence

There is a whole course on Silence as well as the book, **Silence** by Robert Sardello. Thus, here, we will only give the most basic practice for entering into the Silence. By the Silence, we do not mean 'being inwardly quiet', though that is a part of it. Silence is an actual, palpable, bodily kind of sensation, a Presence. Silence is always, always here and is the ground of whatever we might experience figurally – and not just auditory sounds. Everything of the world, or Earth, comes out of the 'sounding' of the Silence. Practically everyone has had an encounter with the Silence. Usually in the natural world. But, it is possible to be present with the Silence under any circumstances, even in the 'noisiest' places.

The medium of heart Presence is the Silence. Heart Presence as an actual power cannot be fully experienced except from within the Silence.

An initial capacity to be, for a time, within the Silence is not difficult to develop. As with all of the practices, we are not trying to make anything happen. We are developing ways of attention that make it possible to experience what is already happening but cannot be effective because we are not present and conscious in ways that are in keeping with the nature of the phenomena.

Here is a simple practice for entering into the Presence of the Silence:

This practice is to be done directly following upon the heart alignment practice.

With eyes closed, place your attention at any specific region at the periphery of the body. Attention is something very, very different than thinking. It is an actual placing of where you inwardly 'are' over to the periphery of the body. Try this a couple of times.

When you have the sense of what attention is like – that it is a bit like a very subtle 'object' that can be placed wherever you intend, then place your attention at the periphery of the body and notice what that is like. It is as if one is being very lightly touched. It is a palpable sensation of a kind of caressing Presence. Then, shift your attention to various regions of the periphery of the body and notice this same sensation is present no matter where you place your attention. Then, allow that sensation to be felt around the whole of your body – you will feel as if you are being lightly held, lightly, subtly embraced. This is the Presence of the Silence. Stay there for a while. Your whole bodily being will relax and there will be a particular subtle but distinct feeling, the distinct sensation of healing. It is not a healing of 'this or that' that may be a symptom you bodily experience. It is simply a central quality of the Silence.

From being within the Silence to being within the heart is a very quick and easy matter. The instructions are simple:

From the felt sense of being within the Silence, now place your attention within the center of your heart. Stay within the heart for as long as you feel comfortable and do not find your break being there with thoughts. If you do find you have left the heart, return by placing your attention within the center of the heart.

(Your physical heart is located very near the center of the chest. We tend to think of it as on the left side of the body, but only a portion is there.)

Notice what it is like being within the heart; you are now in the realm of feeling. It is not 'having' a feeling, but being within feeling as an 'autonomous' region of the soul. We can also descriptively say that this is the region of imaginal consciousness. Whatever we experience within the heart is utterly real, but not 'actual'. That is, what lives in the heart is not just a representation of what we experience outside. It is a creating of what we experience in imaginal form – which is not at all necessarily a visual image. It is feeling.

Spend time within the heart, just noticing what it is like. You can explore the interior of the heart. In fact it is very important to do so. But you explore it with your attention, not by thinking about where you are.

A Necessary Excursion into the Realm of Feeling.
Feeling as Subtle Touch

Feeling is the ground of experience rather than any thematic focus of experience. Think of the way in which the Gestalt Psychologists spoke of figure/ground. The body that I am aware of is a figural phenomenon, something that I focus on and have ideas about, and even felt-ideas of/. But the felt-sense of bodying-forth is not one of the properties of the figural body. The body that I am aware within, is a field awareness that has no actual or perceptual or imagined "hard" boundaries, but exits as an ongoing process of being-within awareness.

Feeling is that soul region where life (etheric forces) first crosses over into experience. Feelings, in the ordinary sense have no relation to this meaning, and refer to emotions. Feelings occur in a **twilight** consciousness. Another word, an accurate one, is **disposition;** another descriptive term is **Mood.** These terms give the sense that feeling is a ground-experience, not a kind of perceptual experience, not even an inner perceptual experience.

Feeling is experienced as the very ground of consciousness, as Mood. The way we speak of mood is usually actually emotion, or it can be the awareness we have of the existence of body-as-feeling, that is mood. This second aspect of feeling makes it difficult sometimes to distinguish feeling and emotion. For every realm of feeling, we can also specify the same emotion. There can be moods of anger, joy, peace, reverence, happiness, etc, and there can also be the emotions of anger, joy, peace, and even reverence or happiness. Further, a common characteristic of each of these modes of consciousness is that they both, when present, completely pervade our awareness. But, each in a different way. An emotion is experienced as coming into us, as suppressing the fullness of awarness, narrowing aweness to that one emotion and, in effect, replacing consciousness with that one emotion. We then become the emotion. Emotions usurp the sense of freedom.

Feeling, on the other hand, pervades consciousness in such a way that we experience ourselves within the feeling without losing the sense of who we are. Our central being, our I, pervades the feeling without obscuring the feeling in any way, and the feeling does not obscure the sense of the I. It is as if we are possessed by emotions, but not by feeling. Emotion is autonomous and beyond us; so is feeling, but feeling does not eradicate or bring about a dimming of the I the way that emotions do. Emotion has an eruptive character. Feeling is much stiller, calmer. Think, for example of the expansive opening of oneself in a transport of joy, the flight-at-any-price in panicky fear, the desire to sink to the floor in shame, the convulsive stuggle to be free in anxiety. Emotion takes over completely. So does feeling, but without the loss of our own spirit-presence.

Both feeling and emotion are bodily experiences, but much more strongly so with emotion – the expansion or contraction of the blood vessels, glandular secretions, reactions of the viscera. In emotion it is as if consciousness refuses to do its normal duties, as if it disconnects itself wholly or partially and is overpowered. In emotion, the personal dignity of the individual vanishes. We give ourselves up to primal powers which now explode without guidance.

Moving Deeper into Heart Presence
From Heart Attention into Pure Body -Awareness and Pure Heart-Awareness.

Thus far we have shifted the center of consciousness from the head to the heart. This sift is an alteration of the range of possible experience. It is as if when we are solely within mental consciousness, this form of consciousness itself determines what we are able to experience. When awareness shifts to the region of the heart, then we are able to experience a much large range of what is within us and also around us, though we lost linearity in doing so, or at least linearity begins to be more in the background. What we gain, however, is immediacy of know through feeling – that is, by being in subtle touch with whatever heart orients toward. The word 'feeling' conveys perfectly what it is – it is to feel the presence of what heart orients toward; just as when we feel something with our fingers, such as reaching out to touch what a fabric feels like, feeling is to touch – and to be touched.

Staying within heart Presence is still somewhat difficult because up to this point in the practices, we have been relying on our usual sense of the physical body and orienting toward heart in relation to the physical body. However, the physical body as we know it from physiology, anatomy, medicine, and even everyday life is not at all the fullness of the physical body-as experience. This mental sense of the body, and attempting to stay within heart Presence form that mental sense of the body is severely limiting. For example, within this mental sense of the physical body, we will not be able to recognize that the full physical body, and, even more, full heart-presence are neither time nor space bound – and yet are bodied.

When I speak of "heart", I am not speaking out of a sense of the heart as a metaphor without substance, nor of the heart as a substance without metaphor. Nor, however, am I referring to the "heart chakra". I mean the organ of the heart. However, it is necessary for us to remain consistent with what we developed yesterday, and not fall into the pitfall of understanding the organ of the heart as that only physical organ as it is understood by physiology and medicine. Heart is a field of awareness, and it is also the actual organ that beats within our chest. Of that heart, we know from immediate experience that it is something more than described by science and medicine. When we meet someone we love who has been away for a long time, our heart leaps. When we are severely disappointed, our heart sinks. We have all know what a broken heart feels like. These experiences are of the heart, are felt at the place of the organ of the heart, but cannot be accounted for through the understanding of the heart as a pump. A pump cannot do these kinds of actions. And yet, these actions are something more than a turn of language, metaphors without substance.

Alchemy has a way of speaking of the awareness field of the body that solved the difficulty of the split heart. And of differentiating heart-awareness from other kinds of body-awareness. Entering into an alchemical imagination of the body can help us re-orient our present body-awareness.

Heart as the Organ of the Middle

One of the primary accesses to an imagination of the organs is to begin always by paying attention to the location of the organ within the body. The heart is located between the head and the organs of the abdomen. This location is important. We would be decidedly different beings if our heart was located, say in the left leg.

Alchemy spoke of the body as consisting of three primary activities - note, we say activities, for it is important to begin to be able to imagine the organs as the locus of relationships rather than as entities. The three primary bodily activities are the Salt processes, the Mercury processes, and the Sulfur processes.

Salt refers to the activities of the body concerned with solidifying, bringing to form, hardness. The nerve-sense processes of the body are Salt; they are centered primarily in the head region of the body, but also are to be found in each and every organ of the body. These processes have to do with the hardening element, with sclerosis, with head and brain and nerves, with what is cold rather than warm.

The Sulfur processes of the body have to do with the life processes of the body - with warmth, heat, body-forming processes, growth, reproduction, digestion, the transformation of a thought into movement, the metabolism.

These processes are centered primarily in the lower part of the body, the abdomen and genital regions, but they too are to be found occurring in every organ of the body.

The Mercury processes have to do with balance, with rhythm, with the middle region of the body, with heart, breathing, circulation of the blood. The heart is the primary organ of this middle region and its processes having to do with balance.

The Heart as Mercury

Within this picture of the Salt, Mercury, and Sulfur processes of the body, the heart is the primary Mercury process. Thus, the location of the heart in the middle region indicates that the work of this center is to bring balance to the hardening forces of Salt and the dissolving forces of Sulfur. Any heart difficulties, except perhaps certain congenital heart difficulties, concern what happens when there is lack of balance between Salt and Sulfur processes. For example, when brain-nerve processes are two strong, then these forces move too strongly into the region of the heart, and the result is angina or sclerosis. When the Sulfur or metabolic processes are too strong, as for example, when through alcoholism the liver processes become out of balance, then the metabolic or Sulfur processes works too strongly into the middle region, and the result is an enlarged heart, or congestive heart disease.

Note, the heart itself does not become diseased. Heart disease is always a result of imbalance of the other two polarities. This leads us to a second image, also related to Salt, Sulfur, and Mercury. These processes also, at the same time, describe soul and spirit processes. Salt has to do with thinking; Sulfur with willing; and Mercury with feeling. As we proceed, the importance of this imagination will become apparent.

The Salt, Sulfur, and Mercury Processes of the Heart

In the alchemical way of imagining the body, every organ of the body is the whole body; the part is also the whole. Thus, it is possible to speak of the Salt, Sulfur, and Mercury processes of the heart in its activity. It is thus possible to consider, on the one hand, the nerve-sense processes of the heart, which also have to do with the way in which the heart is a certain kind of thinking. Within the heart, the Salt processes relate to the small bundle of nerves at the opening of the right chamber of the heart - known as the sino-atrial node (and, as well, the bundle of nerves known as the auricular-ventricular node of the heart). This bundle of nerves, like all nerves - indicate that the heart has a capacity to sense. What happens is something like this: When blood enters the right chamber of the heart, the valve closes, and for a brief moment, the blood is stopped in the heart chamber. In this brief moment, the nerve bundles senses the qualities of the blood - all kinds of qualities, such as chemical composition, but most importantly, what is sensed is the warmth of the blood. The blood is different temperatures at different places in the body - for, example, the blood is warmest at the place of the liver; it is coldest in the lungs because here there is direct connection with the outer world; and the blood in the brain is colder than that in the abdominal region. If the qualities of the blood are such that the whole of the body is not in balance, then the heart starts beating either faster or slower - an attempt to restore balance. This is really a kind of thinking located within the heart. Then, Sulfur processes also occur in the heart. Sulfur has to do with the soul activity of willing, and with the metabolic activity of the muscles. The heart is also a muscle, and thus we can speak of the will of the heart. There are some extraordinary things about this muscle. First, it is one of two hollow muscles of the body, and only women have them both, for the other hollow muscle is the womb. Thus, there is an intimacy between the heart and the womb, and this intimacy has to do with creating. Women have, I would say, an much more intimate connection to the heart than men, and know in a bodily way that the heart has to do with creation of life in the world as the womb has to do with the creation of life within. Another most important feature of the heart as a muscle is that this muscle is between what are known as smooth muscles and muscles that are striated. Smooth muscles, for example, like those lining the wall of the stomach, are characterized as being involuntary. Striated muscles, such as those of the arms and legs, are characterized as being voluntary. The muscles of the wall of the heart are between smooth and striated, tending toward striated. This indicates the most amazing fact that the heart is gradually evolving toward becoming a conscious organ, able to be worked with voluntarily. When, for example, we say of someone that their heart is open or their heart is closed, this has in fact a physical dimension to it. Another most important aspect of the wall of the heart is that it consists of seven layers of muscles; and at each layer, these muscles are seen to move in a different direction - if one could put all seven layers into a single image, what would be seen is the form of a spiral. This spiral form indicates that the heart is always, always in connection with the spiritual worlds.

Finally, the heart is primarily concerned with the Mercury processes of balance, as already pointed out. Mercury, though, has to do with the soul process of feeling. It does not have to do with emotion - but with feeling. From the other heart processes, it is possible to say that the two ground - feelings of the heart - that from which all of feeling life originates, is the feeling of devotion and the feeling of courage. Devotion - related to the intimate, unending engagement of the heart in its observation of the qualities of the blood; not detached observation, but fully involved, and never resting - this is devotion. Courage has to do with the unending enthusiasm with which the heart is always at work balancing Salt and Sulfur. Since this act of courage is always present, it is difficult to experience; it is experienced only at times when it stops - for example in an attack of angina. At such a time a person feels terrible fear, a fear that cannot be taken away - for example, by trying to calm the person down.

The Heart is Not a Pump; The Heart as the Organ of Spirit

The prevalent medical conception of the heart is that it serves to pump the blood through the body, keeping the blood circulating. The researches of anthroposophical medicine, and particularly those of Rudolf Steiner, indicate that the heart is in fact not primarily a pump. First, it is to be noted that this can be verified through our own experience of the heart. When, for example, we feel a moment of joy, the heart leaps in the chest - and this is more than a metaphor. And when we feel anguish, the heart sinks. A mechanical pump simple does not do this; it just sits there and mechanically beats. Further, when the heart beats, it moves within the body with a torque. A mechanical pump does not move at all. The torque movement of the heart is related to the seven-layered spiraling muscles of the wall of the heart.

Now, in a certain way, the heart does function like a pump, but more like the kind of pump known as the "battering ram" than a pump with cylinders, etc. The pumping action of the heart, however, is not what is responsible for the circulation of the blood in the body. The pump-like action of the heart increases the pressure so that the blood can get from head to toe - it increases pressure but is not primarily responsible for circulation. The interesting question then arises - where does the circulation of the blood come from. Here, we have to look more closely at the capillaries. The capillaries are where blood becomes so fine that it lines up one cell next to another - like in the extremities near the skin. When the blood cells are lined up like this, a surface area is formed, and this surface area - is in close connection with the outer world - these capillaries come very close to the skin. In this close connection with the outer world, it is the circulation of the sun that is responsible for the circulation of the blood in the body - though the circulation of the blood occurs in a different periodicity than the circulation of the sun.

Work with the Following Images

From: ***The Human Organs: Their functional and psychological significance***
By Walter Holtzapfel

Pg. 68 – "We know how strongly the psychological element affects the blood circulation. Anger and shame cause blushing, i.e., they drive the blood into the periphery of the body. Fear and anxiety make a person grow pale – the blood withdraws into the body's interior. If I intend to move a limb, blood flows into the appropriate muscles even before the movement is carried out. If I imagine a tasty dish, my mouth waters because blood flows into the saliva glands, making the saliva flow. All this is in agreement with Rudolf Steiner's statement that in the human soul and spirit the actual impulses of the blood circulation are found.

t is the feelings of the soul which give rise to the movement of the blood; the soul drives the blood, and the heart moves because it is driven by the blood.

….Man today, however, cannot guide his heart as he will; when he feels anxiety, it beats faster, since the feeling acts on the blood and this quickens the motion of the heart.

Pg. 70 – "The most alarming features in patients who have undergone heart transplants are the personality changes reaching even psychotic proportions. The daughter of Dr. Baliberg (the first heart transplant recipient) reported in an interview after her father's death that after his heart transplant a complete personality change had occurred reaching such a dimension that she could hardly recognize him."

N.B. three results of heart transplants: a)rejection, recurrence of the original illness (e.g., Dr. Baliberg's heart illness was due to advanced coronary sclerosis; when he died with the new heart a year and a half later, his new hard showed signs of this disease; did not come with the new heart, which was from a 24 year old healthy young man); b) rcurrence of the illness; change of personality.

    a) rejection – has to do with the etheric body – the wholeness of
       the body
    b) return of the illness – the astral body
    c) the change in personality – the ego, the I.

pg. 76 – The hand is the "limb" of the human middle system. From the point of view of the human threefoldness, the strong and muscular flexor of the thumb represents the will pole, whereas the upper four fingers with their sensitiveness to touch and temperature represent the pole of the nerves and senses.

Pg. 81 – Red blood is not changed into blue blood or vice versa in the heart, but red and blue blood are flowing opposite each other. Therein lies the crux of the human being's ability to look at and to face the self in self-consciousness. Living in the self-related and ever recurring blood circulation, the heart does not come into direct contact with the outer world and this is the characteristic symptom of the human ego. Rudolf Steiner wrote the sentence, "The ego recognizes itself " in the form of a circle and illustrated it with a picture of the snake biting into its own tale.

A. Entering Heart-Awareness

    1. Always begin with the practice of Body-Awarenss (essentially, the practice of entering into the Silence

    2. When you are comfortable within the Silence, place your attention into the center of you heart.

a) describe the difference between 'paying attention to something' and 'the placing of attention – use the example of paying attention to your big toe and placing attention in your big toe

3. Stay within the center of the heart for five or so minutes. Then Describe what it is like to be within the heart, and how heart changes from being within us to us being within the heart. Note how the heart as "outside" is carried out in the iconography of religious statues of Christ and Mary. And also in Alchemy (give out alchemical pictures – from: The Emblems of Daniel Cramer and the Heart Emblems of Paul Kaym?)

B. The Qualities of the Interior of the Heart

The Shared Heart
Relating through the Heart.

Listening, Speaking, and Presence
These are the three aspects of relating through the heart. We bypass all the possible ways of working with the very notion of relationship, what relationships are about, in favor of the practical question of how to relate with others through the place of the heart.

Dwelling within the Silence is the Secret of relating through the heart. There is a chapter in the book on Silence on Relating. Let me shorten what I said in that chapter by quoting Heraclitus:

Not knowing how to listen, neither can they speak.

Relating through the heart begins with listening into the Silence out of which all our thought first rise and take shape. Listening with the Silence makes it possible to listen to what is within the heart of someone else.

If we are not able to listen with the Silence, our words do not re-sound from the depths of the heart but become unaware expressions of our immediate past experience. For most people, "listening" is a mere, brief prelude to speech, in which we are waiting for the other person to finish speaking so that we can speak what we are thinking. We identify with our mental words and inner voice rather than with their silent source. We remain unaware that whatever we speak is colored by the inner tone or mood of our experience.

Listening to the inner Silence give us more time to be aware of all we are experiencing. Being in Silence does not mean cessation of all thought and feeling, or even of 'mental noise.' It means hearing thoughts and feelings through the Silence. We get a chance, then, to hear, to be-aware of how our inner speech might be shaping, coloring, muddying, and obscuring the translucent clarity of our inner Silence. The purpose, then of this inner listening to the Silence is to bring the Silence of the heart into resonance with our speaking.

Rudolf Steiner says this concerning Silence:

the listening skill is extremely important. We must become accustomed to listening in such a way that we quiet our own inner life completely when we listen. Once we are practiced in listening in this way ... we begin to learn how to unite ourselves with the being of the other person and fully enter into it. We begin to hear through the words, into the other person's soul.

As we consistently practice this new habit, sound becomes the medium through which we can perceive soul and spirit ... Then a new sense of hearing comes to life in the soul. The soul becomes capable of hearing "words" from the spiritual world that are not expressed in outer tones and cannot be heard by physical ears. Perception of the "inner word" awakens. Truths are gradually revealed to us out of the spiritual world. We hear ourselves spoken to spiritually.

Whatever we hear from the lips of true spiritual researchers is only what they have brought into experience in this way." There perhaps could not be a better statement indicating the true purpose of relating – to be present in our listening, to the soul and spirit of another person.

The Practice of Listening to the Silence of the Heart.

The Silence of the Heart as the Tone of your Being

The difference between feelings and Feeling: feeling are something that we have; Feeling is something that we do. Feeling is what the heart does. Emotional feelings are transitory. Beneath them are certain qualities of feeling that are uniquely your own that are like deep musical chords. Day-to-day feelings rise and fall. Feeling remains. These feeling tones pervade our being. They are the form our soul takes when combined with the flesh, and are centered in the heart.

A letter of the alphabet is the visible but silence face of a sound. Any body expression is the silence face or image of an inner sound, giving silence but visible sharpe and form to a tone and quality of Feeling. The sounds our bodies utter when we speak are shapings of different tonal frequencies, the expression of inner sounds.

Practice: Insounding.

There is such a large separation from what little sense of silence we have and not only our speaking, but also the incessant inner speaking that goes on in our heads, that we have to make a bridge between the Silence of the heart and speaking, a bridge that helps assure that a resonance is set up between the Silence of the heart and our speech. The practice is one of actively shaping and toning our speaking to resonate with our heart, so that the resonance of the heart can enter into our speech. Here is a practice:

1. Open your mouth and eyes as wide as possible as if about to utter a long and sustained 'AH' sound.

2. Without making any audible sound hear yourself inwardly uttering a sustained AH sound.

3. Now imbue this inner AH sound with a feeling tone and quality of awareness akin to wonder, lightness, light and delight.

4. Let this tone and quality show themselves fully in your eyes and transform your entire facial expression.

5. Now alter your posture slightly or feel for a gesture of your arms that embodies the same quality of feeling awareness.

Now purse your mouth as if to make an sustained 'UH' sound (as in 'trUe'), hear yourself sounding it inwardly and imbuing your inner voice with a low pitched feeling tone bearing a quality of deep awe and reverence. Finally, closing your mouth, and, sealing your lips firmly, hear inwardly humming a deep and sustained 'M' sound. Feel the inner hum permeating your entire body and imbuing your awareness with a quality of fluid warmth. The 'ear' with which you hear yourself uttering the inner AH sound is your INNER EAR, the voice you utter it with is your INNER VOICE, the face you mime it with is an INNER FACE of your soul, and the eye that lets its qualities show through your eyes is your INNER EYE and an inner self or "I".

Feel yourself uttering your whole body as the AH sound, and be aware of how this alters the entire way you feel your body from within – giving it a sense of lightness and translucence. In this way, and not through any repetitive audible chanting of 'AUM' or 'OM', you will come to experience the true meaning of 'Mantra'.

Second Practice.

The first practice, when done through the Felt sense of body and the felt sense of the Silence of the heart, makes it possible for us to feel the quite amazing relation going on between the imaginal space of the heart, inner sound, reaching right to the edge of speaking. After this kind of practice is done regularly for a while our sense of speaking and of listening alters. We experience the presence of heart-feeling within our speaking. Again, though, be aware of the difference between 'feelings' and the heart-realm of Feeling.

Concerning speaking, Rudolf Steiner says:
"If we follow the successive sounds as they occur in a single word….then we can experience all possible shades of feeling."

When we slow down our speech to such a degree that enables us to prolong the enunciation of each sound, we can savor each sound as the embodiment of the Feeling of the heart. Each sound is felt as a distinct person. Here is a practice to enhance this sense of feeling:

Choose a word, personal name or sacred mantra, or, if working alone just allow sounds - vowels or consonants - to come to you one by one.

Looking at yourself in a mirror or facing a partner, silently MOUTH the first sound, taking care to position your jaws, tongue, lips in exactly the way you would form to utter the sound, but instead MIME it in an exaggerated way – forming the 'Mudra' of the sound.

Hear yourself uttering the sound inwardly. At the same time savour the 'onomatopoeic' quality of the sound – for example the warm, permeating quality of an 'M' sound, the shimmering or showery quality of an 'SH' sound, the languid quality of an 'L' sound, the uplifting quality of an Ah sound or the steadying quality of an Eh sound.

Let the tone and texture, feeling and flavour, of the sound show itself in your eyes, not only MOUTHING the sound but also MIMING its qualities and exaggerating every feature of mouth and eyes in order to give form to the silent face or 'Mukha' of the sound.

Silently MOUTH and MIME the transition from one sound to the next as slowly as possible, so that it shows itself in an incremental MORPHING of your entire facial expression, accompanied by METAMORPHOSIS of your entire bodily sense of self, as both become imbued by the feeling tone or MOOD of the new sound, and its sensual texture.

If looking in a mirror check to see how expressively you give form to each new inner sound. If working with a partner, mirror each other's expression of each sound, and feel the resonance this brings about.

Bringing the Listening of the Heart to our Listening to Others

From the Heart to the Heart of Others

We want to extend speaking and listening through the heart to the way we speak and listen to others. That, is, only at this point do we address the question of the intimacy of the heart. In quite a different way than this theme is typically addressed in psychology.

When we are able to be present through the heart by an inner hearing of the silence, we can then attempt to hear the silence within the heart of another. Martin Heidegger said "To hear what is silent requires a hearing that each of us has and no-one uses correctly."

Listening simultaneously to the silence of our heart and to the silence of the heart of another person requires developing the following capacities of hearing. Being aware of these capacities is already a large step in developing them.

a) The capacity of with-holding
   maintaining a receptive and attuned silence before, after, and during speaking

b) The capacity of hearkening
   Attuning to the qualities or tones of the silence
   Sensing where the speaker is even before he/she speaks
   Tuning in in such a way that the speaker feels encouraged to speak what is really important at any given time.
   Does the speaker feel able to speak authentically from themselves.
   Listening to you, not simply to what is said

c) The capacity of heeding

learning to hear the tonality of your exact choice of words. Taking the time to respond inwardly to the implicit as well as the explicit message conveyed.

d) The Capacity of Hosting

ability to listen as if only listening to this person and absolutely nothing else –eg. Not inner listening to what is going on in their head.

It is as if you re both lisening to the "between".

e) The Capacity of Whole-Being

Listening in such a way that makes it possible for us to slow down our speaking, to listen before we speak, to hear our own words more deeply.

f) The Capacity to hear the un-spoken

hear those words that conceal more than reveal

hearing not only what you say, but what you fear to say.

g) The Capacity of Holding

Do you feel held in the inner gaze of the listening intent?

Do you feel it is

your whole being that the listener is in contact with?

h) The Capacity of Beholding

Do you feel that the listener is looking inside themselves as they are listening,

not just looking at or for you.

i) The Capacity of Harboring

Do the listener's questions say something rathern than merely asking for something to be said? Questions that are full rather than empty shells.

j) The Capacity of Holding Open

Are the listener's questions really open, or are they interpretive? Does the question help you into wordless feelng?

Facing the World with Soul

Second Edition

New Forward and Epilogue

Forward

"Non Nobis Solum Sed Toti Mundo Nati"

"Not for ourselves were we born, but for the sake of the world." This great medieval saying serves as the motto for the work of the School of Spiritual Psychology, which I, along with Cheryl Sanders lead. This School began in 1992 as a direct result of the publication of the first edition of this book and continues, now some eleven years later. The work of the school consists in fostering embodied spirit-soul consciousness that is open and receptive to the autonomous beings of the spiritual worlds and has as its purpose care of the Soul of the World. This book intends to inspire others to find ways of serving soul in the world. It has been heartening to hear of instances of such inspiration. An individual in Washington read the book, and on the basis of what he learned in the chapter on food started a natural food restaurant with a new sense of the soul of food. Work on imagining the soul of the city continues in Dallas, under the apt guidance of Dr. Gail Thomas, who is really the originator of working in practical ways with the soul of the world. A friend in Detroit has worked with the chapter on violence in his position as minister and councilor, instituting programs that have beauty at the center of the effort. A number of students are now pursuing imaginative and scholarly work to develop an understanding of the soul of the world. Many people have written me to say that the chapter on disease has changed the way they approach their illnesses. A builder has told me he now seeks to design homes in a way that is hospitable to soul.

We do not have to be social activists to feel that some sort of balance has to be brought into the world so occupied by material gain and loss, violence, wars, disease, natural catastrophes, political and corporate machinations, and terror. While there are amazing deeds of heroism and courage meeting these world difficulties, those of us who are not directly involved, but certainly directly affected, can do much that can be of real help. We can develop the soul capacities that encourages the world to move in harmony with its spiritual destiny rather than retrench into further isolation, policing, fear intensification, and removing the conditions needed for the inner development of the freedom of spirit.

This writing offers one form of bringing the balancing factor of soul into a world adrift. It is an extended meditative look at the world through the perspective of soul. On the one hand, it is diagnostic. Soul has been and continues to be left out of the way we collectively approach the sectors of life making up civilization and culture. We need to know the consequences of that exclusion. On the other hand, this book is curative. It suggests that developing the capacities of sensibility to depth, imagination of the heart, and seeing through of being, our doing falls unwittingly into the same kind of consciousness that has created the many problems we confront. These problems would not go away if the spirit-soul had a voice in the making of culture, but we would not feel that we alone, with backs turned to the spiritual worlds, can solve all our problems and continue with the kind of 'progress' now characterizing civilization.

Facing the world with soul is an act of sacred service. Indeed, one of the most significant directions of the work of the School of Spiritual Psychology stemming from this book is the program in Sacred Service now offered by the School. Eleven years later, we might even re-title this new edition **Facing the World with Sacred Service,** for the spirit-soul's inherent action when turned outward rather than inward is the action of service, but service re-imagined. Re-imagined in a way that brings the spiritual worlds into the circuit of serving, and re-imagined in a way that soul is served through soul.

There is light deep within the soul. Until that light turns outward, we are so focused on ourselves that we cannot see the soul being of others or the soul being of the world. The inner light of the soul illuminates only our own images or those of the collective unconscious. There has to be enough freed light to shine into the outer world. When this happens, we begin to see the inner qualities of all that surrounds us. We begin to have a sense of the world soul. Beyond a certain limit, inner work that is self-focused becomes self-absorption. There is always more to discover about ourselves, but it takes sensitivity and attention to gradually discover that we learn most about ourselves when we are serving the soul being of the world. Perhaps less sensitivity is needed now because the suffering of the world is so evident.

How do we know when we are in connection with the soul of the world? We know because we begin to find ourselves engaging in a new kind of imagination. We develop an ironic imagination. The ironic imagination is able to hold contradictories together without seeking to resolve the contradictions, holding them until something new, unknown and unexpected, comes from holding the tension. I weep at the destruction I see in the world and I sing. I do not propose tearing down the faceless cities we inhabit or propose new forms of education, or decry technology and extol nature. You will notice that nowhere in this book is there a proposal for new programs or taking up standard forms of activism. Ironic imagination holds that nothing changes until we can fully take in what is here and hold it in tension with what is possible.

Too often, spiritual imagination takes flight from the world and cannot seem to hold together the realm of being with the realm of doing. I once had a dream that showed me this necessity. In the dream, I was in an interior courtyard. A man had fallen to the ground, suffering from a heart attack. I was attempting to do something by pounding on his chest, trying to resuscitate him. I looked up and saw through a window inside a building where a woman was playing a harp, in a way, not doing anything to be of help. The harpist was looking directly at the stricken man, and she was singing. Nothing in the dream indicated that what the harpist or I was doing was misdirected or in error. Both were needed, and needed at the same time; that is, an imagination that encompasses both is needed. The dream put together these two ways of presence –doing and being, and let them live in ironic contradiction. We try as hard as we can to do something to improve the world while at the same time we do not get caught in the notion that, we, though our efforts alone, can affect change. That is the kind of imagination that forms this writing. We have the task, the inner work, of taking in and holding all that is visible of the world, and holding it in tension with all that is invisible and mysterious. That gives room for other, unknown and surprising factors to enter to bring about change. This is the way of the virtues of faith, hope, and love, for we do not practice these virtues directly, but, by developing ironic imagination, open a space for them to enter and do their transformative work of bringing the earthly world into coherence with the spiritual worlds.

The ironic imagination has to be prepared for. The mind can think about contradictories, but it cannot hold them and embrace them. The soul can. But it has to expand a great deal for it to be able to do so. This soul expansion takes the form of loneliness, darkness, and silence. We see terrible destructiveness in the world. Not only all the violence and the terror, but also the numbing comfort and psychopathic doubling, the immensity of concentrated political and economic power. We prepare for the ironic imagination by feeling how alone we are in knowing that nothing can change without the conscious presence of soul as a central factor in life. We can only look on, feel the darkness, enter into silence, and wait. Then, slowly, almost imperceptibly, the dawn arises. We see soul where it did not seem to be. It is there in our cities and our architecture, in our education, our technology, and in our diseases. We do not try to put soul into the world, but learn how to apprehend it. Soul, it has to be understood, does not make things better – it makes them more complete. And that is the necessary condition for types of change that will not produce further suffering under the guise of improvement.

When ironic imagination awakens, we do not at first see the soul qualities of the world. Not at first. Rather, we see our own brokenness. The state of the world reflects back to us our own inner state. We see that what is out there is in here. That is a great gift because then we don't go around projecting the world's problems on everyone else. It is not a matter of taking blame for the destruction we see. That would be egotistical. Rather, it is the moment of awakening to the reality that our soul and the world soul are inextricably intertwined. It is also the moment of awakening to the fact that whatever we do to know our own inner life more fully will resonate in some way in the world.

When we can feel that our soul and the world soul function as a unity and can thus feel the suffering of the soul of the world as if it were our own suffering, this intersection, felt in this way, is already an act of sacred service. It is sacred service in two ways. First, because it is not an attempt to do something that we think will be of help. That form of service always has the dangers of egotism, of doing something to help others or the world because it makes me feel better about myself. In this meeting at the intersection, however, there is nothing to do. The meeting, in a way, is felt as an inner emptiness. We only feel the suffering of the soul of the world. That alleviates the major source of suffering – isolation. And second, these moments are moments of sacred service because it is in these moments of emptiness that other forces can enter, spiritual forces that can inspire us to do exactly what is needed without imposing anything of our own desires. And, what we are inspired to do, more often than not, is something very small and imaginative. There are many examples in this writing. Maybe I am inspired to place a flower in a room that lacks any sense of soul. Or, I do a conscious act of meditation in which I enter into the interior of my heart, and from that center radiate a field that surrounds a person diagnosed with an illness without the intent to work against the wisdom of the illness. What is asked for in such moments comes to us rather than being planned by us.

The measure of the success of our attending to the soul of the world is the failure to desire success. We are being asked to alter our criteria for determining the outcome of what we do. We cannot apply the same criteria for soul work as we do for ordinary functional activity. If we desire for something to happen by being present through soul to soul, that is an indication that we have left the experience of soul and are back into ordinary consciousness. This stance of refraining from desire, however, is somewhat different than the well-known spiritual dictum that it is important to be detached from outcomes, which usually means being detached from all desire. For soul to do its work we need to be detached from the desire for success, but not detached from desire. Desire is the great net thrown out by God to draw everything back to the source of creation. To be in soul is to be in this large current of desire. Not our own private desire, but the world-force of desire. To attend to the soul of the world thus means that the currents of desire are felt as a bodily experience, primarily in the region of the heart. When we are in soul connection with the suffering of the world, we feel it in our heart. Something very palpable happens. We feel warmth in the region of the heart. We feel a radiating from the center of the heart.

The more we become accustomed to these currents and the stronger they become, the more powerful the work of caring for the soul of the world. Yes, power is involved in soul work. Power is good. In the realm of the soul, for example, intelligence is the power of thought. Satisfaction is the power of feeling. Accomplishment is the power of the will. There is nothing the matter with power. We look at the suffering of the world and see that much of it seems to be the result of actions of power. It is not power per se, but the tendency of power to accumulate itself that is the source of danger and the source of so much suffering. Power changes the world. Power that accumulates detracts from the world because it is only interested in power for power's sake. Many spiritual disciplines try to stay away from power. Soul work with the soul of the world does not. The warmth of the heart, its radiations, is powerful and does something in the world. In soul work it is quite easy to become interested in the enjoyable feelings of being in the heart. It is imperative to learn to focus not on the feelings of the heart but on the qualities radiating from the heart. When we become centered in the feeling it is a sign that soul work for the sake of the world has introverted and become soul work for the sake of personal feeling. This is a form of accumulating power. In the work of sacred service for the sake of the world, the power of power is relinquished. Knowledge, effort, and feelings of satisfaction must never accumulate.

Working through soul to be present to the soul of the world is known only through the heart and never by the action done. From the outside, the things we do in relation to the world do not seem to be any different than the actions anyone else does. No observer will usually be able to tell that you are caring for the soul of the world. What is done is different, but the differences are subtle. Soul work of any kind lies in the art of the subtle. It is the constant effort to work from the balancing center of our being, the heart, but not to exclude the head or the will. And this soul work has deep faith that the radiations from the heart center are powerful and change the field of interactions in the world in ways that are typically initially unknown, that lie in the physics of the indeterminate.

Besides this new forward, this new edition of **Facing the World with Soul** has a chapter- by-chapter epilogue, placed at the end of chapter ten. The epilogue intends to bring out more clearly the practical soul work that can be done in relation to each of the sectors of the world addressed in the book. In addition, the effort of description characterizes these writings. No theory is proposed. I attempt to stay as close to the phenomena addressed as possible and try to allow the phenomena to speak for themselves. Staying close to immediate experience, not inner subjective experience, but what the phenomena reveal, is the highly practical because do so changes our perceptions and thus our actions.

I suggest that you read each chapter and then the epilogue to that chapter before going on to the next chapter. These epilogues, you will see, are not extensions of the chapter per se. Each one develops a new thought, related certainly to the chapter, but not necessarily a linear continuation. You get a chance to see what has developed internally since the first publication, which mainly is the practical, meditative work, the doing of serving the soul of the world.

Epilogue to Letter 1 – The Soul of the World

These epilogues are intended to specify practices in being present to soul qualities in the world. Let us start with the most basic of those practices, learning to enter into the field of silence. In the chapter on the soul of the world, I say; "What must be done to enliven the resonance between ourselves and the soul of the world?......The primary practice is silence, the first aspect of magic"(pg. 24-25). There is far more to silence than being quiet. Silence is a basic phenomenon, like other basic phenomena such as soul, spirit, love, and death. In fact, silence may be the most basic of these phenomena, since it envelopes all the others. It is not a derivative phenomenon. It does not originate from something else; silence does not come from sound as its cessation; if silence were the absence of sound, it would imply that sound is basic and silence comes out of it. But, that is not the way we experience silence. It is experienced as more basic that sound, more primary, and in fact, as the very originating force for sound. All we have to do to verify this is to drop into silence for a moment and feel its presence. It is just there. We do not experience silence starting when we are quiet, but rather, we experience moving into something that is already there. It is all around us, but also everywhere within us; silence is all-pervasive; it is experienced that way when we touch into it.

We also encounter the presence of silence as a particular quality of our body. It is as if silence comes and gently surrounds us as well as pervades us. A particular bodily feeling comes. We feel the boundaries of our body as if something gently presses up against us. This something, which is palpable silence, is always there; it is as if it holds our subtle-body shape in form and without it we would spill into the world like a burst water-balloon. But, when we attend to silence, we feel this presence more actively. It surrounds our body and stirs the silence within our body. When we attend to this enveloping presence, we notice that it cannot be something cognitively known. It is known through the region of the heart. When silence visits we descend from mind to heart.

This subtle envelope of silence has a shape. It is as if our body stands within the form of the vesica. The vesica is the form made where two intersecting circles overlap. It is the middle-form, the almond-shaped form between the two intersecting circles. This form is often seen in sacred art, often surrounding a statue or painting of a holy figure. For example, pictures of Our Lady of Guadalupe show this form surrounding the body of Mary. I do not think this radiating form is the aura as it is often said to be, but rather the field of silence that shapes when we enter into the interior of the heart. This vesica, however, is three-dimensional, so it is somewhat like a transparent cocoon of silence, as if we are in a vessel, maybe the vessel of the heart itself.

While silence announces itself to us in this form, it is not emptiness, but rather an extraordinary fullness that makes possible feeling the interior, the innerness of the body. In silence, we feel our body interiorly as a body of wholeness. This experience is characterized by an inner bodily joy, absence of strain, and an immediate presence to a flow of currents from within the body outward, a flow of force from within that maintains but does not produce this transparent vesica of silence.

The surround of silence becomes the organ for perceiving the silence of the world. To get to this surround it is only necessary to become quiet and then move the center of our consciousness from the region of the head to the interior of the heart and wait. This initial practice may require several months to be able to do with ease. We can tell if our orienting meditation works, not by continuing to sit with eyes closed, but by, after a time, opening them and noticing the world. We can then perceive that the inner silence spreads all around us. The transparent vesica-cocoon has the peculiar quality of maintaining its enveloping presence around us, while at the same time, it now becomes the organ through which we are able to perceived silence in the world.

In silence, we perceived individual things surrounded by fringes of a great quiet. Objects are as if filigreed. Silence wraps around them like lace. This filigree is most apparent with things of nature such as the leaves of a tree, a flying bird, a tree, a boulder, a valley, a stream, a mountain, the sky. Human-made things are also wrapped in silence, but generally it is harder to perceive. These things – such as buildings, bridges, furniture, and so on, do not typically share their silence and seem to sit in it rather passively rather than glow in it as do the things of nature. Only when things are built with a concern for their context do they radiate silence in the manner that natural things do. And, not only things noticed in their individuality glow in silence, but groupings of natural things, such as a grove of trees or the relation between a tree and the building next to it and the grass in front of the building can be seen swathed in the glow of silence. It is as if the filigree extends outward, filling the space between things. Or, the space between things is actually not empty space at all, but is of the substance of silence that comes up against things and gently touches them, setting off a resonance of silence within them.

The perception of silence is, not strictly speaking, visual. All of the senses are in this moment gathered together into a whole. If we attend closely to this moment, it is even possible to shift our attention around each of the senses and experience the presence of silence gently impressing itself into each sense. We feel the touch of silence, experience it within the inner wholeness of our body, and sense its distinct quality of movement, which is like a swirling gentleness. We also hear the silence, smell it, and taste it. Of course, something is happening in this kind of sensing that differentiates it from ordinary sensing. The sensing of silence is not only subtle sensing; it is also an imaginal sensing. That is to say, our sensing becomes elevated to the level of imagination. It is *as if* we smell the silence, touch it, feel its movement, and so on. However, such sensory experience is not imaginary. We are not experiencing something that is not there, but rather are taken into a different level of what is there. The sense-perceptible world is raised to the level of the imaginal for us the moment we cross the threshold of the noisy world into silence. I distinguish here between what is imaginary, which is equivalent to fantasy, and the imaginal, which is the particular way soul phenomena present themselves.

We perceive something of the soul of the world when we are able to reside for a time in silence. The world is then experienced in wonder. The sensory world, when only experienced at a surface level, sensing without soul, can only take us from sensing into an immediate and unconscious soul act of judgment. We do not typically sense the world but rather sense only the outer surfaces of the things of the world and make judgments concerning what we sense. I see a tree with green leaves. I smell a rose. I touch a tabletop. I hear the birds singing in the morning. These declarations, which appear to be reports of sense experiences are in fact judgments.

Since we do not really enter into sensing but use sensing for judging, our powers of judging are acute and developed to a very fine degree. The strengthening of judging that comes from this superficial way of sensing is taken into all areas of our lives. We judge others all the time, not knowing that is what we are doing because it remains sub-conscious. We judge ourselves all the time. We judge what is going on in the world. We have opinions about everything and sense nothing.

Deep and soulful sensing can completely alter daily living. Clarity of knowing depends upon true presence to the depths of reality. How, then, can we develop a practice of soulful sensing? How do we develop the practice of entering into the world of silence through sensing?

Silence is available all the time. It does not go away. We go away from it. We go into the world of noise and sensory disturbance, as if into the vast buzzing of insects. And, having done that both individually and culturally, the soul dulls. It is not simple to turn to silence. It is not just a matter, for example of being more quiet, going inward, getting back in touch with ourselves, disengaging from time to time from the pressures and tensions of life. We have to achieve a certain freedom from ourselves in order to be able to sense soulfully. It's quite simple. How can we touch silence when the soul is filled with noises of every sort? There is the incessant inner talking that goes on. Then, there is the continual churning of the emotions --- angers that have gone unresolved for years, envies, hatred, desires, bad memories, pains and hurts, deceits we have justified to ourselves. And most of all, a sleepiness of soul that makes us value what makes us comfortable above all else, even if we seem to have other noble ideals.

Sometimes the door of silence opens without effort; it opens as a momentary grace, giving the gift of awakening the senses. And sometimes, when our non-abstract and non-intellectual attention is drawn to one of the senses, silence also opens up. When that happens, a shift occurs in which the sensory world is not only vivified, it is also experienced as a living being. A tree suddenly appears as a soul-reality; its trunk and leaves and branches experienced as if they were gestures. Our usual categories of knowing disappear and this tree no longer exists as 'over there' in front of me as an object in the world. We feel as if we were swimming together with the objects of the world. When we get beyond the surface, the sensory world has a certain thickness or depth and this world has a will of its own.

Depth sensing, when it comes as a gift, lasts a short while and then it is if it never happened. In order to reside more permanently in the depth of the sensory world, it is necessary to cultivate certain very specific qualities of soul life that we get a glimpse of with the gift of silence. The more important of these qualities is the sense/soul experience of wonder.

Wonder consists of the capacity to be present to the world in an ongoing attitude of amazement. Wonder is the experience of being present to something and experiencing it as both known and unknown at the same time. You see the green leaves of a tree. Suddenly, you are not separated from what you see. You are taken into their very life, where you sense something of their independent life from within their life itself. There are not just green leaves. "Green leaves" becomes a 'greening' and a 'leafing'. Wonder is not an intellectual quality, but it leads to creative thinking, thinking within the things themselves rather than thinking about them.

When we experience wonder, we are remembering something. This is not ordinary memory. What is the difference, for example, between waking in the morning and hearing the singing of the birds outside and going on with the things we have to do, and hearing the extraordinary difference between the long, lamenting call of the hawk, the crackling of the crow, the sharp chirp of the sparrow? That is wonder. When we hear only with our ears, we hear birds. When we hear with our whole being, we hear something of the soul quality of the song and even have an immediate experience of some other world that is beyond the strangeness and beauty of this realm of creatures as they exist within the folds of nature. In the moment of wonder, we experience an immediate presence of the world of Wisdom from which these extraordinary feathered beings originate. This kind of experience is a memory. Within our sensing of the visible world, we remember the presence of the invisible world. At the same time, this recollection is a self-recollection. We come home to the depths of ourselves.

When we experience wonder, we always feel that what we are present to cannot be put into words. This is the connection of wonder and silence. It is not just that we don't have the right words; there are no words. We are at the very origin of words. Words can come from this experience, original words, but we cannot put words to the experience. When we know through our sensing, which is non-cognitive, immediate knowing, this knowing has a rhythmic quality. The outer sense experience exists in perfect rhythm with the deeper resonance of that event, opening the event to untold depths. We do not experience a thing or an event in the world as static in the moment of wonder. The depth of its life presents itself as an invisible undulating movement. The everyday obviousness of things around us takes on a quality of transparency. Something shines through the things of the world. We see the active being of beauty shining through the mundane. The depth of what we are sensing and the depth of our most intimate self are non-intellectually known, together. Experiencing deep silence is not a subjective experience of an object, event, or another person. Nor is it objective in the usual sense of that word, as presence to something as independent of ourselves. Sensing silence knows the world as ourselves and ourselves as the world.

In wonder, the things we encounter take on the quality of being infinitely remote and infinitely close at the same time. We experience an inner radiating of the inner mystery and glow of things, while at the same time these very things remain at a distance from us and retain their own autonomous character. One small part of the world is sensed as if it were, for the moment, all of the world.

In wonder, the "here" and the "there" come into intimacy, not only with each other and us, but also merge with the "now" and the "then." This experience is difficult to describe because we hardly have adequate language for it. We might speak of it at a moment of "vision", as long as we do not restrict "vision" to the visual. Silence is experienced in a different time; it is not timelessness we experience, but more it is more like time gets spread out into a feeling of spaciousness. It is also as if past, present, and future go on simultaneously. The depth of silence occurs in repose-full time; it is not motionless, but more like motion-at -rest.

Wonder takes us into the depth of silence. There are three qualities to the depth of silence. First, this depth is intimate. Our perception of the things of the world alters in silence from one in which we perceive surfaces and have the impression that there are only things in the world standing side by side, to the perception of something of the utter particularity of each and every thing. There are no 'its' in silence, only the particularity of the 'thou'. Perceiving becomes meeting. Not just any meeting, and it is even something more than an encounter. Meeting through silence can be described as a mutual enveloping, in which the individual things of the world, too, are wrapped in silence, and the first quality of depth is silence meeting silence through inter-enveloping. We are allowed the extraordinary privilege of entering into each other's space of silence. Can you imagine anything more intimate that being together with another in an entwining of hearts in silence?

A peculiar aspect of the intimacy of silence is the absence of negation. Now, there are definitely negative silences. Silence can be terrifying, deadly, hurtful, filled with anger, divisive, cruel. In these instances, however, silence is usurped, used in order to convey or do something to others that actually has nothing to do with the silence. We have all experienced these qualities, specifically in our relations with others, and most of all those with whom we are intimate. But silence itself is never negative. There are aspects of silence that can be emotionally difficult – sometimes it is an overwhelming sadness, a grief, but in all instances the quality of positive intimacy is never broken.

Speaking of this intimacy as positive is not to say that it is something personal. The intimacy excludes our ego. We are, in our ego-being outside observers only. The intimacy focuses on the more impersonal aspects of our being and the being of the things of the world. Our body, externally and internally experienced feels in intimate relation with silence. It is also a soul intimacy, and it is definitely a spiritual experience. But it is not an ego experience. This last realization, that the ego is kept away from the substance of silence, accounts for why there is no negative experience of deep silence. Judgment of any sort has no part in this experience. We experience the full range of emotions in silence, but without the accompanying inner evaluating that goes on in ordinary consciousness.

A second quality of the depth of silence can be described as a particular sense of entering into the world as holy. A good, descriptive word for this quality is liturgical silence. A good place to go to experience this quality is a cathedral or a temple where there are great rhythms of liturgical silence, even when a liturgy is not being performed. When we enter silence we enter a temple, a region where we not only contemplate, but are also being contemplated. The experience of this quality signifies going more deeply into the world of silence, where the initially multiple envelopes of silence surrounding each thing become encompassed or nested within an invisible form that reverberates intimations of a holy source within the particularity of each thing.

Another reason for naming this quality of the depth of silence liturgical, concerns the subtle perception of silence as anything but static and still. The ever-present movement of silence is dramatic in form, and liturgy is always sacred drama. We have dramatic form whenever there is the experience of polarities, opposites, contradictories held together in creative tension. The dramatic quality referred to here concerns, for example, the presence of irresolvable opposites in the experience of silence. Opposites such as perception of the utterly particular in tension with perception of the deepest meaning of the things around us. And the unsolvable tension that silence is mine and not mine at all; of its closeness which is infinitely far; of it being a phenomenon of surfaces and also a phenomenon of depth. We also experience ourselves within and part of an infinite activity that is simultaneously moving and still. Then, there is the dramatic quality of being within a reality while being able to observe it as an objective reality. It is like being within soul and being able to observe it at the same time. And, being able to engage in this kind of observation without splitting off part of oneself to become the observer. There exists a reflective quality to silence. It seems to mirror the dramatic, creating actions of the cosmos, making it a cosmic phenomenon. At the same time, we find ourselves mirrored in silence; we come home to ourselves.

In silence there is anticipation. This is the third quality of the depth of silence. The anticipation is not ours. What does it involve? An anticipation of what? By whom? Partly, in the experience of silence, the answer to this question is not known. Yet, it is the strongest element of the depth of silence. It is as if silence poises and just about speaks. That is the anticipation felt; something about to be said. The saying goes so far as expressing itself as the inner life of the things of the world. In silence we have the immediate experience that all of the space within which the things of the world exist is not empty at all. It is as if all the things of the world are being squeezed out of silence; they are the word, the word that is deeper than any one word or all of the words of all the things of the world. Through the silence we feel the unity of the word, and the things of the world as expressions of the word.

You know what it is like when you have something to say, something that comes quite spontaneously and yet has an urgency to be expressed. That moment before it is said, that is the quality of anticipation that characterizes the depth of silence. A preparedness, an about-to, a coming, or as they used to say in the 60's, a happening.

In perceiving the depth of silence we come to discover the invisible body of the world, the spiritual body within which everything is nurtured into existence every moment. And, we discover ourselves in a new way. We are participants in the great being of silence. We are not detached observers of an independent phenomenon, but exist within what we are observing. This engagement does not make what we can say concerning silence subjective. Typically, we think of ourselves as individual beings, and the world as spreading around us. We take our inner life to be private and subjective. In silence, this relation changes. We no longer exist within the kind of polarity that oscillates between a focus on ourselves one moment and a focus on the outer world the next. The area of silence is more like an ellipse, within which one focus is the being of silence creating our soul-being while the other focus is the inclining of our soul-being toward silence. This picture gives us the beginning of the way to imagine the topography of the spiritual region we are investigating here. Within this vast region what occurs between the individual and silence can no longer be thought of in linear terms nor in terms of any kind of causality.

The intimate connection between silence and the soul of the world is best depicted through the story of the goddess of silence. Hidden away in the *Sacellum Volupiae*, the Roman Sanctuary of Pleasure, is a statue of *Angerona*. Her mouth is bound and sealed. An uplifting finger touching her lips points to her silence and her suffering. Angerona is the goddess of silence.

Angerona was the protecting deity of the ancient city of Rome. She is the goddess of secrecy, as well as of fear and anguish, and was believed to give relief from pain and worry. At the height of her feast day, the day of the Winter Solstice, the sun reaches its weakest moment of the year, and at that same moment the light begins to increase. As they waited for this critical promise of renewal, the goddess' worshipers were reminded of the necessity of honoring the delicacy of the natural balance. She is sometimes referred to as a goddess of death.

The goddess of silence watches over the cyclical renewal of the earth and the cosmos. With her finger raised to her already bound mouth she is doubly cautionary. Be quiet enough to listen, she says, but not to me. Be quiet, while I don't speak. Listen, that is, to everything else. To everything. The cosmos is most eloquent when it speaks in silence.

A connection exists between Anagerona and Sophia, the soul of the world. Angerona is said to be the same as Sige, the goddess Silence, who in the Gnostic creation stories, for example, in the *Pistis Sophia*, is the mother of Sophia. Sophia emanates from Silence and Depth. When we think imaginally rather than causally, we can say that silence is the mother aspect of the soul of the world. Silence is what mothers the soul of the . world.

Epilogue to Letter II – House and City

I have come to realize that the soul of the house and of the city must be combined with a consideration of a third factor, the soul of community. As long as individualism reigns, buildings and cities will be built according to individual and corporate self-interests. Sometimes the word 'soul' is used with respect to an individual house or perhaps an office building, but the term tends to be a clique, though at times a clear sense of soul can be detected amidst all the anonymity. Soul, though, can occur only when enacted between people. Due to the influence of Jung, we have a sense of the soul as individual interiority, but there is a much more ancient tradition, going back at least to the Greeks, of soul as communal. Soul and community rely on each other. Often, people use the word 'community' in speaking about their neighborhood and about the city. The word is typically used inappropriately, without thought, and in a general, abstract and idealized fashion. House and city cannot in themselves have qualities of soul if the community context within which they exist remains unconscious.

"Community" is a symbolic terms and thus many varied meaning cohere in it. Sometimes it refers to a group with a common aim, such as 'the community to fight against crime'. Sometimes it refers to a group with a common identity, such as the 'gay community' or the 'black community'. At other times, the term is used by individuals seeking strength and support, as when people say that they are looking for 'their community'. The word also applies to civic groups, and often to any kind of working group. Little distinction is made between group and community. That distinction is one I want to pursue here. A group that works well together and achieves something for the world is not necessarily a community. Besides what a community can achieve in the world, there are more subtle aspects, the chief one being the enhancement of the soul of house and city.

Individuality tends to be diminished in groups. In order to accomplish a goal, individuals give over to group consensus. I relinquish my individuality so that the group may proceed. While extremely difficult to enact, in a true community everyone finds their individuality enhanced. Not their egotistic individualism but the sense of their individual spirit being recognized and appreciated by others, and its contribution interwoven into the communal enterprise. The true making of community, in fact, hinges on the capacity to recognize something of the true individuality of others. Everyone's view is taken into account and becomes a part of what happens. Community belongs to the future of humanity. Right now it is an ideal, but one that can be worked on in every endeavor where people work to be together.

For community to come about it is necessary to reveal some of the shadow side of people coming together. Why do we want to come together at all? We do so because we cannot stand to be alone. Coming together with others often attempts to heal the hollow places of the soul. We feel better with others around, but then, after, when we are alone, we begin to think of the other people, what they did and didn't do, how self-centered everyone else seems to be, how one person dominates and another manipulates. When such emotions come, it signals that the togetherness experienced was a group and not community.

Many of our idealisms in coming together are based in selfishness. The test for readiness for community consists of the ability to be alone without tasks or distractions. If, when we are alone we become anxious, fidgety, and cannot stand our own silence, then coming together with others is not for the sake of others, but for self-comfort. Further, we are drawing on the soul-substance of others, using it to fill the hollow places in our soul so that we will not feel them. Separateness is not resolved by being in a group; it must be resolved alone. The satisfaction that comes from being with others can become addictive. We need others so that we do not have to confront inner emptiness. And, after a while, when being with others becomes a habit of avoiding ourselves, strife and conflict begins to show up in the group. We cannot feed off of the soul life of others without dire effects.

Starting, belonging, or trying to find community without developing the individual interior conditions necessary for community assures that we will fall unknowingly into the shadow of community. What are these capacities? One has already been mentioned – the capacity to be comfortable with ourselves, alone. This is a necessary condition because it prepares us to be receptive to the spiritual worlds and acknowledges that the spiritual worlds belong in the circuit of the 'us'. We learn other important lessons, too, from confronting ourselves alone. We learn that our idealisms concerning community are full of innocence and as long as they are we are unable to tolerate all the errors and mistakes that, of necessity, occur when people try to come together. We learn to develop an appreciation for our own limitations and those of others; we learn, by looking back over our lives, how we have harmed others and how we are capable of harming others. This sobering knowledge helps reduce the fantasy factor in coming into community and helps in the development of true imagination of what we are seeking. Self-knowledge is essential for community development, and along with that, the ability to be imaginative but objective, the capacity to experience forgiveness as the deepest of cosmic mysteries, and to seek and enter community only if we perceive that it is our destiny to do so, rather than a pressing interest that more than likely serves other soul needs that are being overlooked.

The heart, too, has to be prepared for community. We are best prepared in heart by learning to observe the world with loving care and developing the capacity to see what is there without inserting our desire into what we are observing. In groups you always find people who are over-gregarious, who have so much heart that they take over. Their desire is too zealous, and the group cannot form into community. Little do they know that they are projecting their desire onto the group and while the warmth engendered by their presence helps keep things flowing for a while, it cannot sustain the movement into community. As long as we have not confronted our own desires they eventually come out as likes and dislikes. Unexamined desires also result in a group gravitating toward personalities and the danger that the group sets up either a formal and informal leader. In a community, everyone takes on the role of leader according to the particular leadership qualities that are needed at any given moment.

When our desires are recognized they can be held in check without being suppressed. Desire then turns into interest in others, not for our sake, but for theirs. Then, a new quality of community arises; a healing community emerges. The interest of a community is never self-interest. Self-interests operate by imposing some ideal onto a group, making the group think that the ideal is what they are supposed to be seeking. A community inherently heals because each individual has the good of the other at heart. New forms of wisdom, love, and action characterize community life. Wisdom concerns bringing the spiritual worlds into the circuit of relationships. Love concerns interest in others. The action that is specific to community has little to do with what the community might be about. That is, the soul-spirit action of a community is what I want to describe rather than the aims and goals a community might have. For example, a 'community' might feel that it is a successful community if it fulfills its aim of helping the homeless, or whatever the community is oriented toward doing in the world. But the will aspect of the community has to do with what will forces help make the community be a true community rather than a group. The primary aspect of will here concerns the will to be completely human. Such a statement may sound trite, but I have in mind here the true nobility of being human, working out of the center of the heart, neither ruling over others by means of intellect nor by feelings of false togetherness. The will in community works to unite differences while not annihilating them. Without this aspect of the will to be completely human, hostility toward others arises and battles for power ensue. The purpose of community is not only to be able to do things together that would be very hard to do alone, it is more centrally about bringing more life into the world than could ever be done alone.

What does a community in action look like? First, the members of a community represent every spirit-soul quality imaginable. A community does not have a narrow outlook nor consist of people who all think the same, have the same background, or are selected because they seem to fit with what the community intends to accomplish. Such a diverse group of individuals, further, does not operate by consensus. Consensus often signifies domination by a few personalities or by an abstract idea. A community works by synthesis rather than by consensus. In a synthesis, everything anyone has to offer is taken into the work and given a place. In consensus, some view get left out, supposedly for the sake of the whole of the group. Community synthesis is most difficult and takes a great deal of time. Synthesis, however, is not to be taken literally as it is by many people trying to live community. The sense of synthesis is that everyone is truly heard and the imagination is affected by what everyone says.

A community in practice also works at all levels of soul life. Imagine three planes operating simultaneously – the ream of thoughts, the realm of the heart, and the realm of the soul. Conversation descends from the head to heart to soul and back, with a continual movement between the planes. Most people attempting community do so more or less confined to the head, so there is a lot of intellectual talk and emotional reaction. Or, in order to try and get to these other levels, various games are brought in to try to get people to feel closer. Talk can be action taking place on all three planes. When thinking alone dominates, an abyss is created between oneself and others. When feeling alone dominates, personal reaction takes over and there is the loss of objective understanding. When soul alone dominates the community turns into a therapy group.

Another aspect of community involves the question of what the central imagination the individuals are enacting. For example, most groups trying to become a community are trying to do something in the world for which there is little place, and thus such a group is in the imagination of warriors. What gets enacted as community changes considerably if the group imagination is one of service rather that fighting to get something accomplished. When the group imagination is one of being warriors, changes tend to get imposed onto the world. A community of service works by fostering inner listening for what needs work and listens to what is being asked for by those who need help. This kind of community does not assume it knows what people need.

A community also differs from an organization, though communities are organized. An organization, though, typically has a hierarchical structure or a variation thereof; communities do not. A hierarchical structure assures continuance because one piece can be taken out and replaced with another, as is done in corporations. Members of an organization are expendable. Efficiency of operation is a primary goal, and thus the heart and soul level is obscured. It is necessary that corporate organizations work in this manner in order to provide goods, products, and services in a consistent way. A community, however, functions in a more organic way. A community is more like a plant. It grows, blossoms, and then often goes dormant for a while, coming back when needed. Community does not seek self-perpetuation and in relinquishing that desire has more openness, vitality, energy, and spontaneity. It is able to continually re-invent itself. The elements of community can fructify an organization, but the elements of organization tend to deaden community.

When a community forms, you can tell that something in addition to the members are bringing life. It is as if an angel comes a guides the work of community. It is the angel that makes what we do more than individuals working together and more than group work. The ultimate purpose of community is to bring what we do into harmony with the spiritual worlds, to make a new Heaven and a new Earth.

Epilogue to Letter III – Learning Through Soul

For adults, a great part of our continuing to learn throughout life takes place through reading. In this chapter the magical character of reading was addressed. I want to pursue that magic further here, pointing to some methods through which we can enter into the magical world of books in a such a manner that the soul level opens up for us. I am continually amazed how often my writing is read from a spectator perspective by others and I have come to understand that speaking of soul does not guarantee that what is said will be met with soul. Something written in soul read as if it were information, results in great confusion. When something is written from soul but read as if it were any other kind of text, the response tends to be that the writing is perceived as difficult. It is not; quite the contrary, it is immediate and descriptive. We have to re-learn how to read from soul.

There are several traditions of soul reading, the aim of which is to move away from reading only for information and concepts and instead letting the words become living speaking that impress themselves into the life of the soul. There is the great monastic tradition of *Lexio Divina*. While this form of reading was confined to sacred texts in the monastic tradition, we can learn much from it. In this tradition, reading is a supreme act of *listening*. The words of a text, then, cannot be glossed over, read only for their informational content. Language itself consists of two simultaneous forms happening at the same time. La Lingua, and La Parole, is the way the French linguists speak of these two simultaneous forms. La Lingua concerns the grammatical structure of the language and its content. La Parole concerns the living word. In the tradition of Lexio Divina, the attempt in reading is to hear the living word, as if someone were speaking; and, in fact, someone is – the author, the tradition, maybe even the spiritual beings of the word. To get at this level of reading, it is helpful to speak passages the book you are reading aloud. Feel the texture, the qualities of the words. Slow down your reading. Slow down your reading. Slow down your reading. The soul moves slowly; it loves to move this way, making imaginations of what the words are saying. When you read, try to be in the imagination of being read-to. Imagine what it was like to hear stories when you were a child. Approach any text *as if* it were a story. Get interested in the words…not just hearing through the words into the concepts. Read with your whole body, not just with your eyes.

There is the other great tradition of reading that comes from the Medieval world. This tradition is also centered in the spiritual tradition, the reading of sacred texts. However, this tradition was extended by Dante into the writing and reading of all texts. Every text can be simultaneously read at four levels: the literal level, the moral level, the allegorical level and the anagogical level.

Without going into these levels in detail, notice that the first level is the literal level. The literal level is the words as they present themselves. You have to start at this level. You have to get what is said. Thus, always read a text through for an initial understanding.

Example of the four levels:

If a biblical text says: "Israel went out of Egypt"

1) The literal level --- the Jewish people left Egypt

2) The moral level – This phrase refers to the conversion of a soul from a sinful life.

3) The allegorical level – The text is an allegory speaking of redemption through Christian conversion.

4) The anagogical level – Anagogical means "mystical". The text at this level is speaking of the movement of a life from temporal to eternal states of being.

It is not necessary, nor recommended that you 'analyze' the levels of a text. It is important to try to hear the polyphony of language; to hear that many things are being said in a text, and try to take them all in. The literal level is important, but most people get completely stuck, caught at the literal level when reading a non-fiction text. This difficulty stems from years of education in which the reading was more or less confined to text books, the worst possible kind of reading. And the difficulty stems from education in which literalism is encouraged. If, as a student, you saw through the literal to other levels of a text, you most likely received a bad grade for your effort and genius.

Hearing the levels beyond the literal when reading does not happen as an intellectual act. We hear the text resonating, as if expanding and deepening. We feel it affecting other parts of our being than our intellect and emotions. We feel that we have entered into a mystery, and we feel new worlds opening to us that we are not able to get to on our own. These openings are the spiritual gifts of reading. When something is written in wonder and love, these spiritual acts become the medium through which the words transport us, not out of the world, but to the worlds within the world. And, we become more interiorly active, not less. Fiction, particularly fantasy fiction, takes us into other worlds and completely supports us there so that we do not have to do anything other than enjoy those worlds. But, then, once reading is completed, we fall completely back into the mundane. A multi-leveled, polyphonic text requires concentration, but your soul is being changed through such concentration. New capacities are developing, so that gradually the text opens to the wider world and we see and live differently.

Soul Reading is a particular kind of reading in which, through the literal level one tries to hear, or to live in the listening question: "What is being said to the soul in this speaking"? In order to read in this way, it is necessary to pause a lot in your reading. In the pauses, let what you just read sink down from the region of the head into the region of the heart. Then, listen within and try to be aware of the response you are hearing from within region of the heart. Try, though, to hear, in an inner way, the soul's repeating of what was read, of what was understood mentally when you read the text.

A third imagination of soul reading comes from the practice of hermeneutics. Hermeneutics is the philosophy …and the art of interpretation. Interpretation here, however, does not mean saying what you think something means…making an interpretation. The word "hermeneutics" is based in and is itself saying that reading is the art devised and living in the soul as the gift of Hermes. Hermes…herme..neutics. The word means a "carrying across". Hermes is the messenger. He carries "between" the gods and the mortals. Soul reading is getting into the between, feeling the region in the text that is holy and that is at the same time completely human. Hearing the text in this way, as a kind of message from the spiritual worlds, clothed in the language of the human world. The main work of soul reading is to refrain from restricting our reading a) "This is what I got out of the reading." b) " This is what the author means." c) "Lets discuss the reading together." Try instead to re-say what the reading says, speaking now from the viewpoint of the soul. If, for example, a text says: "The soul resonates" – what does the soul hear in these words? How can you say what you hear the soul saying in these words? Take a text as a mystery --- as something to enter into more and more deeply, not as something to master and take the living blood out of so you can take the informational knowledge and pack it away somewhere. At the same time, respect, respect, the literal level of any text. If you do not 'get' it at the literal level, the soul level of hearing will always be erroneous.

Reading non-fiction imaginatively has an additional inherent difficulty, which is the narrative character of such writing. I have had to use the narrative form to embody soul. Narration, however, inherently distances us from the reality we are trying to enter. Thus, a particular act of reading becomes necessary in order to hear soul resonance within narrative writing. We have to enter into the silence surrounding the writing.

One of the residences of silence is in the intervals of our speaking. Narration, speaking about our experience rather than from within our experience, covers over this most natural region of silence. Not only does narrative-speech run one word into another, one sentence into another, eliminating the sense of the interval, this same pattern installs itself into our inner life. When we first go inward all we find is an endless narrative stream of ourselves talking to ourselves about things and experiences. Even our inner presence to images and feelings are mediated by this same narrator, now serving as a kind of inner docent to the galleries and museums of the mind. We have no genuine inner life if it is all filled with everyday content all of the time. A very first entry into silence concerns developing an appreciation for the pause, for the stumbling, for the inarticulate, for the gaps in our speaking, which narrative writing hides and pretends as if they were not there.

The intervals of speech, those interesting pauses between words, set silence into motion. Silence is certainly not the empty space between the words, not a mere void. When I say a word or a few words, and then pause, not an affected pause, but merely the pause that tries to listen, then the words said set up a rhythm with the silence, a rhythm within which the palpable substance of silence can be felt. In addition, the wave of silence draws to it the next words to be said, and the rhythm of those words, even before said, also enter into the silence as an aspect of its motion. When we read a narrative work, it is helpful to do so by learning to attend to the great silence surrounding each sentence, each paragraph, each chapter, the whole of the book.

You can get to the doorway of silence by the following meditation: close your eyes. Say to yourself a phrase, letting pauses enter into the phrase or sentence. Repeat the phrase or sentence varying the pause between words, like this:

I	enter	the	silence

Or

I	enter	the	silence

Or

I	enter	the	silence

This kind of little word meditation holds secrets. While silence is not something we do but rather a world we enter, we cannot neglect the importance of our part in orienting toward this world. A meditative sentence, such as the one above, sets up a current of silence. However, silence must already be there for this current to take effect. We attract silence to us by a kind of anticipatory act; it gathers through our anticipation of it. In order to enter this meditative sentence, we have to already be oriented toward silence. In terms of the meditative sentence, even before we speak the sentence in an inner way, the sentence already has a silence before it and a silence after it. That is, the sentence is already surrounded by silence when we enter it. If we incline toward this silence before speaking, the silence spreads throughout whatever we read and is evident as the rhythm of speech. Rhythm is the way that silence pervades the spoken word.

Taking passages of a book and reading them aloud attunes us to the silence within which the soul of reading resides. Not all books, of course, lend themselves to this kind of inner work, nor are all books worth such an effort. If a writing has only one level, you will find that this meditative approach to reading does not open anything up because there is nothing to be opened up. But, original writing, not secondary writing, is almost always worth this effort.

Epilogue to Letter IV – Disease

In our age, a false flight from the pain of every sort of illness, nurtured by the strictly modern fantasy that a technical approach to medicine can restore health, has effectively all but eliminated the imagination of illness as bearing value. Even alternative medicine, which has come to prominence in the past five years, is caught in the imagination of health as the norm and illness a deviation from this norm. When the prestigious New England Journal of Medicine reported the results of a telephone survey of 1539 American adults concerning the use of unconventional medical therapy, doctors of conventional medicine were alarmed to learn that 34% of those surveyed had used at least one form of unconventional treatment in the last year. The Journal reluctantly concluded that unconventional medicine has an enormous presence in the U.S. health care system. Some 87 million men and women were willing to pay $10.3 billion out of their own pockets for a kinder medicine. Nonetheless, holistic, complementary, empiric and natural medicines, like conventional medicine, value health and look upon illness as evil.

Health belongs to an intractable polarity, that of health-illness. From this point of view, there can be health only when there is also illness. When we pursue health with the imagination that illness opposes rather than complements it, the significance of illness has no place. Simply stated, illness represents one of the primary ways in which the forgotten, sleeping soul awakens itself by falling into body. This is the view taken by Alfred Ziegler in his wonderful book, **Archetypal Medicine.** The aim of archetypal medicine does not consist of merely ridding the body of pain, suffering, and disease, but rather to take advantage of this bestirring of soul, alleviating physical suffering where possible by loosening the bonds of soul from a too strong immersion in body, without however obliterating individual presence to soul life. Illness can be a call to soul, and eliminating it rather than listening to it obliterates the presence of soul.

Approaching disease through soul awareness differs from a psychology of illness, or psychosomatic medicine as typically practiced, and differs even from an analytic psychology of illness and disease. The craft can be characterized as proceeding by way of archetypal reflection, which, however, does not limit itself to the psyche. Instead, it applies archetypal reflection to the whole person, not just to the psychic realm.

Archetypal reflection belongs belonging to Sophia, or 'wisdom' rather than to logos, or intelligence. Wisdom as a mode of knowing works with polarities without splitting them apart; it knows from within, by communion, is filled with contradictions that do not seek after resolution, contemplates rather than analyzes, functions through the entire body, not just the head, replaces insight with empathy, seriousness with drama, causal logic with imagery. In this mode of knowing under the aegis of Sophia, the human being suffers, not because of a deviation from health, but because suffering belongs to the nature of the unavoidable conflicts entailed in intimate participation with the ever-changing and contradictory nature of the spiritual, cosmic, archetypal, and natural worlds. Changeableness and mutability are here seen to be the essence of the human reality as well as the feminine divine reality of Wisdom or the World Soul which is its prototype.

It might be fruitful to contemplate some of the differences between archetypal reflection on our illness and not only conventional medicine but also some of the alternative medicines to amplify how working with Wisdom contrasts with logic. Conventional medicine views disease through the logic of entities. The nature of these disease entities varies considerably, from the invasion of the body by a bacteria or a virus to an alteration of genes to some factor or other which inhibits the normal functioning of one or more organs. The approach is completely materialistic, relying on the scientific model of cause and effect and treatment that is oriented toward eliminating the cause; and it operates heroically.

Traditional Chinese medicine, which includes acupuncture, acupressure and Chinese herbalism shares some aspects with archetypal view, but also differs in significant respects. Chinese medicine share with archetypal reflection the view that the human organism participates in the life of the cosmos. This participation concentrates on the bodily network of subtle energy channels and energy circulatory patterns which link the human body to energy patterns of the solar system and the stars. Chinese medicine constitutes the empiric aspect of Taoism, a vast philosophical view interrelating energy, consciousness, the body, landscape and cosmos. These interrelationships are held in balance through "Three Treasures" - jing, chi, and shen, or physical substance, life energy, and spirit. The dynamic relation of these three forces are "read" by the practitioner by the feeling of pulses and the signature of an illness determined by the strength or weakness of a pulse. Acupuncture points stimulate or suppress the flow of energy to bring about balance in the system. Illness in this system means blockage of energy and illness has no significance in itself.

Homeopathy founds its understanding of the disease process on what Samuel Hahnemann, the founder of this form of medicine, called the dynamis. The dynamis is a life-giving vital energy that rules and animates the organism. Homeopathic remedies stimulate the dynamis to restore bodily harmony. The remedies, highly diluted plant, animal, and mineral substances, work as healing agents based upon an imagination of similarity: the practitioner discerns the key correspondences between a patient's complex symptom picture and the subtle energies of remedies, utilizing the remedies based on similarity between the symptom picture and the remedy. "Like cures like," says homeopathy. Homeopathy does rely on a certain valuing of illness, insofar as the "illness" of the remedies effects the cure. However, neither the practitioner nor the patient undergoing this treatment enter into illness as a source of value.

Chiropractic therapy, probably the most widely accepted of alternative medicines, is based upon an imagination of the correct alignment of the 24 spinal vertebrae, which is seen as crucial to nervous system function and thus to overall health because the nervous system is said to control and coordinate all internal organs and bodily functions. Daniel David Palmer, the founder of chiropractic therapy, held that structure governs function. If the structure is displaced, illness follows. Treatment consists of physical manipulation to bring the vertebrae into alignment. What misalignment may be saying does not come under consideration.

Herbalism as practiced today is based upon an allopathic model of illness, much the same as conventional medicine. Herbal preparations are selected to oppose and act against existing physical symptoms. The more ancient view of herbalism related the action of herbs on the human organism to the influences of the stars and planets. Some herbs are ruled by the Sun and are good for warming and drying. An herb ruled by Saturn would be good for structure. The correspondences between herbs and the starry worlds, however, is today often not incorporated into the practice. In the West, the seventeenth century compiler of herbology, Nicholas Culpeper, held that correspondences are the key to herbology. He stated: "physic without astrology is like a lamp without oil." Practitioners today may know about the correspondences but do not work out of a deep imagination of the cosmos.

A wide range of alternative medicines focus on working in non-physical domains of the human being. Flower Essence therapy, first developed by Edward Bach, M.D. in the 1930s employs subtle tinctures made from specific blossoming flowers which are said to work on the "soul body" and bring emotional and psychological life into balance. Various forms of Therapeutic Touch work by massaging not the physical body, but the human energy field at a distance of several inches from the body. These forms of treatment also often include having the patient engage in creative visualization, the reporting of images that come while subtle body manipulation is being carried out, and sometimes actively working with these images in active imagination. Similarly, some practitioners work with chakra visualizations. The chakras are subtle energy matrices arranged along the spine which are said to be something like transducers from cosmic energies to human energies. In illness, some of these chakras are said to be blocked or out of balance in relation to each other. Illness is never looked into for what it shows concerning the situation of the soul. New age alternative medicine colludes with conventional medicine without knowing it; the sweetly smiling cosmic hero stands in the camp of the raging warrior.

Conventional medicine and all of the forms of alternative medicine follow a path of medical pragmatism. Whatever works is right. And, all of these practices do work, some of them better for one person, others for another. They all take health as the norm, viewing illness as something gone wrong, and they all work from logic rather than wisdom. Some of the alternative therapies, for example, Chinese medicine, have wisdom as a basis, but wisdom is converted into logic. Individual practitioners may rely more on wisdom and base their practice more on intuition than following the logical rules of the system, but none of the alternative medicines see value in illness and in this respect hold hands with conventional medicine. In the sketch given above, one also notices a propensity to rely upon a very abstract word - energy. I suggest that the archetypal element of these forms of healing hides within that word which has great explanatory power but actually says nothing concerning what is actually happening.

When nature is evoked as the guiding principle of medicine, as often happens in alternative medicine, the underlying imagination of nature appears highly romanticized. Nature's ways are best, whole, healthy, life-giving, life-restoring. And so are the 'energies' of the cosmos. Dark nature is never considered. One does not have to observe nature very carefully, however, to see that She always operates in polarities of life-death. Some examples. Spotted hyenas typically bear twins which are well developed at birth, completely furred, teeth fully developed. Within minutes of birth one of the cubs attacks its twin, killing the other. This deadly conflict is the norm, having nothing to do with food shortages. The female cub usually wins this murderous battle, maintaining female dominance among hyenas. The Amazon's vast armies of ants produces 200,000 tons of formic acid a year, spraying this into the air as part of their communication and defense system. This acid, released into the air makes the rain mildly acid and promotes decay, that is, the death process. Every few years in Norwway, there are population explosions of lemmings. Masses of lemmings descend from the mountains and invade forests and pastures in a suicidal march to the sea. In their march, when progress is blocked by a lake, river, cliffs, the accumulation of lemmings drastically increases and they turn mean. They fight, bite, and kill each other. Assault, battery, child abuse, murder, infanticide and suicide then characterize their behavior. Antarctic penguins, when they are very young, gather in large numbers on the edge of the ice, readying to take their first plunge into the sea. They have only one enemy, leopard seals, who hang around beneath the ice floe, waiting for penguin lunch. The large gathering of penguins watch as one jumps into the water. If the courageous swimmer is eaten, the rest backtrack, noses in the air, as if nothing happened. They then wait for another to take the plunge, until finally one does not disappear forever but bobs up, inviting the rest in.

Everywhere in nature, from plants to insects to birds and animals we find this polarity of life-death. This is more the imagination of nature that guides archetypal reflection on illness, one in which illness and death are integral to each other. Such an understanding of nature helps us to see that both conventional and alternative medicine are not merely guided by a deep-seated fantasy of health as good and illness as bad, but underlying such a false division can be found the fantasy of immortality. Medicine works under the pretence that we really should not have to die, and death is an unfortunate glitch in an otherwise bountiful, good universe.

Health seems to be something literal, substantive, to be brought about by equally substantive things such as counting calories, keeping cholesterol at a certain level, running a certain number of miles a day. But, in fact, health as a thing and the things that bring it about are conceptual ideas that have become literalized. What seems to be so concrete turns out to be highly abstract, having little to do with the body that smells, aches, gurgles, snores, wheezes, farts, excretes and pees, becomes excited, aroused, sometimes feels like lead, sometimes like fire, sometimes not felt at all.

When we actually look at the body in all its concreteness, it becomes apparent that health must be a decidedly puritanical notion. Are we not to be thankful to illness for bringing back smelly breath, festering wounds, belching and bloating, coughing, burning and freezing, saving us from bodily fundamentalism? Here at least imagination begins to have a place. The ill person becomes forced into imagination, forced into the full actuality of the body. A dull ache pounds in the stomach, becomes sharp like a knife during the day, moves from one region to another, disappears for a while after lunch, becomes stronger after drinking wine, produces sleeplessness into the early morning hours, followed by intense dreams of being forced into a cave by a dragon. Suddenly, even the most literal-minded becomes a story-teller, image-maker, poet, sometimes even a genius. Until the diagnosis comes. It turns out to be an ulcer - and then the imagination stops, globed up with Kaopectate. Be grateful for the stirring of soul and utilize soul reflection and imaginative language as the instrument through which somatization can be relieved while imagination retained.

If one tries to begin to work with one's own illnesses in an archetypal way, which may be necessary, given that the practitioners of this art are almost unheard of, it may at first be like entering a dark forest, where shadows constantly pop up as seeming realities. The main shadow to be alert to consists of the tricky inversion of this way of working back into the model of health. Recently, I was speaking with someone who for months had been nauseous, felt pain in the stomach, was weak, and continually losing weight. Conventional medicine could find nothing. The doctors suspected a blockage in the stomach. Another physician suspected a ruptured appendix which however closed itself in some peculiar way. A medical intuitive told her that her inner organs were all enlarged, like obesity introverted. A Jungian told her that hearing the symptoms brought to mind a twisted telephone cord and that what was needed was silence, relaxation, and unwinding. Everyone imposing their subjective imaginings. Notice, however, that in each instance the fantasy of health was operating. Even the Jungian, also an astrologer, who gave the additional diagnosis that this person was suffering from a Virgo attack, was being led by the fantasy of health. The twisted telephone cord can also be seen as the body's necessity for knotting, for complexity, twistedness, entanglement, confusion in communication. Two suggestions arise from this little story. First, beware of the imposition of images, and second, beware of the ever-lurking one-sidedness of health. Rather than concocting images of our condition, it is far better to wait for them to come in their own way.

It takes years to learn a language, and even longer to shift attitudes toward health and illness; longer yet to move from logos to Sophianic imagination. I am not suggesting just another interesting way to work with illness, but rather am speaking of the path of illness. We are impatient with our illnesses, caught in the general speeding up of time characterizing this culture. Archetypal time differs considerably from the clock time by which we order our days. I do not think archetypal imagination takes us into the timeless but rather into the quality of time that can be called duration. The day offers itself as different ratios between duration and tempo. In the present world, duration is fast being lost and tempo accelerates into repetition, pace, and now instantaneousness. Duration has to do with the soul qualities of time, and as long as duration endures there is not the abstraction of time, but the immediate experience of multiple times - work time, play time, love time, prayer time, illness time and many more. Duration dominates the place of the Grand Canyon. Tempo dominates the corporate office. If I walk down the street in New York City, tempo rules. If I go into Central Park, I enter another time where duration enters more strongly. And even within Central Park, the duration of one place differs from that of another - the time of the gardens is different from that of the jogging path. And when I step back onto the street, time again changes. The idea of health chains us evermore to tempo, for the economy of heath care systems, managed care, is to shorten the time of illness in order, not only to cut costs, but to assure that we do not get out of step with the fast paced tempo of daily life. Illness, however, has its own time and timing, which belongs much more to duration than tempo. Recovery time, sick time, grieving time, mourning time, can also be seen as the body's work to heal the disease of measured time, time's one-sidedness.

Epilogue to Letter V – Economics and Money

We who are interested in matters of the soul and how soul can find expression in the world cannot pretend to invent a new economics. Even if it were possible to do so, which would not be particularly difficult, it would not be helpful since no one would listen. We have to find the ways to infiltrate our present economic system and our present imagination of money with a new imagination. We can do this daily, with the money that we have and work with, save and spend, earn and lose. We can infiltrate money with soul. Indeed, this may well be the task we are presented with rather than complaining and watching what is happening to the world through the excesses of greed spawned by an imagination of money founded in fear. We have to try to turn that from the inside rather than expecting that perhaps, after the complete collapse of our current imagination of money and wealth and poverty, a new a better imagination will arise. It will not and cannot unless the kind of consciousness involved in thinking and imagining money transforms into a more spiritual imagination.

For those of us who are interested in soul and spirit, and work to find ways to live in harmony with soul and spirit, money is typically left out of the work. It is kept outside, used to finance our interests in these matters, but not itself subject to inner transformation. In the eleven years of the work of the School of Spiritual Psychology it has become increasingly clear that this sleepiness to money will bring death to soul and spirit endeavors in the world in not too long of a time. People more and more have no time for these endeavors because they have to work too hard for their money and have little or no time for matters of the soul, nor do they have money for what seems to be something that is not 'necessary' to their living.

Modern economics operates out of two central premises. The first is that there is no connection between the earthly worlds and the spiritual worlds. This premise, the premise of strict materialism, results in something quite fascinating --- it is not at all surprising that modern economics begins with a sense of scarcity. It begins with a deep inner feeling of absence, of want, of need, of lack. How could it be otherwise? The sense of scarcity does not rightly reflect reality, the fullness of reality; rather, this first premise reflects only the limitations of the world-view chosen as the basis of a particular sort of economics. The view of scarcity is actually the fear resulting from cutting ourselves off from the gods. There is no scarcity if the divine worlds are taken into account in the forming of an economic world-view. The scarcity that is at the heart of modern economics is not founded on a scarcity of things or resources; it is founded upon the inner feeling of lack due to having expunged the divine worlds. In other words, if there were a sacred economy, there would never be a feeling of lack. Saying this, however, I am not opting to have a world view of abundance as the foundation of economics. If we opt for abundance we are still within the polarity of scarcity-abundance. Behind the imagination of abundance there always lurks the imagination of scarcity. We have to see that something else operates in economics.

A second necessary premise follows from starting with the assumption that material reality alone is the basis of economy and the divine worlds are excluded. Instead of developing an imagination of the Whole, we are confined to an imagination of earth as finite and consisting of parts. Everything, including economics is thus viewed in terms of cause and effect and it is thus imagined that economy can be manipulated by knowing the causes of things like inflation and depression and making adjustments based on the knowledge of those causes. Manipulating interest rates is an example of treating economy as if it were a complex, closed system of cause and effects.

A third aspect of economics follows from these two central premises. What these premises inspire in the soul are fear and greed. Fear of their being limitations on what is available, and greed as the way to build security against this primordial fear. But since the insecurity is not based in the fear of not having enough but in the fear resulting from cutting economy off from the gods, no amount of having can ease the insecurity.

You may say that you certainly do not hold to these premises. I am not speaking of individuals. I am speaking of the system of economics. Those individuals who do not hold to these premises live a constant contradiction, holding on to their soul in spite of an economic system that urges us to forget anything like soul life.

The result of modern economics is that we are all forced to privatize the realms of soul and spirit. These realms are not allowed to circulate in the world. What are allowed to circulate are wants. "I want" and "I need" are the extent of the psychology inherent in modern economics. Desires, cut off from the divine worlds are insatiable. Fulfilling unlimited desires requires wealth and power. Wealth and power used to take from others. Economics as war. The making of a society of war of each against all, everyone struggling for gain or self-preservation. Self-interest is at the center of modern economics.

As long as economy does not become everything, we can individually hold to a completely different world-view than modern economics and watch in utter disgust and amazement at what is happening in the world. The wars; the greed for oil; the greed for money; lying; politics; the devastation of life of Earth – of water, land, trees, air, and all She has to offer.

And we can join in one work or another to stand against this devastation. However, we have no choice but to do so while being forced to use the money that expresses everything that we do not believe in. A most interesting situation. We stand by and have to watch the laws of greed work – greed breed acquisition. If you have an economy of scarcity and greed you have to live by the rules of scarcity and greed. Why do we not see this is necessarily the case?

The vast majority of people do not individually believe in the assumptions of the modern economic system. Why don't we revolt and demand a soul economy? Well, because, in a certain sense the soul, or a certain version of it, is automatically taken into account by the medium of modern economy, money. Since all that constitutes soul is taken out of economics and therefore out of money --- imagination, memory, myth, depth, fantasy, art, poetry, the gods ---- money becomes the projection place for the life of the soul and we thus place all kind of imaginations onto money which do not belong with money itself. Money is power, wealth, freedom, energy, tightness, generosity, sensuality, show, perversion….but not actually. We project the forgotten soul onto money and thus it becomes for us something having the qualities of the divine that money actually excludes. This bit of psychology tells us why we can on the one hand clearly see the materialistic assumptions of economics and see that these premises are totally ridiculous and nonetheless abide by and live within what we do not believe in for one moment --- quite contentedly, except for the knowing anxiety that says that this should not be this way.

It might seem that because money is the screen for projecting all our soul life that money is in fact equal to soul. James Hillman, for examples, thinks so. I do not think that projection of fantasy life constitutes money as soul. The soul of the world is left out with the result that the soul life connected with money is completely self-absorbed soul. Money is intended to be the medium, the carrier of the imagination of the economic realm. If the economic realm is imagined in such a way that there is an opening to the spiritual worlds, then money carries an imagination as having to do with the circulation between the earthly and the heavenly worlds. Money that is not backed by such an imagination is a kind of blank screen for psychic projections that are limited to our desires and fears only.

There is a further interesting difficulty in relation to soul and economy. The origins of money are sacred. Money in the Western world originates as a the receiving of coins at sacrificial ritual to the goddess. Thus, there is a deep memory in humanity that connects money with the sacred realms. This unconscious memory still makes it difficult to see through the materialistic premises of modern economics. We let those premises stand, in part because there is still a sacred feeling to money, even though we know that this is not so. Our money, though, depicts in the pictures and words it carries that there is a connection between money and the sacred realms. Our money says, "In God we trust." Money lies.

An exercise is helpful in bringing to light the way in which money has become the screen for the projection of fantasies. Think of something that you really want to buy, something even that you think that you need badly or must have. Then, write down, without thinking, a list of twenty things that come to mind when you imagine the thing that you desire. This list is all the fantasies that surround the thing you think you need. Once you become aware of the investment of fantasy in the things you think you need, what happens to the desire for that thing?

To develop towards a whole soul economy, the first thing we need to recognize is how economy devoid of soul corrupts. It invites us to use people, step on people to get ahead, rewards ruthlessness, and lose conscience.

An economics of the Whole begins with the assumption of **creativity** rather than scarcity. Creativity is not of our doing. We receive it and pass it on in the world. It requires that we come into inner connection with the soul and spirit worlds. Through genuine creativity, not cleverness, we enter into an open system. In an open system, new ideas come, many possibilities appear, we are not fixed. If you do not feel this way in relation to money, then you are trapped by the closed system..

In an open system, we are open to reality that is beyond us. Openness expands life. We are able to face the uncertain and more importantly, to overcome our own resistance to change. The pressing question is: is it possible to work within an economy that is a closed system and with money that has no connection with the divine worlds in such a way that it is as if we are in an open system? There are only three choices:

a. Live within the present closed system as it is, watching how the soul and spiritual dimensions of our lives become more and more difficult to maintain because of the kinds of demands made by this system of economy.

b. Wait for this closed system of economics to go completely out of control resulting in a time of devastation and depression, hoping that a new system will be more open.

c. Try to work within the present economic system as if it were an open system and see what happens with us individually. We can do this by working with money in different ways --- one such different way is suggested below. We need to recognize, though, that this third alternative, the one followed here, will make an immediate difference in the way you experience money, but it will not immediately have any effect in the larger world. The intention is to let this spiritual current in relation to economy and money affect our souls and work then from the inside outward.

There has to be something that is pan-economic for economy to have a connection, even if remote, to the spiritual worlds. Both wheat and gold served this purpose for a long time. They were a still like the goddess and linked to the goddess. And, if you think of the qualities of wheat and gold, you can see how this is so. Take gold, for example. When gold is used – not possessed, is released into the economy it generated circulation; and it was removed to slow circulation down. It was the balancer in economy. But it could not itself be part of the economy. It was the basis of economy. This is a picture of substituting a substance for a god or goddess. And for a long time, it was seen that such a substance must bear a similarity to the divine.

Gold is a remarkable substance. Gold is present everywhere on earth – in the seas, in the highest strata of the atmosphere and in the earth itself on every continent. It exists as the finest dust and in dense nuggets. Gold has a special infinity to light, radiating it rather than retaining it. It is capable of transformation into the thinnest of gold leaf. On the other hand, it is the heaviest substance known. It is almost twice the weight of lead. (The specific gravity of lead is 11.6; of gold, 19.3). It does not oxidize or combine with any other substance. It remains unto itself. It is the most extendable substance in the world – one gram of gold can be extended into a thread nearly two kilometers long. By its very nature gold mediates between infinite expansion and strong cohesion. It is extraordinarily stable, able to pass back and forth between extremes. It is the substance that is as close on earth as we can get to something of permanent value. That is why it was chosen to be the basis of economy. It cannot be destroyed. Wheat, incidentally, has some of these same qualities.

As a pan-economic foundation for economy, wheat also has interesting properties. It carries ancient memories of the goddess. Two properties make it as immutable and stable as gold. First, it has been observed that good and bad harvests balance each other out over long periods of time, so that it is possible to speak of an average constant harvest. This constant makes it possible to hold grain resources in such a manner that represents a constant in economic life. Second, the grains at the center of the ear of wheat have a uniformity of size and weight. This is the second constant. Then, for many ages, wheat was the background staple of people.

We have to realize that when gold and wheat become of the economy, that is, become substances used as commodities to be bought and sold, then there is no longer a constant to rely on. With the abandonment of the gold standard, economy becomes a pure idea. I mean that there is no standard. Economics is freed from physical substance.

Seeing something of the evolution of money helps us realize that we need some meta-economic backing for money. Seeing that money emancipated from being backed by any substance, we have to leave behind any notion of a meta-economic substance. There have been groups who have tried to introduce such a substance. These groups were successful for the most part, but were shut down by legislative means. For example, a group in Exeter, New Hampshire. Under the leadership of an economist, Ralph Borsodi, a local money was introduced called 'constants.' This ran from June 1972 until January 1974. The Constant was based on a basket of 30 of the world's most important and valuable commodities and worked through checking accounts in a local bank. The scheme ended because of fear that it was an infringement of security insurance laws.

Where we are led, though, is to see that *we need a meta-economic idea* to stand as the ground of economy and thus of money. That the history of money is the history of abstraction is not in itself wrong. The difficulty is that we have lost a background imagination of money. This we can work on individually and see if it changes our own individual relationship to and imagination of money. Such an idea answers the question: Given that money is now everything and anything, a blank slate for our unconscious projections, it is up to each individual to consciously make a very clear choice of what backs the money you have and use, spend and save. Choosing an individual meta-economic idea means that if you live your economic life in relation to this idea you will not be subject to advertising which draws out our unconscious fantasies and attaches them to their products to buy. Nor will you be subject to all the political propaganda surrounding money and the economy, the stock market, investments, insurance, banks.

Your meta-economic idea must be a ***sacred idea***, not something that you personally make up because it suits your needs. This requirement is based on our exploration of the need for an open rather than a closed economic system and on the images of the origins and purpose of money. Your meta-economic idea must also be quite practical and quite specific. It cannot be a general 'feel-good' idea. It is necessary to be able to specify exactly how the idea works.

For example, the Eight Beatitudes form a wonderful meta-economic idea that can change our ongoing relation with money. "Blessed are the poor in spirit, for theirs is the kingdom of heaven." This beatitude invites us to feel our poverty as a spiritual state, as always looking for spirit. It invites us to realize that inner emptiness is a necessity in order to feel the presence of the spiritual worlds. It says that if we fill up inner emptiness we cannot feel the presence of the spiritual worlds. And, in a practical way, this beatitude invites us to get and use money in ways that do not cover our inner emptiness. It does not say you have to literally be poor, but that you have to stay awake to inner emptiness in order to be in connection with the spiritual worlds. The other beatitudes can be similarly worked with in this imagination of a sacred meta-economic idea. There are many other sacred backgrounds that can be individually chosen and worked with to change the sense of money and economics in daily use.

Epilogue to Letter VI – Technology

A particularly important relationship exists between technology and work. We live in a peculiar time with respect to the question of work; while there seems to be fewer and fewer jobs available, at the same time there is more work to be done in the world than ever before. If you look in the Oxford English Dictionary, a striking difference between the words - work and job - is immediately apparent. Work is something whole; it refers not only to the act of doing something, it also refers to the product of what is done, such as a work of art, or a work of architecture; the word, work, also carries a moral connotation, such as good works. While one can also do a good job, that simply means that the specialized operation was carried out in such a way that it was brought to successful completion. The word job is defined as a part or a piece of a work, particularly a part that is done as one's specialization or profession. We see immediately that a job can quite easily lose its connection with work; one can easily get lost in the specificity of what one is doing so that it loses imaginative connection with the whole to which it rightly belongs. In our time, work has been taken over into the realm of technology. It is no surprise, then, that electronic technology has completed altered the way we do our jobs. In some cases, electronic technology has completely changed the face of time honored professions. For example, architecture is now a technical discipline rather than the art it once was. Very few people go through architecture school these days leaning to draw by hand. It is all done by computer, with little understanding how this technology is far more than a substitute for a pencil. It has completely mechanized buildings in their appearance and function. Electronic technology is also rapidly changing medicine, business, education. Every kind of work is turning into a technical job. The difficulty here is that the deeper meaning of these changes goes unrecognized.

Very few people today feel that they are involved in a work. Why is this the case? In order to experience being involved in a work, it is necessary to be united with life, not someone else's life. Work concerns the acts that one does in the world that are united with one's life. A job concerns the acts that we do that require that we becomes forgetful of our own life and labor that serves someone else's interests - whether this be an individual, a business, or a large corporation. This distinction can quite readily become blurred. It is not likely that having a job at the local Burger King is an expression of doing something in the world that brings the fullness of one's life into the world. However, having a job at the top local law firm does not necessarily fully express one's life in the world either. The distinction becomes blurred when one's talents and abilities are called upon for a task, but these talents and abilities are harnessed to accomplish what someone else wants in the world rather than what is demanded by your life. A job originates from and intensifies a one-sidedness that often requires relinquishing the true creativeness that characterizes spirit and the true depth of individuality that characterizes soul. Receiving a salary is the compensation for forgetting who you are. Work, on the other hand, comes from and intensifies the labor involved in becoming a complete human being. Even more, work impresses itself onto the world, leaving the mark of the individual soul in the world. Technical jobs also leave a mark on the world, not just in terms of what has been accomplished, but an alteration of the World-Spirit. Rudolf Steiner has spoken of these world changes in his work, **The Karma of Vocation**. The most serious questions concerning technology are how technology alters the presence of the spirit in the world, and how, increasingly, because of electronic technology it is becoming more and more difficult to experience spiritual qualities in the world.

Look, for example at what happens when stones are made into a house. The stones are taken from a quarry; then they are shaped by a machine, and then they are laid in place by a builder according to a plan. What is happening in this process is that the human spirit is being joined with the raw material. When a new machine is made, in a similar way, the human spirit is joined with the machine; it is there in the machine. It is there in an objective manner. Now the house will eventually wear away, and so will the machine. However, and this may be somewhat difficult to imagine, but Steiner says that the atoms which compose the machine have been changed from the atoms of the metal or other material from which the machine is made because they have been united with the human spirit. While the machine may be thrown away and eventually disintegrates, the atoms do not. And these atoms are forever changed because of having been united with the human spirit.

What is completely bypassed in the way jobs are presently imagined – job talk is limited to jobs as a way of making a living, as a way of making profits, as a way to advance, get a promotion, as a way to save for retirement – concerns understanding that the human spirit enters into the materials with which we work daily - pens, pencils, computers, paper, iron, steel, wood, telephone, video. Because technology intervenes between the human and the product, the human spirit now does not fully enter into the materials of our jobs and the world is not being spiritually changed; rather, it becomes more and more materialistic. Through what we do, soul is either added or subtracted from the world.

As the imagination of work diminishes and the unemployed soul is left wandering in private fantasy while jobs become more and more specialized functions, a concomitant event is also occurring in vocational life - it is rapidly becoming electrified. Through computers, faxes, copiers, cellular phones, communications satellites, E-mail, pagers, we have entered the electronic era. We must try to enter into this development imaginally to see what is going on there with respect to the human soul and spirit in relation to work. What does it mean, for example, that a person can have a thought in New York and that this can be transmitted virtually instantaneously to London, or any part of the world. In terms of the way we have imagined human thought entering into the matter of the world, what is most interesting about the information revolution is that it requires no work. It is just a part of one's job. It is necessary to go beyond the surface and see the implications of this revolution That one can change a thought into a bit of electronic impulse is possible only because the nature of thought is essentially the same thing as electricity. If the two, electronic impulse and thought were not similar, it would not be possible to use one in place of the other. Even more, human thought, in the form of electricity is thus being imprinted upon the atomic world very directly. The entire earth is being turned into a kind of self-functioning electrical apparatus. This electronic apparatus begins even to function on its own, without the need of human thought. For example, when the stock market reaches a certain point of decline, investors do not have to contact their brokers to buy or sell; this happens automatically through electronic sensors. which put into operation buying or selling. Further, almost all that goes on through these electronic means is oriented toward materialistic aims. Materialism thus acquires its own life. A vast web of electronic impulses directly and immediately connected with the atomic structure of the world is transforming the world, not into a work of art, but into the realm of greed.

I put forth this imagination, not as a way of saying that one must stay away from electrical devices; this is impossible, and since we are now surrounded by a world-wide electronic web, we are all in any case affected by it even if we are not ourselves directly involved in these kinds of technology. What is important is the knowledge that this happens. The question becomes one of finding ways to balance this circumstance. But first, it is necessary to fully experience the effects of what is going on in this realm of electricity.

Keeping this imagination of the web of electronic information that completely encirlces us, try to imagine now how this effects soul work. We must, I think, conclude that soul work, the very moment that it enters the world, is subjected to the influence of this invisible electronic web. The result is that seekers keep seeking without experiencing an effect of their inner work. That is to say, inner work may be gratifying to individual life but we are in fact not seeing inner work have much effect in the world. For example, the subtle soul-currents generated in meditation cannot pull the spiritual currents from the spiritual worlds through the more course electronic waves surrounding the globe of Earth. The nature of meditation now changes. Much more is up to us. Human beings used to be able to put out a little effort and receive a response from the spiritual worlds. Now great effort is needed. Meditation, in fact, is no longer a luxury. It must be done as the primary way of balancing the heavy effects of electronic technology.

Epilogue to Letter VII - Things

Approaching soul in the world requires developing the capacity to describe the immediacy of experience. Everything said in this chapter on things is founded on this capacity. It might seem easy to describe experience but it takes a good deal of practice. We now live so much in the realm of theory that our theories shape the way we perceive the world and we do not know that is the case. For example, scientific, biological, and medical conceptions of the human body are now so prevalent, so much part of our culture and of everyday life, that we take the theories of the body put forth by these disciplines as descriptive of the body. We think, for example, that the heart is a pump, when this view of the heart is a theory put forth by William Harvey that has come to be so widely adopted that not only do we take it as reality, we no longer have any immediate experience of the heart. We do not actually experience our heart as a pump. Our heart leaps for joy, sinks in anguish, expands in love, contracts in fear. And, with a little practice it is possible to perceive the world through the heart. A pump cannot function in these ways. We also think that our body is a system of physiology, not recognizing that we do not live a system of physiology but that this is but one way of viewing and understanding the body. And, we think the body is wholly physical, not recognizing that there are spiritual aspects of the body.

Truths are to be found in physiology, but the body we live knows no physiology. Our body is the place from which the world opens up. This is a descriptive statement, immediately verifiable by consulting your experience. The body is also both subject and object, the place from which experience originates, but also an object of experience. The body also gets us around in the world. In the words of the phenomenologist, Maurice Merleau-Ponty, the body is the "I am able." The body is also inherently expressive. Embodiment expresses. Even the lack of expression here is a form of expression. And the human body is a body of time. We, in our bodily movement do not just exist in time, but time lives within the body.

These few statements would be the starting point for a phenomenology of embodiment. It is interesting that such statements might seem to be abstract when in fact they are concrete and descriptive while physiological and medical statements concerning the body are abstract. We live in an upside-down world, and it takes an adjustment to find the way back into experience. Not only the experience of the body, but of nearly any phenomenon you can think of.

A phenomenological approach to the human being and to the world is particularly important for spiritual psychology. Psychology has been particularly subject to theorizing and explanations. We can gain conscious access to soul life, however, only through developing the ability to be present to experience and then attempting to find language for what we experience.

Phenomenology is concerned with being present to what is present. The word itself means "the speech of phenomena". The intention of phenomenology is to allow phenomena of every sort to reveal themselves rather than imposing theories to explain phenomena. As a component of spiritual psychology, phenomenology lets inner experience reveal its own form, character, and content. Inner experience, however, is not subjective. The innerness of the world is simply another perspective, a decisive one for the life of soul and spirit.

There are a number of approaches to phenomenology, the discipline founded by Edmund Husserl in the 19th century. He recognized that human beings were rapidly losing the capacity to be present to the immediacy of the world and others. This immediacy is being replaced by theories. We forget the theories and take the forgotten theories to be reality. The particular approach to phenomenology of importance to spiritual psychology is existential phenomenology. This approach to phenomenology began in the

Netherlands, and was brought to this country primarily by psychologist Adrian Van Kaam.

Existential phenomenology begins with the sense of the inherent intentionality of consciousness – consciousness is always consciousness-of-something. Consciousness always has an object, and the object of consciousness cannot be separated from consciousness itself. This founding principle, based on observation, has the implication that we must always look to particular instances in order to understand the operations of consciousness. If we just speak of 'consciousness' we are speaking an abstraction. For example, emotional consciousness is the bodily and psychic act of holding something in affective regard. We need a sense of what an emotion concerns – what is its world?; its time?…its space? What does the body go through in emotion? For example, when we are in fear, the world contracts. It appears smaller, more constricted. In extreme fear the world becomes flat, as if we were looking at images projected on a screen. The change in the world in fear cannot be separated from the inner experience of fear. Phenomenology is non-dualistic.

Existential phenomenology understands the human being as ex-isting, that is, as standing out in the world. We belong to the world. Human beings are not in the world the way in which apples are in a box. The world is not just a container. We co-exist with the world. We do not create our own reality, but are together with the world and together exist in our fundamental being as creating beings, the mode of perception needed to perceive our living presence in the world. That is, in order to perceive the operation of soul within and within the world, a creative act of perception is needed. This creative act of perception has to be prepared for, we have to develop the capacity to perceive through soul because in our ordinary consciousness this capacity is asleep.

A further aspect of human ex-istence concerns time. Human beings are time beings. We do not just exist in a neutral world with time as an independent factor that is now measured by the clock. Lived-time is very different than clock time. There is work-time, leisure-time, love-time, depression-time, and many, many other kinds of time. Soul-time never heard of the clock.

Phenomenology is not a theory but a method. We have to undergo a discipline to be able to be present to the immediacy of experience. This discipline begins with the conscious work of placing what we already 'know' into brackets, that is consciously attempting to put aside for a while what we know and attempt to be present to the immediacy of experience. This immediacy does not mean going to the level of feelings or of sensations, because these too are now covered over by conceptual constructions. The work is to simply be present to a phenomenon without imposing what we think about it, and let the phenomena itself shape the way we speak it.

Here is an example of a description of an experience. The event was a phone call from a friend in difficulty. After receiving the call, this description was written with the purpose of serving as an example of what a description of immediate experience is like:

"D. calls me in a panic. The panic is palpable; it comes through the phone and is as it leaks out the receiver into my ear and through my body, like liquid ice. He speaks of feeling completely betrayed by four people he has worked with for twelve years as their supervisor, their director. The experience of the call, the initial moment –it is as if a voice comes to me out of the depths of the darkness. This quality of darkness announces itself, as if saying this is not an ordinary call. The darkness is not blackness in spite of the bleakness of the voice. The person calling is located somewhere in that darkness; in fact all that is left of him is a voice, as if supported by the darkness. His voice pushes out of the darkness and gradually becomes more forceful while filled with pleading. I have to work to be able to listen in a way that allows him to speak, not so much to me, as into a different kind of field. I do not feel I am perceived by this person as an individual right now. It is more that a voice in the darkness is searching for some familiarity. My listening is called upon to let the voice from the darkness move out instead of round and round in circles. He needs someone to hear his plight, as if hearing it will turn on a light. He has tangled with these feelings of betrayal alone, as if only inside his head. I feel that I am being dumped on and also that I am going to be asked to do something, and that the call is somewhat manipulative. I work to back away from these feelings and to re-open and remain with the sense of the field that has the qualities of depth. My effort is in that direction. To let the panicked voice find a resting place.

I find it enormously difficult to hold to this deep and open field and he is so caught in the emotion of what has happened to him that it is most difficult to just be in silence together even for a moment. As a way of trying to keep the field open, I, without thinking about it, try to focus on the details of what happened, to hear the story. I find myself doing this because the emotion expressed is so overwhelming that I can feel it crushing the open and dark space of the field. He is full of emotional judgments concerning those four people. How terrible they are. What they have done to him after all that he has done for them. My focus does not get out of the emotion, but gives the emotion something to stick to so that it does not float around in a circular way and go right back into him. But, in the process it feels as if a film of goo oozes onto me and breathing becomes an effort.

I begin to feel his anxiety. The anger is laced with anxiety and both attack. I work to breathe in what is being said into the heart and breath out through the solar plexus. I do this because I feel the anxiety in the solar plexus and I am trying to get free enough of the anxiety of this person that I can just listen. There are only fragmentary moments that I can just listen. I either want to consol or to offer advice about what to do, or offer to do something. It is as if I have to keep fighting off the anger and the anxiety, which come at me as if there were autonomous beings. It is like suddenly being in a swirl; it feels like walking unawares into a hornet's nest. There are too many negative things coming at me. I can't find the space of listening.

I have a moment of feeling that the fears this person is feeling and emotions this person is feeling do not only have to do with what has happened to him. The call is not so much about the betrayal. It is that the betrayal took the ground from beneath my friend and he does not know where he is or what is coming next. An abyss opens up. It is as if the ground is gone. The betrayal severed the support of the past, the support my friend has relied on, but also the immediate support of the ground we stand on. This is a huge transitional time for this person, a liminal time, a threshold. His time with these people is at an end and he is thrown into not knowing where he is or who he is. I have only a slight and momentary sense of this threshold and that sense helps give a contour to the initial experience of a voice coming toward me out of the depths of darkness. In this place, the past is gone and there is no sense of the future. That is what comes to this person. That is the darkness. But I now feel the darkness differently. As the angel of darkness. What comes to my friend is the protection of a mantle of darkness.

He cannot sense this, though. And I cannot say this without objectifying it. I rest, though, in the darkness surrounding his voice now.

This description contains no explanation of what is happening to the person calling or to the person receiving the call. It describes what happens but gives no explanatory theory. There is no clinical diagnosis, no attempt to know the reasons the person experiences this panic. The world is also part of the experience. The experience here is not the subjective experience of the one receiving the telephone call. It is as if the experience has autonomy, it exists quite objectively there in the world.

The whole of this book is based in the phenomenological method. The writing, of course, does not consist of a string of experiences, but the outlook of the writing is phenomenological. In this chapter on things, for example, there is no attempt to explain things, but only to try and give examples of how things present themselves. The intention of such presence is to take us closer to the reality of things and to let them exist in their own right. With this method, we loosen the reins of desire so that we can see things as they are rather than in terms of what they can do for us. The spiritual psychology that characterizes the writing of this book does not have the conveying of information as its primary aim. Rather, the notion is that returning to immediacy of experience is healing, not only of ourselves but also of the phenomena addressed. We do not have to do anything but learn to be present. This approach to the world is simply an extension of what has been known for a very long time by therapeutic psychology; radical receptivity heals.

The phenomenological method utilized by spiritual psychology functions in conjunction with two other methods. Entering into silence, as described in the epilogue to the chapter on the soul of the world is central to the method of spiritual psychology. Being present to what is present and entering into silence occur together. One fosters the other. The second method utilized in conjunction with phenomenology and with silence concerns being present from the place of the heart.

In order to enter the interior space of the heart, it is first necessary to feel an inner alignment. We cannot find the heart center if our consciousness is scattered. The following meditation, which is an adaptation of an exercise suggested by Rudolf Steiner, serves as a method of inner alignment which makes possible moving to the heart. The outer instructions are: "Close your eyes and feel your consciousness centered in the region of your forehead, a spot right behind the surface. When you are present to this region, inwardly say the words "I am." Then, move your consciousness from this region down to the region of the throat, to a spot right behind the surface, and inwardly say the words, "it thinks." Then, move your consciousness back to the place on your forehead; again, move your consciousness down through the region of the throat to the region of your hear, to the interior of the heart, and say the words "she feels". Then move your consciousness again back to the region of your forehead. Then slowly move your consciousness through the region of the throat and then through the region of your heart, and into the region of the solar plexus and inwardly say the words "he wills." Stay still for a few moments and then open your eyes." It is not important to think about what the words mean, but rather to enter into their action, for they are power words. Here is a phenomenological description of doing this exercise:

Upon closing my eyes, it becomes necessary to take a moment and move into stillness. All that is going on inwardly has to stop before it is possible to begin. This moment of stillness is a changing of worlds. At first, when I close my eyes, all of the world is present, though now in the form of thoughts, images, and inner dialogue.

When stillness arrives, the experience of the body moves from an outside point of view to the interior. In this interior, there is visual darkness, but it is a spacious interior. When I stay there for just a moment, it is as if the boundary between myself and the world no longer exists. I am, it seems, in the interior of the world, not just my private interior. The interior spaciousness is not amorphous, but feels egg-shaped. And the interior has depth, what seems like an infinity of depth. This interior, dark depth is flexible. It can center in the region of the head, but when I focus on the whole of my body, the interior expands. This place of expansion is where I start the exercise.

When there is the interior speaking of "I am", it is as if the words come out of the depth of the darkness. I can, on the one hand, feel myself saying the words, but at the same time the words come pouring out of the darkness, as if on their own, as if the darkness has given shape to these words, which come forth as if a liquid. I realize for a second that in usual speaking we are talking words from the outside, not speaking from within ourselves. When spoken from within, this speaking of "I am" is not wholly my own speaking. I also notice that the words resonate, reverberate through the interior space, and it is as if they go back into the dark interior. I also experience an interior current that starts at the center of the head, inside, and radiates outward. As I move consciousness down from the region of the forehead to the region of the throat, it is not a skipping move. I feel consciousness itself moving from forehead down through nasal area, and arriving at the throat. A quite physical sensation. The region of the throat is experienced quite differently than the region of the head. It is a much more subtle region and does not have the sense of an rounded, infinite interior space. Here, the saying of the words "it thinks" does not feel to come from an interior darkness, but from the interior voice itself. The speaking here is one with my voice. Also, the words radiate out more quickly and they do so from the center of the speaking in a left and a right direction from the speaking which is from the center of the throat region. It is almost as if the words, when spoken, gather in a vast current from the outside. That is, this speaking does not feel that it radiates out very much…only a little, where it then becomes joined by currents from the wider world.

When I move consciousness from the throat back to the region of the head, it also feels like whatever was gathered at the region of the throat now move back and joins into the "I am" experience. Again, when consciousness is moved from the head down to the region of the heart, it is experienced physically as moving from head, through the throat region and into the mid-region of the body. The consciousness is centered in the middle of the body, but I can feel the heart becomes immediately engaged—a current moves from the center of the chest to the heart on the left. What immediately happens upon saying the interior words "She feels" is that a strong current runs from this center region out through the arms, down to the fingertips. This movement of current then forms an embracing shape, but one that goes way beyond the boundaries of the body and feels like a gesture of the world. A slight feeling of longing and also of sorrow is felt when these words are interiorly spoken. Also, the feeling in the interior of the chest region is that currents are more like incoming and outgoing waves. A rhythm that was not present in the region of the head or the throat. The rhythm bursts forth the instant the words are said. When consciousness is then moved back again through throat and head, some of that rhythm goes with it, and there is a very slight change in the experience of these two regions. (I want to later, in other instances, try to describe these changes, and how, in fact, moving consciousness up and down like this results in an alteration of the currents of each region.)

As consciousness is moved from the heart region back to the forehead region, it is as if a path, like a tube, of light is forming between these centers so they do not feel like isolated regions. When consciousness is moved from the interior of the forehead down to the solar plexus, and the words "He wills" said interiorly, a current is felt that moves first through the arms and then downward through the legs to the bottom of the feet. Here, the interior words shape an inner space that is a particular kind of energetic space in which currents move from a deep center point outward; an analogy is that it is like a sound emanating from the center of a cave. It is as if these words establish the boundary of the body. The boundary is felt as if from the outside, as if giving the body its shape.

When the sequence is completed, there is a feeling of extreme calm and when I open my eyes, the world is experienced much more from an interior perspective. I do not feel like a spectator, looking at things; the things in around me are resonating within me.

When this exercise is carried out each day – it can be done easily in five to ten minutes, the body gradually changes. It becomes more sensitive. You know when you are out of alignment. You feel scattered, not only in a mental, but also in a bodily way. And, when in alignment, the world is perceived differently. Perception is more vivid. You perceive more of the subtly of the things of the world, and it becomes apparent, though not logical, that things have an interior animation.

Epilogue to Letter VIII – Violence and Beauty

Art, beauty, artistic creation - these do not show anything that is completely new, rather, they transform reality, make it more than what it is, make it what it is intended to be. But, art does not make anything up. Art and beauty, artistic creation, make of the world something that the angel, the spiritual world, can comprehend and find amazing. How does this act of making the things of the world, the ordinary things into sensory things that are at the same time spiritual things come about? How can beauty come about in the world? We take the world in through our senses. We drink it in, and not just for our enjoyment, for our pleasure. The world, received in this way, and then re-created as art, as beauty - that transforms the Earth! Is this not what She wants -- to be transformed into beauty?

Art and beauty are about much more than our emotions, our feelings, the display of our own inner states; it is certainly about more than social problems, social concerns put into allegorical pictures; it is about much more than making a commodity to exist in the economic and social world, something to be displayed in the gallery, in the museums, on the stage, to be looked at as performance, to be written about by people who intellectualize about it, critics. Art and beauty are about much more than the history of art, which seeks to kill, to destroy the potential of art to change the world. And art is much more than how to become a successful artist, which is what art has been reduced to in the present world.

What does beauty do? Where does it come from? Why is beauty a necessity? How does the presence of beauty affect the body, the senses, the soul, the spirit, the world? These questions are to be taken as more functional questing than philosophical pondering. Rudolf Steiner has provided a unique imagination of art and beauty in the context of what he terms 'reverse ritual'. Ritual is usually understood as a means whereby something of the spiritual realms is brought into the earthly realm. Reverse ritual, according to Steiner, characterizes the task and challenge of our time. Instead of performing some action that seeks to bring the spiritual realms down, we must form certain of our actions in such a manner that we elevate these actions to the spiritual realms. Steiner imagines the arts as functioning in this manner. Thus, beauty concerns elevating the senses to the imaginal realms. It is helpful to look at each of the arts in terms of the sensory realm that is elevated. This way of looking gives us fresh and new ways to think about how beauty functions.

Before giving a sketch of the arts in terms of the elevation of the sensory realms, it is helpful to clarify the difference between the beauty of nature and beauty in the realm of art. In the natural world, the beauty of a sunset, the rainbow, a field of yellow flowers, a deer running through the woods, the majesty of a mountain capped with snow - whatever appears beautiful belongs together with the whole. All of the natural world functions as a whole, with each individual thing having its place within the whole. If you see a field of yellow flowers, it is in the context of a particular landscape, and that landscape exists only in relation to other landscapes; it is not divided from the rest of the Earth. The blue of the sky covering the field does not come to an end at the boundaries of the field. The stream running through the field still gurgles with the melodies of the high, rocky mountain from which it came and, in its movement forward, already belongs to the lake to which it is going. If you walk out into the field and cut a bouquet of the yellow flowers and take them home, they still belong to the whole from which they came, and their beauty belongs together with the whole natural world. If you react in awe at the beauty of a lion in the zoo, this beauty is but a shadowy reflection of the beauty of that lion in its natural surroundings. Both the vase of yellow flowers and the lion in the zoo are abstractions - they have been abstracted from their living context. They both belong with the whole of nature.

A work of art is different than the beauty of the natural world. Any work of art exits whole and complete in itself. Here, a single thing is in itself a world. A single painting is completely unlike a single yellow flower in the field. It is completely unique, completely singular; like the flower, it belongs to the sensory world, but unlike the flower, which exists with the world imagination, the work of art, at the same time that it is sensory, is also an idea. We could say, then, that the realm of art exists as a third realm, alongside the realm of the sensory world, which is always particular, and the idea world, which is always general. Such a world is not present as given to us in existing reality. We must create it ourselves.

A work of art does not just express an idea that the artist might have; art does not illustrate an idea; the idea exists within the sensory object that is the work of art. I do not mean that the subjective thoughts of the artist enter into the form of art. Nor do I mean that the work of art expresses or embodies something like an archetypal idea, nor even an archetypal image. Such art, of course, does exist, but it is not the embodying of an archetypal image or idea that makes it art. Art is not a matter of making the imaginative element real, but of imbuing the real with imaginative form. This is what is essential in art - not embodying something imaginative but transforming sensory reality into something imaginative. Reality takes new form with art.

The pleasure we experience with art is spiritual and soul pleasure. Everything that makes an image complete is already inherent in it. In a work of art, again, we do no have an archetypal idea or image in the form of a sensory phenomenon, but we have a sensory phenomenon in the form of an archetypal image. A sensory phenomenon that is at the same time an image, an imaginal reality, satisfies because the sensory object of art is at the same time the fullness of the image. Beauty, then, is with a work of art always something real and direct; it is the spiritual and soul realm directly perceivable because it is sensory. Beauty does not simply express the divine realm in a sensory garment; rather, beauty is the sensory world wearing the garment of the divine. Artists bring the divine to earth, not by letting it flow into the world, but by uplifting the world into the sphere of the divine. In this manner, artists continue the work of creation. The work of art as the sensory world wearing the garment of the spiritual realm does not have to do with the content of art - it is not the what, but the how.

The reason we do not recognize that soul and spirit are completely intertwined with the world which we sense, the reason why soul is relegated to the deep interior and spirit relegated to the wide cosmos, somewhere in the heavens, is because the realm of art has not come to the center of everyday life. If it did, we would gradually come to experience the whole of the world in a quite different way than we do. The deep interior qualities of soul, its depth, its imaginal character, its simultaneity of many things going on at the same time instead of line in linear sequence would begin to be experienced. The ever- active movement, of creation coming into being every moment, the liveliness of everything in the world would begin to be perceived. To try and verify this proposal, we can focus on each of the arts and see that each art puts one of the senses at the center of its concern and shapes this sense into a sensory form imbued with qualities of soul and spirit. Each of the arts, of course, does not involve only one of the senses, but most of them center the act of making on uplifting one sense to the spiritual dimension, and then the rest of the senses gather around in support of the uplifting of that sense. As we go through each of the arts it will be very helpful to make an inner image for yourselves of an instance of each of these arts.

A What Makes Dance Beautiful

Dance works most centrally with the sense of balance. We are able to walk around upright because of the sense of balance. The organ of balance is located in the inner ear, the semi-circular canals, giving us our position in space. But, our sense of balance has undreamed of possibilities. Imagine being present to a beautiful dance performance. The dancers move freely, more freely than we ever could. We could not turn and spin and jump and move that way without falling. The dancers do not just use their sense of balance - their sense of balance, in the dance, is spiritually released. The sense of balance becomes a spiritual picture, an image that pictures balance in its spiritual state, but in a completely sensory way. When we watch the dancers, for that time at least, our sense of balance is also elevated to the spiritual, yet remaining fully in the sensory realm. Dance takes the sensory quality of balance and wraps it in the garments of the spirits of form. The spirits of form are the spirits responsible for bringing everything on earth connected with the course of time. Through the art of dance we see something of a particular spiritual realm, the realm of the spirits of form; this realm does not descend from the spiritual regions, but rather, the sensory realm has been uplifted to this spiritual realm, without every leaving the sensory world. But, the dancers must be true to the dance itself. They must not let their own desires enter into the dance. When we dance, ordinary dance, not dance as an art, we play with the sense of balance and bring in our own desires for pleasure into this sense. The art of dance is never this kind of personal expression.

B. The Art of Movement

An art that is very close to the art of dance, but nevertheless must be distinguished from dance is mime. In mime, it is the sense of movement rather than balance that lies at the center of the art. Through the sense of movement, we sense the movement of our own bodies - from the large movements of our arms and legs to the smaller movements of the neck, or the movement of the chest in and out in breathing, to even the smallest of movements, such as the movement of the eyes. Through the sense of movement we experience the mobility, not only of the body, but of the soul. We move from place to place and yet continually retain the sense that wherever we are, we are the same individual. Wherever you go, there you are. The art of mime uplifts the sense of movement; movement gets poured into form. Movement becomes clothed in the spirit of movement. Again, for movement to be an art, personal wishes and desires have to be held back. In our time, mime as an art is very rare and has lingered on mostly as an amusement. The difference between mime and dance is most interesting to watch. To get a sense of the art, it is necessary to focus, not on the content, but on the how. Notice how mime is more two-dimensional than dance. Even though it is performed in three dimensions, it is as if it occurs on a single plane. It is the quality of this single plane that shows how movement has been uplifted to the spirit of movement.

C. The Art of Sculpture

The sense that lies at the center of the art of sculpture is the life sense. In ordinary life, the life sense senses the liveliness of our body. The life sense is experienced as a quality of well-being in the body. We are usually aware of the life sense only through its disruptions - such as the sensations of hunger, thirst, tiredness. When the life sense operates undisturbed, we experience our body in its well-being. The art of sculpture elevates the life sense into a spiritual form existing within the sensory world. A work of sculpture does not have to have the human body as a content to uplift the life sense to a spiritual form. Any work of sculpture does this; that is what the sculptural imagination is about. A work of sculpture, whether realistic or abstract, can be characterized as a physical form clothed with the spiritual quality of life.

D Architectural Imagination

The question of what architecture imagines is much more difficult to come to than the other forms of art considered thus far. What is it that is working in the imagination of the architect? What capacity is required to imagine making a building? To what aspect of the spiritual realm does architecture aspire? We cannot find this capacity based in any of the senses. Architecture is like the spiritualizing of balance and also like the spiritualizing of movement and also like the spiritualizing of the life sense. Thus, architecture at one and the same time is like dance, like mime, and like sculpture. But, it seems that the spiritualizing of these senses serve, or stand in for something that cannot quite be specified. We cannot say that architecture is a combination of dance, mime, and sculpture. It makes use of these qualities of imagination. But, an architect does not really imagine through these qualities alone. The architect - as an artist, not as an engineer, and not as someone who builds buildings completely out of practical concerns, begins with and out of the capacity of free fantasy. All of the senses are taken up into the realm of fantasy, but really, I think that it is the sense of touch that is at the center of architecture. But, with architecture, you touch with the eyes, feel the movement of a graceful building through a quality like touch, sense the proportion, that is, the balance, as also a kind of touch - all of the senses become endowed with the quality of touch. The only restriction to this free fantasy is that it comes under the force of gravity; it is wholly oriented toward what can stand here on the Earth. Practical concerns only enter later. It must begin with the practice of developing a free, unconstrained imagination. One must be able to imagine all kinds of forms, many of which could never actually be built because they are beyond what is technically feasible. To become an architect in the artistic sense requires a training that frees imagination. This freedom goes so far as to call it pure fantasy. When architecture begins with practical concerns, engineering concerns, economic concerns, personal desires on the part of building according to what others may want, the architectural imagination, the play of free fantasy, is from the outset either constrained or bypassed.

E The Art of Painting

What is the imaginative capacity that makes possible the art of painting? Where does the painter's imagination come from? The capacity to create painting is founded in the sense of vision which has combined with the inner life of the soul. The capacity of soul vision recognizes the soul-being shining through the surface of things. The painter's imagination is able to ensoul everything that appears as color and form. In painting, soul speaks through visual form and color. With painting, the sensory realm of color has inner soul qualities. Here, color, brought into form has an inner depth that is not present in our ordinary seeing of color in the world. The painter's imagination may be turned outward, seeing into the things of the world, seeing beyond the surface of things into their inner qualities; it may also be turned inward, toward seeing within soul life itself. Both kinds of seeing, in distinction from ordinary seeing, is intuitive - intuition as an actual capacity of visionary imagination. In painting, the sensory realm of sight is uplifted into the spiritual realm of intuition. The sense of sight wears the spiritual garment of intuition.

F The Art of Music

Music is centered in the sense of hearing, the sense of sound. But it is not an imitation of sound as ordinarily heard, nor even a variation of this sort of sound. The sense of sound is combined with the inner life of the soul, giving sound a new form than that found in ordinary hearing. The musical imagination creates musical tones out of the soul itself. This musical imagination, the creating of sound from within the soul is called inspiration.

The art of music is founded in the capacity of inspiration, and expresses something of the soul that cannot be expressed in any other way - not through thoughts or concepts - it directly expresses feelings, feelings that are not personal, but all the complicated and powerful feelings that live in the human soul. Music, poured forth into the world, produces something in the world that otherwise would not be there at all. The song of the birds, the sound of the wind through the trees, the trickling of a spring come close to music, but cannot be called true music. There is a great distance between these melodious sounds and music. With music, the sense of sound reaches toward the spiritual realm of inspiration. Inspiration clothes the sensory realm of sound in music.

G The Art of Poetry and Drama

The poetic imagination, which includes both poetry and drama, works with human language and makes possible that human beings express in language something that could never be communicated with the ordinary sense of language. Through rhythm and meter the soul qualities of the will find expression. Poetry is the imagination of the will. This art is perhaps the most mysterious of all. In our ordinary life, we do not really experience the will in a direct way. We know our will only as it gets reflected into an idea, which we then put into action. The source of will lies deep within the body and remains unconscious. We might also say that will lies in the deepest part of the soul and remains unconscious. Will is body and soul together. How do we experience will? We feel an inner urging, which gets reflected as an image or as an idea, which we then put into action. Poetic imagination dives down into the will, right to the very basis and origins of all action, and here, will finds direct expression as the language of poetry and drama. Poetry and drama does not simply use language, but clothes language with the will, gives it a force that it ordinarily does not have. The will, expressed through poetic imagination, as in all art, contains nothing of the personal expression of will, but expresses the force of will itself. The power of poetry and drama stems from this impersonal force of the will.

H. Literature

The art of literature may seem to belong with poetry and drama. But, there are important differences. Poetry and drama are not really meant to be read; poetry speaks and drama is displayed. We read literature, and it is thus a most interior art. The literary imagination works with all of the senses. If a flower is described in a work of literature, you must be able to see and smell and touch the flower when reading. If a gun is part of the story, you must be able to see the gun, touch it. Every sensory experience must be made actual in a work of literature. We do not, of course, actually smell roses when we read of two lovers kissing at night in the midst of a rose garden. So literature elevates all of the senses into the realm of imagination. Literature does not lift the senses to the spiritual realms, but to the soul realm, to the imagination. The whole sensory world is elevated into imagination. But, in addition, imagination in literature is put into the realm of time. A story has a sequence; the real art of literature is that of elevating the senses to the level of imagination and putting imagination into the quality of sequential time, though time in literature is also an imaginal quality; a novel may describe events occurring over many years, and is yet read in an evening.

Epilogue to Letter IX – Food

There is metaphysical significance to food. Perhaps the current condition of obesity characterizing Americans is not a matter of how much we eat and how much protein versus carbohydrate, or the number of calories, but signifies a condition of our spirit. Gluttony is a matter of a deficit of desire. While it may seem like overeating concerns excessive desire for food, it is actually a case of trying to get rid of desire. It is the attempt to squelch desire before it reaches religious proportions. Spiritual psychology approaches eating disorders from this point of view. It is odd that psychology classifies binging and purging as psychological disorders, but looks upon obesity as having nothing to do with the soul and as something that can be handled with discovering a new diet pill or a new program. It is thus necessary to open up the concern for food in the widest way possible. Let me see if I can substantiate the claim that food has a metaphysical dimension.

Food problems are a subset of problems concerning desire. No one has understood desire better than Dante in *The Divine Comedy*. The *Divine Comedy* can in fact be understood as the path of desire. The whole of this work, which is the journey of the soul in life and is not the journey of the soul after death, concerns the purification of desire. The work uses the vast metaphor of the soul after death, but in the work we learn to recognize when, in life, we are in hell, or purgatory, or heaven. What such moments are like. Hell is egotism, where nothing is learned and *me, me, me* prevails. Desires are indulged without learning anything from them and punishment consists of being mercilessly immersed forever in one's egotism. Purgatory is where learning occurs, where desire becomes purified. Purification does not mean one becomes pious but rather that, though learning, desire becomes pure desire, uncontaminated with what we want from it. Heaven is where desire lives without constraint, where Dante learns that desire is the great net thrown out by God to draw all creatures back to the creator. Heaven, in life, is when we are able to operate unencumbered out of our own impulses and we are sufficiently conscious of these impulses that we are not trapped in them. Heaven does not mean being free of desire, but rather free to express all desire as the desire for God.

It is in the *Purgatorio* where we begin to get a sense of the metaphysical significance of food. In Canto 18 Dante speaks of how the world is a great array of people and things that have the capacity to impress the soul, some good, some not. The desire, the longing, is always good. The journey to heaven does not consist in crushing out desire but rather learning to distinguish between the primal desire, the desire for God, from other desires. And, we are instructed not to throw out all the other desires, but rather to learn to see them and live them in conformity with the primal desire. Dante has an orchestral view of desire. All desires meet their ultimate expression when in harmony. Separately, they lose their vitality. Or they separately become far more than they really are. What harmonizes the vast array of desires, is, of course, the great question. And Dante address it, saying that it is free will. That answer does not take us very far without going into the nature of free will, but that cannot be pursued here. I can say that free will has to be understood as our individual spirit freely willing to see all desires in context. I don't think Dante is speaking of willful willing, but receptive willing.

Dante gives this view of desire on the ledge of purgatory where sloth is punished. Sloth is clearly a lack of ardor and passion, and in the poem, at that point, Dante goes to sleep and dreams of a Siren who, with the contribution of his projections, tempts him mightily, nearly stopping the journey. She actually shows up in the dream as a quite unattractive figure, but in the dream Dante looks upon her with longing and she turns into a raving beauty. Half-heartedness is the problem here. We wish that love and pleasure will visit us effortlessly. The whole night scene of going to clubs and hoping to meet someone is in this image. As the country-western song says, "the girls always get prettier at closing time." We are being introduced by Dante into this wonderful insight that what looks like desire is often not desire at all but is something like anti-desire. We expect our desires to be fulfilled magically. A confusion exists between effortless love and unearned love. Effortless love characterizes adolescence, no matter the age. It is that illusory hope that love will drop into our lap. Unearned love is the great mystery of the Universe. The whole of the universe is bathed in love. It is what holds everything together and makes the beauty of the world. But when someone comes up to me and appears in a brief moment as the most beautiful thing I've ever seen and I have to have her, this is not unearned love. It is the illusion of effortless love.

Before getting to the heart of the metaphysical significance of food, Dante first shows us that we must confront the difficulty of possessing and identifying with desires. He does this in canto 20 of the *Purgatorio*, a canto concerned with greed or avarice. The canto tells of King Midas and of Hugh Capet, originator of the Capetian dynasty in France, noted for its avarice. Both the mythical king and Huge Capet sacrifice their daughters for greed. The story of King Midas shows that greed results in a weakening of vital energy. Preoccupation with the material order results in everything going dead. And, when caught in greed, as vitality goes out of life, there is the attempt to have more and more material goods to compensate for this loss of vitality. Having, we see, when it becomes our preoccupation, is a self-desertion, and it is also a desertion of the soul of the world. We fall into spiritual avarice when we try to possess things that cannot be possessed. To think, for example, that I have talent, or that I have children or that I am a teacher are all claims to possess something that cannot be possessed. The problem of having has to be answered by being, not having. I am. That is all that can be said. We must relinquish defined existence in order to come to destined existence. That is, as long as we are identified with something, take it to be ours when it cannot be, we also cannot find our destiny. We are too occupied with illusions of what we think it is.

I am utilizing Dante to put the question of the misuse of food in our time in a much broader context than diet and exercise. Dante's spiritual psychology is impeccable. He keeps us to the wheel, following through each nuance concerning the failures of desire and their reasons. Then, in canto and twenty-three of the *Purgatorio*, he comes to gluttony per se. But to understand it and be transformed by his poetry, by reading this poetry in such a way that you allow your life to be changed, we have to be brought through sloth and greed as the background of gluttony. Gluttony, of course, is not an aberration confined to food. But food is a very good example of its operation.

We cannot trick desire. Sometimes, when we cannot get what we want, we try, mostly unconsciously, to reach for something even more difficult. Many are the ambitious who, not achieving a certain level of capacity, reach beyond it for even something higher. In this manner, many waste their lives because they are not able to confront desire head on and see the larger desire behind any particular desire. I recently was speaking with someone who has for a long time desired to be of help to the endeavor of spiritual psychology. Each time this person offers help, however, the specific thing requested, which is always something very small and limited, is ignored, and in its place the person imagines doing something large and magnificent. We do thing kind of thing all the time, and in doing so do not live in desire but try to escape it.

The paradox of desire is that we want and we cannot have. This is the very nature of desire, how that vast net of God keeps working on us to gather us in and take us back. We become confused because we think we are supposed to get what we desire and think that some outer force is preventing it and somehow we can fix that. Or, in the case of gluttony, we attempt to feed the desire out of existence, which is nothing more than trying to kill desire so that it no longer bothers us. How difficult it is to settle back into the paradox – I desire *and* I cannot have. I sing and I weep. How to joy and weep at the same time. That is living in the desire. Dante sees this and comes one of the great insights of the *Divine Comedy*. We are hungry; that is who man is as a species. That is the beginning of wisdom. We must stay in touch with hunger for that is who we are. The problem with the glutton, as with sloth, is that there is not enough desire. The more desire we feel, the more pain. And the more desire we feel, the closer we are to the spiritual worlds, and the more intense our hunger. The work, though, is to refrain from feeding it because that is the attempt to kill desire. Pain and joy are not dichotomized on the spiritual path. Pleasure-pain is a prism for reflecting or refracting the wholeness of the mystery. If food is a problem, I mean too much food, gluttony, obesity, perhaps it is that we do not have a sufficiently transcendent object of desire.

Food aberrations have to do, from a spiritual point of view, with either trying to sate desire or trying to control it. And when we are pulled in both directions and once we binge and purge. The glutton tries to sate desire. The anorexic tries to control it. Our approach to food reveals much about the mystery of life. It has even more to do with the mystery of the soul. If by chance or conscious spiritual work, we do find the capacity to be our hunger, the mystery of desire is not yet resolved. Whatever remains of desire that is not orchestrated with divine desire for us is metaphorical fat. That is, this blocked up desire signifies our attempt to live off our own resources. Eventually it will be burned up, as it should be. And herein lies another metaphysical source of food problems. Fear of the fires of purification. In canto twenty-five, Dante comes up against this fear. In this canto he spiritualizes the difficulty of desire. He is about to move out of purgatory into heaven, but comes to a wall of fire. He is filled with fear. He says: 'I became like one laid to the grave." Whatever is still left of desire that he has acted upon rather than lived within must be purged here. It is certainly not wrong that we act on desire; it becomes problematic only if we do not learn from those actions. Look in the *Divine Comedy* at the gluttons in hell to have a sense of what that is like. In this canto, though we learn that, paradoxically, it is only desire that can get us through the fires of purification. Dante shows this in a wonderful way.

He is there, stuck, unable to move on to paradise. Vigil, his guide then tricks him. He tells Dante that Beatrice is on the other side of the fire. Well, she is, but when Dante hears this he thinks of the Beatrice he knew years ago, and all the love, all the desire for her, in every sense of the word desire, come pouring back in. The Beatrice on the other side of the fire is the spiritual Beatrice. Dante hears Virgil and imagines the earthly Beatrice. Virgil uses carnal desire, purged of lust, to lure Dante through the fire. The canto works with a wonderful image. As the apple got Adam and Eve out of paradise, Virgil uses the apple to get Dante into paradise. What is the learning here? We cannot solve the problem of desire. That is, as long as we are embodied, desire is with us. Thank goodness! Desire is good. And the transformation of bodily desires of every sort into spiritual desires is ultimately a matter of grace. We cannot do it on our own. There is spiritual greed, spiritual gluttony, which is every bit as difficult as good old fashion earthly gluttony. Our desire for the spiritual realms can fall into all of the twists elaborated here in relation to food.

Epilogue to Letter X – World Soul and Hermetic Consciousness

It might be helpful to round out the presentation on hermetic consciousness with a more phenomenological description of how this form of consciousness is experienced in practice. It must be emphasized, however, that the way I describe such an experience is only one way of undergoing such a state. I am sure there are others, many others, and in addition, each mode is tinted by the particular personality of the person engaging in such a hermetic activity. Thus, this description intends to help get closer to the experience, but do not literalize what is spoken here and take it as the one way in which such experiences always happen.

My experience of hermetic consciousness comes from reading, writing, teaching, and working with people in groups for the past thirty years. It is, however, only in the past seven years that I have become more conscious of the state I am in when working through soul. Let me describe the conditions under which this experience of hermetic consciousness takes place. It is a particular form of consciousness that occurs as a field, a region of consciousness that exists between myself and others. Consciousness here does not mean a private, internal state.

A preliminary work is required in order to be able to enact a hermetic relationship with others in a group. I work very hard to prepare to meet with a group, which takes the form of being present to my experiences surrounding the topic addressed, doing a great deal of reading on that topic, doing extensive writing that is somewhat original, making notes based on that writing, and then making notes based on those notes. Then, as much as possible, I memorize those notes by heart, that is, I take them to heart. Thus, at the beginning, there seems to be a very organized structure.

This preparation, however, is never what is presented to the group; at least, not in the form prepared. And even though the material is well thought through by the time I am finished, the preparation itself, particularly the writing, is really an entry into a different world. I never know what I am writing in advance of the actual act, though I know what I intend to write about. As the writing gets going, it takes its own course and goes its own way. The words that compose the writing are nothing more that bits and pieces of a vast universe pulled down or pulled out from an unknown region. I can, though, describe something of the qualities of what this region is like. Think of this region as a landscape of hermetic exploration.

This region exists as qualities of elemental air. I use this word in an alchemical sense -- as one of the four foundational creating imaginations of the cosmos. The aerial region is a region of pure movement; it is a world of movement, or better said, a world that *is* movement and nothing other than movement, though it is a highly differentiated world of currents flowing every which way. This elemental imagination is primarily a kind of spiritual mobility of the greatest, liveliest, and most exhilarating kind. It is the psyche's experience of openness and novelty. More than anything else, it is this movement that distinguishes the human psyche. This realm of infinite air has nothing to do with the ordinary sense of space around us, nor does it have to do with "outer space." It is non-dimensional space, inner space, where we come into contact with non-dimensional matter, a realm that is wholly dynamic. In this region thinking feels like great streams of air flowing through, and the task is to try and catch as much as possible and translate it into concepts that can be understood through ordinary consciousness.

When I am thinking, or reading, or writing, I am at first, and sometimes for a very long time, caught in an immobilized world. This is the world of thoughts we all ordinarily inhabit. The hermetic state is not there when preparatory work begins. These thoughts feel heavy. These thoughts are like big, heavy, bricks, cinder blocks, and I lift and move one block at a time. These beginning thoughts are always either someone else's thoughts, or my own already thought thoughts, those with which I am already quite familiar. I then begin to notice that a lot of fear accompanies these heavy thoughts; it is like being in a pit, trying to find the way out. Then, when blocks have been lifted, moved around, placed next to and on top of one another.... when this is sufficiently done ....and I cannot ever know when this is the case, and I lift yet another block, suddenly, completely without warning, a blast of elemental air comes, and lo and behold, there I am, right in the midst of movement. When this happens, at the very moment it happens, the feeling of thinking moves down from the head to the center of the chest. It feels like being rhythmically squeezed, right in the region of the heart. The thinking then takes on its own movement. Then, rather than writing, I find myself being written. I find myself in a world that is simultaneously dream and thought.

I know this is another world, because it is not really possible to stay there in an extended way. If I slow down even a bit, trying to find words to express what is going on in that world, then I find myself back in those heavy, lump-thoughts. It is like moving from a graveyard into heaven and then back again.

This world of movement can also be described as a world of aspiration. The psychic region of movement, it can clearly be felt, is not at all random. Nor, however, can we say that this world consists of anything going in straight lines; linearity has no part in this world. I speak of it as a world of aspiration because something new tries to be said, and it comes in from all directions and goes out to the widest inner expanses. This world of movement breathes; it expands and contracts. The real work of staying within this world concerns entering into its rhythm. The moment that I lose its rhythm, then I find myself back in the graveyard. Further, I lose its rhythm either by getting caught in the contraction phase or getting caught in the expansion phase of the rhythmical movement. In the contraction phase, I suddenly find myself back among the heavy cinder blocks of ordinary thought, sitting there, wondering whether where I was just a moment ago was just an airy nothing. If I get caught in the expansion phase, then I begin to find that I cannot retain consciousness of what I am doing. It moves too fast.

The moment the pure mobility of imaginative thinking touches into the body, it is as if a revitalizing occurs. Often, it is difficult to hold the surging current of this mobility when felt in such a completely bodily way. Sometimes, I must stop and rest, like an athlete of the imagination, to get another breath of the fresh elemental air. At such moments, it becomes important to establish a circulation between head and heart. Imaginatively, this circulation is like oxygen now united with the blood. This circulation is necessary because it establishes a mode of conduction between the imaginative realm of mobility and the flesh. When I get transported too far out into the world of imaginative motion, I know this by the response of the flesh, which gasps for air; it grasps for images that can, so to speak, nourish the body.

I am quite convinced that finding mobility of consciousness forms a necessary preparatory work for entering deeper into the hermetic field. We have to be released from our usual and ordinary ways of thinking and acting or else it will not be possible to experience the activity of the field. We have to be released from our habits, which are the exact antithesis of the creative imagination. Others may not prepare in this way I have described. Certainly, there are other ways to journey to the land of the imaginary, ways that are just as true as this one. The way of the elemental earth takes the path through the will to this land and is characterized by firmness of action; the way of elemental fire is the way of the spirit; and the way of elemental water takes the path of feeling. And, the way of elemental air is psyche's way. It is the way that allows us to grow psychically. The way you go depends on the infinity that attracts you.

An aspect of the work needed to enter into the hermetic field that I have barely mentioned concerns language. It is not sufficient to live in the dreamland of flowing thinking. The currents of thinking wish to be expressed as speech, as speaking. The effort of writing, which I have mentioned, is already a step down from the creative speech characteristic of the airy imagination. Speech appears at the psychic high points of the mobile imagination. Such speaking is filled with ambiguity and double meanings. And it is filled with metaphors, though in the land of air, the metaphors are not visual. Words are used in order to go beyond words to thought. And thought goes beyond thought into the land of the moving psyche.

I mentioned earlier that while I have been working with groups for thirty years, it is only in the past seven that this has become conscious hermetic work. The other 23 years were preparatory to the preparation just described. These years consisted of learning to read in such a way that the spiritual voice of the author could be heard, speaking from the imaginative world. The informational part of a text is just the graveyard holding the corpse of the author, which must be raised into life like Lazarus, for a book to become living. And these years also consisted of emptying as much as possible my own thoughts, at least for brief spans of time, and becoming speechless enough to hear the speech of creative thinking coming from the land of spiritual imagination. And these years consisted of working to unite the whole of my life, the whole of my being with imagination's mobility. Finally, and perhaps most important, these years consisted of working to develop capacities to be objective in the realms of the inner life – my own, and that of others. This objectivity is more like that of an artist than that of the scientist. Thinking is one of the arts.

The preparation for entry into the hermetic field is a preparation for newness. The aerial imagination forms the basis for a psychology of newness, of what has not yet happened. However, it recognizes such newness as a substantial reality and not just subjective wishing. To step into the hermetic realm, rather than asking that we clear away the blocks in our psyche stemming from frustrated desires, we instead enter into the current of desire itself. The aerial world I have been describing is simply another way to describe the dynamic of desire. While psychoanalysis and all its variations work to *clear away* everything that might hinder the psyche's future, an initiation into the aerial imagination, into the domain of pure mobility, is an entry into future forms. The weight of a heavy past can be best lifted by the spirits of imagination. Thus, the work of preparation described thus far can be considered a kind of therapy of ascent, learning how to let ourselves be uplifted, rather than the heroic task of trying to lift ourselves out of the heaviness of our past.

We typically experience desire primarily in its aspects of hindrance. A kind of pleasure is in fact associated with this hindrance. We feel the friction between something that is drawing us and the blocks within us that prevent us from reaching what attracts us. This friction is experienced as a pleasurable, though also painful bodily sensation. Little do we know that this sensation is not genuine desire but is desire hindered. Little do we know that we become trapped in seeking the pleasures of hindrance rather than the true happiness of unencumbered desire. Unencumbered desire, rather than the frustrated pleasures of the body, can be found in the realm of the radiant air. In other words, desire needs to be imagined as a psychic place that we can learn to go to, a place of aerial light, of golden air, the light of the dawn, new beginnings, in which we are bathed in the possibilities of the future. In this light, the enlightening soul is born. The turbulence of frictional desire needs to be replaced, gradually, ever so gradually, by the serenity of bathing the soul in the living current of the aerial world of desire if we are to find the way to the in-between regions inhabited by Hermes.

Modern psychoanalytic and Jungian practitioners have, in recent years, discovered a field of the soul. They have done so by learning to concentrate on the subtle qualities of the interaction between therapist and patient rather than what supposedly goes on within the soul of the patient.

Classically, this domain of interaction is known as the transference. Transference concerns the feelings going on between therapist and patient, feelings that belong neither to the patient alone, nor to the therapist alone, but is a third, a field between them. Both are together immersed in this field. When therapy reaches a point where this field is entered, strong feelings of desire are experienced. A field of desire has formed, now known as the interactive field.

The field of desire psychoanalysis calls transference is not the same as the field of desire I have been describing. It inclines more toward the field of frictional desire rather than radiant desire. Following this field carefully takes the therapist and patient into the shared unconscious relationship that goes much deeper than the shared conscious relationship. Indeed, a field is entered, something that is quite independent of either the therapist or the patient. There is no doubt that concentrating on this interactive field and particularly on the images that arise for both therapist and patient revealing the dynamics of that field, can be healing. It can be healing because both therapist and patient find the way out of their own subjectivity into a more psychically objective realm. The process of doing so is typically long and arduous. The process that I have described thus far is also long and arduous. The difference lies in direction. Does one wish to go into the radiant cosmos or into the velvety underworld? Spiritual psychology adds upward mobility to the descent that characterizes depth psychology. You can go deep into the heavens as well as deep into the underworld.

The way into the radiant cosmos does not ignore the darkness of frictional desire. I am not suggesting aerial escapism. Once the luminous field of the soul is entered, it then becomes possible to look at and enter into any sort of memory, any sort of pain or longing or darkness from a new point of view.

This description of hermetic imagination as aerial imagination implies that there is a movement from ordinary thinking to imaginal thinking. Images are involved. Because our prevailing notion of images is that they are some sort of form, different certainly than the forms around us in the waking world of usual consciousness, but nonetheless forms, let me try to give an example of speaking an image as form and speaking that same image from the perspective of the aerial imagination. There is a strong tendency to think that images are pictures to look at. Let us, for a moment, engage the aerial imagination in a heightened way so our visual prejudice will not sneak in and infect the air.

First, an image spoken in terms of visual imagination. Suppose I look at a painting on a wall. It is a landscape painting. It pictures a strong, flowing stream, blue, stirred into whiteness, moving from a higher region to the left, and down toward the right. On the far side of the swiftly flowing stream is a hill, a beautiful hill of dark green tall grasses, sloping steeply down to the stream. And on this side of the stream, more dark green grass, filled though with small blue flowers sitting atop long green stems. A hint of the blue sky forms the background of this pleasant painting.

The aerial imagination perceived the activity of the painting more so than its content. It is as if the content trails along after the activity. The aerial imagination of this painting would have to be spoken something like this: downard flowing white capping blue rushing, cutting through greening sloping hill ushering a welcoming field of flowering blue reaching toward its sky blue likeness.

The first image concentrates the visual imagination. The second image concentrates the dynamic imagination, of which the aerial imagination is the prime example. The animation of the image, we can see when we bring it out and let it speak loudly, comes from the aerial imagination. The formal imagination always risks missing the animation or makes animation a matter of cinematic movement rather than subtle qualities interior to the image.

Once we have released ourselves from the notion that images are like pictures to be seen, that is, release ourselves from the tyranny of the visual imagination, images as formed content, and begin to be able to feel and experience images as motions of soul, images as activity rather than as forms that do this and that, we are on the way to imaginal thinking. And just as images change from content to action with the aerial imagination, hermetic, imaginal thinking is characterized by its constant and prevalent interiority of motion, action, movement. What we usually call thinking is not thinking at all but rather the stringing together of already completed thoughts. We typically engage in "thoughting" not thinking. We use thinked thoughts. Just as we neglect images as motion and focus only on the matter, the structure, and the form of images, even more so do we confuse thinking with what is thought about. That is, when we are thinking about something, we mistake what we think about with the thinking itself; the thinking activity goes unnoticed and thus we move further and further away from the possibility of thinking being open to the worlds of the gods, from which thinking originates. We do not think. Thinking occurs through us. Coming to this experience is central to hermetic consciousness.

Made in the USA
Monee, IL
23 June 2021